ANDREW RAWSON

THE VIETNAM WAR HANDBOOK

US ARMED FORCES IN VIETNAM

The History Press

First published in the United Kingdom in 2008 by The History Press
Cirencester Road · Chalford · Stroud · Gloucestershire · GL6 8PE

British Library Cataloguing in Publication Data
A catalogue record for this book is available from the British Library.

ISBN 978-0-7509-4697-1

All photographs, unless otherwise noted, are from the National Archives and
Records Administration Photograph Collection, College Park, Maryland,
USA. They are from the US Army Signal Corps, US Marine Corps, US Air
Force and US Navy collections. Credits refer to the relevant photograph
collection and image number.

Typeset in Sabon
Typesetting and origination by
The History Press.
Printed and bound in Malta.

CONTENTS

CHAPTER ONE

BACKGROUND TO A LONG WAR

FRENCH RULE TO COMMUNIST THREAT

The United States' first contact with Ho Chi Minh, North Vietnam's future leader, came during the Second World War. Minh's resistance fighters were engaged with the Japanese forces occupying French Indochina and as part of their struggle they gathered intelligence and rescued downed American pilots. At the cessation of hostilities US Army officers looked on while Ho Chi Minh rejected French rule of Indochina and declared Vietnam's independence.

America's support for Vietnam changed course in August 1950 when a small team of personnel arrived in Saigon to set up Military Assistance Advisory Group, Indochina, ready to distribute military aid delivered to Southeast Asia. Four months later equipment and supplies started to arrive, allowing the Vietnamese Army to expand in its growing fight alongside the French against the Viet Minh, Ho Chi Minh's Communists.

For the next three years the French engaged Minh's troops and they struggled to come to terms with a different kind of warfare, guerilla warfare. In November 1953 General Navarre decided to draw them into open battle, deploying a large concentration of troops at Dien Bien Phu near the Laos border. The Viet Minh soldiers took up the challenge, occupying the hills surrounding the French positions, and slowly tightened their stranglehold. Heavy fighting and dwindling supplies took their toll on the French and after six months they were forced to surrender on 7 May 1954. Two months later hostilities came to an end as Vietnam was split into two at the 17th Parallel.

The communists controlled the north while the French handed over the south to a new democratic regime led by President Ngo Dinh Diem. However, the Viet Minh continued the struggle in the south and it soon became clear that the South Vietnamese Armed Forces needed assistance to protect their borders and maintain internal security. The first group of US military advisors reached South Vietnam in March 1955 and eight months later Military Assistance Advisory Group, Vietnam, was organized to supervise a range of training programs to help the South Vietnamese.

The United States kept a close eye on developments in Southeast Asia, concerned by the worldwide spread of Communism (America was also extremely sensitive to home-grown Communism at this time) and it believed that if one country fell under its control, the rest of the area would follow; a theory branded the 'Domino Effect'. Four years passed before events descended into a deepening circle of violence following North Vietnam's announcement that it was changing its strategy from a political struggle to an armed struggle. President Dwight Eisenhower made the United States' first public commitment to support South Vietnam's fight for independence in April 1959 but it had little effect on Ho Chi Minh's followers and three months later two American servicemen were killed during an attack by Vietnamese Communists (now known as the Viet Cong).

North Vietnam began to step up the pressure in April 1960, in the hope of toppling the South Vietnamese government, and it began sending trained soldiers to the south to organize attacks while military conscription was introduced in the north. At the end of the year it announced that a new organization, the National Liberation Front, had been formed to lead the struggle in the south.

The beginning of 1961 saw John F. Kennedy elected as President of the United States and he continued Eisenhower's support, pledging further military assistance at the end of the year in response to a call for help from the South Vietnamese president. A new organization, Military Assistance Command, Vietnam, was formed in February 1962 to control the increase of American advisors and support personnel supervising the build-up of US war material.

The world's attention was briefly centered on Cuba the following October as America confronted the Soviets over the deployment of missiles close to its shores, a confrontation which ended in a desperate nuclear standoff between Presidents Kennedy and Khrushchev. However, trouble was never far away in South Vietnam and on 1 November 1963 President Diem's unpopular government was toppled by a military coup; the President was killed by his own soldiers.

Three weeks later, President Kennedy was assassinated on 22 November in Dallas, Texas, leaving Lyndon B. Johnson to take control of the uncertain situation in the United States and the countries it supported. He did not have to wait long before his resolve was tested.

North Vietnam began sending regular troops into South Vietnam in April 1964 to take advantage of the chaos left by the coup. An attack against a US base at Nam Dong on 6 July showed that the Viet Cong was determined to seize control whatever the cost and a month later they made a second hostile move against US military personnel.

US Navy ships had been patrolling off the coast of North Vietnam, monitoring vessel movements and coastal defenses since February 1964 and at the end of July they were given permission to shell targets in the Gulf of Tonkin. On 2 August, North Vietnamese patrol boats attacked the destroyer, USS *Maddox* and while F-8 Crusader fighter planes from USS *Ticonderoga* sank one of the boats, it marked the first time that North Vietnamese and American servicemen had openly engaged each other (undercover operations involving Special Forces teams had been underway for some time). A second destroyer, USS *Turner Joy*, joined *Maddox* later that evening and patrolling resumed but two days later the North Vietnamese allegedly made a second attack (several key witnesses later reported that the second attack never took place).

President Johnson acted immediately on the information available, ordering retaltory airstrikes against North Vietnamese naval bases and a fuel depot. He also presented the Tonkin Gulf Resolution and on 7 August, the United States Congress and Senate passed it, authorizing the President to deploy US Armed Forces to defend the non-Communist nations of Southeast Asia.

Johnson was elected President on 3 November, and two months later he was called upon to use his Resolution when the Viet Cong attacked US military installations in Pleiku. US Navy planes based on carriers stationed in the South China Sea responded by attacking targets across North

A US advisor watches while a Vietnamese officer plans how to cross a river during a river crossing. (111-CC-22791)

The first Marines land on the beach near Da Nang on 8 March 1965. (127-GVC-A183727)

Vietnam. With the threat of attacks against military installations mounting, Johnson increased the stakes, ordering the deployment of ground troops to protect them. 9th Marine Expeditionary Brigade landed at Da Nang on 8 March where the bemused Marines were greeted by government officials and cheering civilians carrying garlands of flowers. In May 173rd Airborne Brigade, the first US Army unit to deploy, arrived at Bien Hoa to the north of Saigon. It was the start of an eight year commitment of US ground troops to South Vietnam, one that would cost thousands of lives, force many more to leave their homes and change the lives of everyone who was involved.

South Vietnam with both its military and provincial areas outlined.

GEOGRAPHY AND WEATHER

The terrain and the weather in South Vietnam affected the nature of warfare waged by the Viet Cong and the North Vietnamese Army. The United States Armed Forces had prepared for a war against the Soviet Union, across the open plains of northern Europe; in Southeast Asia they encountered every type of terrain ranging from rugged mountains covered by thick jungle to flooded paddy fields and river deltas.

South Vietnam is long and thin with an extensive coastline extending over 900 miles from North Vietnam in the north to Cambodia in the Gulf of Siam to the south. It is only around 100 miles wide for much of its length, narrowing to 40 miles at the Demilitarized Zone, next to the 17th Parallel, the border with North Vietnam.

Temperatures are high all year round throughout most of the country, except in the mountainous region running down the Laotian border. Humidity is always high while monsoons and tropical cyclones alternately sweep the northern and the southern regions. Hue, the ancient capital of the north, is soaked with an average of 116in of rain between November and February while Saigon, South Vietnam's capital in the south, has an average of 58in of rain between June and September.

South Vietnam's terrain is varied but the country can be split into three distinct areas.

CENTRAL HIGHLANDS

An inland chain of mountains, ranging from 100 to 200 miles wide, sits astride South Vietnam's border with Cambodia and Laos. The mountains are covered by tropical forests and while some areas have multi-canopy trees hiding tall elephant grass others are secondary growth areas with a denser coverage of smaller trees and thick undergrowth. Occasional bamboo thickets, rubber plantations and farms are scattered across the area. A large plateau, known as the Central Highlands, has peaks ranging from 600 to 1,600ft to the north of Ban Me Thuot while the mountains to the south rise as high as 3,000ft. Rugged spurs and river valleys jut out to the east, in many places almost to the sea, restricting north and south movement to the coastal plain.

CENTRAL LOWLANDS

A narrow coastal area, rarely more than 40 miles wide, separates the mountains from the sea. The lowlands are heavily populated and the farmers live in small villages and hamlets, tending their crops and paddy fields. Sand dunes line the coast and fishermen earn a living from the shallow coastal waters.

MEKONG DELTA

The area south of Saigon is crisscrossed by a network of rivers, including the Mekong, the Dong Nai, the Saigon, and the Vain Co Dong. Canals were added

Terrain varied from mountains covered by thick forests . . . (127-GVC-A372128)

. . . to expanses of marshland and paddy fields cut by canals and streams. (111-CC-40405)

by the French, creating large expanses of paddy fields and areas of high ground where the villagers live. The northern edge of the delta, an area known as the Plain of Reeds, is a large expanse of mud covered by mangrove patches. The Delta floods during the monsoon season, leaving extensive areas under water. The southern tip of the Mekong Delta is known as the Ca Mau Peninsula.

CAMPAIGNS AND PHASES

United States military involvement began with a small number of advisors in March 1962 and over the next seven years the number of troops engaged increased to over half a million. Starting in April 1969, major units were withdrawn as the pacification and Vietnamization programs allowed the South Vietnamese Army (ARVN) to take over offensive operations. The thirteen years of US military activity was later divided into the seventeen distinct phases and campaigns:

ADVISORY PHASE:
15 MARCH 1962 TO 7 MARCH 1965

US Military Assistance Command, Vietnam, battled to help the South Vietnamese Army improve internal security and national defense with field advisors and Special Forces detachments. Thousands of civilians were gathered into protected strategic hamlets but they proved to be unpopular and provoked unrest for the government as it struggled with political turmoil and corruption.

DEFENSE:
8 MARCH 1965 TO 24 DECEMBER 1965

Following attacks on military installations, US troops were deployed across South Vietnam. While the Marine Corps deployed in the north, the Army took over the Central Highlands, the coast and Saigon, leaving the ARVN operating in the Mekong Delta.

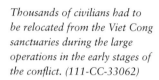

Thousands of civilians had to be relocated from the Viet Cong sanctuaries during the large operations in the early stages of the conflict. (111-CC-33062)

Ground operations were consolidated under US Army Vietnam (USARV) and while engineers began establishing bases and ports, troops kept the Viet Cong at bay. In October a large enemy attack on Plei Me near the Ia Drang Valley marked the start of an advance on Qui Nhon and an attempt to cut the country in two. The recently deployed 1st Cavalry Division retaliated in a month long campaign.

COUNTEROFFENSIVE, PHASE I:
25 DECEMBER 1965 TO 30 JUNE 1966

With troops in position across the country, it was time to expand the search and destroy operations into Viet Cong held areas. United States and Allied troops were deployed as follows:

III Marine Amphibious Force with the South Vietnamese I Corps in the north
I Field Force with the South Vietnamese II Corps in the center
II Field Force with the South Vietnamese III Corps around Saigon
South Vietnamese IV Corps covering the Mekong Delta

Operations improved the security around base camps and across populated areas, protecting the rice harvests and limiting Viet Cong activity.

In February and March 3d Marine Division and 173d Airborne Brigade moved near to the Demilitarized Zone to stop North Vietnamese troops crossing into South Vietnam. B-52s began bombing along the Laos border for the first time in April.

COUNTEROFFENSIVE, PHASE II:
1 JULY 1966 TO 31 MAY 1967

The Joint Chiefs of Staff declared their objectives as ground troops fought a war of attrition in South Vietnam and the Navy and Air Force continued air strikes against the north:

Stop the North Vietnamese control and support of insurgency in South Vietnam and Laos
Assist the South Vietnam in defeating Viet Cong and North Vietnamese forces
Assist the pacification of South Vietnam so the government could extend control

Eighteen large operations, including White Wing/Masher, Hastings, Attleboro and Junction City, were carried out across the country as United States and Allied troops worked together to drive the Viet Cong from their sanctuaries.

COUNTEROFFENSIVE, PHASE III:
1 JUNE 1967 TO 29 JANUARY 1968

By June 1967 US forces had risen to nearly 450,000 personnel and major operations continued as the South Vietnamese Armed Forces started to conduct their own. Vietnamese Special Forces took over a number of Special Forces camps in the Central Highlands but when North Vietnamese attacks began to threaten their existence, sixteen American battalions had to be deployed to restore the situation.

TET COUNTEROFFENSIVE:
30 JANUARY 1968 TO 1 APRIL 1968

Starting on 30 January, over 80,000 North Vietnamese Army and Viet Cong units attacked a wide range of targets across the country during the Tet holiday period. They infiltrated or fired on the majority of cities and provincial capitals, attacking the US Embassy and the Presidential Palace in Saigon and both the Vietnamese Joint General Staff's headquarters and Tan Son Nhut air base on the outskirts; many military installations were also attacked. The US Marines Corps base at Khe Sanh was besieged for over ten weeks while Dak To Special Forces camp in the Central Highlands was repeatedly attacked. US and Allied troops reacted quickly and in many places the fighting was over within days, however, there was extended street fighting in urban areas and it took over a month to clear Hue.

The Tet offensive was a major military defeat for the Communists and the Viet Cong never recovered from the losses it sustained. Most attacks were crushed in the first few hours and anticipated public uprisings did not happen. However, the US public was shocked by the level of violence they saw and many felt betrayed by the generals and politicians who had assured them that the war was being won. As public support for the war diminished in America, thousands of South Vietnamese refugees faced a bleak future.

COUNTEROFFENSIVE, PHASE IV:
2 APRIL 1968 TO 30 JUNE 1968

Battalion-size operations took place between April and June 1968 as US and Allied forces continued their counteroffensive against the scattered remnants of the Viet Cong and North Vietnamese forces. In the north, Operation Pegasus relieved Khe Sanh Combat Base while Operation Delaware regained temporary control of the A Shau Valley, forcing the NVA to end attacks across I Corps.

The emphasis then moved to III Corps as the Viet Cong launched a series of attacks against Saigon on 5 May (the attacks were known as Mini-Tet). The attacks were small and after a few isolated battles around the edge of the city, the NVA and the Viet Cong withdrew.

COUNTEROFFENSIVE, PHASE V:
1 JULY 1968 TO 1 NOVEMBER 1968.

The NVA's final offensive on 17 August was quickly stopped and US troops began concentrating on support for the South Vietnamese government's pacification programs. US and ARVN troops restored control of populated areas, allowing government units to move in. Regional and Popular Forces started to take over responsibility for security while the police and civil authorities systematically screened the population for Viet Cong sympathizers.

President Johnson announced that the bombing campaign over North Vietnam would end in October while the NLF and South Vietnam were invited to join peace talks in Paris for the first time.

COUNTEROFFENSIVE, PHASE VI:
2 NOVEMBER 1968 TO 22 FEBRUARY 1969

President Richard Nixon was elected in November 1968 and two months later he announced the phased withdrawal of US combat troops, coinciding with the start of peace negotiations in Paris. As soon as the populated areas had been cleared, the Accelerated Pacification Campaign extended operations into the countryside, hunting down the Viet Cong's leadership as its units scattered. Meanwhile, ground operations to corner large units operating along the border continued.

TET 69 AND COUNTEROFFENSIVE:
23 FEBRUARY 1969 TO 8 JUNE 1969

On 23 February NVA attacks against military installations across I Corps were stopped. American troop strength peaked at 543,400 in April and although there were over seventy ground operations, the NVA and Viet Cong avoided major contacts.

SUMMER AND FALL 1969:
9 JUNE 1969 TO 31 OCTOBER 1969

US troop numbers fell to 505,500 by October as President Nixon announced more withdrawals. The remaining ground troops were engaged in small unit actions, tracking down fragmented Viet Cong units and fending off isolated attacks on fire bases.

The attack on the US Embassy during the Tet Offensive shocked the American people; Ambassador Ellsworth Bunker inspects the damage. (111-CC-46024)

WINTER AND SPRING 1970:
1 NOVEMBER 1969 TO 30 APRIL 1970

As Army and Marine Corps units continued to withdraw, Vietnamization improved the effectiveness of the South Vietnamese Armed Forces. US and allied forces concentrated their efforts on the Viet Cong's base camps and tried to reduce the number of attacks against military installations.

SANCTUARY COUNTEROFFENSIVE:
1 MAY 1970 TO 30 JUNE 1970

The situation was under control in South Vietnam and attentions turned to NVA bases in Cambodia. As the North Vietnamese and Viet Cong advanced on Phnom Penh, Cambodia's capital, Marshal Lon Nol appealed for help; President Nixon did not hesitate and removed restrictions on crossing the border. US and ARVN troops launched eight separate invasions in May and June, discovering large bases and huge quantities of material.

COUNTEROFFENSIVE, PHASE VII:
1 JULY 1970 TO 30 JUNE 1971

Starting on 30 January, Vietnamese troops advanced from I Corps into Laos aiming to cut the Ho Chi Minh Trail and attack bases around Techepone. Despite large amounts of US fire and air support, Operation Lam Son 719 failed to achieve its objectives and the ARVN fell back in disarray; it did, however, interrupt the North Vietnamese Army's plans to attack in March 1971.

CONSOLIDATION I:
1 JULY 1971 TO 30 NOVEMBER 1971

South Vietnam assumed full control of ground operations as the US Armed Forces handed over responsibility for them on 11 July (101st Airborne Division would carry out the final operation, Jefferson Glen, in October). Phase I of Vietnamization came to an end on 11 August when President Nixon announced that the remaining 191,000 US troops were deployed in a defensive role.

When the American forces had withdrawn they thought they were leaving trained and well-equipped Armed Forces: but could they stop the North Vietnamese? (111-CC-81753)

CONSOLIDATION II:
1 DECEMBER 1971 TO 29 MARCH 1972

The final stages of Vietnamization were carried out, leaving around 25,000 US troops behind to protect US military installations. Meanwhile, the air attacks on North Vietnam were stepped up to disrupt anticipated offensives against South Vietnam and Cambodia.

Both sides exchanged peace proposals during the period but little headway was made. President Nixon proposed to withdraw all US and Allied troops within six months of an agreement being made: the Communists wanted all troops removed and US aid to Indochina.

CEASEFIRE: 30 MARCH 1972 TO 28 JANUARY 1973

The NVA launched a conventional offensive on 30 March 1972, capturing large areas. South Vietnamese troops counterattacked, recapturing Quang Tri City in September, while US Army helicopters and planes struck the NVA supply routes.

With time running out, American advisors working with the South Vietnamese Air Force made their final preparations before they withdrew. The final seven battalions protecting US military installations left but many support and service support units remained behind to help the South Vietnamese stopped.

DEPLOYMENT OF COMBAT TROOPS

THE 2½ WARS CONCEPT

President Kennedy's administration began planning for a new kind of strategy in 1961, expanding the American Armed Forces to face a number of threats around the world. The strategy was known as the 2½ Wars Strategic Concept and by 1965 there were the equivalent of over twenty-five active and reserve divisions ready to deploy either to Europe to face the Soviets or to Asia to face the Chinese. The possibility of a counterinsurgency threat anywhere in the world was counted as half a war.

Initially Vietnam was seen as the half war but the conflict escalated and between March 1965 and April 1968 the Army alone deployed the equivalent of nine divisions and four independent brigades where they are joined by a large number of Allied troops.

By 1967 reinforcements for Europe and the Strategic Reserve had been deployed. Shortages of trained officers and men, the limitations of the twelve-month tour and President Johnson's refusal to mobilize the Reserves severely stretched the Armed Forces. It left the US troops deployed dangerously thinly across Germany and Korea. Units arrived in the following order:

1965

March 8	9th Marine Expeditionary Brigade lands at Da Nang
May	3d Marine Division headquarters arrived at Da Nang to take control of its units
	173d Airborne Brigade arrives at Bien Hoa, and is joined by an Australian battalion
July 29	1st Brigade, 101st Airborne Division deploys
September	1st Cavalry Division (Airmobile) arrives
	Korea's Capital Division and Marine Brigade arrive
October	1st Infantry Division arrives

1966

February	1st Marine Division headquarters takes command of its units at Chu Lai
March	25th Infantry Division deploys and a second Australian battalion deploys
August	196th Light Infantry Brigade deploys
September	4th Infantry Division arrives
	Korea's 9th Infantry Division deploys
December	9th Infantry Division and 199th Light Infantry Brigade deploy

1967

May	A New Zealand company deploys, and is joined by a second company in December
September	The 23d American Division starts to form with 196th Light Infantry Brigade
	A regiment from Thailand deploys
October	198th Light Infantry Brigade joins the American Division
November	101st Airborne Division (Airmobile) joins its 1st Brigade
December	11th Light Infantry Brigade joins the American Division. Australia deploys 3d Battalion Royal Australian Regiment to join the Australian Task Force in III Corps. New Zealand deploys an Infantry Company to III Corps.

1968

February	3d Brigade, 82d Airborne Division deploys following the Tet Offensive
April 30	US military personnel in South Vietnam peaks at 543,400
July	Thailand's commitment increases to a division

US TROOP NUMBERS

From just a few dozen military staff in March 1955, the number of troops serving in South Vietnam grew to 543,400 by the end of April 1969. The election of President Nixon in November 1968 marked the beginning of the end of American involvement in Vietnam. His adminstration imposed

Thousands of troops poured into South Vietnam between 1965 and 1968; many arrived by ship. (111-CC-31462)

Vietnamization on the US Armed Forces, so they could hand over responsibility for the fighting to the South Vietnamese. Units started to withdraw in the summer of 1969 as the Armed Forces began looking at a new strategy, the 1½ Wars Strategic Concept. Over the next three years units left the country and by the end of 1973 only fifty advisors were left. The following table shows the number of troops deployed at the end of each year:

INCREASING NUMBERS		DECREASING NUMBERS	
1959	760	1969	475,200
1960	900	1970	334,600
1961	3,200	1971	156,800
1962	11,300	1972	24,200
1963	16,300	1973	50
1964	23,000	1974	50
1965	184,000		
1966	385,300		
1967	486,600		
1968	536,000		

US Marines were the last troops to leave South Vietnam on 30 April 1975 as they helped to evacuate the US Embassy in Saigon during Operation Frequent Wind.

CHAPTER 2

COMMAND AND CONTROL

The number of servicemen and women serving in Vietnam grew from a few dozen advisors to over half a million between 1950 and 1968. Command and control had to reorganize several times to cope with the increase as the United States Armed Forces' role changed from advising to conducting large multi-battalion operations across the country.

MILITARY ASSISTANCE ADVISORY GROUP, INDOCHINA (MAAG – INDOCHINA)

A small military assistance advisory group of 128 men arrived in Saigon on 3 August 1950 and by November it had been formed into Military Assistance Advisory Group, Indochina. On 23 December the United States signed military aid agreements for Vietnam, Laos and Cambodia; the commitment would cost $2.6 billion over the next fifteen years. The Group distributed and maintained equipment but it had no authority to train their South Vietnamese counterparts.

General Navarre, the French commander, took advantage of the aid to go on the offensive against the Communist Viet Minh, deploying a large force at Dien Bien Phu in November 1953 to precipitate a decisive battle. It was decisive. After a six-month-long siege the garrison surrendered on 8 May 1954, ending French military operations.

On 20 July the Geneva Accords officially ended the fighting in Indochina and although neither the United States nor South Vietnam formally acknowledged them, the United States agreed to adhere to the terms laid down, including the following:

Vietnam would be split at the 17th Parallel
Laos and Cambodia would be granted independence
New troops and equipment could not be moved into Vietnam
Neither North nor South Vietnam could establish new military bases
New types of arms, ammunition and equipment were forbidden, except as replacements
The number of advisors and their staff was fixed at 542 French and 342 Americans

The Geneva Accords left President Eisenhower's administration in a dilemma. France was looking for direct armed support, but he was unable to act without Congress approval and support from the rest of the Southeast Asia Treaty Organization (SEATO), the alliance formed to counter the Communist threat. Another way of supporting South Vietnam had to be found.

The losing struggle against the Viet Cong is etched on the face of this South Vietnamese Ranger captain. (111-SC-616827)

General John O'Daniel took over as the commander of MAAG, Indochina, on 12 April 1954 and arranged clearance with the French commander, General Ely, for US advisors to start training the Vietnamese Armed Forces. The agreement was ratified by the President's special envoy, General J. Lawton Collins, and on 1 February 1955 the new Training Relations and Instruction Mission (TRIM) started work. While Army and Air Force advisors helped the South Vietnamese Armed Forces out in the field to defend their country, Naval advisors supervised the evacuation of hundreds of thousands of civilians from the north to the south before the border closed in May 1955. French involvement finally came to an end in August 1955 when their High Commissioner left Saigon.

While Vietnam was dealing with the end of French rule, Cambodia declared itself an independent state on 25 September 1954. The following May it agreed to accept military aid from the United States and Military Assistance Advisory Group, Cambodia, was organized in Phnom Penh to supervise the delivery of military aid.

MAAG, INDOCHINA'S COMMANDERS

Brigadier General Francis G. Brink	October 1950
Major General Thomas J.H. Trapnell	August 1952
Lieutenant General John W. O'Daniel	April 1954

MILITARY ASSISTANCE ADVISORY GROUP, VIETNAM (MAAG, VIETNAM)

The departure of the French and the Cambodian situation called for the reorganization of the military assistance in Vietnam and on 1 November 1955 Military Assistance Advisory Group, Indochina, was renamed Military Assistance Advisory Group, Vietnam. TRIM was renamed Combat Arms Training and Organization Division and Temporary Equipment Recovery Mission (TERM) was established to salvage American material left behind by the French. By May 1960 the number of staff had been raised to 685.

South Vietnam faced turbulent times in the late 1950s. The Army suffered widespread corruption and it was opposed by several religious sects and a criminal group known as the Binh Xuyen. While the Montagnards living in the Central Highlands refused to recognize the government, the influx of over one million Catholic refugees from North Vietnam upset the country's balance of power.

President Diem's refusal to hold a referendum in 1956 stopped the Communists seizing power through the ballot box but terrorist activity against the South Vietnamese government intensified. Elections in the fall of 1959 did not stop the unrest (many claimed results were falsified) and President Diem was forced to announce that his country was at war with the Viet Cong as MAAG, Vietnam, began teaching his troops anti-guerrilla tactics.

The new United States President, John F. Kennedy, pledged increased military and economic aid for South Vietnam while a new policy group, known as the Country Team, devised a Counterinsurgency Plan to improve the South Vietnamese Army, train a Civil Guard and a Self Defense Corps while US Special Forces teams trained a new Vietnamese Ranger force.

In October 1961 a team headed by General Maxwell D. Taylor made the following recommendations to improve the situation in South Vietnam:

Expansion of the Vietnamese Armed Forces and the number of US advisors
US combat support, in particular tactical aircraft and helicopters
Support for the strategic hamlet program, moving villagers out of Viet Cong control

The suggestions were approved but as MAAG, Vietnam's, headquarters mushroomed to 2,394 staff, the existing command structure could not cope. A new type of command structure was needed.

Although US Military Assistance Command, Vietnam, was established to take over control of military operations on 8 February 1962, MAAG, Vietnam, continued to control the field advisors (3,400 at the beginning of 1963) until it was disbanded on 15 May 1964.

The heat and humidity have taken their toll on this American advisor and he takes a short break while his Vietnamese unit crosses a river. (111-SC-616-825)

General Westmoreland is briefed on the deteriorating situation by two advisors. (111-SC-616823)

Ambassador Taylor and General Westmoreland give statements to the press following attacks on Qui Nhon base in February 1965; the attacks led to retaliatory air attacks on North Vietnam. (111-CC-31914)

MAAG, VIETNAM'S COMMANDERS

Lieutenant General Samuel Williams	November 1955
Lieutenant General Lionel C. McGarr	September 1960
Major General Charles J. Timmes	July 1962

US MILITARY ASSISTANCE COMMAND, VIETNAM (MACV)

US Military Assistance Command, Vietnam, was established as a temporary measure to supervise the counterinsurgency effort against the Viet Cong, allowing MAAG, Vietnam, to continue work on the Military Assistance Program. The commander, General Paul Harkins, was responsible for policy, operations and assistance of the South Vietnamese Armed Forces, advising their government on military and security matters. The Command also had an Army commander to control operations (the Naval and Air Force involvement were still only small) while the Navy's Support Activity provided logistical support from Saigon. The intention was that MACV would be disbanded once order had been restored but as the situation deteriorated, the two headquarters increasingly came into conflict.

In March 1964 General Paul Harkins requested full control over all Army activities to ease the problems and two months later MAAG, Vietnam, was closed down as MACV took over responsibility for the Military Assistance Program. On 20 June 1964, General William C. Westmoreland became commander of US Military Assistance Command, Vietnam, with responsibility for all military activities in Vietnam. It would eventually have the following subordinate commands:

III Marine Amphibious Force	Ran Marine operations in I Corps
I Field Forces Vietnam	Controlled operations in II Corps Tactical Zone
II Field Forces Vietnam	Ran operations in III Corps and later IV Corps Tactical Zone
XXIV Corps	Controlled Army operations in I Corps after 1968
USARV	Controlled administrative and logistical Army units
5th Special Forces Group	Ran countrywide Special Forces operations from Nha Trang
Field Advisory Element	Ran South Vietnamese Armed Forces advisory activities
CORDS	The Civil Operations and Rural Development Support programs
Naval Forces, Vietnam	Controlled warships off the coast and aircraft carrier wings
Seventh Air Force	Commanded land-based air wings, including those in Thailand

MACV headquarters moved out of Saigon in 1967 as part of operation MOOSE (Move Out Of Saigon Expeditiously), part of General Westmoreland's plan to reduce the US military presence in Vietnam's towns and cities. It relocated to Tan Son Nhut, north of the capital, remaining there until it finally closed down on 29 March 1973.

MACV, VIETNAM COMMANDERS

General Paul Harkins	February 1962
General William Westmoreland	June 1964
General Creighton Abrams	July 1968
General Frederick Weyand	June 1972

FIELD ADVISORY ELEMENT, MACV

Advisors provided the link between the American and South Vietnamese military at all levels with the help of interpreters. In many isolated areas they were the first Americans the Vietnamese had encountered and although they initially faced many problems, hard work and initiative overcame them and the majority developed a close bond with their Vietnamese counterparts. Advisors accompanied troops on operations and they were able to call on American artillery, helicopter and air support. Although they did not have the authority to command the Vietnamese troops, advisors often stepped in to help steady a shaken unit.

To begin with field army advisory teams were allocated to each regiment and they gave advice and assistance with training, operational planning, communications, logistics, medical evacuation and intelligence. Advisors also worked with each province, providing help with psychological warfare and civil affairs.

In 1964 teams were allocated to battalions while others joined the districts around Saigon, increasing the number of advisors to over 4,700; eventually each district had an advisory team. Over 350 new teams were created in 1968 to advise Regional and Popular Forces platoons on village defense, bringing the total to over 9,400 advisors. The advisory teams' role took on a new importance as the American troops handed over to the Vietnamese and prepared to withdraw.

FIELD FORCES

The US Army level of command for controlling divisions and support troops across a large area was the Corps. However, the situation in Vietnam demanded a headquarters capable of controlling the tactical situation while it advised the South Vietnamese Armed Forces. It also had to deal with the supply problems inherent with operating in a hostile country while pacifying the civilian population. General Westmoreland chose the title Field Force to avoid confusion with the South Vietnamese Corps zones and the two were organized in March 1966. I Field Force took control of II Corps while II Field Force covered III and IV Corps (I Corps was under III Marine Amphibious Force control).

American advisors worked closely with the ARVN during the Military Assistance period. (111-CC-27764)

A Field Force Headquarters was far more flexible than the traditional Corps organization and it managed additional units as they moved into and out of the area. The Artillery Headquarters and Headquarters Battalion was responsible for heavy artillery support across the Field Force's area and the two Artillery Groups each had a number of heavy batteries, including self-propelled 175mm guns and 8in howitzers. The batteries had a list of pre-planned missions which could be fired at short notice and they were used to protect military installations (both US and ARVN), lines of communications and population centers; combat units could also request support. A Chemical Detachment Battalion was armed with heavy mortars.

Operational communications were controlled by a Signal Battalion while an Army Security Agency Battalion dealt with confidential wireless and radio traffic. A Military Intelligence Detachment coordinated the interpretation of intelligence material while a Psychological Operations Battalion provided support for units in the field.

The Civil Affairs Company and two Public Information Detachments, one for each Corps, organized civil programs while the Military History Detachment recorded events.

The Transportation Company provided vehicles for the Field Force staff while the Military Police Company covered security issues. An Army Postal Unit dealt with mail, both military and personal.

I FIELD FORCE, VIETNAM (I FFV)

A provisional field force headquarters, titled Task Force ALPHA, was organized at Nha Trang in August 1965 to counter the NVA's threat to the Central Highlands. It was renamed Field Forces, Vietnam, the following month, with control over all US and Allied forces. It was renamed I Field Force, Vietnam, covering II Corps when II Field Force was organized.

I Field Force took over command of the following combat units when it came into existence: 1st Cavalry Division, 3d Brigade, 25th Infantry Division and 1st Brigade, 101st Airborne Division. It also commanded 5th Special Forces Group's Company B while fixed wing and helicopter support was provided by 17th Aviation Group. The following combat units joined I Field Force later:

4th Infantry Division after July 1966
52d Artillery Group in January 1967 and 41st Artillery Group in May 1967
173d Airborne Brigade after May 1967
Task Force South (Provisional) was formed in July 1968 with 173rd Airborne Brigade and brigades from 4th Division and 101st Airborne Division

The Field Force Headquarters closed in 30 April 1971 but many of the staff went on to serve with Second Regional Assistance Command (SRAC) and US Army Forces, Military Region 2, the two new organizations created to deal with Vietnamization and redeployment.

An advisor discusses the outcome of an armored personnel carrier field exercise with the squadron's officer. (111-CC-22793)

General Westmoreland congratulates a group of Air Cavalry troopers after Operation Thayer II. (111-CC-78503)

II FIELD FORCE, VIETNAM (II FFV)

II Field Force was organized at Bien Hoa, near Long Binh, to control operations in III Corps. It would later extend its area to cover IV Corps and became the largest combat command in Vietnam, coordinating US, Allied and ARVN operations around Saigon, along the Cambodian border and across the Mekong Delta. Capital Military Assistance Command was organized in June 1968 to secure Saigon and the surrounding provinces.

II Field Force took command of 1st Infantry Division, 25th Infantry Division and 173d Airborne Brigade when it formed; it also controlled 5th Special Forces Group's Company A. 12th Aviation Group provided fixed wing and helicopter support while 23d Artillery Group took control of the artillery; 54th Artillery Group joined in October 1966. The following combat units joined later:

196th Infantry Brigade and 11th Armored Cavalry Regiment from October 1966
9th Infantry Division and 199th Infantry Brigade after December 1966
3d Brigade, 101st Airborne Division after December 1967
1st Cavalry Division and 3d Brigade, 82d Airborne Division after October 1968

Field Force II headquarters closed in May 1971 but many of the staff went on to serve with Third Regional Assistance Command (TRAC).

CORPS TACTICAL ZONE AND MILITARY REGION US ARMY ADVISORS

In June 1966 senior US Army advisors were added to each of the South Vietnamese Corps area. Most were either colonels or brigadier generals but in October 1970 four lieutenant generals took over when the role became the responsibility of the senior general in each Military Region (Military Regions had the same number as the Corps). IV Corps was renamed Delta Military Assistance Command in April 1968 and then Military Region 4 in October 1970.

THE MARINES AND THE ARMY IN I CORPS

9th Marine Expeditionary Brigade had been activated after the Gulf of Tonkin incident in August 1964 as a reaction force to any further attacks on US bases. Following attacks against Da Nang base in February 1965, President Johnson agreed to have two Marine battalions deployed to protect US installations in the northern sector of South Vietnam. 1st Marine Battalion Landing Team landed on 8 March but rather than enemy fire, the Marines were met by dignitaries and schoolgirls carrying garlands of flowers as they waded out of the surf.

US Marines had been deployed first because of their ability to supply themselves from ships and landing craft by Logisitics over the Beach (LOTB) methods. This allowed them to operate without ports and airfields and by the end of the month 5,000 Marines had formed a perimeter around Da Nang base. To begin with they had strict orders not to engage the Viet Cong but as enemy activity increased in the area, the order was reversed and on 22 April the Marines carried out their first helicopter assault landing near Da Nang air base.

III Marine Expeditionary Force was renamed III Marine Amphibious Force (III MAF) on 7 May and its commander, Major General William R. Collins, was placed in command of all US Marine and Army units in I Corps area.

3d Marine Expeditionary Brigade was landing near Chu Lai (it was briefly renamed 3d Marine Amphibious Brigade) at the same time, extending US activity across I Corps and 3d Marine Division headquarters were ashore by the 30th, the day Major-General Lewis Walt took over as commanding general of III MAF. By 7 June over 16,500 Marines had landed as fighting intensified around Da Nang and Phu Bai.

A series of helicopter and amphibious assaults extended the Marines' hold on the coast of I Corps over the next nine months and in March 1966 Force Logistic Command had to be activated at Da Nang to supply ongoing operations and prepare for the imminent arrival of the 1st Marine Division in the Chu Lai area at the end of the month.

Although the Marines were able to keep enemy activity under control for the next twelve months, by the spring of 1967 it was clear that Army troops would have to be sent north to reinforce I Corps. Task Force Oregon, a division-sized organization comprising three separate brigades and an assortment of support troops, reached Quang Ngai on 12 April and took over responsibility for the southern part of Quang Tin Province. The move allowed 1st Marine Division to move north to the Demilitarized Zone and permitted 1st Cavalry Division to extend its area of operations along the coast area of Binh Dinh Province, opening Highway 1.

Task Force Oregon was headquartered at Chu Lai and ran operations around Chu Lai and Quang Ngai until 23d Infantry Division (American) was formed on 22 September 1967.

NVA activity continued to increase over the winter of 1967/8 and the Tet Offensive in February 1968 meant a further increase in Army units in I Corps as 1st Cavalry Division and 101st Airborne Division joined the battle for Hue and Quang Tri. MACV set up a Forward Headquarters on 9 February to coordinate Army operations in I Corps; it was renamed Provisional Corps, Vietnam, on 10 March 1968. Even though the NVA and Viet Cong attacks subsided, it was obvious that I Corps needed a permanent Army presence and XXIV Corps was activated at Phu Bai on 15 August 1968 to replace the Provisional Corps. Despite remonstrations from some quarters, the Corps reported to III MAF as it controlled combat operations immediately south of the Demilitarized Zone; III MAF controlled support and civil activities across I Corps as well as combat operations south of XXIV Corps' area of activity.

27th Marine Regiment was the first to leave Vietnam in September 1968 and 3rd Marine Division followed between July and November 1969. 1st Marine Division started to send units home the following spring and on 14 April 1971 III MAF disbanded as 1st Marine Regiment prepared to be the last combat unit to leave. XXIV Corps had moved to Da Nang in March 1970 but it controlled Army units until June 1972 when its assets joined First Regional Assistance Command (FRAC), the new command overseeing the final handover to the Vietnamese Armed Forces.

MILITARY ASSISTANCE COMMANDS

The Tet offensive in February 1968 exposed weaknesses in the Vietnamese defense of Saigon and the lack of coordination between the military and police forces. The situation was rectified by the appointment of a new military governor for the Saigon area and Gia Dinh Province in June 1968 while the Vietnamese Army commander of the Capital Military District acted as his deputy.

General Abrams and Commander Zumwaltz attend the handing over of sixty-four gunboats to the South Vietnamese Navy. (111-CC-58664)

II Field Force had set up a temporary command group called Hurricane Forward in February 1968 and a Task Force was reestablished following a second NVA offensive in May. It was organized as Capital Military Assistance Command the following month.

Delta Military Assistance Command was organized in April 1969 to coordinate activities across the Mekong Delta.

COORDINATION AND COOPERATION

US Military Forces had to cooperate at all levels with their Allies, in particular the South Vietnamese Army. General Westmoreland originally suggested establishing a combined US-ARVN headquarters but the South Vietnamese Army staff objected to the idea and US commanders had to coordinate operations through one of the nine advisory groups out in the field. Representatives on the Vietnamese General Staff dealt with high-level issues. Intelligence collected by American and Vietnamese sources was pooled and assessed at the Combined Intelligence Center, Vietnam.

While South Korean troops controlled their own operations following the guidelines set down by the Free World Military Assistance Council, Free World Military Forces from Australia, New Zealand, the Philippines and Thailand were under American control.

A DIFFERENT KIND OF WAR

In previous wars success and failure could often judged on the amount of territory captured or lost. In Vietnam, statistics became important and new terminology and reports appeared while commanders tried to maintain the pressure on an elusive enemy. Increasing the time combat units spent in the field improved Operational Effectiveness while higher numbers of enemy killed or prisoners taken increased Operational Efficiency. Eventually, divisional staff had to compile eighteen different statistical summaries, so they could be discussed at Weekly Operational Review and Analysis briefings.

OPERATIONAL EFFECTIVENESS

Divisions fought a constant struggle to maintain the numbers of men in the field and continual studies were made to improve their organization. The standard organization of seven rifle battalions and two mechanized infantry battalions did not suit the terrain in some areas. Some mechanized battalions had to be dismounted while others were exchanged between divisions, moving to areas where they could be deployed.

The three-rifle company battalions were also reorganized into four-rifle company organization to increase effectiveness and battalions changed over the winter of 1968 and 1969; divisions generally gained 33 per cent in rifle strength. It was also found that four-battalion brigades were very effective but divisions rarely used them because it created an ineffective two-battalion brigade.

As divisions settled into their areas, the number of defensive missions grew as units organized routine patrols, base security and convoy escorts. Units had to be rotated to stop the men becoming complacent and enemy activity had to be monitored so that troops were deployed effectively.

Divisions had to keep a constant watch on the use of their manpower. Rotations, excessive numbers of men deployed on base and administrative duties and long-term minor illnesses severely limited the number of men in the field:

5 per cent	Losses due to rotation and casualties were slow to be replaced
10 per cent	Infantry soldiers diverted from line units to brigade and battalion headquarters
15 per cent	Fire base perimeter security duties and morale boosting facilities

Poor management could reduce a company's paper strength from 164 down to 120 (known as the Paddy Strength).

Commanders also had to monitor recurrent diseases as malaria, diarrhea and foot diseases could debilitate hundreds of men if preventive programs and sanitary conditions were not controlled.

OPERATIONAL EFFICIENCY

Operations in Vietnam were designed to sweep areas (known as search-and-destroy and later clear-and-search operations) and commanders could only rely on the number of Viet Cong or North Vietnamese soldiers killed (known as the body count) or captured and the amount of material seized to measure their success. A high body count soon became recognized as an important factor in operations as statistics took on a new importance. Commanders were under constant pressure to return high body counts, but results could be misleading. In many areas the Viet Cong chose to hide while they regrouped and a successful unit which had cleared its area would see its body count fall.

A battalion commander outlines the tactical situation in his operational area to his brigadier during 101st Airborne Division's Operation Cook.

Brigade commanders were continually looking to reinforce successes and improve on failures as the Viet Cong responded with new tactics. The nature of the war in Vietnam made it difficult to carry out operational studies and it took skill and experience to draw the correct conclusions from them. One of the main indicators used was a comparison between the number of enemy killed compared with their own casualties, often called the Exchange Ratio or, more controversially, the Kill Ratio.

Well-led and motivated units had consistent positive results rather than the occasional big encounter. Poor results could mean either that the unit needed extra training and a change in tactics or the enemy had moved out of its area of operations.

The number of enemy killed following a sighting was known as the Contact Success Ratio. A high number meant that units were using the right tactics while a low number showed that the enemy was consistently evading contact.

CONSTANT PRESSURE CONCEPT

The NVA and the Viet Cong suffered heavy losses during the large US operations in 1967 and many units went into hiding. Although results could be rewarding, it took time to plan a large operation; time which the NVA and the Viet Cong soldiers used to rest while political cadres gathered new recruits. The Constant Pressure Concept was introduced as a solution.

Company and platoon-sized operations could be organized quickly and they were more responsive to intelligence leads. The risk of using smaller units was higher but well thought-out contingency plans made it acceptable even though the operations put extra pressure on junior officers. Constant searches of an area made it impossible for the NVA and Viet Cong to regroup, making units difficult to command and the fragmented groups eventually disintegrated under the pressure.

CHAPTER 3

THOSE WHO SERVED

Over 9 million men and women served in the Armed Services between 1964 and 1973; 2,594,000 of them were posted to Vietnam. More than 1.7 million were drafted during the same period and while four out of five men serving in Vietnam in 1965 were volunteers, by 1970 the number had fallen to 30 per cent. The majority of draftees served in the Army and while around 40,000 served in the Marine Corps, the Navy and Air Force continued only to accept volunteers.

VOLUNTEERS

Some men volunteered at their local Armed Forces Recruiting Stations so they could time their service and plan their education or career around it. They could also choose their Military Occupation Specialty (MOS) providing their Armed Forces Classification Test score was high enough. Men served for three years and they were then in the Standby Reserve for three years. They could be mobilized if there was a war or a national emergency, however, Vietnam was only classified as a conflict and Reservists were never recalled. Men were discharged at the end of their six-year military obligation.

Over one million men volunteered to serve in the National Guard or the Organized Reserves and after six months of training they attended monthly weekend drills, training courses and a two-week summer camp for the next six years. Only a small number of National Guard units were posted to Vietnam but several were deployed to deal with the violent anti-war demonstrations at college campuses across the United States during the latter stages of the conflict.

THE SELECTIVE SERVICE SYSTEM

All males had to register at one of the 4,000 draft boards when they reached the age of 18; 17-year-olds could enlist if they had their parents' permission but they had to wait until they were eligible for service in Vietnam. Draft boards were given a monthly quota and men were eligible to be called until the age of 27. The oldest were drafted at the beginning of the conflict but the situation was reversed in June 1967 so that 18-year-olds were called first, in the belief that it was easier to draft men before they started college, careers or families. The number of men called every year varied considerably and while numbers peaked at over 380,000 in 1966, they had dropped rapidly by 1970. Draftees served for two years followed by four years on the Reserve.

While the Army accepted thousands of of draftees, the Marine Corps was more selective, preferring to accept volunteers; the Air Force and Navy only accepted volunteers.

New recruits receive training with the .30 machine gun during their Advanced Infantry Training. (111-SC-618815)

THE LOTTERY

In 1969 a lottery was introduced to make the selection of draftees impartial and registrants born between 1 January 1944 and 31 December 1950 (men aged 18–26) were included. Capsules containing dates were drawn live on radio and television and paired with a lottery number. Each state and county had to fulfil its draft quota and the numerical sequence determined who would be drafted first. The first draw was held on 1 December 1969 and millions watched as Congressman Alexander Pirnie drew the numbers. The lottery ended in 1973.

CLASSIFICATION

After men had received their Registration Certificate, or Draft Card, they were called for their classification tests where they completed questionnaires and underwent the Armed Forces Physical Examination. The following areas were checked:

P - Physical capacity or stamina
U - Upper extremities
L - Lower extremities
H - Hearing and ears
E - Eyes
S - Psychiatric

Men had to be awarded 1, the top mark, in all six categories to qualify for the combat arms (the artillery accepted 2 for hearing). The combined results determined the man's classification and it was printed on a results card complete with the following statement:

This is your Notice of Classification, advising you of the determination of your selective service local board that you have been classified in accordance with Selective Service Regulations . . .

Class I-A meant that a man a good chance of being drafted and while the rest of Class I and all of Class II were deferred to a later date, Classes III and IV were classified exempt from military service due to personal, employment or medical reasons. A minority lied about their personal circumstances or tried to fake the result of the physical but the majority accepted the result. The boards were supposed to operate impartially but there were suspicions that different criteria were applied across the country. The following list outlines the main classifications and what they signified:

CLASS I

I-A: Available for military service and almost certain to be drafted

I-A-O: Conscientious objector available for non-combat military service

I-C: Member of the Armed Forces, Environmental Science Services Administration or the Public Health Service

I-D: Member of the reserves or a student undergoing military training

I-O: Conscientious objector available for civilian work in hospitals or other service work

I-S: Student deferral; lasted until graduation from high school, the end of a college or university academic year or their 20th birthday; deferment could be lost if grades dropped

I-W: Conscientious objector performing civilian health work or other service work

I-Y: Qualified for military service only in time of war or a national emergency

CLASS II

II-A: Deferred due to a civilian occupation (engineering, defense work, teaching, police)

II-C: Deferred due to an agricultural occupation

II-S: Deferred student on special studies

CLASS III

III-A: Extreme hardship deferment or the registrant had a dependent child

CLASS IV

IV-A: Sufficient prior active service or a sole surviving son

IV-B: Official deferred by law

IV-C: Alien not currently liable for military service (many were later reclassified and served)

IV-D: Minister of religion or divinity student

IV-F: Physically, mentally or morally unfit; some imitated an illness to avoid being drafted

CLASS V

V-A: Over the age of liability for military service

There have been many discussions about how men from different social and racial backgrounds were allocated to units but statistics indicate that the Armed Forces in Vietnam generally represented the national population in both areas. However, the upper and middle classes were more likely to be exempted or deferred due to their reserved occupations or continuing education while the lower classes were more likely to be classified I-A. While only 40 per cent of college graduates went to Vietnam, around 65 per cent of high-school graduates and dropouts served. The Army often capitalized on a man's education, assigning him to the appropriate arm or service to develop his skills; it meant that high-school graduates and dropouts were usually assigned to combat units. The racial and social composition of society in America meant that many Blacks and Hispanics fell into this category and consequently suffered higher casualties.

DRAFT DODGERS

Thousands (numbers vary from 50,000 to over 100,000) refused to be caught up in their country's war for a variety of reasons, including political, personal or religious beliefs, and many did not register with their draft board. Some draft dodgers ignored the registration letter and tried to avoid being arrested while thousands emigrated to Canada to escape the authorities (meanwhile, hundreds of Canadians enlisted in the American Armed Forces). Others openly defied authority and publically burnt their draft cards at one of the many anti-war demonstrations.

SWEARING IN

Volunteers, draftees, Guardsmen and Reservists from all Armed Services gathered to be sworn in together by an officer. With their right hand raised, they pledged to defend America from all enemies, foreign and domestic, and to obey all lawful orders of those appointed over them. The declaration ended with the words 'Congratulations, you are a member of the Armed Forces of the United States.' Whatever route the man had taken to join, there was no turning back. Once the leaving parties with friends and farewells with family members were over, the man was left alone to comtemplate his new life as a serviceman as he climbed on the chartered bus heading for one of the Armed Forces training centers.

BECOMING A SOLDIER

BASIC TRAINING

The recruits were met by drill sergeants with their distinctive Smokey Bear hats (drill instructors in the Marines) at the reception station and they were subjected to shouts and curses as they started Zero Week, a round of tests, inoculations and equipment issues; they also received a severe haircut.

Men were allocated to a company billet area with three buildings and a parade ground. They slept in the austere surroundings of the barrack block and their belongings were kept in foot lockers. They had to work together to keep their area spotless and punishment drills or physical exercise were dealt out to anyone who stepped out of line. The men dined in the mess hall; the administration building had offices, an orderly room, a supply room and the arms cage.

Men learnt how to drill, practiced formations and learnt the basics of service life. Hours were filled with inspections, exercised, long distance marching, formation marching and rifle drill. Courses covered self-defense and confidence training, first aid, tactical training and rifle marksmanship with the M14.

As the weeks passed, the drill sergeants encouraged platoons to compete, increasing the sense of teamwork, and singled out promising candidates as squad leaders and platoon sergeants. The eight-week course ended with a graduation ceremony and a short break before the next stage of their training began.

ADVANCED INFANTRY TRAINING

Men assigned to the infantry were posted to one of the many schools to begin training in their specialist area; some attended a two-week Leadership Preparation Course so they could serve as squad leaders and platoon guides. The men were organized into training companies with three rifle platoons and a support weapons platoon armed with mortar and recoilless rifle crews.

The eight-week course continued to inflict physical exercise, drill and inspections on the men but courses were more intensive, and they were dedicated to squad tactics, hand-to-hand combat, patrolling and navigation. The men were given instruction on all types of weapons ranging from pistols and grenade launchers to rocket launchers and the .50-caliber machine gun, but the most time was spent on the M14 rifle and the M60 machine gun. Other subjects included survival and escape training, radio procedures, mines and booby traps and for the first time the men were given specific information on the type of warfare they would encounter in Vietnam. Some trainees volunteered for the Basic Airborne Course at Fort Benning provided they passed the three-week Airborne Physical Fitness Test and carried out five parachute jumps.

During the later years of the conflict, many instructors were veterans and they passed on their knowledge during the week-long Vietnam orientation training course. Men were taught about the Viet Cong's tactics and given extra tuition on patrolling, navigation and booby traps; the week's course ended with a simulated cordon and search operation on a mock-up Vietnamese village.

Towards the end of the course the men were told their destination and for most it was Vietnam; draftees had thirty days' leave while volunteers often went to Stateside units first to complete their training. Men bound for other postings were only given two weeks' leave.

NON-COMMISSIONED OFFICERS' CANDIDATE COURSE

Promising candidates who had passed the Leadership Preparation Course could go on to take the NCO Candidate Course. By 1967 there was a shortage of NCOs in Vietnam and the decision was taken to train promising candidates as squad leaders. Over 20,000 infantry NCOs passed the course over the next four years and the majority went to Vietnam where they had to work hard before they were accepted by time-served senior NCOs and the grunts.

Potential squad leaders practice an assault landing on a 'hot' landing zone at an NCO academy. (111-SC-645319)

MARINE CORPS

Officers went to the processing center at Quantico, Virginia, while other ranks went to one of the three centers at San Diego, California, and Parris Island, South Carolina. Commandant General David M. Shoup summarized the Corps' attitude to training recruits with the following list of actions the drill instructors would carry out: 'receive, degrade, sanitize, immunize, clothe, equip, train, pain, scold, mold, sand and polish'.

The initial ten-week program was split into five phases, Receiving, Forming, and Phases I, II and III. During the two initial stages recruits lived and trained together in platoons and they learnt the basics; respect for authority, how to take care of themselves, and teamwork. Phase I was three weeks of drill, exercise, marching and getting used to their equipment while Phase II included two weeks of further drills, use of the rifle and marksmanship, followed by a week on mess and maintenance duties. Phase III had examinations, intensive exercise, swimming instruction and hand-to-hand combat, concluding with an overnight exercise and a military field meet.

Following the graduation parade, men were assigned their Military Occupational Specialties (MOSs) and many went to the two Infantry Training Regiments at Camp Pendleton or Camp Lejeune where they had further training similar to the Army's Advanced Infantry Training.

THE OFFICER CORPS

In 1965 many higher level officers were veterans of the Second World War or Korea, while others had seen service across Europe during the Cold War era. Junior officers had joined efficient and well-equipped Regular Army forces where they learnt how to fight on the open plains of Europe. Few had experienced counterinsurgency warfare and officers had to adapt to the new battlefield where it took time, patience and skills to learn how to fight in the jungles and paddy fields of South Vietnam.

Junior officers were the vital link in the chain of command during the small-scale platoon and company battles in Vietnam. They had to control their men in a difficult enviroment, where they were often isolated for long periods as they relied on tenuous radio links to keep in touch with their commanders. An officer could call upon a devastating amount of fire support but he had to use it wisely in populated areas where the villagers and the enemy dressed the same.

Although there was an abundance of experienced junior officers during the early days, the rapid expansion of the Armed Forces and the annual rotation system put a tremendous strain on the number available and eventually virtually all serving officers went to Vietnam, some several times. Steps were taken to increase the number of junior officers available but additional training could not replace experience. By the end of the conflict, experienced men sometimes refused to take orders from their new officer. Racial tensions also increased as the Civil Rights movement gained momentum in the States, and many white, middle-class officers faced difficulties dealing with the issues among their men. A few men took their disobedience a stage further by attempting to wound or kill their officer, a practice known as fragging.

Despite the problems, the overwhelming majority of junior officers (many of them in their early twenties) worked hard to gain their men's respect as they tried to achieve difficult objectives. Sometimes the young officer had tough decisions to make, decisions that could cost men's lives. Many lieutenants and captains spent their first six months serving with a combat unit before transferring to a staff post; a situation that was often resented by the enlisted men. However, nearly 3,000 captains and lieutenants lost their lives in Vietnam.

Although senior officers had a reputation for having an easy life in their safe and comfortable base areas, many served alongside their men during operations or risked their lives flying overhead in their command helicopters. Over 100 lieutenant-colonels and over 200 majors were killed in action.

Army officers were trained at one of three types of establishment. The US Military Academy at West Point trained the professional officers (known as lifers), but the demands placed on Officer Corps by the rapid expansion of the Armed Forces meant that it could not cope.

Reserve Officers Training Corps (ROTC) Programs were present on many university campuses in 1965 but as support for the war waned and students staged anti-war protests, numbers fell and some programs were withdrawn. Courses were four years long and many joined to help pay their tuition fees. Candidates attended military lectures, drills and summer courses before they were commissioned. A twelve-week Officer Basic Course at Fort Benning and specialized branch training followed; distinguished graduates could apply for Regular Army commissions. Graduates served for six years.

College graduates could attend the twenty-three week course at the Officers Candidate School (OCS) if they had attended college for two years. Experienced non-commissioned officers could also attend the course as battlefield commissions were rarely issued in Vietnam. As the number of junior officers dwindled, standards had to be lowered to keep up the numbers of men.

A helicopter crew practice their riot control skills using talcum powder to simulate tear gas at a training center known as 'Riotsville'. (111-SC-647265)

WARRANT OFFICERS

Warrant officers commanded by warrant rather than through commission and there were four grades, with W-1 being the highest. These officers traditionally held technical posts, and the shortage of helicopter pilots in Vietnam led to an expansion of the warrant officer program. Many trained as aviators or air crew and over 1,200 were killed in action.

These new arrivals have just touched down at Long Binh Air Base clutching their personnel files. (111-CC-64733)

ENLISTED PERSONNEL

The men who went to Vietnam in 1965 were volunteers. Many of them had seen combat in Korea while some of the senior NCOs were veterans of the Second World War. They had extensive training and were working along a chosen career path, and many had experienced overseas service in Europe or other theaters.

The combination of several factors radically changed the Armed Forces over the next eight years. The rapid deployment of troops to Vietnam meant that many units deployed before they were combat ready. While 9th Infantry Division had to have twelve weeks cut off their training schedule, the new 1st Cavalry Division (Airmobile) was still training when it received the order to sail.

The combination of mounting casualties, a ban on using Reserve units and the twelve-month rotation system led to serious personnel shortages, particularly in skilled occupations, leaving some combat units well below their authorized strengths. The continued deployment of new units meant that the Armed Forces were constantly searching for experienced personnel from other theaters. Although the training centers were full and their training cycles had been cut to increase numbers, experienced NCOs and men had to be replaced by inexperienced soldiers, many of them serving beyond their rank.

As the conflict continued, new problems arose. Opposition to the war increased and anti-war riots at college campuses sometimes resulted in violent clashes with the National Guard. The draft system often appeared to be unfair and the introduction of the lottery system did little to alleviate the resentment felt by some as many attempted to avoid the draft. A higher proportion of those being drafted came from the poorer classes, particularly among the Black and Hispanic communities, at a time when Civil Rights issues were at the forefront of United States politics.

While opposition to the war grew, the US Armed Services had their own problems to deal with. The scaling down of units started in the summer of 1969 and the increase in the ratio of logistics personnel to combat troops was a constant source of resentment for the men in the field. As the number of operations reduced and units resorted to security duties, the problems increased. While men had to be self-disciplined to survive in the field, boredom set in when they were confined to base. The lack of experienced officers often allowed peer pressure to take over and disobedience, drug abuse and racial problems multiplied.

By 1970 most draftees thought serving with the Armed Forces was a waste of their time and they just wanted to survive their tour of Vietnam and get back to their lives. However, most still served dutifully, displaying the same skills and courage associated with previous wars, far different from the disobedient and drug-dependent stereotypes portrayed in many films.

Over 2,300 staff sergeants and over 5,100 sergeants were killed in action. Nearly 11,500 corporals and over 12,800 privates, first class, were killed in action.

CHAPTER 4

COMBAT ARMS

THE INFANTRY DIVISION

Infantry Divisions were commanded by a Headquarters and Headquarters Company. The three Brigades also had Headquarters and Headquarters Companies to control the three infantry battalions, although the number could range from two up to five as battalions were temporarily assigned for operations.

The Division Artillery Headquarters and Headquarters Battery controlled the divisional artillery, typically three six-gun 105mm towed howitzer battalions, one supporting each brigade, and a dual 155mm towed howitzer and 8in self-propelled M110 howitzer battalion. Extra battalions could be attached during operations and the division could call for support from the Field Force's heavy artillery. A Chemical Detachment was equipped with heavy mortars.

The division's Aviation Battalion's two Airmobile Companies (a third was sometimes attached) usually had insufficient helicopters to support them and the area Combat Aviation Battalion provided support during operations. The Air Cavalry Troop carried out aerial surveillance.

The Armored Cavalry Squadron, consisting of three ground cavalry troops and one air cavalry troop, was intended to be used for reconnaissance, however, the air cavalry was often attached to the Aviation Battalion. Two Long Range Patrol Companies and a Ranger Company carried out low-key reconnaissance missions, often spending long periods out in the field monitoring targets.

The Engineer Battalion's Headquarters and Headquarters Company controlled four combat engineer companies which were usually spread across the Divisional Area; it also had a Bridge Company. The Signal Battalion maintained radio and wire communications across a large area and its personnel were often assigned to units in the field. An Army Security Agency Company dealt with confidential signals, working alongside the Military Intelligence Company.

The Division Support Command Headquarters and Headquarters Company was responsible for keeping the division fed and moving, organizing the Supply and Transport Battalion and the Maintenance Battalion. An Administration Company kept the divisional records while the Military Police Company maintained base security and law and order.

INFANTRY DIVISIONS IN VIETNAM

In Vietnam divisions were often as much as 25 per cent over strength but the extra numbers did little to increase the number of men in the field, and companies often operated under strength. The extra men were used to carry out a range of functions unique to the counterinsurgency war encountered in South Vietnam. A whole range of new procedures had to be administered, extra intelligence functions had to be manned, while civil action projects and

An infantry captain briefs his company before they climb into their helicopters. (111-CC-34250)

Infantry land on a hilltop, ready to protect engineers while they construct a fire support base. (111-CC-45146)

liaison duties with the Vietnamese all had to be staffed. The nature of guerilla warfare meant that all the division's installations and fire bases had to be protected, while roads and logistics convoys also needed to be covered.

Extra personnel were needed to cover the high turnover of men caused by the twelve-month tour; on average over 1,500 men were leaving a division at any one time and their replacements had to be trained. Battle casualties and a high rate of sickness caused by the inhospitable climate also took their toll.

9th Division conducted a survey of its companies operating in the Mekong Delta in the spring of 1968 and it discovered that around 30 per cent of combat troops were absent from operations for the following reasons:

1. 15 per cent were engaged in base security or morale-boosting activities, including messes and PXs; they were often men who were only fit for light duties
2. 10 per cent had been diverted to brigade and battalion headquarters duties
3. 5 per cent were coming to the end of their tour

A paper strength of 164 was reduced to an operating strength (known as Paddy Strength) of 120 and divisional personnel officers were given the task of increasing the numbers in the field.

It soon became apparent that standard organizations had to be altered to adapt to the new style of warfare. Brigades were often given a fourth battalion to increase their area of operations while battalions were organized into four rifle companies, with one covering base and convoy security while the rest operated in the field. By 1967 the infantry division numbered approximately 18,500 men.

Heavy weapons had little use out in the field where they were restricted to roads or helicopter transport and the infantry had to rely on helicopter gunships, tactical aircraft or the artillery stationed at the fire bases for support.

INFANTRY BATTALION

The infantry battalion had thirty-seven officers, two warrant officers and 810 enlisted men.

Typically officers and warrant officers carried revolvers while the enlisted riflemen carried M14s until they were replaced by M16s. Machine gunners and their assistants carried pistols for personal protection. The grenadiers carried their M79 grenade launchers and a pistol, however, some carried an M16.

BATTALION HEADQUARTERS COMPANY

The company had fifteen officers, two warrant officers and 147 enlisted men. Two M60 machine guns and eight M79 grenade launchers provided fire support. The company was organized into specialized companies and sections responsible for keeping the rifle companies in contact with headquarters and each other, keeping them supplied and for dealing with casualties.

COMMUNICATIONS PLATOON
The signals officer and the communications chief organized the staff working to install, operate and maintain the battalion's radio, wire and courier communications systems. The platoon had administration, wire and radio sections.

SUPPLY SECTION
The section dealt with requisitions of supplies and then distributed them to the company supply sections. It was supervised by the S-4 officer, assisted by a property book officer and the battalion supply sergeant. A company needed the following supplies:

Class I: Rations and water
Class II: Clothing and individual equipment
Class III: Petroleum, oil, and lubricants (obtained by the support platoon)
Class IV: Construction materials
Class V: Ammunition
Class VI: Personal demand (PX) items
Class VII: Major items including vehicles
Class VII: Medical supplies (obtained by the medical platoon)
Class IX: Spares for repairs (obtained by the maintenance platoon).
             The section was also responsible for water supplies and distributing maps.

Above: *The point man of a patrol edges warily forward through thick jungle.*
(111-CC-34395)

Right: *A possible sighting of Viet Cong in the distance brings a platoon to a halt.*
(111-CC-51624)

SUPPORT PLATOON

The platoon operated the battalion transport, delivering rations, water, ammunition, petroleum, oil, and lubricants to the companies. It had a platoon headquarters, an ammunition section, a Petrol, Oil and Lubricants (POL) section, a transportation section, and a mess section. The platoon leader was assisted by a platoon sergeant and a mess sergeant who organized the drivers and cooks.

MAINTENANCE PLATOON

The platoon inspected, tested, serviced and repaired equipment; it also recovered disabled vehicles. It was organized into administration, recovery and services sections while maintenance teams accompanied companies in the field. The maintenance officer was assisted by a maintenance technician and a motor sergeant while they supervised a variety of maintenance and repair specialists.

MEDICAL PLATOON

The platoon gave medical support, treating and evacuating casualties as well as stopping the spread of diseases. It was divided into a platoon headquarters, a medical treatment section, an ambulance section, and a combat medical section. The battalion surgeon was assisted by an operations officer and a physician's assistant and they organized the NCOs, corpsmen and nurses working at the battalion aid station. Combat aidmen were assigned to each platoon during operations to administer first aid to casualties until the medevac helicopter arrived. They also dealt with minor injuries and illnesses contracted in the field.

The Heavy Mortar Platoon was armed with 4.2in mortars while the Anti-Tank Platoon had 106mm recoilless rifles. The battalion headquarters also had a Recon Platoon, with an officer leading forty-eight men organized into eight six-man squads, a Ground Surveillance Section for monitoring activity across the battalion's area and an Air Control Team to coordinate air support.

RIFLE COMPANIES

The Battalion was originally organized into three Rifle Companies (A–C) and a Combat Support Company (D) but a fourth Rifle Company (D) was formed to improve operational effectiveness in 1967; the Support Company was designated E. Few Battalions deployed the Support Company as a whole while the heavy weapons platoons were usually kept with the Headquarters Company. Nine 2½-ton, four ¾-ton and nine ¼-ton trucks provided company transport.

Each company had six officers and 158 enlisted men and the headquarters platoon ran three rifle platoons and a weapons platoon. Six M60 machine Guns, three 81mm mortars and twenty-four M79 grenade launchers gave fire support while five ¼-ton trucks provided transport.

COMPANY HEADQUARTERS

The company commander, a captain, was assisted by an executive officer, a lieutenant, a first sergeant and a clerk. Communications were organized by the communications chief, two radio operators, two wiremen and a field radio mechanic. They operated two AN/VRC-47s and two AN/GRA-39s mounted on ¼-ton utility trucks and ¼-ton cargo trailers; they also operated three-man pack AN/PRC-25s. Supplies were organized by the supply sergeant and equipment clerk while the armorer dealt with weapons. The company supplies were carried in a 2½-ton truck and a 1½-ton cargo trailer.

RIFLE PLATOON

The Rifle Platoon had one officer and forty-three enlisted men organized into a headquarters, three rifle squads and a weapons squad.

Headquarters: A lieutenant and platoon sergeant led the platoon and they kept in touch with their squads with two short-range AN/PRC-6 radios and the company headquarters with a longer range AN/PRC-25 radio; they were maintained by the radio operator.

Rifle Squads: Squad leaders, assisted by a rifleman carrying an AN/PRC-6 radio, ran each of the three rifle squads. Each squad had two teams with team

As usual, the Viet Cong go into hiding, leaving the platoon to follow up and investigate. (111-CC-35682)

Huey helicopters fly in to collect a platoon and take them to the next landing zone. (111-CC-34613)

leaders. Each team had an automatic rifleman armed with a rifle and bipod, a grenadier carrying an M79 and a pistol and a rifleman armed with an M14 or M16.

Weapons Squad: The squad leader used an AN/PRC-6 radio to keep in contact with the platoon leader. The squad had two M60 machine guns operated by a gunner and his assistant. Two bearers kept the weapons supplied with belts of ammunition. Two 90mm recoilless rifles were operated by gunners and assistant gunners.

The 90mm recoilless rifles were often left behind at base or in the night defensive position and the crews either carried an M60 machine gun or extra ammunition.

WEAPONS PLATOON

The standard Weapons Platoon encountered a number of difficulties in Vietnam and its deployment had to be carefully orchestrated. The platoon transport was restricted to roads while mortars could not be used in the jungle and the teams could not carry sufficient ammunition for sustained fire. Security also posed a problem and the weapons usually stayed at the company fire base or were moved to night defensive positions by helicopter.

Platoon Headquarters: The lieutenant and platoon sergeant organized the mortar section and the anti-tank section. A ¼-ton utility truck and ¼-ton cargo trailer carried the platoon's AN/GRC-125 radio and the operator.

Mortar Section Headquarters: The section leader led three 81mm Mortar Squads. Three observation teams, each with a Forward Observer and a radio operator, adjusted the fall of shot via their AN/PRC-25 radio. Two fire direction computers carried out calculations and relayed their instructions to the squads via their AN/PRC-25 radios. Two ¾-ton cargo trucks and trailers carried the section's equipment.

Mortar Squad: Each mortar team had a squad leader, gunner and an assistant gunner operating an 81mm mortar. Two ammunition carriers kept the mortar supplied.

Anti-tank Section Headquarters: The section leader led two anti-tank squads equipped with 106mm recoilless rifles.

Anti-tank Squad: The squad leader directed the gunner and assistant gunner. An ammunition carrier kept the 106mm recoilless rifle supplied. The squad kept in contact with its headquarters with an AN/GRC-125 radio mounted in a ¼-ton utility truck. Recoilless rifles were usually confined to base and used for perimeter defense while the infantry used lightweight, single-shot LAW anti-tank missile launchers in the field to destroy bunkers.

COMBAT SUPPORT COMPANY

The company had four officers and ninety-six enlisted men organized into a company headquarters, a mortar platoon and an assault platoon armed with flamethrowers. The Headquarters was organized along the same lines as the infantry company headquarters and transport was provided by four ¾-ton trucks and four ¼-ton trucks.

4.2in (107mm) Mortar Platoon: An officer and seven men led four squads, each armed with a 4.2in mortar manned by six crewmen. The platoon usually attached a forward observation team to the company headquarters and they kept in touch with the Forward Observer and his operator via the platoon AN/PRC-25 radio.

Assault Platoon: An officer led twelve four-man flamethrower teams.

LIGHT INFANTRY BRIGADES

Four light infantry brigades served in Vietnam. 11th, 196th and 198th Brigades were eventually amalgamated to form 23d American Division, while 199th Brigade always served as an independent brigade. Light Brigades had 280 officers, forty-one warrant officers and 4,293 enlisted men organized into a brigade headquarters and four battalions. Battalions were organized along the same lines as the regular infantry battalions and they had thirty-seven officers, one warrant officer and 731 enlisted men organized into a Headquarters and Headquarters Company, three rifle companies and a Combat Support Company. The battalion was sometimes reorganized into four rifle companies in Vietnam to increase operational flexibility.

RECONNAISSANCE UNITS

RANGER INFANTRY COMPANY

The Long Range Patrol Company carried out long-range patrols (LRPs) and long-range reconnaissance patrols (LRRPs) searching for enemy base camps and trails across the division's operational area. Patrols often followed up information provided by aerial photographs or other intelligence leads, confirming if a target was worth engaging. By the end of 1967 each division had a LRP company, and numbers continued to grow until there was enough for each brigade.

The LRPs and LRRPs were renamed in January 1969 with all companies becoming part of 75th Infantry Regiment (the famous Merrill's Marauders during the Second World War); the title LRP was also changed to Ranger.

A Ranger blends into the background as he moves slowly through thick undergrowth. (111-CC-72581)

The Divisional Ranger Company had three officers and 115 enlisted men organized into a headquarters and two platoons. The Company Headquarters had an officer assisted by seventeen enlisted men dealing with intelligence, operations, logistics and communications. Each platoon had a headquarters, and the officer and his enlisted assistant coordinated eight six-man patrols. Officers were armed with pistols while the men carried M16 rifles; the company also had thirty-two M79 grenade launchers. Company transport was provided by nine ¼-ton trucks.

Field Force Ranger Companies were larger, with around 200 officers and men; Company H serving 1st Cavalry Division was the same strength. Brigade Companies were smaller, with sixty-one officers and men.

KIT CARSON OR TIGER SCOUTS

Viet Cong and NVA soldiers who had defected (known as Hoi Chanhs) were sometimes recruited to work with the US combat troops as riflemen or scouts. By 1968 a division could have up to 250 Tiger Scouts, deploying two with each platoon, and numbers continued to increase as the number of defectors grew.

Due to language difficulties, they were often mistrusted by the American troops and it took time to build up a good working relationship. The Scouts' knowledge of the enemy's techniques and the local terrain could make them a valuable asset as they talked to villagers and interrogated prisoners.

DOG UNITS

Sentry dogs were highly intelligent and loyal to their handlers and were used to guard base perimeters. Scout Dog Platoons worked with combat troops in the field, and their keen sense of smell and hearing was useful for detecting the enemy. They also sniffed out booby traps, tunnels and supply caches. A platoon usually worked with each infantry brigade.

Five-man Combat Tracker Teams were organized for each division and many brigades to search for trails following the Tet Offensive in February 1968. Over 1,500 dogs were being used by the Army by 1968; nearly 200 were killed or injured in action.

THE MARINE DIVISION

Two Marine divisions, the 1st and 3d, served in Vietnam and there were many similarities between the organizations of the Army and Marine divisions. The infantry were organized into three regiments (the equivalent of an Army brigade), each with three battalions. (All Marine regiments, both infantry and artillery were designated by number only.) The regiment was led by a Headquarters Company with eighteen officers and 200 enlisted men; two naval officers and two enlisted men acted as a liaison team. It was organized into the Regimental Headquarters, the Company Headquarters which had a command post security platoon, a communications platoon and a scout-sniper platoon.

Two extra infantry regiments from the 5th Marine Division were sent to Vietnam to serve with 1st Marine Division. Battalions often served with other regiments during operations to increase the number of troops in an area. Eventually the Marines deployed a battalion to serve with Seventh Fleet as the

Above: *Marines hit the dirt as an air strike hits a group of Viet Cong probing 7th Regiment's perimeter. (127-GVC-A189884)*

Left: *The crew of an M60 machine gun open fire during 1st Regiment's defence of Con Thien fire base. (127-GVC-370563)*

Special Landing Force, and it carried out amphibious landings along the coast of South Vietnam; the battalion was rotated on a regular basis.

The Marine Battalion was led by a Headquarters and Service Company comprising 329 Marine personnel and fifty-six US Navy liaison personnel. It had eight 81mm mortars and eight 106mm recoilless rifles. The battalion's four rifle companies each had a paper strength of six officers and 210 enlisted men led by a company headquarters with nine staff, including the captain, a lieutenant executive officer, a first sergeant, a gunnery sergeant, an armorer, a supply sergeant and several administrative clerks. 1st Battalion's companies were designated A to D, 2nd Battalion's companies were designated E to H and 3rd Battalion's companies were designated I -M; the letter J was not used.

Each of the company's three rifle platoons had forty-six enlisted men led by a lieutenant who was assisted by a staff sergeant, a radio operator, a guide, and a medical corpsman. The platoon had three rifle squads with fourteen men organized into four-man fire-teams; team leaders directed the automatic rifleman, and two riflemen. Men were armed with the M14 rifle until they were replaced by the M16; one man in the squad carried an M79 grenade launcher.

Each rifle company had a weapons platoon organized into a platoon command group and three weapons sections. The 60mm mortar section had three M19 mortars, the M60 machine-gun section had three two-gun squads while the assault section had three squads, each organized into two teams, equipped with M20 rocket launchers; they were soon replaced by the M72 light anti-armor-weapon.

Each division also had a Reconnaissance Battalion organized into four rifle companies and a Force Recon Company; they were used for intelligence gathering and reconnaissance missions.

The Marine Division was supported by an Artillery Regiment with 202 officers and 2,555 enlisted Marines as well as fifteen naval officers and forty-five enlisted men. The Regiment was controlled by a Headquarters Battery and it was organized into three Direct Support Artillery Battalions and one General Support Artillery Battalion. Two extra battalions from 5th Marine Division increased the amount of firepower available to 1st Marine Division.

The Direct Support Artillery Battalion was controlled by a Headquarters Battery with seventeen officers, 142 enlisted men, four naval officers and two other ranks. The battalion had three batteries each armed with six towed 105mm howitzers and they were manned by nine officers, 131 enlisted men and two naval personnel. It also had a battery of six weapons unique to the Marine Division, the lightweight M98 howtar, a 4.2in mortar barrel mounted on the carriage of a 75mm pack howitzer; the battery had four officers, eighty-nine enlisted men and two naval personnel.

The General Support Artillery Battalion was also controlled by a Headquarters Battery with thirteen officers, 144 enlisted men, one naval officer and three other ranks. The battalion had three batteries, each armed with six 155mm howitzers and they were manned by five officers, 117 enlisted men and two naval personnel. Although the batteries had officially converted to the self-propelled M109 155mm howitzer, both Marine divisions took two self-propelled batteries and one towed 155mm battery to Vietnam; the towed battery was still kept for airmobile operations when the third self-propelled battery was deployed.

Each division was supported by a tank battalion with forty officers and 617 enlisted Marines as well as one Navy officer and fourteen men. The headquarters and support company was equipped with two M48 tanks, nine M67A2 tanks equipped with flamethrowers and an M51 tank recovery vehicle. The battalion had three tank companies, each with seventeen M48 tanks, and an anti-tank company equipped with twenty Ontos, tracked anti-tank weapons armed with six 106 recoilless rifles.

Marines were expected to carry out amphibious operations and the Landing Vehicle Tracked, Personnel (LVTP) had been designed to operate on land and in the water, replacing the outdated landing craft. An Amphibious Tractor Battalion of LVTPs, and their variations, supported each division. The headquarters and support company had three command vehicles, twelve personnel carrying vehicles, eight engineer vehicles and a single recovery vehicle (extra recovery vehicles accompanied the battalion during operations). The infantry were carried by two companies, each equipped with three command vehicles, forty-four personnel carrying vehicles and a recovery vehicle. An armored amphibian company supported the battalion and its twelve vehicles were armed with 105mm howitzers for providing indirect fire support.

ARTILLERY

Each Field Force had an artillery headquarters to coordinate heavy artillery activity under its command while Field Artillery Groups controlled part of its area. A range of artillery served with each group but it was primarily the heavier 8in and 175mm self-propelled howitzers which carried out many fire missions. They were usually based in a static role and covered many stationary targets, including fire bases, military installations and government buildings, responding if they came under attack. They could also add their firepower to any operation in their range if clearance was given.

MARINE ARTILLERY

1st Field Artillery Group arrived in November 1966 to coordinate the artillery serving with 1st and 3d Marine Divisions. Additional Army artillery units moved north and by the end of 1967 forty-five batteries were covering I Corps and the DMZ.

155mm howitzers and their crews are protected by embankments and fences at Fire Support Base Concord. (111-CC-58170)

XXX CORPS ARTILLERY AND
I FIELD FORCE VIETNAM ARTILLERY

XXX Corps Artillery arrived at Nha Trang in November 1965 to support Task Force ALPHA but it was renamed I Field Force, Vietnam, Artillery in March 1966 when the two Field Forces were organized. A provisional Forward Task Force headquarters served at Qui Nhon between December 1966 and April 1967 and in December 1970 a Provisional I Field Force Artillery Group was established in Dalat. The headquarters became the basis for Second Army Regional Command Artillery in April 1971 and it was soon renamed US Army Artillery Force, Military Region 2; it left Vietnam in June 1972.

41st Field Artillery Group was based at Phu Cat from April 1967 to November 1969, to cover the northern coastal area of II Corps. The following battalions served with the Group:

105mm towed howitzers:	7/13th, 2/17th and 5/27th Battalions
155mm towed howitzers:	1/30th and 6/84th Battalions
8in self-propelled howitzers:	7/15th, 3/18th and 6/32d Battalions
175mm self-propelled guns:	5/22d Battalion
Self-propelled automatic weapons:	4/60th Battalion with a battery of quad M55 .50-caliber machine guns of Battery E, 41st Artillery

52d Field Artillery Group was based at Pleiku in the Central Highlands from June 1966 to June 1971. The following battalions served with the Group:

105mm self-propelled howitzers:	3/6th, 7/13th and 2/17th Battalions
155mm towed howitzers:	1/30th, 6/84th and 1/92d Battalions
8in self-propelled howitzers:	7/15th Battalion
175mm self-propelled guns:	6/14th and 5/22d Battalions

II FIELD FORCE VIETNAM ARTILLERY

The Field Force Headquarters was based at Bien Hoa from March 1966 to May 1971, to support units across III and IV Corps.

23d Field Artillery Group was based at Phu Loi from November 1965 and moved to Long Binh in May 1971, it left Vietnam in January 1972. The following battalions served with the Group:

As calls for artillery support come through on the radio, the coordinates are plotted and the new mission is calculated. (111-CC-43351)

105mm towed howitzers:	7/9th, 2/13th, 6/15th Battalions
155mm towed howitzers:	2/11th, 2/12th, 5/42d and 3/197th Battalions
155mm self-propelled howitzers:	1/27th and 2/35th Battalions
8in self-propelled howitzers:	7/8th, 6/27th Battalions
175mm self-propelled guns:	2/32d Battalion
Automatic weapons:	5/2d Self-Propelled Battalion armed M42A1 dual 40mm anti-aircraft guns and a battery of quad M55 50-caliber machine guns of Battery D, 71st Artillery

54th Field Artillery Group served at Xuan Loc, east of Saigon, from October 1966 and Bien Hoa from the end of 1968; it left Vietnam in November 1969. The following battalions served with the Group:

105mm towed howitzers:	7/9th and 6/77th Battalions
155mm towed howitzers:	3/16th Battalion
155mm self-propelled howitzers:	2/35th Battalion
8in self-propelled howitzers:	7/8th, 6/27th and 1/83d Battalions
175mm self-propelled guns:	2/32d Battalion

I CORPS ARTILLERY

108th Artillery Group was organized at Dong Ha in October 1967 to coordinate Task Force Oregon's artillery. It worked for MACV Forward Headquarters during the Tet Offensive and came under XXIV Corps command the following summer. The Group moved to Phu Bai in September 1970 and left Vietnam in November 1971. The following battalions served with the Group:

105mm towed howitzers:	6th Battalion, 33d Artillery
105mm self-propelled howitzers:	1st Battalion, 40th Artillery
155mm self-propelled howitzers:	2d Battalion, 138th Artillery (Kentucky National Guard)
175mm guns and 8in howitzers:	8th Battalion, 4th Artillery, 1st Battalion, 39th Artillery, 1st Battalion, 83d Artillery and 2d Battalion, 94th Artillery
Self-propelled 8in howitzer:	1st Battalion, 83d Artillery
Self-propelled automatic weapons:	1st Battalion, 44th Artillery

TARGET ACQUISITION

A network of radar and sensors was installed across South Vietnam to monitor enemy movement and artillery was often fired at positive readings. Sound ranging devices and flash ranging devices could locate mortar and rocket launch sites from the noise or flight path of the projectiles. The following target acquisition units were deployed to Vietnam:

108th Artillery Group: Battery C and F, 2d Battalion, 26th Artillery
XXIV Corps: Battery F, 2d Battalion, 26th Artillery monitored the Demilitarized Zone
I Field Force: Headquarters battery, 8th Battalion, 26th Artillery
II Field Force: Headquarters battery, 8th Battalion 25th Artillery

Capital Military Assistance Command: Battery D, 25th Artillery covered Saigon from September 1969; it transferred to II Field Force Headquarters the following March.

ARTILLERY BATTALION ORGANIZATION

Officers and warrant officers were generally armed with pistols or revolvers while the enlisted men carried M14 or M16 rifles. Each battalion had a number of M60 machine guns and M79 grenade launchers for close fire support.

105MM TOWED HOWITZER BATTALION

Each battalion had a Service and Battery Headquarters and four batteries, designated A, B, C and D. The Service and Battery Headquarters had twenty officers, three warrant officers and 158 men. Transport consisted of sixteen 2½-ton trucks, twenty ¾-ton trucks and twenty ¼-ton trucks. A 5-ton wrecker and a 5-ton truck were available to tow disabled vehicles.

Each battery had six 105mm howitzers manned by eight officers and 107 enlisted men. Transport was provided by thirteen 2½-ton trucks, four ¾-ton trucks and five ¼-ton trucks.

155MM TOWED HOWITZER BATTALION

The battalion had a Headquarters and Battery Headquarters, three 155mm batteries designated A, B and C, and a Service Battery, designated D. The Headquarters and Battery Headquarters had seventeen officers, three warrant officers and 113 enlisted men. Company transport operated seven 2½-ton trucks, twenty ¾-ton trucks and ten ¼-ton trucks.

The howitzer batteries had six 155mm towed howitzers manned by six officers and 119 enlisted men. Transport was provided by ten 5-ton trucks, three 2½-ton trucks, four ¾-ton trucks and five ¼-ton trucks. The Service Battery kept the battalion supplied and maintained. It had two officers, three

The crew of a 105mm howitzer fire marking rounds at a landing zone during Operation Bolling. (111-CC-43353)

warrant officers and eighty-five enlisted men. Two light carriers were used as command posts while four cargo carriers hauled ammunition. Transport was provided by ten 5-ton trucks, nine 2½-ton trucks, three ¾-ton trucks and three ¼-ton trucks; a 5-ton wrecker could retrieve disabled vehicles.

155MM/8IN BATTALION

Each battalion had a Service and Battery Headquarters, three 155mm self-propelled howitzer batteries designated A, B and C, and a Service Battery, designated D, armed with 8in self-propelled howitzers. The Service and Battery Headquarters had seventeen officers, two warrant officers and 144 men. Transport consisted of twelve 5-ton trucks, nine 2½-ton trucks, fifteen ¾-ton trucks and fourteen ¼-ton trucks. A 5-ton wrecker was available to tow disabled vehicles.

The three howitzer batteries had six 155mm M109 howitzers manned by four officers and 109 enlisted men. Transport was provided by nine 5-ton trucks, three 2½-ton trucks, two ¾-ton trucks and two ¼-ton trucks. The Service Battery had four 8in self-propelled howitzers manned by four officers and 110 enlisted men. Two light carriers were used as command posts while four cargo carriers hauled ammunition. Transport was provided by six 5-ton trucks, five 2½-ton trucks, two ¾-ton trucks and two ¼-ton trucks.

175MM AND 8IN MIXED SELF-PROPELLED BATTALIONS

Each battalion had a Service and Battery Headquarters, three self-propelled howitzer batteries designated A, B and C, while D Battery was the service battery. The Service and Battery Headquarters had seventeen officers, three warrant officers and 115 men. Seven 2½-ton trucks, twenty-one ¾-ton trucks and ten ¼-ton trucks provided transport.

The howitzer batteries had four self-propelled howitzers capable of being armed with either the M107 175mm gun for accurate short-range shots or the M110 8in for long-range fire. They were manned by six officers and 112 enlisted men. Transport was provided five 2½-ton trucks, four ¾-ton trucks and six ¼-ton trucks. An M577 armored personnel carrier was used as a command vehicle while four 6-ton cargo carriers supplied the howitzers with ammunition. The Service Battery had two officers, three warrant officers and seventy-one enlisted men. Transport was provided by eight 2½-ton trucks, three ¾-ton trucks and three ¼-ton trucks. A 5-ton wrecker and an M578 Recovery Vehicle could retrieve disabled vehicles.

ARTILLERY SUPPORT

Traditionally batteries had been deployed in safe areas behind a rigid front line but in South Vietnam, over half of artillery missions were fired towards friendly troops or into areas surrounded by friendly units. As batteries were spread out across a number of fire support bases, fire control had to be decentralized. Detailed defensive plans were needed to protect installations while offensive operations required flexible planning. Artillery officers had to work closely with the infantry units in the field as helicopters moved their units across the battlefield at speed.

While the divisional artillery commanders were kept busy supporting operations, corps level headquarters provided area coverage. Population centers, logistics areas, supply routes and possible enemy base camps and trails were added to the target list so fire missions could be fired at a moment's notice.

A platoon adjusts the artillery fire mission on an adjacent hilltop. (111-CC-39773)

ARTILLERY LIAISON

Forward Observers (FOs), trained to spot targets and adjust fire for artillery batteries, were attached to each company. They were also experienced in assessing targets and choosing the most effective type of ordnance and firing pattern to use. They often had to adjust fire missions by sound alone in dense undergrowth or jungles, sometimes climbing trees to get a better view. Many FOs were responsible for map reading for the infantry, counting paces as they followed a compass bearing and asking for smoke rounds to be fired at known points to check their bearings. They also had to keep track of the company's platoons and squads to avoid friendly fire incidents.

The Artillery Liaison Officer (ALO) coordinated the Forward Observers for the infantry battalion and his artillery plan had to be flexible in case the operational needs changed. He summarized potential targets provided by the FOs and forwarded them to the Brigade Artillery Liaison Section for clearance. The Brigade Artillery Liaison Section also forwarded requests for fire support from the Field Artillery Groups and made recommendations for tactical air or naval support. Prearranged targets were calculated and circulated so the artillery could fire at target references, cutting response times and reducing errors; the references also acted as a simple code.

A Chinook helicopter delivers ammunition to a new fire base. (111-CC-43358)

Division, Corps and Field Force Fire Support Coordinators organized fire support during major operations and the Corps Coordinator integrated the air, naval and ground fire plans. The Air Force had full control above 5,000ft but aircraft flying any lower needed allocated flight paths to avoid artillery fire. Many battalions had an Air Advisor monitoring artillery fire and aircraft movements.

Artillery Air Observers were grouped at divisional level (at group level for non-divisional artillery), and each observer was allocated an area during an operation so that he could become familiar with the terrain. Observers carried out visual surveillance of suspect areas and could assist the Forward Observers during fire missions.

Once an operation was underway the battalion fire plans could vary considerably as new contacts appeared and the brigade redeployed its companies. Platoons and companies needed rapid and precise fire support and company liaison officers often spoke directly to the battery commander. The Battalion Fire Plan was rarely referred to when a unit was operating in a free-fire zone, and higher headquarters rarely knew what missions its batteries were firing. This decentralized system worked well if operating procedures were followed, however, the stresses of combat, carelessness and human error could lead to mistakes, resulting in friendly and civilian casualties.

CLEARANCES AND 'FRIENDLY FIRE'
Requests for artillery support had to be cleared by several military and civilian headquarters, taking up valuable time. Combined Fire Support Control

Centers coordinated clearances, agreeing which areas were free-fire zones in advance of an operation.

Artillery units were usually banned from firing into populated areas but the Viet Cong often sited weapons around them and they required special clearances before returning fire. Fire missions aimed at targets within 600m of friendly troops needed special clearance and the observer used the words 'Danger Close' to alert the artillery; the ranging round had to be an air burst of smoke or white phosphorous so that it could be adjusted safely. Barrages were known to be directed as close as 200m of a friendly position in an emergency if the ground commander gave clearance.

FIRING PROCEDURES

The Forward Observer requested a fire mission to support his unit with the following information:

> The target's map coordinates in code and his own unit's coordinates
> The most effective type of shell, the preferred fuse and the desired fire-pattern

After verifying the coordinates, the Battalion Fire Direction Coordinator plotted the target coordinates and calculated the gun's horizontal angle (known as deflection), the barrel's vertical angle (known as quadrant elevation) and the size of powder charge and relayed the information to the battery. The gun crews then went into action, aiming and loading their gun; the commander notified the Coordinator as soon as his weapon was ready to fire. The following is a typical list of commands issued to a howitzer battery as it prepared to fire:

COMMAND	ACTION TAKEN
Battery Adjust	Battery alerted
Azimuth 3,600	Guns swung round to point towards the target
Shell HE	Load required round (high explosive)
Charge 6	Powder charge required for the range*
Fuse – Quick	Type of Fuse (point detonating in this case)
Number Three one round	Instructions for range firing gun (Number 3)
Battery round in for effect	Battery fire for effect to follow
Deflection 3,460	The gunner adjusted the barrel left or right
Quadrant 536	The Assistant Gunner raised or lowered the barrel
Number Three – Fire!	The ranging gun begin firing

* 8in howitzers used charges while 175mm guns used zones

The Coordinator announced *SHOT* to alert the Forward Observer, followed by *SPLASH* seconds before impact so he could watch the explosions. Ranging rounds were used to adjust the gun on to the target and then the order *FIRE FOR EFFECT* was given and the gun crews fired as fast as directed until the Coordinator gave the order to CEASE FIRE.

TYPES OF FIRE MISSIONS

Contact Fire: Called by an infantry unit under fire; these were given the highest priority.

Time on Target (TOT): Several batteries calculated the time their rounds would be in the air and fired their guns so they would simultaneously hit the target; a mixture of ground and air bursts could devastate a small area.

Above: *A 175mm howitzer fires harassment rounds.* (111-CC-43794)

Right: *105mm howitzers point in all directions on a mountain top fire base during 1st Cavalry Division's Operation Thayer.* (111-CC-36509)

Zone and Sweep: The battery fired five salvoes in an X pattern; the first salvo marked the center while the rest hit the four compass points so the bursts covered the maximum area.

Convoy Protection: Fire missions were planned to hit likely ambush points along a route.

Defensive Fire Missions: Used to protect fire bases and military installations.

Counter-mortar and Rocket Fire Missions: Prearranged missions aimed at likely launch sites.

Harassment and Interdiction: Unobserved fire fired randomly at likely targets.

Illumination: Parachute flares fired to light up an area; two were often exploded simultaneously a short distance apart to eliminate shadows.

Precision Fire: A single gun firing at a small target; the precise 8in howitzer was often used.

Mini and Mirco Arc Light: B-52 Arc Light bombing missions delivered a devastating amount of ordnance against targets but they took time to organize. During the siege of Khe Sanh at the beginning of 1968 mini and micro versions, coordinating artillery and air missions, were developed. They were timed so that artillery hit half the target while an air strike hit the other half. The mini Arc Light took 45 minutes to organize and it devastated an area of around 1,000m by 500m. The micro version covered a smaller area with less ordnance but it only took 10 minutes to arrange.

THE ARTILLERY RAID

Occasionally the infantry wanted to pursue the enemy beyond the range of their fire bases so the artillery raid was devised to provide support. Helicopters flew a battery and ammunition to a chosen area with little or no preparation. The guns would fire on predetermined targets and then be lifted out before the enemy could react.

Although the raids could be planned and executed in only a few hours, they could be hazardous and had to be carefully coordinated. A typical raid had six 105mm howitzers, three 155mm howitzers and a rifle company for protection.

MAINTENANCE AND SUPPLY

Maintenance teams carried out routine inspections of the guns and dealt with unexpected problems, flying out to fire bases to carry out their work. Towed howitzers were easy to maintain and could be airlifted by helicopter to a repair depot, but a disabled self-propelled weapon was a problem, especially if they were operating outside the fire base perimeter. Security had to be arranged until a maintenance repair team repaired the gun or towed it back to base.

With artillery able to move quickly by airlifts, the problem of keeping batteries supplied had to be considered and helicopters were often used to stock up a fire base with ammunition before the guns arrived; truck convoys were used when possible.

ARMORED AND AIR CAVALRY

Each infantry division had an Armored Cavalry Squadron responsible for reconnaissance, intelligence gathering and security missions. (Note: The cavalry squadron was the equivalent of an infantry battalion, while the cavalry troop equated to an infantry company; both arms used the term platoon.)

CAVALRY DEPLOYMENT

DIVISION	SQUADRON	DIVISION	SQUADRON
1st Infantry	1/4th Cavalry	23d Infantry	1/1st Cavalry
4th Infantry	1/10th Cavalry	25th Infantry	3/4th Cavalry
9th Infantry	3/5th Cavalry	101st Airborne	2/17th Cavalry

1/1st Cavalry served with Task Force Oregon before joining 23d Division

Reorganization of 101st Airborne Division's cavalry squadron to airmobile status started in December 1968 but Troops A, B and C (airmobile) did not arrive until the following March; Troop D was added in December 1971.

Independent brigades were served by a single troop of air cavalry.

BRIGADE	TROOP	SQUADRON
1st Brigade, 5th Infantry	Troop A	4/12th Cavalry
3d Brigade, 82d Airborne	Troop B	1/17th Cavalry
1st Brigade 101st Airborne	Troop A	4/12th Cavalry
11th Infantry Brigade (Light)	Troop E	1st Cavalry
173d Airborne Brigade	Troop E	17th Cavalry
196th Infantry Brigade's (Light)	Troop F	17th Cavalry
198th Infantry Brigade (Light)	Troop H	17th Cavalry
199th Infantry Brigade (Light)	Troop D	17th Cavalry

SQUADRON ORGANIZATION

The squadron had twenty-one officers, two warrant officers and 240 enlisted men organized into a headquarters troop and three armored cavalry troops, A, B and C. The troops were equipped with M113A1 armored personnel carriers (APCs) for reconnaissance and M48A3 tanks (replaced by the M551 Sheridan) for firepower. Troop D was an Air Cavalry Squadron armed with observation, transport and helicopter gunships for aerial reconnaissance.

The headquarters troop rode in six M577 command carriers and ten M113 personnel carriers; four M132 flamethrower carriers dealt with bunkers. Ten 6-ton cargo carriers distributed ammunition while two M88 recovery vehicles and three 5-ton wrecker trucks recovered disabled vehicles. Ten 5-ton, fifteen 2½-ton, seven ¾-ton trucks and eighteen ¼-ton utility trucks provided transport.

THE ARMORED CAVALRY TROOP

The Troop was organized into a headquarters and three platoons and although organization often varied, it had around five officers and 192 enlisted men. Twenty-two M113s acted as command vehicles and personnel carriers. Nine M48 tanks gave direct close support while three M125 81mm mortar carriers gave indirect support. Transport was provided by one 2½-ton, one ¾-ton and three ¼-ton utility trucks; an M88 recovery vehicle recovered damaged vehicles.

The troop headquarters had four M113s. A captain ran his troop from the headquarters (APC) while the forward artillery observer, a lieutenant, kept in contact with the divisional artillery through the radio operator. The crew of the communications APC controlled the radio net while two radar APCs could set up ground surveillance radar to cover the troop's perimeter.

Each platoon was led by a lieutenant and he led six M113s, one mortar carrier and three tanks. The scout section had four APCs organized into two squads to locate targets, so the tank section and the infantry APC could move in to engage it, while the mortar APC gave indirect fire support or fired smoke.

In action the driver continued to operate the M113 while the vehicle commander fired the .50-cal and the two observers fired the M-60 machine guns (one acted as loader if he had no targets on his side). Each crew member had an M16 rifle and the vehicle carried an M79 grenade launcher. The platoon usually rode on and fought from their vehicles, however, the infantry APC carried a squad to search inaccessible areas. The M125A1 81mm Mortar Carrier provided indirect fire support for the platoon.

The tank section had three M48A3s and it was led by the lead tank's commander; his two tanks were controlled by tank commanders. All three tanks had a driver, a gunner and a loader. The M48s were replaced by the lighter and faster M551 Sheridan, starting in 1969.

Mines were a constant worry for the cavalry troop and the APC crews often reinforced the floor of their vehicles with sandbags. Four-man engineer teams were often assigned to each troop to sweep for mines.

Each troop had a medic team when it was on operations and they either rode with the radar M113s or the squadron loaned them an M113 as an armored ambulance. A casualty clearing station would usually be set up next to the communications M113 so the medics could call in helicopters to retrieve the wounded.

THE AIR CAVALRY TROOP

The armored cavalry squadron had one air cavalry troop with fourteen officers, thirty-three warrant officers and 147 enlisted men. The air cavalry troop was the aerial version of the cavalry squadron and its helicopters could carry out reconnaissance and security missions over a large area. It was organized into three platoons equipped with different types of helicopters:

Scout platoon: Five OH-6A observation helicopters armed with a minigun.
Aero rifle platoon: Six UH-1D utility/transport helicopters each carrying a rifle squad.
Weapons platoon: Seven UH-1B helicopters armed with machine guns and rockets; they had been replaced by AH-1 Cobra attack helicopters by the end of 1967.

1st Cavalry Division's air cavalry squadron had a full squadron of air cavalry, 1st Squadron, 9th Cavalry, to cover its larger area of operations and it was organized into three troops, each with three platoons. Maintenance sections kept the helicopters in the air.

Experience showed that different pairs of helicopters, or teams, suited different types of missions:

Red Team: Two UH-1 or AH-1 gunships for maximum firepower on offensive missions.

White Team: Two OH-6 observation helicopters for reconnaissance missions; one flew low searching the ground for targets while the other watched from overhead.

Pink Team: An OH-6 observation helicopter flew low over the area, while an armed UH-1 or AH-1 flew overhead, acting as navigator and radio relay.

Blue Team: Two unarmed UH-1s carry rifle squads on security or intelligence missions.

The divisional commander could call upon his Air Cavalry Troop to carry out a variety of missions:

Intelligence Mission: The helicopters flew over targets reporting enemy positions, assessing landing zones and bomb damage.

Fire Base Construction: Helicopter teams protected the engineers while they built a fire base. An aero rifle platoon protected the engineer team and then took over ground security as the aero rifle platoon patrolled the surrounding area.

Fire Base Security: Teams provided aerial security, identifying and engaging targets.

A wire screen protects this M113. The crew can take cover in their bunker. (111-CC-64235)

Operation Security: Helicopter crews watched for impending counterattacks.

Rapid Reaction Force: Red Teams added their fire power to assaults and ambushes.

Artillery Protection: The rifle platoon provided security during artillery raids.

Crash Recovery: The Air Cavalry was usually the first on the scene when a plane or helicopter crashed and they would either extract the stricken crew or provide protection until help arrived.

THE AIR CAVALRY BRIGADE

In September 1970 1st Cavalry Division formed the unofficial 9th Air Cavalry Brigade to keep watch over a large section of the Cambodian border, northwest of Saigon. The Brigade reinforced the division's Air Cavalry Squadron and added the division's Ranger Company and a Tracker Dog platoon to track sightings. The unit was formally activated in December when Field Force II added its Air Cavalry Squadron to the Brigade; it left with the majority of the division the following February.

AVIATION

Throughout the summer of 1962 the Howze Board examined Army aviation requirements and considered how the helicopter could be incorporated into combat operations. It proposed forming an air assault division with 459 fixed wing and rotary aircraft compared to the 100 usually deployed with an infantry division. It would be supported by flying artillery supplied by twenty-four Mohawks and thirty-six Hueys.

11th Air Assault Division worked with 10th Air Transport Brigade, experimenting with the airmobile concept, using helicopters to move troops over large distances while air cavalry took over the role of reconnaissance and pursuit; Caribous and Chinooks would keep the assault units supplied. The new concept did pose problems. The number of Army aviators had to increase dramatically while new tactics had to be practiced. As the situation deteriorated in Vietnam, there was insufficient time to train the new 1st Cavalry (Air Assault) Division and although it was only raised in July 1965, troops were soon boarding ships for Vietnam. The fact that their Hueys and Chinooks each needed over 1,300 modifications before they could be loaded only added to the Cavalry's problems.

While the 11th Air Assault Division was experimenting with airmobile tactics in the United States, the helicopter crews training Vietnamese pilots were developing their own techniques. Experiments with armed UH-1 Huey helicopters had been underway since September 1962 but results fell on deaf ears in the United States. *Eagle Flight*s of five armed Hueys escorting seven unarmed transport Hueys to the landing zone had been tried, while a command helicopter controlled the landing from the air and a medevac helicopter evacuated casualties.

AVIATION CONTROL

Army Aviation grew to control over 600 planes and over 3,500 helicopters. A Provisional Aviation Group was formed in April 1965 to control Army aviation units and four months later it was organized as 12th Aviation Group. 17th Group was added in December to take over II Corps' area but by the spring of 1966 a new level of command was required to coordinate the

aviation assets across the country and 1st Aviation Brigade was soon formed at Tan Son Nhut. The Brigade was based at Long Bing after December 1967 and it expanded to control four Combat Aviation Groups, one for each Corps Tactical Zone. It grew to be one one of the largest commands in Vietnam and at its peak in the summer of 1968 had over 25,000 officers and men flying over 3,500 helicopters and over 600 fixed-wing aircraft.

The Group returned to Tan Son Nhut in December 1972 and while ground troops were withdrawn at a steady rate, many aviation units stayed behind to support the ARVN. The Brigade eventually left Vietnam the following March.

Helicopters were extremely versatile and could be used for a variety of missions, including defoliating jungle areas with Agent Orange. (111-CC-59950)

CORPS AVIATION GROUPS

I Corps: Falcon Provisional Aviation Group was formed in September 1967 to support Task Force Oregon. It was soon numbered 16th Group and joined 23d Division; it left Vietnam in November 1971. 11th Group served at Da Nang from April 1971 to March 1973.

II Corps: 17th Aviation Group was based at Nha Trang, Tuy Hoa and finally Pleiku between December 1965 and March 1973.

III Corps: 12th Aviation Group was based at Tan Son Nhut and then Long Binh from August 1965 to March 1973.

IV Corps: Delta Provisional Aviation Group, later known as 164th Aviation Group, was based at Can Tho from December 1967 to March 1973.

Aviation Control: 165th Aviation Group was formed in February 1969 to take over the aviation control center at Long Binh; it left Vietnam in January 1972.

ALLOCATING HELICOPTER ASSETS

Infantry divisions had a single aviation battalion for troop lifts but it never had enough helicopters. The Field Force Headquarters (XXIV Corps Headquarters in I Corps after 1968) allocated helicopter assets to the divisions and infantry commanders requested a wide variety of missions once they appreciated the versatility of the helicopter. To begin with, requests were forwarded on a daily basis but it was difficult to conduct long term planning and there was a tendency to give successful units more helicopters. Before long they were assigned on a monthly basis to spread their influence across a wider area.

Airmobile divisions had three aviation battalions and they needed their own Aviation Group to control the large numbers of helicopters operating across their area.

1st Cavalry Division: 11th Group controlled the division's three aviation battalions; it moved to I Corps when the division left in April 1971.

101st Airborne Division: 160th Aviation Group was organized at Bien Hoa to control the division's aviation battalions when it became airmobile in July 1968. It moved to Phu Bai during the Tet Offensive and was it renamed 101st Group in June 1969; it left Vietnam in January 1972.

COMBAT AVIATION BATTALIONS

The battalions controlled a variety of helicopter and fixed wing companies and their organization varied to suit the local requirements. In general Combat Aviation Battalions controlled a number of UH-1 Huey utility helicopter companies and a fixed wing CV-2 Caribou transport company in 1965.

The Caribous had transferred to combat support battalions by the end of 1966 (they later came under US Air Force command) and they were replaced by CH-47 Chinook transport companies. Huey helicopter gunships were soon added and AH-1G Cobra attack helicopters started to appear at the end of 1967.

COMBAT SUPPORT AVIATION BATTALIONS

The battalions started with surveillance and utility planes for reconnaissance and transport missions. They were soon joined by a variety of helicopter companies as the battalion's role increased. Assault Helicopter Companies took over the majority of the battalion's missions in 1971.

FIXED WING SUPPORT BATTALIONS

Battalions controlled a mixture of surveillance and utility fixed wing companies to begin with; they later took control of a variety of helicopter and fixed wing support companies.

DIVISIONAL AVIATION BATTALIONS

Each Division had its own aviation battalion. The battalions had two
airmobile companies and an air cavalry troop.

DIVISION	BATTALION	DIVISION	BATTALION
1st	1st	23d	123d
4th	4th	25th	25th
9th	9th	101st	101st

101st Battalion joined 160th Aviation Group in July 1968 when 101st Airbone
Division was converted to Airmobile status; a third Airmobile Company and an
Aerial Weapons Company armed with AH-1 Cobras were added.

THE AVIATOR SHORTAGE

By 1966 there was a serious shortage of Army aviators and the situation
became critical when many were due to return to the States at the end of their
twelve-month tour. Pilots were only supposed to fly for 90 hours per month,
but many clocked up over 100 hours and the unit's flight surgeon had to make
sure that his men did not suffer from flying fatigue. Attempts to get reservists to
volunteer failed and trained pilots had to be recalled from Europe and Korea.
The number of graduates was nearly quadrupled and a new pilot course was
started at Fort Rucker for non-college graduates training to become warrant
officers. Helicopter units also suffered from a shortage of experienced crew
chiefs and mechanics. Once in Vietnam a pilot had to take part in further
training before he was allowed to fly his own helicopter. After 25 hours of non-
combat flying he flew as a co-pilot on combat missions until he was judged to
be fully competent.

CLOTHING

To begin with crews wore fatigues or US Air Force issue coveralls and leather
gloves until in 1968 a two-piece Nomex uniform made with fire retardant
material was introduced. The early helicopters had no armor and while some

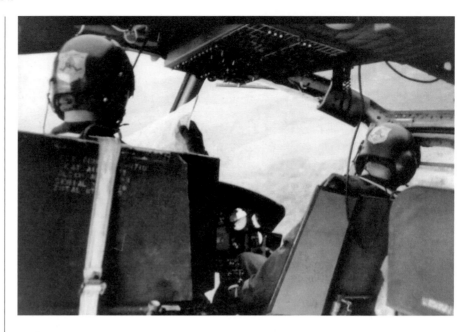

Seat armor protects these two pilots as they fly their command and control helicopter on a security mission. (111-CC-68575)

pilots wore Korean War vintage flak jackets, others made their own. Bullet-proof seats were introduced for the UH-1 helicopters and body armor was introduced in 1965. Aircrews wore flak vests while the pilot and co-pilot wore chest protectors known as chicken plate.

Pilots wore the 1959 model APH-5 flight helmet until the AFH-1 appeared in 1967, however, many aircrew found that it was too small. The SPH-4 helmet, which was designed to reduce noise, appeared in 1969.

HELICOPTER GUNSHIPS

Helicopters could be directed by the infantry commander and they were able to deliver close-range aimed fire at ground targets. They were extremely responsive and could immediately be redirected to different areas. The crews also had an extensive view of the area and were able to direct the ground commander to new targets..

The UH-1B and UH-1C utility helicopters could be equipped with a range of armament systems, including machine guns, rocket launchers and grenade launchers. They could also drop smoke to screen friendly troops or CS gas to drive enemy troops out of their positions; at night they were able to drop flares to light up an area. The AH-1G Huey Cobra was a specially designed high-speed attack helicopter with integrated weapons systems that could be aimed by the pilot.

Although helicopters were an unstable gun platform, an experienced crew could deliver accurate fire. Bad weather, particularly low cloud during the monsoon season, restricted their use and in the early stages of the war helicopters were rarely deployed at night. The amount of ammunition the UH-1 had to carry limited the amount of fuel the B Model could take onboard, but later models overcame the problem.

Tactics were developed as pilots learnt to land their machines in hot landing zones while their gunners performed acrobatics as they fired at the surrounding area. Gunners fired directly at obvious targets and although it was easier to aim when the pilot flew straight towards the target, the helicopter was vulnerable. Flying past at low level was far safer, but the gunner had to track the target.

Suppressive fire was far more common and the pilots either flew past at low level or hovered at a distance while the gunners fired at an area. During an assault landing the door gunners with each wave of helicopters targeted the perimeter of the landing zone as the squads jumped off and ran for cover.

Helicopter gunships were also included in the ground commander's fire plan and the pilots could give direct fire support while acting as observers. The infantry marked their perimeters and the target with colored smoke or white phosphorus as the helicopters approached. Most firing runs were made either parallel to their perimeter or heading directly towards them so the helicopter's guns would point away from their position if it came under fire. Pilots rarely fired while over their own troops to save them from being showered by hundreds of shell cases and rocket caps.

AVIATION MAINTENANCE AND SUPPORT

Most maintenance work was carried out at night and the Division Aviation Officer tried to keep as many helicopters in the air as possible. Every evening he reported how many were available and his maintenance plans for the night so operations could be planned; the morning report finalized details. Helicopters were maintenance intensive and although one hour of maintenance per hour of flight was the desired ratio, it could often rise to 10 hours.

To begin with some units could only fly half their helicopters at any one time but improvements increased the numbers to over 80 per cent. 34th General Support Group was organized at Tan Son Nhut in January 1966 to coordinate support for all types of aviation units and civilian contractors worked alongside Army personnel to keep hundreds of aircraft and helicopters airborne; the Group left Vietnam in November 1972.

In April 1966 USNS *Corpus Christi Bay*, a converted seaplane tender, reached Cam Ranh Bay and started work as a floating maintenance facility. The crew could refer to a huge onboard library of drawings and images and they could broadcast information to maintenance facilities via closed circuit television. In September 1966 the ship relocated to Qui Nhon to be nearer to the 1st Cavalry Division, its main customer.

Above: *A door gunner keeps watch as his helicopter flies low above paddy fields.* (111-CC-27904)

Left: *A helicopter stands idle inside its maintenance hangar while it is checked over.* (111-CC-64996)

These Dust-Off helicopters at 3d Field Hospital are protected by well-spaced revetments. (111-CC-62502)

HELIPORT CONSTRUCTION

Helicopter rotors produced dust storms and the debris restricted the pilot's visibility during takeoffs and landings so helipads needed special treatment to prevent accidents. The crews preferred aluminum or steel planking pads but these were too expensive and diesel was often used to limit the dust at firebases; larger facilities used peneprime, a specialist dust suppressant.

1st Cavalry Division (Airmobile) needed a huge facility for all its gunships and transport helicopters, and An Khe in the Central Highlands was chosen. Engineers worked around the clock to build runways, helipads and facilities while Vietnamese labor removed vegetation and tree stumps by hand to retain the grass. The base had soon acquired the nickname 'the Golf Course'.

Helicopters were vulnerable to mortar and rocket attacks and pilots had to space their machines out to reduce the chances of extensive damage from single missiles. Permanent shelters were impractical due to the number of times a unit moved so a variety of temporary blast walls were built using earth, sandbags, fiberglass containers and timber to begin with. Corrugated steel revetments filled with earth were then used until pre-cast concrete units appeared in 1970.

STATISTICS

From an experimental introduction, the helicopter became an indispensable part of the Armed Forces, with hundreds of flights being flown every day. The total of Army, Marine Corps and Navy sorties flown in Vietnam illustrates the machine's diversity:

Command and control sorties	21,098,000
Troop landing sorties	7,547,000
Gunship sorties	3,932,000
Cargo sorties	3,548,000
Total sorties flown	36,125,000

Inevitably, many helicopters were shot down, often as the pilot sat helpless while he guided his craft to the ground. Even a minor malfunction could lead to catastrophe and although pilots were trained to land a stricken helicopter on open terrain, the dynamics of the machine and the rough terrain made it extremely difficult. Casualties were consequently high:

Helicopter pilots killed in action	1,069
Helicopters lost due to enemy action	2,076
Helicopters lost in accidents	2,566

ARMOR

To begin with US Command believed that most of Vietnam's countryside was unsuitable for armor. The mixture of jungles and mountains in the north would restrict vehicles to the poor road network while the extensive paddy fields and wetlands did the same in the south. The deployment of two tank battalions, 2d Battalion, 34th Armor Regiment, with 4th Division and 1st Battalion, 69th Armor Regiment with 25th Division (they were exchanged in August 1967) soon proved that armor had a valuable role to play. Commanders discovered that the M48s were very effective at providing direct fire support for the infantry as they forged their way through the undergrowth heading towards an enemy position. The battalions were soon deploying squadrons across the country where their tanks worked alongside armored personnel carriers, clearing roads, protecting convoys and entering enemy held areas.

Armor proved to be so successful that a third battalion, 1st Battalion, 77th Armored Regiment, was deployed with 1st Brigade, 5th Infantry Division (Mechanized). The Brigade had been specially organized for Vietnam and its combination of firepower and mobility was used to support Marine operations south of the Demilitarized Zone.

Tanks were also deployed with the divisional Armored Cavalry Squadrons and the largest armored unit deployed to Vietnam, 11th Cavalry Regiment, had fifty-one M48A3 tanks.

ARMORED BATTALION ORGANIZATION

The battalions were reorganized for deployment to Vietnam and the Headquarters and Headquarters Company had sixteen officers, one warrant officer and 139 enlisted men. It was armed with three M48 tanks and nine M113 carriers while four M106 carriers armed with 4.2in mortars provided indirect fire support. Five 2½-ton trucks and twelve ¼-ton utility trucks provided transport.

The battalion had three tank companies, A, B and C, each with five officers and eighty-seven enlisted men. It was armed with seventeen M48 tanks, nine of them equipped with xenon searchlights so they could operate at night. An M88 recovery vehicle was able to recover disabled tanks while an M113 carrier took supplies to the crews when they were operating in the field. The battalion transport included one 2½-ton truck, one ¾-ton truck and three ¼-ton utility trucks.

The battalion's service company, Company D, had six officers, two warrant officers and 152 enlisted men. Two M48 Launched Scissor Bridges could provide temporary bridges across narrow watercourses while two M113 carriers moved supplies. The company also had two M88 recovery vehicles and two 5-ton wrecker trucks to carry out servicing and repairs. Transport was provided by twenty 5-ton, five 2½-ton and five ¾-ton trucks and twelve ¼-ton utility trucks.

M48 tanks add their firepower to the blocking force covering the Saigon River during Operation Cedar Falls. (111-CC38110)

DEPLOYMENT

2d Battalion, 34th Armor arrived in September 1966 and while Company A joined 25th Division at Cu Chi and Company B joined 1st Division at Phu Loi, Company C was sent north to I Corps. It was withdrawn in December 1970.

1st Battalion, 69th Armor Regiment arrived in March 1966 and its companies served across II Corps. Company B was engaged in the only tank-to-tank combat when North Vietnamese PT-76 tanks attacked one of its night defensive positions in March 1969. It was withdrawn in April 1970.

1st Battalion, 77th Armored Regiment, served with 1st Brigade, 5th Infantry Division (Mechanized) in I Corps from June 1968 to August 1971.

Company D, 16th Armor company, deployed its M56 self-propelled Scorpions as mobile anti-tank weapons with 173d Airborne Brigade in May 1965. The company was reformed as the Tuy Hoa Provisional Armor Company in April 1969 and it worked across Binh Dinh Province until it withdrew from Vietnam in November 1969.

RIVERINE OPERATIONS

In the summer of 1966 MACV decided it would deploy a mixed force of infantry, artillery, landing craft and shallow draft ships to engage the Viet Cong in the Mekong Delta. The force would be known as the Mobile Riverine Force and its new base, at the junction of the Song My Tho River and the Kinh Xang Canal west of My Tho, would be known as Dong Tam or 'Friendship' in Vietnamese.

Over 17 million cu yd of fill were dredged to form a turning basin and it was used to build a 600-acre area of dry land for the base facilities complete with a port, landing craft ramps, airstrip and heliport. Work started at the beginning of 1967 and it intensified after the Tet offensive so that 9th Division could move in by July 1968.

The base could accommodate 12,500 men and as the base started to take shape the combat troops joined the engineers, helping to build their billets.

Two troop carriers beach on a riverbank so the men inside can begin their operation.
(127-GVC-A42551)

The buildings eventually covered over 1 million sq ft and were served by 13 miles of road; the heliport alone covered 21,000 sq yd and had 174 helicopter revetments, five hangars and several fuel storage areas. Power and water purification plants were added to increase the base's self-sufficiency and a Medical Unit Self-contained Transportable (MUST) hospital facility was built to handle casualties. Dong Tam cost $8million, but before long 9th Division had scattered the Viet Cong units across the Delta and units were soon handing areas over to the Regional and Popular Forces.

THE MOBILE RIVERINE FORCE

Mobile Riverine Force began operations in June 1967 with Task Force 117's flotilla of four command boats, fifty-two armored troop carriers, ten monitors, and two refuelers. The Task Force was spilt as follows:

River Assault Squadrons 9: River Assault Division 91 and River Assault Division 92
River Assault Squadrons 11: River Assault Division 111 and River Assault Division 112

Each division was led by a Command Control Boat and they had thirteen Armored Troop Carriers, three Monitors, and eight Assault Support Patrol Boats; a refueler accompanied each squadron.

While an LST supply ship carried ammunition for the barge-mounted artillery, LCU landing craft transported a battery of 155mm self-propelled artillery as support while LCM-8 landing craft carried ammunition.

Temporary bases were established to extend the flotilla's range and they were designed along the same lines as a fire support base, only with extra waterway facilities. The anchorage could be over a mile long and while river traffic was restricted, curfews kept the local population away at night. One company protected the base and it had to patrol the area, monitor the curfew and watch the river for mines and enemy divers.

OPERATIONS

Operations were planned by the joint staffs of 9th Division's 2d Brigade and Task Force 117. The brigade assessed intelligence collected by its Mobile Intelligence Civil Affairs Team and choose targets, while the flotilla's Riverine Survey Team checked if the rivers and canals could be navigated. The 9th Division's engineers also checked bridge clearances with the Vietnamese while the planners had to consider the tides and navigability of rivers.

A loading schedule, a movement timetable and a plan of assault had to be drawn up and agreed. The flotilla's craft had to be able to land on the riverbank and there had to be nearby moorings for the barge-mounted artillery. While the flotilla team prepared a waterway map with navigation information, ambush points, known bunkers and suspect minefields, the brigade team produced the operational plan. The final briefing was held on the Mobile Riverine Force flagship as the troops boarded their craft.

Operations were often based on the hammer and anvil concept. An infantry force provided the anvil and it was inserted by helicopter to block the main escape route, using concertina wire to block narrow waterways. The riverine force then landed and deployed quickly, acting as the hammer as it drove the enemy before it. Helicopter gunships covered the flanks. The operation was run from the flotilla flagship while the brigade command group coordinated helicopter lifts, artillery and air strikes from a nearby fire support base. The brigade and battalion commanders often watched the operation from their command helicopters.

Bulk cargo and ammunition was loaded on ammunition barges in advance so they could join the flotilla at allotted times. A rifle company filled three armored troop carriers, one platoon to each carrier, and it took 20 minutes to load them. The carriers then rendezvoused with the command ship, the monitors and the refuelers so they could set off in convoy at the specified time. Before long the Riverine Force could move 5,000 men over 100 miles in a 24-hour period and then launch an assault 30 minutes after anchoring.

Two Assault Support Boats led the flotilla, sweeping the river for mines. Drag hooks were used to catch them and, with the help of a high-speed winch, the crews tried to cut the mooring wires with the steel cables. They also fired at danger points to try and prematurely trigger an ambush. The Viet Cong soon installed warning systems along some rivers and canals and the number of ambushes increased.

The battalion followed behind, sailing in three sections, each with three Armored Troop Carriers and a Monitor (the battalion's fourth company was usually at a nearby fire base). An assault boat brought up the rear.

The artillery shelled the landing area, moving its fire inland as the flotilla drew close. As the armored troop carriers made their final approach, the minesweepers and monitors fired at the riverbank. When possible, carriers landed simultaneously so the rifle company could move off quickly to its first objective as artillery, helicopter gunships and air strikes paved the way.

A landing zone was cleared as soon as possible so that helicopters could bring in supplies and remove casualties while plans were made for the flotilla to protect the beach if the battalion was planning to stay overnight.

Landing craft were converted to carry two 105mm howitzers. They had ammunition storage at each end of the craft, while the crew quarters were in the center. An LCM-8, housing the battery command post, was moored alongside and it was able to use its engines to push the landing craft into position.

Placing artillery close to a riverine operation was always difficult in the swampy delta so a special platform large enough for a 105mm howitzer, ammunition and its crew was developed. The legs had a large metal foot suitable for soft ground and they could be adjusted to level the platform. A CH-47 helicopter carried the platform, artillery piece, ammunition and crew to their new location in four lifts.

When the operation was over the men either walked or were taken by helicopter back to the flotilla where they established a narrow defensive perimeter along the riverbank. The boats usually waited at a different location, where trees and undergrowth restricted the enemy's field of fire and colored smoke and radio messages guided the men to the boats as they flew pennants (they shone colored lights at night) so platoons loaded together. Once everyone was aboard, the boats assembled in convoy and returned to base, preferably via a different river to the approach route.

CHAPTER FIVE

COMBAT SUPPORT

There were three types of Combat Support units: engineering, military police and communications. In Army areas the Field Forces delegated responsibilities to Engineer Groups, Military Police Groups and Signals Groups, while each division had units covering its own operational areas. In Vietnam the Marine Corps consolidated its Combat Support units into a Force Logistics Command including the divisional service battalions, two military police battalions, a communications battalion and a motor transport battalion. The organization of the battalions had to be altered drastically to suit operational needs across I Corps.

ENGINEERS

During the advisory period, work was carried out by civilian contractors, but the increase in Viet Cong activity made it too dangerous for them. Although the number of troops in Vietnam at the start of 1965 was 23,000 men, there were still fewer than 100 Army engineers after General Westmoreland's request for another 2,400 was refused; only another eighty were deployed. There was always a shortage of trained men caused by a lack of forward planning and the engineers were overstretched as the number of troops increased.

173d Airborne Brigade's engineers carve out a small landing zone with chain saws so resupply helicopters can land during Operation Cedar Falls. (111-CC-37992)

The decision to rely on the draft hit the engineers hard. Over 100,000 Reservist engineers could not be recalled to fight while the civilian units working at Army bases could not be deployed. Many engineers had to be moved from other theaters and retrained before they deployed to Vietnam. New units had to be formed and others were restructured while large amounts of equipment had to be procured.

ARMY ENGINEER BRIGADES

18th Engineer Brigade arrived at Tan Son Nhut in September 1965 and it took over all engineering schemes across II and III Corps, coordinating work, deciding priorities and ordering materials. It also gave engineering support to the two Field Forces. Over the next twelve months five Engineer Groups were deployed to Vietnam to oversee the following projects:

Expanding existing deep-draft ports and building new shallow-draft ports
Constructing new depots, off-loading areas and logistical facilities at the ports
Building new jet-capable airfields and forward landing strips for transport aircraft
Restoring the existing road network, expanding it to connect the bases to the ports

18th Brigade moved to Dong Ba Thin, near Cam Ranh Bay, in December 1966, to concentrate on I Field Force's area while Provisional Engineer Command worked for II Field Force. 18th Brigade expanded into I Corps when Task Force Oregon moved into the southern provinces. It left Vietnam in September 1971. 20th Engineer Brigade took over from Provisional Engineer Command at Bien Hoa and took control of work across III and IV Corps in August 1967; it left Vietnam in September 1971.

ENGINEER GROUPS

Construction Engineer Groups designed, planned and supervised construction projects, controlling up to five construction battalions at a time. 937th Combat Engineer Group planned and coordinated the combat support activities of up to six engineer battalions working in the Central Highlands. However, it did not design projects. The Engineer Groups were based at the following locations:

I Corps: Three heavy Marine Engineer battalions worked alongside the two divisional engineer battalions and the Navy's Seebee Construction Battalions. The Army based 45th Group at Phu Bai and 35th Group at Da Nang in 1968.
II Corps, North: 937th Group was based at Qui Nhon before moving to Pleiku and then Phu Tai. 45th Group was based at Tuy Hoa before moving to Qui Nhon and then to I Corps.
II Corps, South: 35th Group was based at Phan Rang and Cam Ranh Bay while 34th Group was at Vung Tau.
III Corps: 159th Group at Bien Hoa and then Long Binh where it was joined by 79th Group.
IV Corps: 34th Group at Bin Thuy.

COMBAT ENGINEER BATTALIONS

Two types of Combat Engineer Battalions provided engineer support in the Army's forward areas, covering the work carried out by the divisional engineers. They worked on base and airfield construction, road clearing and bridge building. They would also build defensive positions or demolish obstacles; occasionally they would fight alongside the infantry if their base was under attack.

The larger Combat Engineer Battalion had thirty-nine officers and 755 enlisted men organized into a Headquarters Company and four Combat Companies. They operated ten bulldozers, four graders, thirteen loaders, three cranes and a concrete mixer; the equipment could all be carried by heavy transport planes. A smaller Combat Engineer Battalion had thirty-three officers and 586 enlisted men organized into a headquarters company and three combat companies. It was equipped with seven bulldozers, three graders, three loaders and two cranes.

CONSTRUCTION ENGINEER BATTALIONS

Two types of Construction Engineer Battalions worked on larger projects, building structures, roads and airfields at the Army's military installations. They also maintained the lines of communication across the country, repairing and building roads, bridges, pipelines and railways.

One type had thirty-one officers and 850 enlisted men organized into a Headquarters Company and three Engineer Construction Companies. It operated twenty-four scrapers, thirteen bulldozers, nine graders, six concrete mixers, eight cranes, a rock crusher and machinery for vertical construction. The engineer equipment and maintenance company and the direct support maintenance section serviced the battalion's equipment.

The second type of battalion had thirty-eight officers and 867 enlisted men organized along the same lines, however, it did not have a maintenance section and it only had twelve scrapers. Some battalions specialized in heavy construction while others concentrated on lightweight building projects, often supervising combat and support troops while they built their own facilities.

The three heavy Marine Engineer battalions had between 900 and 1,000 officers and men.

ENGINEERING COMPANIES

A large number of specialized engineering companies were deployed to Vietnam. Light Equipment Companies provided support for engineer combat battalions when they needed extra equipment. They had six cranes, nine graders, four scoop loaders, two concrete mixers, nine scrapers and four bulldozers; they also had quarrying equipment for producing aggregate.

Port Construction Companies had specialist marine equipment for building port and beach landing projects; a diving section carried out underwater construction and maintenance.

Pipeline Construction Support Companies installed and maintained fuel pipelines connecting the port storage tanks to major bases.

Water Supply and Water Supply Support Companies controlled rainwater stocks and drilled for new sources.

Cartography was an engineering function and the combat troops needed accurate maps for navigation and coordinating fire support.

Corps Topographic Companies installed a network of survey markers across the country so that maps could be produced with the help of aerial photography.

A Combat Engineer team set to work repairing a damaged bridge in the Central Highlands. (111-CC-69974)

BASE CONSTRUCTION AND MAINTENANCE

CONSTRUCTION

The first three considerations when building a base were land acquisition, security and the organization of the local labor force. Protracted negotiations were needed with government officials to minimize the amount of disruption to the local population. Combat troops also had to protect the engineers while they cleared the surrounding area. A village was sometimes built alongside to house refugees who could provide a labor force, and the Vietnamese were trained to operate contractor's heavy equipment at some bases. Eventually over 15,000 people lived at the village built next to the bases at Cam Rahn Bay; the majority worked for the Americans.

A shortage of raw materials was always a restraining factor and it took time to secure supplies. Quarries had to be found for building aggregate and the Viet Cong had to be cleared from local forests before sawmills could be set up. Fresh water was always in short supply and local sources either had to be boiled or purified until deep wells had been sunk.

A lot of work was carried out at night due to the hot weather and concreting operations had to take place during the evening while the men rested during the hottest part of the day. Before long, hard standings for motor vehicles, storage areas and supply dumps started to appear and they were connected by temporary roads until permanent concrete and asphalt ones could be built. Accommodation was low down on the list of priorities and the men lived in tents and dugouts for several months. When pre-packed billet units arrived, units were encouraged to spend their spare time building their own accommodation under engineer supervision.

MAINTENANCE

Combat units maintained their own bases but no plans had been made to employ a long-term maintenance workforce. The Armed Forces often did not have the men to spare to carry out repairs and maintenance, ranging from fire protection to pest control (Reserve units carried out the tasks at Stateside bases), so civilian maintenance contractors had to be employed. The Navy and the Air Force had kept the majority of their maintenance units, but they both still employed thousands of local laborers to construct their military installations.

The Army's 1st Logistical Command administered contracts, while Pacific Architects and Engineers recruited and organized American, foreign and Vietnamese labor. By 1968 over 24,000 employees were working at 120 locations, costing $100 million per year. Building and maintenance at the bases were grouped together under the US Army Engineer Construction Agency in March 1968 and the Agency's work was taken over by US Army Engineer Command in March 1970.

An engineer team prepares a tunnel section for demolition in the Iron Triangle. (111-CC-38318)

ROADS AND RAILWAYS

By 1965 most of the 6,000km of roads across Vietnam were impassable, either due to neglect or to Viet Cong activity. Roads were important for supporting combat operations and while aviation assets worked at full capacity many units relied on road convoys to survive. Work began on essential repairs in 1966 and by the following year the Central Highways and Waterways Coordination Committee had drawn up a program of work.

Sixteen engineer battalions worked on the US Army's part of the highway program and by April 1968 work of the main roads was being supervised by the MACV's Director of Construction. The plan was to finish the majority of the program by 1971, with the Vietnamese completing work three years later. By 1968, Army engineers alone were building 5½km of road a week and by October 1970 over 2,300km had been completed.

Construction Support Companies extracted rock and aggregate from quarries and by 1970 more than 150,000 tons a week were being produced. The companies also operated asphalting equipment, surfacing roads which limited Viet Cong mining activity. Dump Truck Companies, equipped with forty-eight 5-ton dump trucks, carried materials around the country. Panel Bridge Companies fabricated concrete bridge sections, which could be lifted into position by helicopter, while Float Bridge Companies specialized in installing pontoon bridges. The Marine Corps had two Bridge Companies covering the same activities.

The French railway system had been severely damaged by Viet Cong activity and bad weather. US engineers started work in December 1966 and before long trains were carrying materials for construction projects. By 1971 South Vietnam's railways were carrying over two million passengers a year.

LAND CLEARING AND ROME PLOWS

Huge Rome Plow bulldozers equipped with armored cabs and sharpened blades were used to carve swathes through the jungles where the Viet Cong hid, limiting movement and destroying sanctuaries. They cut their lanes in defined patterns, sometimes starting with a huge circle to isolate an area, following up with a series of spokes to carve the sanctuary into manageable areas. The bulldozers were also used to clear alongside roads to deny the enemy cover before work started in the sanctuaries.

Clearing operations began in the Iron Triangle in May 1967 when 169th Engineer Battalion arrived. In the summer of 1967 another three land-clearing platoons equipped with thirty Rome Plows arrived. With a mechanized infantry company (or armored cavalry squadron) and a tank platoon for protection the bulldozers flattened bunkers and ripped open tunnels. By January 1969 there were six companies operating across the country.

The tanks led while the infantry covered the flanks and a second tank section brought up the rear. To begin with an area was shelled before the

A column of Rome Plows cut a swathe through a jungle stripped of greenery by Agent Orange defoliant. (111-CC-67282)

bulldozers moved in, cutting swathes through the undergrowth while the infantry and tanks fired into the surrounding jungle. Later on the infantry and tanks swept the area before the bulldozers moved in to reduce the chance of an ambush.

DIVISIONAL ENGINEER BATTALIONS

Each division had a battalion of engineers for building or destroying structures and defensive positions. They could build base camps, fire support bases, landing zones and bridges. Teams could also repair roads, sweeping them for mines on a daily basis. Engineer teams usually accompanied an infantry company during operations, taking along explosives to destroy enemy camps and supplies while teams specializing in searching tunnels, known as the tunnel rats were on hand to search underground complexes. Engineers were trained to fight alongside the infantry if required.

The battalion had forty-six officers and 901 enlisted men organized into a Headquarters and Headquarters Company and four Combat Engineer Companies. They were equipped with fifty-eight 5-ton dump trucks, twelve bulldozers, twelve loaders, four cranes and four graders. The bridge company had aluminum floor sections for bridging small obstacles and repairing roads or airfields.

DIVISION	BATTALION	DIVISION	BATTALION
1st Cavalry	8th	25th Infantry	65th
1st Infantry	1st	101st Airborne	326th
4th Infantry	4th	1st Marine Division	1st Engineer
9th Infantry	15th	3d Marine Division	3d Engineer
23d Infantry	26th		

1st Cavalry Division's engineer battalion, the 8th, operated with helicopters and radios and could build landing zones, helipads and airfields across a wide area. It had thirty-eight officers and 582 enlisted men organized into a Headquarters and Headquarters Company and three Combat Engineer Companies. The battalion was equipped with forty-two ¾-ton dump trucks, light enough to be carried by helicopter, and fourteen scrapers and graders which could be split into helicopter-sized loads.

Independent brigades were served by engineering companies as was the 11th Armored Cavalry.

BRIGADE	COMPANY	BRIGADE	COMPANY
11th Brigade	6th	1st / 5th Division	A, 7th Battalion
196th Brigade	175th	3d, 82d Airborne	C, 307th Battalion
198th Brigade	555th	173d Airborne	173d
199th Brigade	87th	11th Armored	919th

Companies were added as extra engineering support to the following divisions:

501st Company served with 1st Cavalry Division
571st Company served with 9th Division
54th Company served with 25th Division

MILITARY POLICE

The Military Police (MPs) were responsible for base security, highway checkpoints, escorting military convoys and maintaining law and order at military installations. To begin with they operated with lightly armed jeeps but they were vulnerable to attack in built up areas. The arrival of V-100 armored cars and M113 APCs in the summer of 1967 provided welcome protection; many were stationed in Saigon.

Waterborne units maintained security at the ports and along the rivers and coastlines, stopping unauthorized craft and searching for enemy divers. While fast-moving patrol boats armed with .50-caliber machine guns guarded the ports, shallow draft Boston Whalers watched the coast.

A military policeman checks a visitor's papers while his colleague looks beneath the car for explosives outside the American Embassy in Saigon. (111-CC-31814)

A Military Police Emergency Alert Force deploys following a bombing incident in Saigon; the team would administer first aid, evacuate the wounded and provide crowd control. (111-CC-31859)

The police also had to deal with many civil and criminal problems unique to the conflict in Southeast Asia. Conflicts between soldiers on leave and the local population had to be resolved while large numbers of refugees had to be controlled. Military Police detachments often assisted divisional MP companies during cordon and search operations. Armored cars and jeeps would form a cordon and start rounding up detainees with the help of searchlights and loudspeakers while others set up a temporary interrogation center.

The Military Police also conducted criminal investigations, and the number of incidents of black marketeering and drug dealing rose rapidly as morale declined during the final stages of the American withdrawal.

560th Company started providing cover for US installations in September 1962 and it was joined by 504th and 716th MP Battalions in 1965. 89th MP Group took over in March 1966, but it was replaced when 18th MP Brigade took command of all activities across Vietnam six months later, splitting the country between 16th and 89th MP Groups. 16th MP Group covered I and II Corps from Nha Trang and then Da Nang after October 1970 while 89th MP Group covered III and IV Corps from Long Binh. Two Marine Military Police battalions carried out similar duties for III Marine Amphibious Force. A number of specially organized Military Police companies escorted convoys while others guarded bases, some with the help of sentry dogs.

A provisional Military Police Group was organized in November 1966 to investigate crimes committed by soldiers and it was replaced by 8th Military Police Group at Long Binh in August 1968. The group worked with the Divisional Provost Marshal Sections across the country. The Group also ran Long Binh Jail (known as LBJ Ranch, after President Johnson's initials), a second jail was added at Da Nang later in the war. The Group handed over operation to the US Army Criminal Investigation Center, Vietnam Field Office, when it left Vietnam in July 1972.

DIVISIONAL MILITARY POLICE

Each Army division had a Military Police Company while Marine divisions had a battalion; they were responsible for base security, law and order, and traffic control on the division's base camps.

DIVISION	COMPANY	DIVISION	COMPANY
1st Cavalry	545th	25th Infantry	25th
1st Infantry	1st	101st Airborne	101st
4th Infantry	4th	1st Marine	1st Marine Battalion
9th Infantry	9th	3d Marine	3d Marine Battalion
23d Infantry	23rd		

199th Brigade was supported by 152d Platoon.

SIGNALS

ARMY COMMUNICATIONS

A small communications station was set up for the Military Assistance and Advisory Group (MAAG) in Saigon in 1951 and a single-channel radio link to Clark Air Base in the Philippines kept Washington informed about the situation in Vietnam. After the French defeat in 1954 the Army's STARCOM communications station took on a new significance and both the transmitter and receiver had to be moved to improve communications.

As the US Army's advisory role increased, so did radio traffic and in November 1961 the STARCOM Facility at Phu Lam, on the western outskirts of Saigon, became the new location for radio transmitters. Long-range communications across the country were maintained by the Backporch system, involving tropospheric scatter radio signals, while the Wetwash Integrated Wideband Communications System linked the cities. Overseas communications were improved by the installation of an undersea cable to the Philippines linked to a switchboard and paper tape relays at Nha Trang. By January 1964 the system was already handling 6,000 messages a day but the number of communications increased dramatically following the Gulf of Tonkin Incident in August. A satellite terminal was immediately airlifted to Phu Lam (the operating unit was named Phu Lam Signal Battalion, USASTRATCOM, the following summer and renamed USASTRATCOM Signal Support Agency, Phu Lam, in 1970).

By 1965 IBM punch cards were replacing the paper tape relays on the data relay systems. The Automatic Digital Network ended the reliance on paper tape and punch cards in 1968, providing a fast, reliable and secure system for over 40,000 messages a day. Virtually all signals were sent via AUTODIN by the end of 1969 as High Frequency radio was phased out.

Phu Lam's Automatic Secure Voice Communications (AUTOSEVOCOM) Company played an important part in bringing hostilities to an end as it relayed messages to Paris during the peace negotiations. Signal Support Agency, Phu Lam, was reorganized as 60th Signal Battalion just before it was closed in June 1972.

SIGNALS COMMAND

39th Signal Battalion reached Vietnam in March 1962 and took over responsibility for communications support, operating and maintaining telephones, teletypewriters, data and facsimile lines. Army Strategic Communications Command, Vietnam, STRATCOM, began laying down the framework for a vast communications system in July 1965, controlling units as they installed, operated and maintained the expanding network. 1st Signal Brigade arrived in Saigon in April 1966 and it took over all communications in Vietnam and Thailand while responsibility for Southeast Asia's part of the worldwide Defense Communications System was handed over to the Regional Communications Group. The Brigade would eventually build, install, operate and maintain an extensive communications and electronics system at over 200 sites. The Brigade moved to Long Binh in October 1967 and left Vietnam in November 1972.

REGIONAL COMMUNICATIONS GROUP

In May 1966 USASTRATCOM Long Lines Battalion North and Long Lines Battalion South began installing a multichannel communications system across Vietnam. The battalions were formally organized when the Regional Communications Group, Vietnam, was set up at Saigon in July 1966. The Group had a staff skilled in operating the communications and electronics system. It was renamed the US Army Strategic Communications Regional Group, Vietnam, in April 1968 and it ran the Integrated Communications System from Tan Son Nhut. In June 1969 the Long Lines Battalions were called renamed Command Radio and Cable Signal Battalions:

Huge tropospheric antennas were part of the long range communications system across the northern half of the country. (111-CC-65457)

North Battalion became 361st Battalion covering I and II Corps areas from Cam Ranh Bay
South Battalion became 369th Battalion covering III and IV Corps areas from Vung Tau

The Battalions left in June 1971 and the Group closed down in July 1972. Three Regional Facilities supported the Regional Communications Group:

US Army Strategic Communications Facility, Phu Lam from November 1964
US Army Strategic Communications Facility, Nha Trang from November 1965
US Army Strategic Communications Facility, Da Nang from August 1966

They were renamed Provisional Signal Battalions in June 1967 and closed in September 1970.

SIGNAL GROUPS

Signal Groups coordinated installation, operation, training and maintenance, controlling a number of signal battalions across a Corps area.

2nd Signal Group arrived at Tan Son Nhut in June 1965, but it handed over II Corps area to 21st Signal Group when it arrived at Nha Trang twelve months later. 2d Group moved to Long Binh in January 1967 and 160th Group took over the Saigon-Long Binh area in May where it ran the Southeast Asia Signal School as well as the Saigon and Long Binh Signal Support Agencies.

I Corps Tactical Signal Group was formed at Phu Bai in September 1968 to run XXIV Corps communications. It was replaced by 12th Signal Group in July 1969 and the group moved to Da Nang in September 1970.

ARMY AND CORPS SIGNALS

69th Signal Battalion started running MACV's signals in the Saigon-Long Binh area in November 1965. It formed the basis for the Saigon Signal Support Agency in June 1970 and left Vietnam in November 1972.

Two battalions maintained communications for the Field Forces, linking them to the divisions and artillery under their command. They operated wire telephones, radio teletype and the Military Affiliate Radio System, known as MARS. A Provisional Signal Battalion briefly covered the outlying areas of II Corps in 1969. Three Radio Battalions maintained radio communications for the Marine Corps in I Corps area.

SIGNAL SUPPORT AND MODIFIED SUPPORT BATTALIONS

Signal Support Battalions operated multichannel telephone, teletypewriter, data and facsimile systems from their signal centers. Combat Area Battalions operated communications centers at base camps, keeping the Corps Headquarters and combat units in contact. Four extra Modified Support Battalions were raised in October 1966 to take control of the Corps' communications systems. Battalions had five companies, each covering an area of responsibility:

Command Communications Center Company
Area Communications Center Company
Telephone Operations Company
Radio Company
Signal Support Agency

This signal site at the top of Black Virgin Mountain covered both 1st Division's and 25th Division's area, west of Saigon. (111-CC-60857)

DIVISIONAL SIGNALS

The Signal Battalion was the hub of the Army division during operations and the personnel used every means possible to keep the divisional and brigade headquarters in contact with the units in the field. A Communications Battalion carried out the same functions in Marine divisions while Radio Battalions were responsible for signal intelligence activities, in particular signal intercepts.

Signal centers operated wire and radio systems (linked by integration stations) with trunk lines to higher echelons and local lines to their subordinates. Personnel were often scattered across the division's area of operations and the battalions with the two Airmobile Divisions (1st Cavalry and 101st Airborne) needed additional personnel and equipment to cover their extended areas.

DIVISION	BATTALION	DIVISION	BATTALION
1st Cavalry	13th	25th Infantry	125th
1st Infantry	121st	101st Airborne	501st
4th Infantry	124th	1st Marine	1st and 5th
9th Infantry	125th	3d Marine	7th
23d Infantry	523d		

11th, 196th and 198th Brigades did not bring signal companies to Vietnam; other independent brigades were served by signal companies:

BRIGADE	COMPANY	BRIGADE	COMPANY
199th Brigade	313th	3d, 82d Airborne	58th
1st / 5th Division	298th	173d Airborne	534th and 173d

A captain of the 1st Cavalry Division keeps in contact with his command helicopter hovering overhead. (111-CC-35286)

A 4th Division platoon commander keeps track of his squads with a tiny AN/PRT-4 transmitter and AN/PRR-9 helmet mounted receiver during Operation MacArthur. (111-CC-49700)

SIGNAL EQUIPMENT

The first units to arrive had difficulties upgrading from the AN/GRC-3 and AN/GRC-8 series of radios to the new AN/VRC-12 series. As they were not compatible, units converted en masse; many other items of signaling equipment also had to be upgraded at the same time including the new series of VRC-12 vehicle-mounted radios. Units arriving later were always short of new equipment and while independent brigades were found to have inadequate signal organizations, everybody's equipment suffered in the hot and humid conditions.

DIVISIONAL AND BRIGADE RADIOS

Multi-channel secure teletypewriter circuits and GRC-19 radios were replaced in 1966 and 1967 by AN/GRC-106 High Frequency single sideband radio set sfitted with new radio teletypewriter configurations. The AN/MRC-69 radio relay carrier terminal set gave the division twenty-four telephone channels and twelve teletypewriter channels and it could be combined with the MRC-73 single terminal, the MCC-6 telegraph telephone terminal and the MRC-54 radio repeater.

Airmobile and airborne divisions used lightweight MRC-111 and MRC-112 systems which could be carried by helicopters or fitted on a ¼-ton truck. They were replaced by the lighter AN/GRC-163, with its longer range, in January 1968. Battalions used the MRC-69 and MRC-122 while the AN/GRC-46 and AN/VSC-1 AM radio teletypewriters were used to send secure printed communications.

Signal battalion commanders had to use their initiative to cover their area with FM and many were soon relying on multi-channel radios, a modification of the mobile MRC-34Y2 terminal, which could be mounted in a trailer or carried by helicopter.

PLATOON RADIOS

The AN/PRC-8-10 radio was replaced by the lighter AN/PRC-25 radio in the summer of 1965. There was a PRC-25 man-pack version and a VRC-53 vehicle-mounted version (the GRC-125 radio was designed to be carried by either). The improved AN/PRC-77 radio appeared later, again in three variants: the PRC-77 man-pack, the vehicle-mounted VRC-64 and the GRC-160, either method.

SQUAD RADIOS

The AN/PRC-6 squad radio, with its hand-held receiver and transmitter, was replaced by the AN/PRT-4 two-channel radio in 1967. The new system had a tiny AN/PRR-9 helmet-mounted receiver. They had a maximum range of 1,000m which was reduced to 500m in adverse terrain.

CHAPTER 6

SPECIAL FORCES

Throughout the 1950s, small teams from 1st Special Forces Group (Airborne) and 14th Special Forces Detachment had been training Vietnamese specialist units. By 1960 thirty men were working with the Vietnamese Rangers (the Biet Dong Quan) and the predecessor of the Vietnamese Special Forces (Lac Luong Dec Biet) known as the Joint Observations Battalion.

THE CIVILIAN IRREGULAR DEFENSE GROUP (CIDG) PROGRAM

At the beginning of 1961 a Special Forces detachment began studying the situation along the border with Cambodia and Laos, in particular across the Central Highlands. It soon became clear that the trust and assistance of the local population, known as the Montagnards, had to be gained if Viet Cong control was to be reduced. The Montagnards were old enemies of the Vietnamese and the Special Forces teams began providing civil assistance, starting with the Rhade tribe in Darlac Province.

Before long the villagers were receiving basic military training and building primitive fortifications while a central Strike Force was organized to deal with Viet Cong attacks. During the summer of 1962 Navy Construction Units, known as SeeBees, built a chain of camps along the border where detachments working for US Army Special Forces (Provisional), Vietnam, were based.

By July 1963, there were four B-Detachments (twenty-five-man teams) and thirty-seven A-Detachments (twelve-man teams) as the Special Forces officially took control of the CIDG Program under the name Operation Switchback; operations also turned from defense into attack. Trail watchers, later called Border Surveillance Teams or Mountain Scouts, carried out patrols and ambushes while the Special Forces detachments led the CIDG troops on raids. Order was quickly restored following a brief Montagnard rebellion against the government in September 1964 and the camps' presence grew to be a real problem for the Viet Cong, so much so that they often tried to overrun them.

The 5th Special Forces Group (Airborne) arrived in October 1964 and established a command chain of Detachments to cover South Vietnam. A C-Detachment (equivalent to an infantry company) ran operations in each of the four Corps areas while twelve B-Detachments covered Provinces and rapid reaction troops. Forty-eight A-Detachments were stationed around the country, many of them stationed in camps along the border. By the end of 1965 the Group had over 1,500 personnel working with 30,000 CIDG irregulars.

The CIDG troops were recruited from many different backgrounds and while some groups were hostile towards the Vietnamese due to religious or cultural differences, they were all loyal to their Special Forces commanders.

A unit of CIDG troops wait to exchange their obsolete rifles for new automatic weapons at their local Special Forces camp. (111-CC-44759)

The Mon-Khmer and Malayo-Polynesian Montagnards populated the Central Highlands while Chinese Mongoloids lived along the coast and in the Cholon district of Saigon; Cambodians in the Cambodian border area of the Mekong Delta were also trained to fight. Two religious sects, the Cao Dai and the Hinayana Buddhists from the Delta area also served with the CIDG despite their differences with the government.

Outside the borders of South Vietnam, the Laotian Meo tribes and the Nung Chinese, many of them exiles from North Vietnam, fought with the Special Forces.

Special Forces camps were often isolated and reliant on air supply, and planes either landed on small airstrips or dropped cargo by parachute. Camps often came under attack and they had to be fortified with embankments, barbed wire, claymore mines and flares while the men lived in bunkers; sentries had to keep constant watch. By October 1966 there were ninety-seven Special Forces camps across South Vietnam.

5th Special Forces Group began reducing its personnel in April 1970 and by the end of the year thousands of trained CIDG troops based at thirty-seven camps along the border had been handed over to the South Vietnamese Rangers. The Group finally withdrew from Nha Trang in March 1971.

DETACHMENT ORGANIZATIONS

C-DETACHMENT

The C-Detachment was the equivalent to an infantry company and it covered operations across a Corps area. It had seventeen men and they controlled between two and five B-detachments and their attached A-Detachments:

Command:	Commanding Officer (Lieutenant Colonel)
Control:	Executive Officer (Major) and Sergeant Major
Administration:	Adjutant (Captain), S-1, and Administrative Supervisor
Intelligence:	Captain, S-2, and Sergeant

Operations: Captain, S-3, and Sergeant

Supply: Captain, S-4, and Assistant Supply Sergeant

Communications: Radio Operator Supervisor, four Chief Radio Operators and a Senior Field Radio Repairman

B-DETACHMENT

The B-Detachment was the equivalent of an infantry platoon and it typically controlled operations across a province. Detachments had been reorganized to suit the operations in Vietnam and the team of twenty-five men commanded between four and ten A-Detachments.

Command: Detachment Commander (Major)

Control: Executive Officer (Captain) and Sergeant Major

Administration: Adjutant (Captain) and Administrative Supervisor

Intelligence: Officer (Captain), Sergeant and Intelligence Analyst

Operations: Officer (Captain), Sergeant, Assistant Operations Sergeant and Clerk

Supply: Officer (Captain), Supply Sergeant and Assistant Supply Sergeant

Weaponry: Heavy Weapons Leader and Light Weapons Leader

Demolitions/ Engineer: Sergeant

Communications: Radio Operator Supervisor and three Chief Radio Operators

Medical: Medical Specialist

Local Advisors: Civic Action Officer and Regional Forces/Popular Forces Advisor

A Special Forces officer discusses problems with a village elder at a refugee camp.(111-CC-43913)

Special Forces and CIDG troops worked together closely as they patrolled the Central Highlands searching for Viet Cong activity. (111-CC-44758)

A Special Forces medic keeps a close watch while a CIDG medic applies medication to an injured child. (111-CC-45178)

A-DETACHMENT

Many of the twelve-man A-Detachments lived in the Special Forces camps, working alongside the CIDG personnel while carrying out civic actions across the district. Typically they were organized as follows but extra personnel could be added for some missions:

Command:	Commander (Captain) and Executive Officer (1st Lieutenant)
Operations:	Master Sergeant
Weaponry:	Heavy Weapons Leader and Light Weapons Leader
Intelligence:	Sergeant
Medical:	Specialist and Assistant Medical Specialist
Communications:	Radio Operator Supervisor and Chief Radio Operator
Demolitions/Engineer:	Sergeant and Specialist

COMPANY AND DETACHMENT DEPLOYMENTS

The Company coordinated Special Forces missions across a Corps area. A lieutenant-colonel commanded a C-detachment which in turn controlled several B-Detachments and the local mobile strike forces; each B-Detachment ran a number of A-Detachments based at the Special Forces camps along the border. An administrative detachment supported each company.

I CORPS AND COMPANY C

Company C ran operations along I Corps' border, including the camps near the Demilitarized Zone, from November 1964 to November 1970. The Company and C-1 Operations Detachment were both based at Da Nang.

B-13 Detachment controlled I Corps' operations from Kham Duc in Quang Duc Province between November 1964 and June 1965, handing over its camps to the Marines. B-11 Detachment briefly ran C-1 Detachment's operations from Quang Ngai city between March and October 1966. Following the Tet Offensive, B-16 Detachment began new operations across Quang Nam Province from its base in Da Nang. B-11 Detachment covered the southern part of I Corps from Chu Lai when the Marines started to withdraw in July 1969.

Between August and November 1970, 3,350 CIDG men based at eight camps were handed over to the Vietnamese Rangers.

II CORPS AND COMPANY B

Company B ran a network of camps in the Central Highlands between November 1964 and January 1971. The Company and C-2 Operations Detachment were both based in Pleiku.

A well-developed Special Forces camp is home for detachment A-236 close to the Cambodian border. (111-CC-62982)

B-23 Detachment started operations in Darlac Province and it was based at Ban Me Thuot after November 1964. B-22 Detachment covered Binh Dinh Province from An Khe after July 1965 and it moved to Pleiku twelve months later; it moved to I Corps in June 1969. B-24 coordinated operations across Kontum Province after January 1966. B-20 took command of the Mike Strike Force based at Pleiku in November 1967.

Between August 1970 and January 1971, 5,000 CIDG personnel based at twelve camps were handed over to the Vietnamese Rangers.

III CORPS AND COMPANY A

Company A ran operations along III Corps' border from November 1964 to January 1971. C-3 Operations detachment was based at Bien Hoa while the administrative detachment was at Ho Ngoc Tau, south-east of Saigon.

In March B-32 Detachment arrived at Tay Ninh followed by B-34 Detachment at Song Be in Phuoc Long Province and B-33 Detachment at Hon Quan in Binh Long Province. B-31 Detachment was based at Phuoc Vinh to control operations across War Zone C. B-35 Detachment arrived at Hiep Hoa in April 1966 to control operations in Hau Nghia Province but it moved to Duc Hoa at the end of the year. B-36 Detachment covered operations east of the capital from Long Hai in Phuoc Tuy Province after September 1967.

Nine CIDG camps and over 3,000 men were handed over to the Vietnamese Rangers from August 1970 to January 1971 as the Special Forces detachments withdrew.

IV CORPS AND COMPANY D

Between November 1964 and December 1970 Company D covered operations in the Mekong Delta, particularly in the Seven Mountains region near the border. C4-Detachment was based at Can Tho and some A-Detachments were equipped with fiberglass hovercraft so they could navigate waterways, paddy fields and swamps at high speed.

In March 1965 B-40 Detachment was deployed to Can Tho in Phong Dinh Province while B-42 Detachment was deployed in Chau Doc Province. B-43 Detachment arrived at Cao Lamh in Kien Phong Province in February 1967, strengthening operations along the Cambodian border; it moved to Chi Lang in Chau Doc Province in April 1969.

Eight CIDG Camps and 2,800 men were handed over to the Vietnamese Rangers between August and December 1970.

SPECIAL PROJECTS AND COMPANY E (PROVISIONAL)

The company was organized at Nha Trang in March 1965 with a C-5 Operations Detachment to run Project Omega (B-50), Project Sigma (B-56), Project Gamma (B-57) and the Dong Ba Thin training center (B-51). It also organized the defense of 5th Special Forces Group's headquarters at Nha Trang. The Company was disbanded in September 1967.

SON TAY PRISON RAID

One of 5th Special Forces Group's final missions took place on 20 and 21 November 1970 when a team of US Army Special Forces and USAF Special

A C-7A transport plane touches down at a Special Forces camp in the Central Highlands. (USAF-106231)

Operations and rescue personnel raided Son Tay Prison near Hanoi. It was believed that over 100 American servicemen were being held in appalling conditions and six helicopters flew the team to the site while Navy planes made a diversionary raid. The raid had been meticulously planned, however the prisoners had been moved a few days before due to flooding and the team returned empty-handed but safe.

LONG-RANGE RECONNAISSANCE

It was soon found that the A-Detachments working along the border were spread too thin, allowing the Viet Cong to infiltrate in great numbers. While some CIDG leaders were too passive, the Vietnamese Special Forces leaders were reluctant to deploy their men effectively and they rarely sent out patrols at night. Before long it was clear that it was impossible to cover the border with static camps and work started on training long-range reconnaissance teams. The new B-Detachments had the following additional staff:

A Plans Officer replaced the Executive Officer
Two extra Intelligence Sergeants and two Operations Sergeants
A Reconnaissance Supervisor controlling sixteen Reconnaissance Team Advisors

B-52 DETACHMENT – PROJECT DELTA

In May 1964 an A-Detachment covertly organized Project Leaping Lena at Nha Trang and began training Vietnamese Special Forces and CIDG troops to carry out long-range reconnaissance missions. The project was renamed Delta in June 1965 as it increased in size; B-52 Detachment took command. Twelve reconnaissance teams and six (later doubled to twelve) CIDG Roadrunner teams were trained to operate anywhere across the country on MACV's orders.

The teams watched trails, set ambushes, reported targets and assessed damage. Teams were also involved in covert hunter-killer missions and special purpose raids. A South Vietnamese Airborne Ranger Battalion was kept on standby to engage lucrative targets or rescue trapped teams. A company of Nungs protected the unit's camp.

On General Westmoreland's orders, B-52 Detachment opened MACV Recondo School in September 1966 to train selected soldiers in long-range patrol tactics. Classes were taught at Nha Trang while field exercises were held on Hon Tre Island. B-52 Detachment was disbanded in June 1970 but the school continued to train recruits until the end of the year; over 3,300 men had graduated by the time the school closed down.

B-50 DETACHMENT – PROJECT OMEGA AND B-56 – DETACHMENT PROJECT SIGMA

The Omega and Sigma projects were activated in October 1966 to increase the range of Project Delta. Omega covered I Field Force's area from Ban Me Thuot while Sigma covered II Field Force's area from Ho Ngoc Tau.

The two detachments started with four Roadrunner teams trained to gather intelligence on enemy troop movements while larger reconnaissance teams followed up setting ambushes. Three commando companies carried out reconnaissance in force missions and one company was always ready to extract a threatened team; a fourth company protected the two base camps. Project Sigma closed down in May 1971, Project Omega followed in June 1972.

B-57 DETACHMENT – PROJECT GAMMA

The Detachment was organized at Saigon in June 1967 to gather intelligence on the situation in Cambodia, in particular the NVA bases located there. The project closed down in March 1970, ahead of the Cambodian invasion.

B-36 DETACHMENT (PROVISIONAL) – PROJECT RAPID FIRE

The Detachment was activated at Long Ha in August 1967 to allow II Field Force to cover III Corps after B-56 Sigma Detachment joined MACV Special Operation Group. The detachment was converted to a Mobile Strike Force Command in May 1968.

B-55 DETACHMENT – RAPID REACTION RESERVE

A Nung security company was put in control of security measures at Nha Trang in November 1964 and after August 1965 it was expanded into B-55 Detachment, controlling 5th Mobile Strike Force Command, a rapid reaction reserve for the Special Forces camps along the border. The headquarters were staffed by US Special Forces and Chinese Nungs and the men came from many ethnic minority groups, nearly half of them were airborne qualified. The Detachment had a 227-man headquarters and service company, four 552-man battalions and a 135-man reconnaissance company. The Detachment was also often used to extract non-Special Forces units. Although many operations were small, company-sized actions, battalions were sometimes deployed in dangerous areas and the Detachment was occasionally deployed en masse. It was disbanded in December 1970.

A student from the Vietnamese Mobile Strike Force learns how to operate an airboat. (111-SC-66736)

MIKE FORCES AND MOBILE GUERRILLA FORCES

North Vietnamese troops often targeted the Special Forces A-Detachments and their CIDG camps across the Central Highlands, hoping to destroy them. 5th Special Forces Group responded by forming an Eagle Flight at Pleiku so its helicopter transports and gunships could reinforce a threatened camp. The reaction force was soon expanded into five Mobile Strike Forces, or MIKE Forces, deployed as follows:

I Corps MIKE Force: Da Nang under Detachment A-113; Montagnards
II Corps MIKE Force: Pleiku under Detachment A-119; Montagnards
III CORPS MIKE Force: Bien Hoa under Detachment A-302; Viets, Cambodians and Nungs
IV Corps MIKE Force: Don Phuc under Detachment A-430; primarily Nungs and Cambodians
5th Special Forces (Airborne) MIKE Force: based at Nha Trang under Detachment A-503

Mobile Guerrilla Forces were formed in 1966 and they were trained to operate independently for long periods. Starting in October, they carried out a series of operations codenamed Blackjack, sweeping Viet Cong-held areas looking for base camps and supply caches. Each Mobile Guerrilla Force had a Special Forces A-Detachment leading a 150-strong MIKE Force Company and a 34-man Combat Reconnaissance Platoon.

Several of the camps along I Corps' border came under attack during the Tet Offensive and Khe Sanh camp became the focus of the world's attention while the Marines held it during a prolonged siege. Special Forces-led CIDG troops were engaged in the battles for the towns and cities and they were particularly effective at ambushing the Viet Cong as they withdrew into the Highlands.

A member of the South Vietnamese Special Forces works alongside a Montagnard as they fire a 4.2-inch mortar at suspected Viet Cong positions. (111-CC-49863)

MOBILE STRIKE FORCE COMMANDS

In recognition of their efforts, the Mobile Guerrilla Forces and MIKE Forces were merged into Mobile Strike Force Commands in March 1968 and they were allowed to play a greater role in securing their own areas; they were also issued with modern weapons, including M16 rifles.

Each Command had a Headquarters and Headquarters Company, a number of 552-man battalions and a 135-man reconnaissance company. The 227-strong headquarters and service company included elite Vietnamese CIDG members and highly trained, airborne-qualified Chinese Nung and Cambodian personnel.

1st Strike Force reported to B-16 Detachment at Da Nang; it covered I Corps with two Battalions.

2d Strike Force reported to B-20 Detachment at Pleiku and covered II Corps with five battalions.

3d Strike Force reported to B-36 Detachment at Bien Hoa and covered III Corps with three battalions.

4th Strike Force reported to B-40 Detachment at Don Phuc and covered IV Corps with three battalions; it also had an airboat company for covering flooded areas.

5th Strike Force had four battalions based at the Nha Trang headquarters, they could be deployed anywhere across the country.

CLASSIFIED OPERATIONS

The South Vietnamese government had formed a secret service in 1958 and five years later it was renamed the Vietnamese Special Forces Command with substantial support from the US Central Intelligence Agency. It was again renamed the Vietnamese Special Exploitation Service in April 1964 when the American-led Studies and Observation Group began operating at Cholon on behalf of Military Assistance Command, Vietnam. MACV-SOG, as it was known, took over highly classified missions across Southeast Asia from the CIA.

The Studies and Observation Group was a cover name chosen to give the impression that its staff were engaged in collecting and studying information on standard military operations. In fact the group was engaged in a wide variety of covert missions and its personnel often used unconventional and controversial methods to achieve their objectives, including sabotage, psychological warfare, kidnapping and assassination. The types of missions it conducted included the following:

Disrupting movements along the Ho Chi Minh Trail
Training agents to raise resistance movements in North Vietnam
Broadcasting anti-communist propaganda; known as gray psychological operations
Spreading false information; known as black psychological operations
Monitoring information on captured and missing American servicemen
Conducting rescue missions to retrieve personnel and sensitive material

To begin with the Group was based in Cholon but it later moved into Saigon, eventually growing to include 2,000 Americans (mostly US Special Forces) and over 8,000 highly trained indigenous troops. It was divided into several study groups, Ground, Maritime, Air, Airborne and Psychological.

Ground reconnaissance missions were carried out by over seventy teams. The smallest, the Spike Recon Team, had three US Special Forces men and nine indigenous men responsible for locating targets for air strikes, monitoring trails and setting ambushes. Larger Hatchet Forces had five US Special Forces men and thirty indigenous personnel and they were used to follow up intelligence leads; they could also be called upon to rescue trapped Spike Teams. The largest unit was the Search, Location and Annihilation Mission Company, or SLAM Company. They were called upon to carry out the largest missions, often following up promising intelligence information.

The Maritime Group was based at Da Nang and it could call upon Navy SEALS teams equipped with fast patrol boats and Vietnamese Underwater Demolition Teams (UDT). The Air Studies Group based at Nha Trang provided air support, operated by 90th Special Operations Wing. It had squadrons of UH-1F 'Green Hornet' helicopters, H-34 helicopters, and C-130 transport planes; a covert C-123 aircraft squadron was piloted by Chinese crews. The Airborne Operations Group was based alongside the training center at Long Thanh.

In September 1967 the Special Exploitation Service was renamed the Strategic Technical Directorate and two months later, MACV-SOG divided its operations between three Command and Control headquarters:

Command and Control North was based at Da Nang: teams had been crossing border into North Vietnam since February 1964 and eighteen months later entered Laos to work alongside Meo tribesmen, pinpointing targets along the Ho Chi Minh Trail.
Command and Control Central was based at Kontum: teams monitored the Ho Chi Minh Trail through the Laotain Highlands and across the border into Cambodia.
Command and Control South was based at Ban Me Thuot: teams began working in northeast Cambodia in May 1967.

The Command and Control Headquarters were replaced by Task Force Advisory Elements in March 1972 in line with the Vietnamization program:

Task Force 1 Advisory Element was based at Quan Loi in the north until October 1972
Task Force 2 Advisory Element was based at Kontum until October 1972
Task Force 3 Advisory Element was based at Ban Me Thuot until April 1972

MACV-SOG left Vietnam in April 1972, handing over operations to Strategic Technical Directorate Assistance Team 158. It too closed down twelve months later.

TRAINING

TRAINING IN SOUTH VIETNAM

B-51 Detachment was established at Dong Ba Thin in April 1964 and it started training the Vietnamese Special Forces and CIDG personnel for the Mobile Strike Forces. In September 1968 the two functions separated when the Special Forces facilities relocated to An Khe and the Mobile Strike Force training center moved to Hon Tre Island; the Special Forces returned to Dong Ba Thin twelve months later. B-51 disbanded in March 1971.

A helicopter has delivered a Thanksgiving dinner to this A-Detachment during an operation in War Zone D. (111-CC-37044)

B-53 Detachment was activated at the Vietnamese Rangers training center at Long Thanh in February 1964. It acted as the Special Missions Advisory Force and was deployed on top secret missions throughout the conflict. Between March 1971 and April 1972 it trained Vietnamese Special Forces and Rangers personnel to operate on their own as part of the Vietnamization program.

TRAINING IN LAOS

Twelve Special Forces teams from 77th Special Forces Group (Airborne) started working covertly with the Laotian Army in 1959 under Operation White Star, helping to prevent a coup the following year. As numbers rose to over 400 and new teams started helping the indigenous tribes to defend themselves against the Pathet Lao, the men were allowed to wear their uniforms for the first time. An agreement was drawn up in July 1962 and although the Special Forces teams withdrew, many of the Pathet Lao stayed behind. They would soon make sure that the Laotian government did not object to the movement of North Vietnamese troops and equipment along the Ho Chi Minh Trail.

TRAINING IN CAMBODIA

With the situation in Cambodia deteriorating, the US Army Vietnam Individual Training Group was established in March 1971 and it set up four centers where Special Forces personnel taught Cambodian volunteers basic tactics and weaponry skills. Training was intensive and the new recruits only had fifteen weeks to learn how to operate as infantry battalions. It was renamed the Forces Armée Nationale Khmer Training Command, or FANK, in May 1972 and continued to train personnel until December 1972. Field Training Command then took over and used mobile teams to work with recruits. It left Vietnam three months later.

CHAPTER 7

INTELLIGENCE

The conflict in Vietnam was a guerilla, or counterinsurgency, war where the enemy often mingled with the local population or hid in the jungle. Intelligence was extremely important, but it took time to collect and assess. The US command had to rely on Vietnamese agencies to begin with, but it soon had its own sources, some conventional, some covert, some controversial, for collecting evidence. Whether they were effective at collecting data and if it was then acted on correctly is difficult to assess. Three Military Intelligence Groups were organized to coordinate intelligence activities across Southeast Asia:

135th Military Intelligence Group was based with the South Vietnamese Security Service and its bilingual staff coordinated long-range and special operations. It assessed intelligence and planned operations to destroy enemy espionage activities. The Group also dealt with interrogations for Military Assistance Command, Vietnam.

149th Military Intelligence Group controlled military intelligence units aiming to capture material on long-range operations. Captured documents would be translated, examined and assessed and used to aid interrogations. Personnel also worked with their South Vietnamese counterparts.

525th Military Intelligence Group coordinated administration and personnel issues for military intelligence units across Vietnam. In December 1967 it organized six Provisional Battalions to improve military intelligence communications. A Combat Intelligence Battalion served from April to September 1968 to deal with the mass of information captured during the Tet Offensive.

COMBINED INTELLIGENCE CENTER

The Target Research and Analysis Center opened in January 1965 to identify targets for B-52 Arc Light missions. It eventually grew into the US Army's main facility for collecting and analyzing intelligence. Specialized staff began to arrive at the end of 1966 to start the ILEX Program, gathering intelligence on the Viet Cong infrastructure in the Mekong Delta before 9th Division moved into the area. The program eventually became a pilot scheme for the Phoenix Program.

The number of staff had grown to over 500 US and 100 Vietnamese intelligence personnel by January 1967 when the Combined Intelligence Center opened. Its first major intelligence coup occurred during the same month when 500,000 documents, including the Viet Cong's long-range campaign plans and a large amount of code and signal intelligence, were captured during Operation Cedar Falls. A month later film footage of senior Viet Cong leaders was seized during Operation Junction City. 519th Military Intelligence Battalion ran the Center and intelligence material was forwarded to one of the three collection centers to be examined.

COMBINED DOCUMENT EXPLOITATION CENTER

The Center opened in October 1966 and 300 US and Vietnamese Military personnel assessed documents, aided by civilian workers. The Center had five branches: Administration, Translation, Evaluation, Operations, Storage and Retrieval. US soldiers systematically gathered intelligence material but it took time to convince the ARVN troops to collect captured documents. Over 10,000 pages (over ½ ton) a day were arriving at the Center by 1967 and each document was checked to see if it was worth translating (around 10 per cent were). They were then graded and distributed:

Alpha   Intelligence needed immediately in the field; forwarded to the relevant unit
Bravo   Strategically important; translated and summarized for planning operations
Charlie Low intelligence value; usually filed untranslated
Delta   Propaganda information; forwarded to psyops
             Foreign currency: kept for paying agents or bribery
Echo   Communications information, including codes

Translated documents were then microfilmed, filed and indexed on computer.

COMBINED MILITARY INTERROGATION CENTER

Prisoners were initially interrogated in the field when they were captured and the Center had traveling teams working with combat units. Teams were dispatched to deal with large numbers of prisoners while significant captives were taken to the Center in Saigon for further questioning.

Troops check through captured material for possible intelligence leads during Operation Cook. (111-CC-43032)

Captured documents were translated, analyzed and filed at the Combined Document Exploitation Center. (111-CC-46831)

The Center also handled Viet Cong ralliers (known as Hoi Chanhs) training many as Kit Carson Scouts so they could act as guides for US troops. Many Scouts were later employed in the Provincial Reconnaissance Units spearheading the controversial Phoenix Program.

COMBINED MATERIAL EXPLOITATION CENTER

Captured weapons were forwarded to the center for evaluation. Teams supervised the safe return of large caches and assessed large immoveable items in the field.

COMBINED INTELLIGENCE CENTER

The Combined Intelligence Center also had four branches specializing in collecting particular types of intelligence:

ORDER OF BATTLE BRANCH
The Ground Order of Battle Section had five teams, one with each Corps and a fifth covering North Vietnam, Laos and Cambodia. They gathered information on enemy units, adding it to the *Monthly Order of Battle Summary*, while new information was circulated on a daily basis. The Order of Battle Studies Section had four teams studying the enemy's techniques. The Strength, Composition and Disposition Team studied how units operated while the Combat Effectiveness Team and the Tactics and Training Team scrutinized new tactics and proposed countermeasures to defeat them. The Logistics Team examined the Viet Cong and NVA supply chain. The Political Order of Battle Section deployed teams to each Viet Cong military region so they could become familiar with its leaders and command structure.

AREA ANALYSIS BRANCH
The branch had six sections collecting and analyzing data for operational planning. The Mapping Section updated military maps and indexed Viet

A Vietnamese interpreter helps a soldier of 173d Brigade interrogate a Viet Cong suspect during Operation Cedar Falls. (111-CC-38325)

Cong place names. The Cultural Features Section collected information on the country's infrastructure while the Terrain Section gathered data on soils, drainage and vegetation. The Lines of Communication Section had teams specializing in highways, railways and waterways while the Entry Zones Section had teams assessing the potential of areas for new airfields, helicopter landing zones and parachute drop zones; other teams studied beaches and potential ports. The Weather Section produced regular weather reports and forecasts.

IMAGERY INTERPRETATION BRANCH
The branch used its range of photographic and equipment to produce detailed 1:50,000 aerial photographs from film taken by reconnaissance planes.

TECHNICAL INTELLIGENCE BRANCH
The branch designed and tested new weapons and equipment, producing field manuals. Sections covered Engineer, Ordnance, Chemical, Quartermaster, Medical, Signals and Transportation. It also analyzed captured enemy hardware.

The Combined Intelligence Center also ran the Combined Intelligence School, training US advisors and their Vietnamese counterparts in intelligence gathering, agent recruitment and handling.

AERIAL RECONNAISSANCE

1st Military Intelligence Battalion worked with the US Air Force at Tan Son Nhut air base. Personnel accompanied observation planes and helicopters on reconnaissance missions, directing the pilots to potential targets, they then analyzed the aerial photographs. Companies were established to coordinate the collection and interpretation of aerial photographs; a dedicated Aerial Surveillance Company was organized in July 1971.

ELECTRONIC INTELLIGENCE

A range of electronic sensors was used in Vietnam to monitor movement in isolated areas. Some were placed by patrols while others were jettisoned from planes or helicopters so they embedded themselves in the ground. Seismic, acoustic and magnetic sensors were used and they were often laid in strings along trails to monitor movement. Once a sensor had picked up a reading, the intelligence team could watch the enemy's movements and assess the size of the column, calling in artillery, mortar or helicopter gunships at an opportune moment.

In 1967 work began on a 40km barrier, known as the McNamara Wall (named after the US Defense Minister, Robert McNamara) along the Demilitarized Zone to reduce the number of ground patrols needed to watch this dangerous area. The plan was to construct a string of strongpoints, observation posts and minefields to stem the movement of troops from North Vietnam, while an extensive network of sensors provided warnings. Work came to a halt at the beginning of 1968 as the number of US troops in the area increased dramatically, severely stretching the logistics system in I Corps. South Vietnamese units were able to man the completed areas of the wall, releasing US troops for ground operations while the sensors placed around Khe Sanh base proved to be extremely useful during the prolonged siege at the beginning of 1968.

Spare sensors were distributed across the rest of South Vietnam and during the latter years of the conflict, as US ground troops began to withdraw, sensors played an increasing role in the defense of military installations.

INTELLIGENCE ASSESSMENT

Processed intelligence was forwarded to the Military Assistance Command headquarters where the four branches of the Intelligence Division analyzed, summarized and distributed it. The Current Intelligence and Indications Branch gave Military Assistance Command headquarters daily briefings, summarizing recent events and making predictions. The Order of Battle Branch analyzed unit information, updating the Viet Cong and North Vietnamese orders of battle, distributing copies to 400 offices. It also published a range of manuals on the Viet Cong and the North Vietnamese. The Estimates Branch assessed Viet Cong and North Vietnamese tactics so counter-tactics could be studied and forwarded to combat units. Strategic Resources Branch analyzed political intelligence.

INTELLIGENCE AND THE TET OFFENSIVE

The Tet offensive, launched on 31 January 1968, was undoubtably a turning point in the war but what warnings did the American military have and how did it react? A document captured in November 1967 by 101st Airborne Division indicating that an countrywide attack was imminent was circulated to many offices around the country. Several Viet Cong prisoners also told their interrogators that they expected the country to be liberated during the Tet celebratory period. Finally, intelligence reports noted a build-up of enemy movements along the Ho Chi Minh trail and north of the Demilitarized Zone, leading the senior intelligence officer to warn General Westmoreland of an attack. The assessment was that the North Vietnamese Army would attack the Special Forces and CIDG camps along the borders, as they had done before, and these were duly reinforced.

What the intelligence sources had failed to recognize was the wholesale distribution of weapons, ammunition and supplies across the countryside and the infiltration of troops who were organizing assistance from the Viet Cong, ahead of their comrades arrival. Thousands of soldiers used the tunnel systems stretching from the border towards the capital while others mingled with the masses moving across the country to visit their families for the Tet celebrations.

Since ground troops had been deployed in March 1965, the American military had been presenting promising reports from Vietnam and the American people were used to hearing that steady progress was being made in the battle against the Viet Cong and the NVA.

When the attacks began, the news that this defeated enemy could attack provincial cities, military installations and the American embassy in Saigon shocked everyone. The military quickly had the situation in hand in many areas, but images of protracted fighting at Khe Sanh and in parts of Saigon and Hue appearing on American television sets rocked the people's support for the conflict. Although the Viet Cong was decimated and the NVA had to fall back across the borders, the public's confidence in their politicians and generals never recovered.

COUNTERINTELLIGENCE DIVISION

The Division followed up intelligence leads, and its three branches, Personnel Security, Counterintelligence and Security of Military Information, conducted investigations and security checks. Security was extremely important and the Division supervised the transfer of classified documents and worked with the Army Security Agency to maintain secure communications links.

By September 1966 the number of security checks and missions had increased to such an extent that 135th Military Intelligence Group took over responsibility for counterintelligence, helping to improve security at military installations.

The Division also advised the South Vietnamese Military Security Service and teams worked in all provinces. The Viet Cong was known to have sympathizers in government and military positions so information for US personnel only was circulated on NOFORN (no foreigners) documents.

The Division also kept files on captured and missing American personnel in the early days; they were eventually handed over the the Defense Intelligence Agency.

DIVISIONAL INTELLIGENCE

Once the masses of information had been analyzed and summarized, it could be forwarded to the divisional headquarters so the staff could make use of it. Divisions carried out Command and Staff Briefings twice a day, discussing recent and proposed operations and the new intelligence updates. A large map displaying friendly and enemy activity over the past 72 hours was the focus of the briefing and colored symbols summarized intelligence leads. Divisional commanders tried to give each brigade a target every day and minor leads often turned up new evidence.

It took time to establish a network of agents and results were often disappointing as double agents and infiltrators gave false leads and threatened or killed informers. The Division Prisoner Collection Point and the Chieu Hoi Centers were often good sources for new recruits.

Cooperation with the South Vietnamese Army was often poor until Intelligence Operations Coordination Centers were set up so combat units could work together.

PSYCHOLOGICAL OPERATIONS (PSYOPS)

7th Psychological Operations Group sent a team to Vietnam to start operations in October 1965. 4th Group took over in December 1967 and it was based at Tan Son Nhut until October 1971. The Groups worked on trying to convince the VC and NVA to surrender rather than fight. Tactical Propaganda Companies operated in the field between February 1966 and January 1968 and Psychological Operations Battalions were organized to work at Corps level in December 1967. They used many methods, ranging from broadcasting messages by radio or helicopter-mounted loudspeakers to dropping leaflets over Viet Cong strongholds. Personnel often worked closely worked with combat units during operations.

A C-47 transport plane drops leaflets during a Psyops operation. (111-CC-64674)

An ARVN Political Warfare Company broadcasts pro-government propaganda to villagers in the Mekong Delta. (111-CC-49888)

The results of psychological operations were difficult to analyze. If a Viet Cong unit had strong leadership and was well fed and armed, results were poor. The political cadre kept a close eye on the men in their unit, warning them that the Americans would torture or kill prisoners; anyone found in possession of a psyops leaflet would be punished. Scattered units often produced good results.

THE CONSTANT PRESSURE CONCEPT

When General Creighton W. Abrams took over command of Military Assistance Command, Vietnam, in July 1968 he was a supporter of the Constant Pressure Concept. While intelligence units targeted the Viet Cong infrastructure under the Phoenix (Phung Hiang) Program, combat units attacked troops hiding in the sanctuaries and along the border.

By September 1969 the strategy was working to such an extent that the Vietnamese Regional Forces were allowed to take over patrolling large areas around Saigon, allowing ARVN units to participate in more combat operations.

THE PHOENIX PROGRAM

Following the success of the ILEX Program, which had assessed the Viet Cong's infrastructure in the Mekong Delta, the decision was taken to extend the Program countrywide. Planning for the Phoenix (from the Vietnamese

Phung Hiang) Program started at the end of 1967 but the Tet Offensive gave it added importance and by the summer of 1968 Intelligence and Operations Coordinating Centers had been set up in each province and district. Over 400 US Advisors eventually worked on the Program alongside Vietnamese staff.

The Centers began by assembling information collected by the National Police, Police Special Branch, Military Security Service, Provincial Recon Units and the division operating in the area. While a suspect database was set up, informants were recruited and the Situation Section assessed each district's current situation, preparing a second database of available support and the Viet Cong's recent activities; it also proposed the best course of action.

As the Program got under way, the Center was looking to arrest or kill Viet Cong commanders, leaving the lower ranks leaderless. Suspects had two cards, one organized by name, the other by village, and they were constantly updated as case officers began studying individuals or organizations. A case file (called a Target Folder) was set up for each suspect with copies of all relevant pieces of intelligence and the Information Summary summarized their details and offences. Case officers could request specific intelligence to fill gaps in the information.

Once the case officer was confident that the file had sufficient information to apprehend a suspect, he forwarded an Operations Plan to the Province Security Committee. The plan outlined the best course of action, the support required, a level of security, and what outcome was required. Once the head of the Province or District Intelligence and Operations Coordinating Center had approved the operation, the relevant service, either a Provincial Reconnaissance Unit, a Special Forces unit or a SEAL team, was notified. If possible the suspect was taken alive so he could be interrogated and encouraged to work for the government (Chuoi Huoi). Some hardcore members were executed. The Phoenix Program proved to be highly effective at decimating the Viet Cong structure but its controversial methods were condemned across the United States.

A suspect is interrogated for useful intelligence on Viet Cong activities in the Mekong Delta. (111-CC-52565)

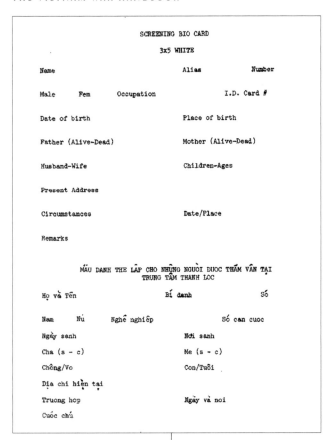

SCREENING BIO CARD

3x5 WHITE

Name   Alias   Number

Male   Fem   Occupation   I.D. Card #

Date of birth   Place of birth

Father (Alive-Dead)   Mother (Alive-Dead)

Husband-Wife   Children-Ages

Present Address

Circumstances   Date/Place

Remarks

MẪU DANH THẺ LẬP CHO NHỮNG NGƯỜI ĐƯỢC THẨM VẤN TẠI
TRUNG TÂM THANH LỌC

Họ và Tên   Bí danh   Số

Nam   Nữ   Nghề nghiệp   Số can cước

Ngày sanh   Nơi sanh

Cha (s - c)   Me (s - c)

Chồng/Vợ   Con/Tuổi

Địa chỉ hiện tại

Trường hợp   Ngày và noi

Cước chú

BLACK LIST CARD

3x5 WHITE

V.C. AT LARGE

Name   Alias(s)

Age   Distinguishing features

Position in VC

Last known location, date

Family information

Additional remarks, Source of information, Date/Place

MẪU DANH THẺ LẬP CHO NHỮNG TÊN VIỆT-CONG HÃY CÒN TẠI ĐÀO

VIỆT CỘNG TẠI ĐÀO

Họ và tên   Bí danh và bí số

Tuổi   Nhận dạng đặc biệt

Địa chỉ trong hàng ngũ VC

Ngày và noi có mặt lần chót

Tin túc gia đình

Cước chú, Nguồn tin, Ngày và noi

Left: *Each civilian had a White Card listing their personal details.*

Right: *A Black Card for Viet Cong suspects.*

MILITARY INTELLIGENCE CLOSES DOWN

525th Military Intelligence Group handed over to the Defense Attache's Office when it left Vietnam. The intelligence section continued to monitor North Vietnamese military activity and it warned of their offensive in the spring of 1975. The section worked alongside the Joint Casualty Resolution Center, locating captured and missing personnel. Negotiations with the North Vietnamese government attempted to secure the return of remains or information on the last known movements of the missing. In many cases they were unsuccessful.

The intelligence's final difficult task came in April 1975 as the NVA closed in on Saigon: the evacuation of hundreds of Vietnamese who had worked for American intelligence forces. Not only was their knowledge vital but they faced certain death as collaborators. Although some escaped to the waiting American fleet, the majority were left behind, lost in the chaotic scenes of South Vietnam's final downfall.

CHAPTER 8

SUPPORT SERVICES

The support services were responsible for keeping the Armed Forces in the field, operating and maintaining the equipment needed to deliver supplies, evacuating and treating the wounded and sick, and finally dealing with the enormous amount of administration generated during the Vietnam conflict.

DELIVERING SUPPLIES

South Vietnam had few natural resources of its own and the United States Armed Forces had to develop a sophisticated logistics chain, starting with suppliers in America and across Southeast Asia. Ammunition, equipment and supplies had to be transported across the Pacific Ocean and then distributed across the country by road or air, often to isolated firebases and outposts.

THE EARLY DAYS

US Army Ryukyu Islands (Provisional) Support Group was set up in February 1962 to provide support for aviation units arriving in Vietnam and it relied on US Army, Ryukyu Islands, based in Okinawa, for supplies and equipment. By July 1965, it had grown from an eleven-man team to over 300 personnel as it reorganized into US Army Support Group under MACV control and it took over the administration and logistics of all Army units. Army numbers grew enormously while the Group was in existence, increasing the quantity and diversity of supplies, and in March 1964 it had expanded to Support Command status. In July 1965 the large increase in combat troops deploying to South Vietnam called for another reorganization and the Support Command was renamed Headquarters of US Army, Vietnam (USARV); logistics functions were taken over by the new 1st Logistical Command.

ESTABLISHING THE NAVAL SUPPLY CHAIN

The US Merchant Marine, Military Sea Transportation Service (MSTS) had a long history in Vietnam, beginning with Operation Passage to Freedom, the evacuation of 300,000 refugees and 200,000 tons of cargo from the north to the south, following the ceasefire between France and the Viet Minh in 1954. As the American involvement increased in 1965, so did the MSTS, and its fleet of ships grew to over 300 freighters and tankers. It included 100 Victory ships of the National Defense Reserve Fleet which had been taken out of mothballs and assigned to private companies. Charter agreements for delivering supplies

Helicopter crews remove the protective covers from their Chinooks after a long sea crossing. (111-CC-47174)

to South Vietnam were drawn up with commercial shipping firms and their civilian crews were given US Navy grades and rank identification.

The Service was renamed the Military Sealift Command and it would eventually carry 95 per cent of the supplies needed by the United States Armed Services, shipping everything from guns, tanks, trucks, vessels, helicopters and planes, to food, ammunition, fuel and medical supplies. It also carried the majority of troops across the Pacific during the deployment stage of the conflict (air travel eventually took over). The Marine Corps relied on its own Amphibious Force Logistic Command based at Da Nang.

It took over three weeks for the ships to make the 10,000-mile crossing but only half the supplies were taken directly to Vietnam, the rest were delivered to staging posts across the Pacific. There was an enormous backlog of ships during the early stages of the conflict until the engineers built the deepwater anchorages and many ships had to anchor offshore to ease storage problems. Roll-on/roll-off ships and container ships were used where possible to speed up loading and unloading. Eventually, the ports were able to handle the non-stop Pacific shuttle service provided by the MSTS and by 1968 it peaked at over 20 million tons a year (costing over $600 million); equivalent to 56,000 tons a day.

Although US combat troops had left by 1973, the Military Sealift Command still had a role to play during the final days of South Vietnam. Thousands of refugees gathered at the ports in March and April as the NVA swept across the country, hoping to escape on one of the cargo ships (three ships evacuated 90,000 from Da Nang on 28 March alone). One final crisis took place on 12 May 1975 when the Khmer Rouge boarded and seized the SS *Mayaguez*. Several US Marines were killed rescuing the crew; they were the last servicemen to die in action during the conflict.

DEVELOPING THE PORTS

Before 1965 the port facilities in South Vietnam were extremely limited. Saigon was the only deep draft port and only one berth had been permanently allocated to US forces while the small pier in Cam Ranh Bay could only handle two vessels. With the road network in poor shape and convoys under attack, the safest way to distribute supplies was to move them by sea or air and within months, landing ships originally designed to carry tanks (LSTs) were ferrying supplies to the shallow ports of Qui Nhon, Vung Tau, and Nha Trang while smaller landing craft and barges delivered cargo to the beaches along the coast. Supplies for the Marine Corps were delivered to a new port at Da Nang built by the Navy's Construction Battalions.

Engineers worked around the clock to develop deep water facilities at the three subsidiary ports but berthing space was always in short supply and while vital supplies were loaded directly on to landing craft and barges out at sea, many ships had to wait for several weeks before they could dock.

Meanwhile, a fleet of dredges moved 60 million cu m of material to create channels, reclaim areas, lay pipes and produce stockpiles of sand while engineers built piers, wharves and landing craft ramps at the ports. Huge depots were built alongside to store the supplies while fuel tankers pumped their cargo straight into storage tanks.

DISTRIBUTING MARINE SUPPLIES

Standard supply items and many supply functions were carried out by Naval Support Activity, Da Nang, on behalf of the Marine Corps and eventually over 11,000 officers and enlisted men worked alongside 6,700 Vietnamese laborers; equal numbers also worked for civilian contractors. The main port was at Da Nang while 350 craft delivered supplies to shipment points at Cua Viet, Dong Ha, Hue, Tan My, Sa Huynh and Chu Lai along the coast. The Naval Support Activity eventually kept 190,000 troops supplied. As the Marines began to withdraw, the Navy handed over its supply functions to the Army, and had completely withdrawn by June 1970.

The Marine Corps Force Logistic Command based northwest of Da Nang was organized around the Headquarters and Service Battalion, Supply Battalion and Maintenance Battalion of 1st Force Service Regiment. The Command included 1st and 3d Service Battalions and while Force Logistics Support Group Alpha supported 1st Marine Division Force Logistics Support Group Bravo supported 3d Marine Division (it also covered 1st Marine Division when it began to withdraw in November 1969).

1st and 11th Motor Transport Battalions delivered supplies to 1st Division while 3d and 9th Battalions supported 3d Division; Force Logistic Command controlled 7th Motor Transport Battalion. Trucks were organized into 'Rough Rider' convoys and their crews often had to fight their way through ambushes to reach their destination.

The Marine Shore Party Battalions were originally organized to control amphibious landings, however they had soon expanded their role to support helicopter operations, preparing supplies, marking landing zones and supervising the unloading of troops and cargo.

DISTRIBUTING ARMY SUPPLIES

1st Logistical Command was organized at Saigon in April 1965 to coordinate the delivery of supplies to Army units serving in II and III Corps and it eventually covered I Corps and IV Corps. US Army Support Commands, based in Da Nang, Qui Nhon, Cam Ranh Bay and Saigon, ran operations on its behalf. Countrywide procurement was handled by the US Army Procurement Agency while stock control was coordinated by the US Army Inventory Control Center. 1st Logistical Command merged with US Army, Vietnam, in June 1970 and left the country six months later.

SUPPORT COMMANDS AND GENERAL SUPPORT GROUPS

A Quartermaster Group took control of Army supply and maintenance in August 1965 and it was renamed 29th General Support Group the following summer when quartermaster activities were reorganized. As supply and maintenance expanded, the country was split into Support Commands, one at each of the major ports.

Additional General Support Groups, also known as Sub Area Commands, arrived over the winter of 1966/7 to coordinate operations at smaller ports and inland depots. Each Support Command controlled the following functions:

A Terminal Transportation Command offloaded ships and moved supplies to the depots
A Field Depot stored and issued supplies; they were later called US Army Depots
An Ordnance Battalion dealt with ammunition stocks
Quartermaster Battalions dealt with fuel stocks
A Motor Transport Transportation Group coordinated transport to inland bases
Direct Support and General Support Maintenance Battalions kept vehicles on the road

Companies were despatched to carry out work for the General Support Groups. The Groups also ran the post, camp and station facilities for the Support Commands.

Vietnamese laborers help to unload armored personnel carriers belonging to the 11th Cavalry Regiment. (111-CC-36312)

I Corps: 15th Support Brigade supported Task Force Oregon when Army troops were first deployed to I Corps. Da Nang Support Command was established to support MACV Forward as more troops arrived following the Tet Offensive and it delivered supplies to Hue and Chu Lai. 80th Group covered Army units operating in the southern part of I Corps while 26th Group supported Army units operating in the northern part of I Corps from Quang Tri; it later moved to Phu Bai.

II Corps, North: Qui Nhon Support Command delivered supplies to Tuy Hoa, An Khe and Pleiku. 593d Group covered the coastal area from Qui Nhon while 45th Group covered the Central Highlands from Pleiku.

II Corps, South: Cam Ranh Bay Support Command delivered supplies to Nha Trang, Phan Rang and Ban Me Thout. 54th Group covered the area north of Cam Ranh Bay from Nha Trang. 26th Group covered the area south of Cam Rahn Bay from Tuy Hoa.

III and IV Corps: Saigon Support Command delivered supplies to Long Binh, Vung Tau, Tay Ninh and Can Tho. 29th Quartermaster Group arrived at Long Binh in August 1965 to cover III Corps but it was renamed 29th General Support Group in July 1966. 53d General Support Group assisted in III Corps, expanding to cover IV Corps with bases at Dong Tam and Can Tho.

ARMY AVIATION MAINTENANCE AND SUPPORT

34th General Support Group supported Army aviation units from Tan Son Nhut. Civilians and Army personnel worked alongside each other to repair and service aircraft.

TERMINAL TRANSPORTATION COMMANDS

Terminal Transportation Commands organized the unloading of cargo from the deep draft vessels and either reloaded it on to shallow-draft vessels or delivered it to the nearby depot.

Terminal Transportation Battalions were in charge of operating the cargo handling equipment.

4th Terminal Transportation Command organized operations at Saigon and Cam Ranh Bay starting in August 1965 and helped to distribute cargo to Qui Nhon, Nha Be, Phan Rang, Nha Trang and Vung Tau. The Command also organized the Army Air Cargo Terminal at Tan Son Nhut.

New commands arrived at Qui Nhon, Cam Rahn Bay and Saigon in October 1966 as 4th Command reduced its operations to cover Saigon Port, Newport Terminal, Vung Tau port and nearby ammunition depots.

I Corps: The US Navy complex at Da Nang also served the Marines and the Air Force but the influx of Army units in 1968 put added strain on the base. Landing craft could carry supplies to the shallow-draft ports at Chu Lai and Hue. A small port at Dong Ha supplied Marine and Army units operating near the DMZ. 863d Provisional Command organized Army transport operations at Da Nang port in April 1970; 5th Command replaced it a month later.

II Corps, North: Qui Nhon was developed into a major port and cargo handling operations were run by 5th Terminal Transportation Command.

II Corps, South: Cam Ranh Bay became the largest logistical storage area in Vietnam and while landing craft carried supplies to Nha Trang, Phan Rang and Tuy Hoa, transport planes used one of the six airstrips around Cam Rahn. 124th Terminal Transportation Command ran operations.

III and IV Corps: Saigon's port was soon overwhelmed and a new facility, named Newport, was built upstream. Landing craft delivered supplies to Long Binh and Can Tho while transport planes used one of the nearby eight airstrips. Vung Tau port was added in 1966 so landing craft could ferry supplies into the Saigon area while Cat Lai was developed into an ammunition offloading port. 125th Terminal Transportation Command ran the Saigon area.

INTER-COASTAL OPERATIONS

Landing craft and amphibious vehicles were used to deliver cargo from the deepwater ports to a nearby shallow-draft port or beach, an operation known as Logistics over the Shore (LOTS).

The two heavy boat companies operated two main types of shallow-draft craft:

LCUs (Landing Craft, Utility): the craft could carry 184 tons
BARCs (Barge Amphibious Resupply Cargo), later called the LARC LX: this amphibious vehicle could carry 60 tons and was able to land safely in heavy surf

The Tet Offensive severely disrupted the lines of communication supplying I Corps and with both 1st Cavalry Division and 101st Airborne Division moving into the area, supplies would increase to 2,500 tons a day. A huge Logistics over the Shore operation based at Wunder Beach, 20 miles northeast of Hue, was quickly established and a makeshift port was soon handling 1,000 tons per day.

Landing craft and amphibious lighters ferry supplies from ships waiting offshore to the beach at Vung Ro Bay. (111-CC-36366)

ARMY DEPOTS

Depots were established at the ports to receive, store and issue all types of stores. Depots were organized into several Directorates:

Administration, Plans and Operations, and Security
Maintenance and Supply
Services, Transport and Storage associated with warehousing

Keeping track of what stores were available and what had to be ordered was an enormous task and Data Processing and Quality Assurance Directorates were organized when computers were introduced. Depots were originally numbered but they were renamed after their locations in 1968.

Shipments of cargo had to be broken down into lorry or plane-sized loads so the transportation battalions could deliver it to the divisional base camps. Combat units consumed the same amount of food and drink every day but the amount of ammunition required increased considerably during operations. Spares for maintenance and repairs had to be ordered according to a unit's needs.

I Corps: A Field Depot was established at Da Nang in February 1968 to supply MACV Forward Headquarters. It was upgraded to a full Army Depot in March 1970.
II Corps, North: 58th Depot ran the depot at Qui Nhon.
II Corps, South: 504th Army Depot ran operations at Cam Ranh Bay.
III and IV Corps: 506th Army Depot was based at Long Binh. By the end of 1971 it was supplying Army units across the whole country and later transferred to USARV/ MACV Support Command when civilian contractors took over.

ORDNANCE

Ordnance units were trained to deal with the off-loading, storage and distribution of ammunition at specially designed depots. 52d Ordnance Group acted as part of the Directorate of Ammunition for 1st Logistical Command from March 1966, setting up ammunition facilities across the country. 60th Ordnance Group was deployed at Bien Hoa to control ordnance maintenance and supply units in September 1965, including 169th Ordnance Battalion at Qui Nhon. The two Groups left when it became clear that the Ordnance Battalions would report directly to the General Support Groups.

I Corps: 336th Ordnance Battalion (Arkansas Reserve) worked at Da Nang depot.
II Corps, North: 184th Ordnance Battalion worked at Qui Nhon depot.
II Corps, South: 191st Ordnance Battalion worked at Cam Rahn depot.
III and IV Corps: 3d Battalion worked at Long Binh, Tan Son Nhut and Vung Tau depots.

PETROLEUM OPERATIONS – THE QUARTERMASTER BATTALIONS

543d Quartermaster Group arrived in at Cholon near Saigon in November 1965 to supervise the supply of POL (petrol, oil, lubricants) across Vietnam. It was disbanded when Quartermaster Battalions took control of distribution for the Support Commands in July 1966.

MOTOR TRANSPORT TRANSPORTATION GROUPS

A transportation group commanded several motor transport battalions, coordinating convoy operations for the Support Command. Motor Transport Transportation Battalions operated the lorries as they carried supplies from the ports to inland depots or divisional bases. They operated a mixture of light and medium truck companies.

I Corps: 8th Group ran XXIV Corps' transport from Da Nang after November 1970.
II Corps, North: 8th Group.
II Corps, South: 500th Group.
III and IV Corps: 48th Group; Delta Logistical Support Activity took over IV Corps' area in August 1970.

A convoy carrying ammunition to Pleiku ordnance storage area. (111-CC-63787)

A C-130 aircraft dropping urgently required ammunition and rations during Operation Junction City. (111-CC-38750)

8th Transportation Group had the difficult task of operating convoys along Route 19 between the coastal city of Qui Nhon and bases in the Central Highlands. Convoys, numbering over seventy vehicles, had to negotiate over 150 miles of difficult road on the road to Pleiku, including the An Khe and Mang Giang mountain passes, an area known as Ambush Alley.

The crews decided to fight back and turned their vehicles into gun trucks, arming themselves with discarded or repaired weapons and adding armor plate to their cabs. Jeeps armed with M60 machine guns drove ahead of the convoys and despite ambushes, snipers, mines and damaged bridges, the Group delivered 12,000 tons of cargo and 80,000 gallons of fuel every week during major operations.

MAINTENANCE

Some Ordnance Battalions were converted into Direct Support Maintenance Battalions in July 1966 to repair and maintain equipment used by non-divisional units; they also supervised Direct Maintenance Companies. They reported to Support Commands if they were working in the base areas and to General Support Groups when they were operating in the field.

General Support Maintenance Battalions coordinated the General Support Companies operating in a Support Command's area. They dealt with administration, training and deployment of the companies.

Maintenance Companies worked at many of the depots and base camps, servicing the heavy and light equipment operated by the Supply and Service Battalions. Some specialized companies provided avionics support while others dealt with equipment processing. Many Provisional Companies were formed into Service Battalions while they operated in the forward areas.

DIVISIONAL SUPPORT

Each division had an Adjutant-General Company, a Maintenance Battalion, a Supply and Transport Battalion and a Medical Battalion to carry out the support functions in its operational area.

ADMINISTRATION

Adjutant-General Companies were responsible for all personnel matters. As divisions settled into their new area and developed base camps and fire bases, the allocation of personnel became more complex. The style of warfare encountered in Vietnam was completely different to that envisaged when the division Tables of Organization and Equipment (TOEs) were laid down and many changes were made as units adapted to their new roles.

Many units were unofficially restructured from the official TOE, causing problems for the Adjutant-General Company, as staff tried to keep track of personnel. The change of the infantry battalions from three-rifle and one support company to four-rifle companies is just one example. They also had to deal with the constant rotation of men, monitoring the departure of those coming to the end of their tour while assigning new arrivals as their replacements.

DIVISION	COMPANY	DIVISION	COMPANY
1st Cavalry	15th	23d Infantry	23d
1st Infantry	1st	25th Infantry	25th
4th Infantry	4th	101st Airborne	101st
9th Infantry	9th		

MAINTENANCE

Equipment suffered in the harsh Vietnamese climate and the maintenance workshops were kept busy servicing and repairing everything from rifles to howitzers. The headquarters usually based teams at the scattered firebases (aircraft, medical and communication security equipment were maintained by separate workshops).

DIVISION	COMPANY	DIVISION	COMPANY
1st Cavalry	27th	9th Infantry	709th
1st Infantry	701st	23d Infantry	723d
4th Infantry	704th	25th Infantry	725th

801st Maintenance Battalion was added to 101st Airborne Division as part of its conversion to airmobile status.

SUPPLY AND TRANSPORT

The Supply and Transport Battalion performed two functions to keep its division fed, clothed, armed and moving. The first was to administer storage facilities, ordering, receiving, and distributing everything from uniforms and ammunition to fuel and building materials (the two exceptions were communication security and aircraft spares). The battalion trucks and personnel delivered the supplies to the men in the field when possible. The administrative staff arranged with the Aviation Battalion to get food and ammunition flown to the outlying firebases.

Soldiers fill out paperwork so they can receive new clothing and equipment. (111-CC-52395)

Above: *Supplies are unloaded from a Huey helicopter during 173d Airborne Brigade's Operation Daytona.* (111-CC-40018)

Right: *A Marine keeps a look-out for snipers while an aidman attends to a wounded man during 3d Marine Division's Operation Georgia.* (127-GVC-K37042)

The Supply and Service Battalions with the two Airmobile Divisions (1st Cavalry and 101st Airborne) developed a kit so units could set up a fire base in a day. Sandbags, timber, corrugated steel sections and concertina wire were packed ready to be flown out to the landing zone.

DIVISION	BATTALION	DIVISION	BATTALION
1st Cavalry	15th	9th Infantry	9th
1st Infantry	1st	23d Infantry	23d
4th Infantry	4th	25th Infantry	25th

426th Supply and Transport Battalion was added to 101st Airborne Division as part of its conversion to airmobile status.

MEDICAL SUPPORT

The Medical Battalion was responsible for the day to day coordination of the welfare of the division personnel, making sure that the maximum number of men were available for duty. It organized the collection and immediate treatment of casualties from the field and administered medication to the sick. Those needing further attention were then evacuated to the field or surgical hospitals. It had to ensure that the divisional units had medical supplies and equipment, and carried out basic maintenace and repairs. The battalion also maintained personnel medical records, and monitored sickness levels, in particular malaria control.

1st Cavalry Division had twelve aeromedical evacuation helicopters to cover its extended area of operations but the rest of the divisions relied on air ambulances to evacuate their casualties.

DIVISION	BATTALION	DIVISION	BATTALION
1st Cavalry	15th	23d Infantry	23d
1st Infantry	1st	25th Infantry	25th
4th Infantry	4th	101st Airborne	326th
9th Infantry	9th		

BRIGADE SUPPORT

The support functions of the independent brigades were grouped together under Support Battalions which were organized into four companies, one for each function. Each company carried out the same functions as the battalions serving the divisions only on a smaller scale:

Company A:	Administration
Company B:	Maintenance
Company C:	Supply and service
Company D:	Medical support and Headquarters

Mechanized, Airmobile and Airborne Support Battalions also maintained and supplied specialized equipment for their brigades.

BRIGADE	COMPANY	BRIGADE	COMPANY
11th Brigade	6th	1st / 5th Division	75th
196th Brigade	9th	3d / 82d Airborne	82d Airborne
198th Brigade	8th	173d Airborne	173d Airborne
199th Brigade	7th		

101st Airborne Division deployed its 1st Brigade before the rest of the division while a number of divisions left brigades behind when they left Vietnam. These independent brigades were supported by a Brigade Support Battalion.

DIVISION	BRIGADE	SUPPORT BATTALION
1st Cavalry	3d	215th Airmobile
9th Infantry	3d	99th
25th Division	2d	225th
101st Airborne	1st	101st Airborne

EVACUATING THE WOUNDED

MARINE CORPS ORGANIZATION

1st and 3d Medical Battalions ran hospitals, each with 240 beds, for the two divisions while 1st Hospital Company operated a 100-bed facility at Da Nang. Two Navy hospital ships, the *Sanctuary* and the *Repose*, were anchored off the coast and they could each take up to 750 casualties during periods of heavy fighting. The large Naval Support Activity Hospital at Da Nang could also treat over 700 patients at a time while many wounded Marines were taken to the US Army's Evacuation Hospital based in the town after March 1968.

ARMY COMMAND AND CONTROL

1st Logistical Command arrived in Saigon in March 1965 and took over all support activities, including medical support, south of Chu Lai. As the size of the US Army commitment increased, so did the need for a dedicated medical command and 44th Medical Brigade arrived at Truong Quoc Dung, Saigon, in April 1966. The Brigade took over 43d Medical Group covering II Corps from Nha Trang and 68th Group covering III and IV Corps from Long Binh; 32d Medical Depot ordered and issued supplies. 55th Medical Group became operational at Qui Nhon in June 1966 to control the northern half of II Corps.

44th Brigade reported directly to USARV after August 1967 and 67th Medical Group became operational at Bien Hoa in October 1967; it moved north to Da Nang to support Army troops in I Corps in February 1968. Brigade Headquarters moved to Long Binh in March 1970 where it was given the new title US Army Medical Command, Vietnam, as it merged with the Surgeon General's Office. The Command was scaled down to Group level and in April 1972 became US Army Health Services Group; the Group covered the final withdrawal and eventually left in March 1973.

Medical Groups were responsible for coordinating the hospitalization and evacuation of the wounded and sick from a Corps area; they also organized medical support for units operating in the field.

I Corps: 67th Group was based at Da Nang after February 1968.
II Corps, North: 43d Group operated out of Nha Trang.
II Corps, South: 55th Group was based at Qui Nhon.
III and IV Corps: 68th Group was based at Long Binh and 67th Group operated out of Bien Hoa until it redeployed to I Corps.

RETRIEVING THE WOUNDED

When a man (or men) was injured out in the field, the aidman administered first aid and organized evacuation to the nearest hospital by air ambulance. His radio call would detail the number of patients, their injuries, the unit's map reference and the situation on the ground, including any enemy positions. During large operations a medical regulating officer coordinated air ambulances' movements, directing them to the appropriate medical facility.

Each air ambulance company had twenty-five UH-1 Huey helicopters modified to carry six stretchers or nine sitting patients; the company was split into four detachments of six. The ambulances were called Dust Offs after the radio call sign of Major Charles Kelly, MSC, an Air Ambulance pilot who was killed in action in July 1964. A single detachment covered the whole country during the advisory period but by the end of 1968 there were 116 air ambulances.

On receiving the call for a Dust Off, a standby crew was alerted and directed to the unit where waiting men would use their radio and colored smoke to guide the helicopter; quite often ambulances would be diverted from a routine mission to reduce the flight time. The Viet Cong knew that the American soldiers always called for an air ambulance when they had a wounded man and they took the opportunity to target the incoming helicopter. Dust Off pilots either had to make a high-speed approach or fly in a tight circle on to the landing zone to minimize the risk and they were rarely on the ground for more than a minute. The Marine Corps responded by organizing flights comprising two evacuation helicopters guarded by two gunships and some were always kept on standby.

As soon as the helicopter had taken off and was flying on a steady course, the medical aidman on board began administering treatment, evaluating the condition of the injured men. There was only one hospital in each Corps Zone in 1965 but as more opened, the choice was increased. The helicopter crew radioed the aidman's information to control, which in turn was given the destination by the medical regulating office. When 44th Medical Brigade took over regulating across the country it was able to route helicopters to other corps areas. They were directed to where the relevant care was available rather than the closest facility when possible. Physicians sometimes spoke directly to the crew for further information on the casualties.

A Dust-Off helicopter prepares to land and pick up casualties during Task Force Oregon's Operation Cook in Quang Ngai Province. (111-CC-43089)

Marines carry a wounded buddy to a waiting CH-34 Seahorse helicopter during Operation Georgia. (127-GVC-K37037)

A Navy corpsman administers first aid to casualties during the flight to the hospital. (127-GVC-A704371)

The average flight time to hospital was around 30 minutes and the crew radioed instructions ahead so a team would be waiting to offload the wounded while the surgical team prepared their theater. The air ambulance crews prided themselves on retrieving casualties from the field in the shortest time possible and an injured man could expect to be on the operating table within an hour of being wounded. Over 95 per cent of men delivered to a hospital survived.

CARE OF THE WOUNDED

The surgeons and their medical teams in Vietnam could usually count on working in a well-established, fully equipped and air-conditioned hospital far from the battlefield. An injured man could expect to be receiving a similar standard of care to that which he would have received in a Stateside hospital.

Each surgical team had a number of specialists including a neurosurgeon, an ophthalmologist, an oral surgeon, an otolaryngologist and a plastic surgeon. A high degree of professionalism was also maintained despite the rapid turnover of medical officers and new staff had to train with experienced teams to understand the realities of combat surgery before taking over their own team. Numerous studies also helped the medical service to manage its staff and supplies, and the distribution of casualties.

New techniques were always being investigated by the Surgical Research Team and while the number of amputations dropped dramatically, frozen blood plasma helped many casualties survive the trauma of being evacuated from the battlefield. The team also introduced new equipment: tissue adhesives and aerosol spray antibiotics for use in the field were just two.

Nearly a million and a half volunteers from military bases across the Pacific Ocean donated blood as the monthly requirement increased to 38,000 units and 24,000 transfusions a month. To begin with only low-titer group O blood was sent to Vietnam so that it was impossible to give the wrong blood to a patient, but as the number of casualties grew, so did stocks of all groups at the evacuation hospitals. By April 1968 fresh frozen plasma was being used to slow blood loss following surgery and transfusions. Facilities experienced problems keeping blood in the hot, humid climate and while new freezers were developed for the hospitals, styrofoam packed boxes were used in the field.

HOSPITALS

The 100-bed 8th Field Hospital based at Nha Trang dealt with all casualties across Vietnam until April 1965. There was a rapid increase in bed space when combat troops were deployed and by the end of the year there were 1,627 beds. The number continued to rise throughout 1966 and 1967 and the policy of keeping as many short-term wounded and the sick (disease accounted for 70 per cent of casualties admitted) in-country saved resources. By December 1968, there were 5,283 beds, including a huge convalescent base at Cam Rahn Bay.

SURGICAL HOSPITALS

These were often the first to treat a critically injured man or the seriously ill and they carried out immediate resuscitative surgery or administered medical treatment as soon as the man was carried off the helicopter. The surgical team

93d Evacuation Hospital at Long Binh received casualties from across III Corps' area. (111-CC-35828)

Ambulances wait outside 3d Field Hospital at Tan Son Nhut base. (111-CC-74596)93d

aimed to stabilize the casualty and cared for him until he was fit enough to be taken to one of the larger evacuation hospitals for further medical attention.

Surgical hospitals were small, having between thirty-five and seventy beds, and there were two types. The original Mobile Army Surgical Hospitals (MASH) needed concrete foundations and services so they could operate a sterile facility and it was several weeks before they were operational. Moving facilities around the country was difficult and time consuming so many were converted into the new Self-Contained, Transportable, or MUST, Surgical Hospitals. The hospital had three units that could be airlifted to a new location and made operational in days:

Surgical Unit: An expanding rigid-panel shelter with accordion sides
Ward Unit: A double-walled fabric shelter that was inflated by air to form ward space
Power Unit: A gas turbine engine provided power for the hospital

FIELD HOSPITALS

Field hospitals usually dealt with the men needing minor medical attention or a few hours' rest before they returned to their units. During busy periods Dust Off helicopters often delivered serious casualties to a nearby field hospital in the hope that immediate medical attention would save a man's life. The hospital also dealt with the overflow from the divisional field hospitals during offensive operations. The medical teams would stabilize the injured and administer aid to the sick until transport was available to take them to the appropriate facility. Field hospitals varied in size from fewer than 100 to more than 300 beds.

SEMI-MOBILE EVACUATION HOSPITALS

Evacuation hospitals accepted wounded and sick patients from all units in its area and took care of them, performing further surgery if required. According to their condition, patients would either be sent to the convalescent center at Cam Ranh Bay or evacuated out of Vietnam when fit enough to travel. The hospitals also dealt with casualites brought in by units serving in the immediate area.

MOVING PATIENTS AROUND THE COUNTRY

Once a patient had received surgery and had been stabilized, he often needed to be taken to another hospital either to recuperate or be prepared for evacuation out of Vietnam. Patients were often moved around the country to free up bed space, particularly during offensives. 658th and 667th Team Area Control Headquarters were set up at Long Binh in May 1967 to coordinate casualty evacuation across Vietnam. Ambulance Companies transported patients around the large bases, either between medical facilities or to waiting helicopters or planes so they could be moved to another hospital. Clearing Companies cared for patients while they waited to be evacuated and during the flight.

During the early months of the conflict the US Air Force used returning cargo planes to evacuate casualties but the system became unworkable as operations increased in size. 903d Aeromedical Evacuation Squadron was activated to make regular in-country evacuation flights in 1967 and its modified C-118 cargo aircraft carried over 10,000 patients during the Tet Offensive in February 1968.

CONVALESCENTS

Injured and sick patients unlikely to recover quickly were evacuated by specially modified aircraft to hospitals across the United States so they did not occupy valuable bed space in Vietnam. However, many soldiers just needed time for their wounds to heal before they could be put through an exercise program.

To begin with a man's recovery time was assessed and if it was longer than fifteen days he might be evacuated as soon as he was fit enough for the journey. It could be extended to thirty days in some cases. When 6th Convalescent Center became operational with 1,300 beds at Cam Ranh Bay in May 1966 the limit could be raised to thirty days and thousands of men spent time at the Center as they fought to return to full fitness. The Center closed down in October 1971.

SURVIVAL STATISTICS

Between 1965 and 1970 nearly 195,000 men were admitted to hospitals and other medical facilities; over 5,000 died; a much lower percentage than other conflicts due to the advanced medical care. While many casualties survived because of the rapid evacuation by helicopter, mortally wounded men, who would normally have died in transit, also often survived the flight to the hospitals.

On average, two-thirds of the hospital beds in Vietnam at any one time were occupied while half of those across the Pacific were also full. A third of the men returned to duty almost immediately but the rest spent on average nine weeks recovering in hospital. Altogether 85 per cent of casualties returned to duty, half in Vietnam and the rest either served in the Pacific theater or in the United States; about 10 per cent were admitted to a Veteran's Administration hospital or were discharged. The rest did not survive.

WOUNDING

The nature of wounds caused by the weapons in Vietnam were often more deadly than previous wars, but the number of men killed immediately in action was lower than previous conflicts at less than 20 per cent.

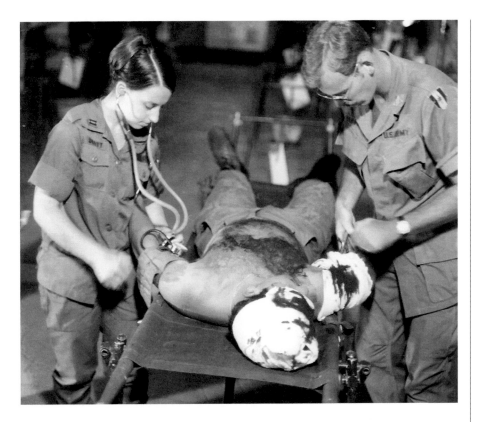

Many female nurses worked in the hospitals; here one is helping to remove field dressings from a badly injured patient as he is prepared for surgery. (111-CC-61548)

The lightweight rounds fired by the M16 and AK47 tended to disintegrate as they entered the body, causing severe internal damage before leaving a large exit wound, while automatic fire often resulted in multiple wounds. Meanwhile, the close impact of an exploding mine or booby trap often left a gaping wound filled with debris. It meant that there was little that the medics could do other than stop the bleeding and stabilize the patient before administering morphine to prevent him going into shock. He then had to hope that a medevac helicopter arrived as soon as possible.

Although it was widely known that helmets reduced the number of head wounds by up to a third, they were heavy and uncomfortable out on patrol and many men preferred to wear lightweight boonie hats. Flak vests were equally successful at stopping fragments and spent bullets but again many men preferred to leave them back at base when they were operating in the jungle.

Men trapped in a burning bunker or armored personnel carrier often died from their injuries while over half of burns victims were caused by accidents. The affected area was treated with Sulfamylon ointment to stop infection and the casualty was evacuated to 106th General Hospital's burns unit in Japan as quickly as possible.

During the early offensive operations small arms fire accounted for nearly half of all wounds, but by 1970, when many men were engaged in holding military installations, around 80 per cent of wounds were caused by mortars and rockets. The average percentages for the whole conflict are as follows:

WEAPON	DEATHS	WOUNDS
Small arms	51	16
Fragments	36	65
Booby traps, mines	11	17
Other	2	2

THE FLIGHT SURGEONS

Flight surgeons were trained in the specialized field of aviation medicine. As well as being able to deal with injuries and sickness, they were trained to monitor the mental state of aviation crews, particularly pilots. Flying a helicopter under fire was extremely stressful and the surgeon worked with unit planners to check pilots' flight programs and often accompanied flights to observe the crews. There was no room for error and any sign of fatigue resulted in a pilot being stood down for a short time; many pilots tried to hide the strain because they wanted to continue flying. The surgeon would then work on a recovery program to get him back in the air as soon as possible.

Flyer fatigue, particularly that involving helicopter pilots, was a new area of medicine encountered for the first time in Vietnam. As the number of helicopters grew and the hours pilots flew (between 100 and 150 a month by 1967) so did the concerns and in some cases it limited airmobile operations. No one knew how long a man could fly while subjected to heat, noise, vibration, dust and enemy fire. Bad weather added to the pilots' problems and as the number of night missions increased, so did the stress they faced.

Around 70 per cent of accidents were due to pilot error and until 1968 more aircrew were killed or injured by accidents than from enemy action and it was clear that many crashes were caused by pilot fatigue. Flight surgeons were often involved with aircraft crash investigation teams.

The introduction of regular schedules and one rest day a week reduced fatigue and ultimately increased the number of men on duty. However, the problem was never completely solved. Attempts to carry out routine physicals were sometimes frustrated by a lack of facilities and support from the unit commanders. An outbreak of infectious disease among aviation personnel was extremely serious and it was the flight surgeon's responsibility to give medical advice. Even a mild case of diarrhea grounded a pilot and in April 1968 1st Cavalry Division was crippled by an outbreak of gastroenteritis caused by contaminated water. Administering medication caused its own problems, in particular the malaria tablet, as the drug could affect a pilot's ability to fly; the flight surgeon's specialist knowledge helped to prevent accidents.

Close monitoring by flight surgeons did help to reduce many problems but he often came into conflict with the operation planners as he tried to reduce flying time. It was simply a case of too many operations and too few pilots.

CHAPTER 9

DIVISIONAL ORGANIZATION AND OPERATIONS

The brigade of each division and each independent brigade have their arrival date, their headquarters location and their departure date listed. The infantry and artillery units under their command, and the dates they served, are also given; combat units attached to the division follow at the end of the listings.

Divisions carried out dozens of extended operations and hundreds of small operations during their stay in Vietnam. Some lasted no more than a few hours, others lasted several weeks, a few lasted months. They varied in size, scope, objective and many operations were combined between more than one division; they all had a name. Listed below are dates, operational names and location of many of these operations.

1ST CAVALRY DIVISION (AIRMOBILE) *THE FIRST TEAM*

1ST BRIGADE DEPLOYMENTS
Arrived at An Khe in September 1965
Moved to Bien Hoa and Tay Ninh in May 1969
Entered Cambodia in June 1970, returning to
Bien Hoa in July
Left Vietnam in March 1971

1ST BRIGADE UNITS
1/8th Cavalry: to January 1970
2/8th Cavalry: to July 1968
1/12th Cavalry: to February 1969
2/5th Cavalry: August 1968 to February 1969
2/8th Cavalry: March 1969
1/5th Cavalry: March 1969 to January 1970
2/12th Cavalry: March 1969 to January 1970
2/5th Cavalry: from February 1970
2/7th Cavalry: from February 1970
2d Battalion, 19th Artillery, 105mm
    towed howitzers

2D BRIGADE DEPLOYMENTS
Arrived at An Khe in September 1965
Moved to Bien Hoa in June 1969
Entered Cambodia in June 1970
Moved to Song Be in December 1970
Left Vietnam in March 1971

2D BRIGADE UNITS
1/5th Cavalry: to February 1969
2/5th Cavalry: to July 1968
2/12th Cavalry: to September 1967
5/7th Cavalry: October 1967 to July 1968
2/7th Cavalry: August 1968 to February 1969
2/8th Cavalry: August 1968 to February 1969

1st Cavalry Division (Airmobile) insignia.

2D BRIGADE UNITS

2/5th Cavalry: March 1969 to January 1970

5/7th Cavalry: from March 1969

1/12th Cavalry: from February 1970

2/12th Cavalry: February 1970 to February 1971

1st Battalion, 77th Artillery, 105mm towed howitzers

3D BRIGADE DEPLOYMENTS

Arrived at An Khe in September 1965

Moved to Bien Hoa in May 1969

Deployed to Quan Loi in January 1970

Entered Cambodia in June

Returned to Bien Hoa in September

The Brigade became a separate command
 in May 1971

3D BRIGADE UNITS

1/7th Cavalry: full tour

2/7th Cavalry: to July 1968

5/7th Cavalry: August 1966 to September 1967

2/12th Cavalry: October 1967 to February 1969

5/7th Cavalry: August 1968 to February 1969

2/7th Cavalry: March 1969 to January 1970

1/12th Cavalry: March 1969 to January 1970

1/5th Cavalry: February 1970 to April 1971

1/8th Cavalry: February 1970 to March 1971

2/12th Cavalry: from March 1971

1st Battalion, 21st Artillery, 105mm towed howitzers

DIVISIONAL ARTILLERY

2d Battalion, 20th Artillery, was an aerial rocket artillery battalion equipped with armed helicopters while Battery E of the 82d Artillery was an aviation artillery battery.

1st Battalion, 30th Artillery, and its 155mm towed howitzers joined in February 1968.

OPERATIONS

1965

WHOLE DIVISION

1 Oct–13 Nov   Good Friend II: cleared Qui Nhon area for ROK Capitol Division

1ST BRIGADE

10–12 Oct   Shiny Bayonet: assault into the Suaica River Valley

14–17 Oct   Lonesome End: secured Highway 1 and around Binh Dinh

19 Oct–28 Nov   All The Way: relieved Plei Me camp and secured Highway 19

20 Oct–7 Nov   Indian Scout: cleared the Binh Dinh area for the ROK Tiger Division

The golf course at An Khe was 1st Cavalry Division's home during the early years of the conflict. (11-CC-33915)

A Huey helicopter delivers troops to a hilltop position so they can check out a suspected Viet Cong outpost during Operation Oregon. (111-CC-39768)

14–15 Nov	Corn: search and destroy operation in Binh Dinh province
6–20 Dec	Charger Sweep I, Sweeping Mustang and Scalping Mustang
10–26 Dec	Quick Kick and Cherokee Trail: security in Pleiku and Kontum provinces

2D BRIGADE

9–16 Oct	Cobra: security of Route 19 across Binh Dinh
10–12 Oct	Shiny Bayonet: assault into the Suaica River valley
13–31 Oct	Happy Valley: pacification of Vinh Thanh Valley (Happy Valley)
16 Oct–1 Nov	Settlement: patrolling Highway 19 around An Khe
19 Oct–28 Nov	Silver Bayonet II: relieved Plei Me camp and secured Highway 19
Dec	Ox Trail, Give Up and Fishhook

3D BRIGADE

1–9 Oct	Blue Bonnet and Red Bayonet: securing Highway 19
10–14 Oct	Shiny Bayonet and Concord: assault into the Suaica River valley
19 Oct–28 Nov	Silver Bayonet I: assault into the Ia Drang Valley
Dec	Clean House and Scalping Mustang

1966
WHOLE DIVISION

24 Jan– 6 Mar	Masher/White Wing: across Bong Son Plain in Binh Dinh province

1ST BRIGADE

7–28 Mar	Jim Bowie: Upper Dak Som River Valley, Binh Dinh
25 Mar–10 Apr	Lincoln I, II and III: Chu Pong and Ia Drang river areas
11 Apr–3 May	Mosby I and II: reconnaissance along the border
16 May–5 Jun	Crazy Horse: Vinh Thanh and Soui Ca Valleys in Binh Dinh
1–21 Jun	Hawthorne: Dak To and Tou Morong areas of Kontum province
20 Jun–2 Jul	Nathan Hale: north of Tuy Hoa in Phu Yen province
2–30 Jul	Henry Clay: along the Cambodian border

1–25 Aug	Paul Revere II: Chu Pong War Zone in Pleiku province
9 Sept–24 Oct	Thayer I: south of Bong Son
13 Sept–2 Oct	Oliver Wendell Holmes: Binh Dinh province
24 Oct	Start of Thayer II: coast of Binh Dinh province

2D BRIGADE

All year	Matador I and II: security across Binh Dinh, Pleiku and Kontum
12–25 Jan	Short Fuse: Tay Ninh Province
16 Feb–5 Mar	Eagle's Claw and Black Horse: Binh Dinh Province
14–21 Mar	Wyatt Earp, Buchanan I and II: security of Route 19
21 Mar–5 May	Benning / Trail Boss: security operation
3 May–21 Jun	Lewis, Clark and Hooker I: reconnaissance across Pleiku and Kontum
13 Sept–2 Oct	Oliver Wendell Holmes: search and destroy
18 Oct–31 Dec	Paul Revere III: Pleiku Province
18–31 Oct	Travis: airlifted to support Operation Paul Revere IV

3D BRIGADE

7–28 Mar	Jim Bowie: Upper Dak Som River Valley, Binh Dinh province
25 Mar–10 Apr	Lincoln I, II and III: Chu Pong and Ia Drang River areas near the Cambodian border in Darlac, Pleiku and Phu Bon provinces
11 Apr–3 May	Mosby I and II: reconnaissance in force along Pleiku and Kontum borders with Cambodia
26 Apr–27 May	Bee Bee and Davy Crockett: Bong Son area, Binh Dinh province
20 Jun–2 Jul	Nathan Hale: north of Tuy Hoa in Phu Yen province
2 Jul–1 Aug	Henry Clay and Hayes: reconnaissance along the Cambodian border
1–25 Aug	Paul Revere II: Chu Pong War Zone in Pleiku province
9 Sept–12 Feb	Thayer I and II: south of Bong Son along the coast of Binh Dinh province

1967

12 Feb–19 Jan	Pershing I: northern coastal plain, Kim Son and Luoi Ci Valleys
27–31 Jan	Bullseye V: 2d Brigade reconnaissance in force in Bong Son Plain
7–22 Apr	Lejune: search and destroy operation in Quang Ngai province
9–10 Apr	Dazzlem: defense of Camp Radcliff in Binh Dinh province
6 June–12 Oct	Greely: 3d Brigade at Dak To in Kontum province
19 Sept	Bolling begins: secured the Tuy Hao Basin in Phu Yen province
4 Oct	Wallowa began: 3d Brigade in Quang Nam and Quang Tin provinces
Nov	MacArthur: 1st Brigade at Dak To Special Forces camp
11 Nov	Wheeler/Wallowa: year-long sweeping operations across Quang Nam and Quang Tin provinces

1968

19 Jan–1 Mar	Pershing II: 1st Brigade continued Pershing I
21 Jan–31 Mar	Jeb Stuart: search and destroy around Quang Tri, Hue and Phu Bai
31 Jan–25 Feb	Tet Offensive: heavily engaged in Hue City
28 Feb–9 Dec	Napoleon/ Saline: keeping Dong Ha port open
18 Apr–17 May	Delaware: assault into the A Shau Valley, Thua Thien province
8–16 May	Concordia Square: 2d Brigade in Quang Tri Province
17 May–3 Nov	Jeb Stuart III: securing the rice harvests in Quang Tri and Thua Thien
17 May–28 Feb	Nevada Eagle: clearing central Thua Thien province
4–20 Aug	Somerset Plain: operation in the A Shau Valley

10 Sept–15 Nov   Commanche Falls I, II and III: clearing Quang Tri and Thua Thien

26 Oct–20 Nov   Liberty Canyon: redeployment of the division to III Corps where it joined Toan Thang II (Total Victory), securing the provinces around Saigon

16 Nov–19 Apr   Sheridan Sabre, Cheyenne Sabre and Nahavo Warhorse: securing Hau Nghia Province

1969

16 Feb–31 Oct   Toan Thang III: securing the area west of Saigon

12 Apr–14 May   Montana Raider: clearing War Zones C and D

22 June–31 Jan   Kentucky Cougar: 3d Brigade in Gia Dinh, Tay Ninh, and Binh Long

1 Nov   Toan Thang IV began

1970

5–8 Jan   Flying Finn: 1st Brigade in War Zone C

29 Apr–22 July   Toan Thang (Total Victory) 42: invasion of Cambodia from III Corps

1 May–30 June   Toan Thang 43: invasion of the Fishhook in Cambodia

6 May–27 June   Toan Thang 45: invasion of Cambodia from Phuoc Long Province

1971

March to May   Keystone Robin (Charlie): all but 3d Brigade left Vietnam

3D BRIGADE DEPLOYMENTS	3D BRIGADE UNITS
May 1971 Based at Bien Hoa	1/7th Cavalry: to August 1972
The brigade left in June 1972 leaving	2/5th Cavalry: to May 1972
Task Force Garry Owen based	2/8th Cavalry: to June 1972
around 1/7th Cavalry; it too left in	1/12th Cavalry: to June 1972
August	1st Battalion, 21st Artillery 105mm towed howitzers

27 Sept–2 Oct   Katum: 3d Brigade in Tay Ninh Province

1972

1 May–30 June   Keystone Pheasant: 3d Brigade left Vietnam

1st Infantry Division's insignia.

1ST INFANTRY DIVISION
THE BIG RED ONE

2d Brigade was the first Army Infantry Brigade to arrive in Vietnam in July 1965, the rest of the division followed three months later.

1ST BRIGADE DEPLOYMENTS

Arrived at Bien Hoa in October 1965
December 1965 moved to Phuoc Vinh
March 1968 moved to Quan Loi
September 1969 moved to Dau Tieng
Returned to Phuoc Vinh in December
Moved to Dau Tieng in January 1970
Reloacted to Lai Khe in March and
  then Di An before it left in April 1970

1ST BRIGADE UNITS

1/28th Infantry: full tour
1/16th Infantry: to November 1966
2/28th Infantry: to November 1966
1/2d Infantry: from December 1966
1/26th Infantry: December 1966 to January 1970
2/2d Infantry (Mech): from February 1970
1st Battalion, 5th Artillery, 105mm towed
  howitzers

2D BRIGADE DEPLOYMENTS

Landed at Qui Nhon and Nha Trang in
  July 1965
October moved to Bien Hoa
Moved to Phu Loi in December
Returned to Bien Hoa in March 1966
Moved to Lai Khe in December 1969
Moved to Di An in March 1970
Left Vietnam in April 1970

2D BRIGADE UNITS

1/16th Infantry: full tour
2/18th Infantry: full tour
1/18th Infantry: to January 1970
1/16th Infantry (Mech): from February 1970
1st Battalion, 7th Artillery, 105mm
  towed howitzers

3D BRIGADE DEPLOYMENTS

Arrived at Bien Hoa in October 1965
Moved to Ben Cat and Lai Khe in
  December
February 1970 moved to Dau Tieng
Returned to Lai Khe in March and then
  Di An before it left in April 1970

3D BRIGADE UNITS

1/2d Infantry: to November 1966
1/26th Infantry: to November 1966
1/16th Infantry: December 1966 to January
  1970 (Mechanized after October 1968)
2/28th Infantry: December 1966 to January 1970
2/2d Infantry: to January 1970 (Mech in
  January 1967)
1/18th Infantry: from February 1970
1/26th Infantry: from February 1970
2d Battalion, 33d Artillery, 105mm towed howitzers

DIVISIONAL ARTILLERY

8th Battalion, 6th Artillery, 155mm towed and 8in self-propelled howitzers,
Battery D, 25th Artillery (Target Acquisition)
6th Battalion, 15th Artillery, 105mm towed howitzers was attached May 1967–July 1968

OPERATIONS

1965

Binh Duong, Bien Hoa and Long Khanh Provinces, north of Saigon

1ST BRIGADE IN BINH DUONG PROVINCE

Oct	Black Lion, Checkmate, Depth, Hot Foot, Flip Flop, Fly Low, Ranger I, Bethlehem and Triple Trouble
Nov–Dec	Turkey Shoot, Riviera, Gladiator, Frisk I and II, Feline and Jingle Bells

2D BRIGADE

19–20 Aug	Barracuda
29 Sept–25 Oct	Red One, Checkerboard and Hopscotch
1 Nov–17 Jan	Viper, Dagger, Custer Flats, Copperhead and Smash

3D BRIGADE

17 Oct–Nov	Bushmaster Bravo, Big Horn, Binder I, II, III and IV
10 Nov–11 Feb	Road Runner I to VI, Beaver and Rebel Rouser: securing Highway 13
14 Nov–9 Dec	Bushmaster I and II: south of the Michelin rubber plantation
15 Nov–12 Dec	Docket I, Rabbit Hunt and Bear Trap: search and destroy operations

1966

Tay Ninh, Binh Duong, Bien Hoa and Long Khanh Provinces, northwest of Saigon

1ST BRIGADE

3 Jan–9 Feb	Quick Kick I, II, III and IV: search and destroy operations
15 Jan–1 Apr	Red Ball IV, V, VI, VII: supply convoy protection
7 Feb–2 Mar	Rolling Stone and Breezeway: security for construction on Route 13
7 Mar–7 Apr	Silver City, Waycross and York
Apr and May	Miami and Providence: road clearing across Bien Hoa province
24 Apr–17 May	Birmingham: search and destroy in War Zone C
30 May–9 Jun	Adelaide I, II and III: opening Route 16 from Phuoc Vinh to Di An
12 Jul–3 Sept	El Paso III, El Dorado and Amarillo: operations in Binh Duong province
4–6 Sept	Cranston: convoy protection from Lai Khe to Phu Loi
23 Sept–9 Dec	Longview, Boyd, Little Rock, Bismarck: securing Route 16 to Phuoc Vinh

2D BRIGADE

17 Jan–18 June	Pioneer I and II: in Bien Hoa Province
28 Jan–15 Feb	Mallet: opened Route 15 through Long Khanh Province
21–27 Feb	Mastiff: search and destroy in the Michelin plantation and Boi Loi woods
1–27 Mar	Hattiesburg, Salem, Wheaton and Monroe: Tay Ninh Province
30 Mar–15 Apr	Abilene: operations across Phuoc Tuy and Long Khanh Provinces
17 Apr–5 May	Lexington I, II and III: search and destroy in Rung Sat Special Zone
20–22 Apr	Omaha: secured Route 13 from Lai Khe to Chon Thanh
5 May–8 Feb	Lam Son II: security across Binh Duong and Bien Hoa Provinces
30 May–6 Jun	Reno: search and destroy operation
2–14 Aug	Cheyenne: securing Route 13 from Lai Khe to An Loc
19–22 Aug	Castine: search and destroy operation
4 Sept–8 Oct	Baton Rouge: search and destroy operation in Rung Sat Special Zone
14 Sept–25 Nov	Attleboro: large operation in War Zone C, Tay Ninh Province
21 Oct–5 Nov	Allentown: search and destroy east of Saigon
27 Nov–23 Dec	Charleston: search and destroy operations

3D BRIGADE

7–14 Jan	Crimp and Buckskin: operations in the Iron Triangle and Ho Bo Woods
8–19 Feb	Bald Eagle and Belt Line: search and destroy and securing Route 13
21–27 Feb	Mastiff: search and destroy in the Michelin plantation and Boi Loi woods

A platoon prepares to move through the mist to check out the results of an artillery strike during Operation Abilene. (111-CC-34049)

1–29 Mar	Beer Barrel, Cocoa Beach, Boston, Los Angeles, Toledo, Tampa, Palestine, Brownsville, Bismarck, Brunswick and Olympia: securing Routes 13 and 16
30 Mar–15 Apr	Abilene: search and destroy operation in Long Khanh province
15–23 Apr	Bolivar, Otsego, Chatanooga and Bowie: road security around Lai Khe
24 Apr–17 May	Birmingham and Hollingsworth: search and destroy in War Zone C
19 May– 13 Jul	El Paso I and II: reinforce Loc Ninh Special Forces camp
July	Springfield I and II, Cedar Rapids I and II: search and destroy operations
2 Aug–3 Sept	Cheyenne, Belfast and Decatur: securing Route 13 to An Loc
6–12 Sept	Bangor and Huntsville: operations in Binh Duong Province
14 Sept–25 Nov	Attleboro: search and destroy operation in War Zone C
3–10 Oct	Decatur, Norwalk and Tulsa: clearing Route 13 to An Loc
16 Oct–22 Dec	Shenandoah I, Leeds and Santa Cruz: across Binh Duong province

1967

9–27 Jan	Niagara/Cedar Falls: 2d and 3d Brigades swept through the Iron Triangle
21 Feb–14 May	Junction City: 1st Division formed blocking positions north and east of War Zone C, Tay Ninh province

8 Feb–31 Jan	Lam Son 67: 2d and 3d Brigades secure Binh Duong and Bien Hoa provinces
14–21 Feb	Tucson: search and destroy in the Michelin plantation and Long Nguyen Secret Zone in Binh Long province
23 Apr–7 June	Manhattan: 3d Brigade swept Boi Loi woods and Long Nguyen forest
17 May–28 Sept	Dallas, Bluefield I and II, Billings and Paul Bunyan: 1st Brigade clearing War Zone D
27 Sept–19 Nov	Shenandoah II: clearing Highway 13 in Binh Duong province

1968

20–27 Jan	Atalla: search and destroy operation in Binh Long province
31 Jan–7 Mar	Tet Offensive strikes the heart of Saigon; battles rage across the city for several days but the NVA and VC are forced to withdraw to Cholon
1 Feb–10 Mar	Lam Son 68: 2d Brigade secured Bien Hoa and Binh Duong provinces
10 Mar–8 Apr	Resolve to Win (Quyet Thang): securing the area around Saigon
16–17 Mar	San Francisco: 3d Brigade search and destroy operation
3–7 Apr	Atlas I, Carlisle and Waterford: securing Binh Long province
7 Apr–31 May	Complete Victory (Toan Thang): secure the provinces around Saigon
1 June–16 Feb	Toan Thang II: securing the provinces north and west of Saigon

1969

17 Feb–31 Oct	Toan Thang II: securing III Corps
18 Mar–10 Apr	Atlas Wedge and Atlas Power: 3d Brigade in Michelin rubber plantation
Nov	Toan Thang IV began in III Corps
21–29 Nov	While Away: 2d Brigade security operation in Bien Hoa Province

1970

III CORPS, NORTH AND NORTHWEST OF SAIGON

| 1 Feb–15 Apr | Keystone Blue Jay: Increment III redeployment of 1st Infantry Division |

After evacuating the villagers and clearing the tunnels of supplies and weapons in a Viet Cong-held hamlet, it is time to raze the buildings to the ground. (111-CC-33057)

4th Infantry Division insignia.

4TH INFANTRY DIVISION

1ST BRIGADE DEPLOYMENTS
Arrived at Tuy Hoa in October 1966
Moved to Pleiku in July 1967
At Tuy Hoa in August 1967
Returned to Pleiku in September
Moved to An Khe in February 1970
Left Vietnam in December 1970

1ST BRIGADE UNITS
1/8th Infantry: to April 1970
3/8th Infantry: to April 1969
3/12th Infantry: to January 1970
1/14th Infantry: from February to December 1970
3/8th Infantry: February to December 1970
6th Battalion, 29th Artillery, 105mm towed howitzers

2D BRIGADE DEPLOYMENTS
Arrived at Pleiku in August 1966
Remained in the Central Highlands
Moved to An Khe in July 1970
Left Vietnam in December 1970

2D BRIGADE UNITS
2/8th Infantry: to April 1970 (Mech after May 1967)
1/12th Infantry: to April 1970
1/22d Infantry: July 1966 to October 1970
3/8th Infantry: May 1969 to January 1970
1/35th Infantry: March and April 1970
2/35th Infantry: March and April 1970
4th Battalion, 42d Artillery, 105mm towed howitzers

3D BRIGADE DEPLOYMENTS
Arrived at Bear Cat in November 1966
Moved to Dau Tieng in December
Transferred to Pleiku in July 1967
Moved to Cu Chi and Tay Ninh in
  August 1967

3D BRIGADE UNITS
2/12th Infantry: full tour
2/22d Infantry (Mech): full tour
3/22d Infantry: full tour
2d Battalion, 77th Artillery, 105mm towed howitzers

In August 1967 the Brigade was exchanged with 25th Division's 3d Brigade

3D BRIGADE DEPLOYMENTS
Joined at Pleiku
Stationed at Dak To in March 1968
Covered Pleiku and Kontum Province
  from April 1968
Left Vietnam in April 1970

3D BRIGADE UNITS
1/14th Infantry: to January 1970
1/35th Infantry: to January 1970
2/35th Infantry: to January 1970
1/50th Infantry (Mech): March and April 1968
2/8th Infantry (Mech): February to April 1970
3/12th Infantry: February to April 1970
2d Battalion, 9th Artillery, 105mm towed howitzers

DIVISIONAL ARTILLERY
5th Battalion, 16th Artillery, 155mm towed/8in self-propelled howitzers
2/8th Infantry (Mech) and 3/12th Infantry were based at Pleiku under 4th Division's
  direct control from May to December 1970

OPERATIONS

1966
1ST BRIGADE
26 Oct–30 Mar   Adams: secured the rice harvest in Phu Yen province

2D BRIGADE
21 Jul–5 Sept   John Paul Jones: secured Tuy Hoa and Vung Ro Bay
4 Sept–25 Oct   Seward: secured the rice harvest in Phu Yen province
End Oct   Operation Paul Revere III and IV in the Chu Pon and Ia Drang areas

Purple smoke guides a resupply helicopter into the landing zone. (111-CC-65033)

3D BRIGADE

Oct	Reinforced Operation Attleboro in War Zone C, Tay Ninh Province
25 Oct–28 Nov	Bremerton: search and destroy operation in Rung Sat Special Zone
28 Nov–14 May	Fort Nisqually: moved to Dau Tieng to start operations in Binh Duong
30 Nov	Fairfax: a battalion joined the ARVN around Saigon

1967

1ST BRIGADE IN PLEIKU AND KONTUM PROVINCES, II CORPS

5 Apr–12 Oct	Francis Marion: stopping NVA infiltration in the Central Highlands
26 Apr–22 May	Hancock I: search and destroy operation north of Ban Me Thout
16 Jun–12 Oct	Greely: protecting Dak To Special Forces Camp
12 Oct	MacArthur: combination of Operations Greenly and Francis Marion

2D BRIGADE IN PLEIKU AND KONTUM PROVINCES, II CORPS

1 Jan–5 Apr	Sam Houston: search and destroy operation and border surveillance
5 Apr–12 Oct	Francis Marion: stopping NVA infiltration in the Central Highlands

3D BRIGADE IN III CORPS

1–20 Feb	Gadsen: search and destroy in War Zone C, Tay Ninh Province
21 Feb–14 May	Junction City: search for the Central Office for South Vietnam
23 Apr–7 June	Manhattan: Boi Loi woods and Long Nguyen forest
13–18 May	Ahina: search and destroy in Tay Ninh Province, War Zone C
June	Moved to I Corps with Task Force Oregon

1968

1ST BRIGADE

All year	MacArthur: sweeping the Central Highlands
May and June	Mathews: operation in Kontum Province

A guide runs to greet members of 4th Division's War Dog detachment as they come into land. (111-CC-55987)

2D BRIGADE

All year	MacArthur: sweeping the Central Highlands

3D BRIGADE

20 Jan–1 Mar	Pershing II: securing Binh Dinh province
1–31 Mar	Patrick: continuation of Pershing II
31 Mar–31 Jan	Cochise Green/Dan Sinh: Binh Dinh and Quang Ngai provinces

1969

1 Feb	Operation Hines: start of sweeps across the Central Highlands, each brigade covered a province with a number of smaller named operations. Separate security operations also took place along the road network

1ST BRIGADE ACROSS BINH DINH PROVINCE

1–28 Feb	Wayne Arrow, Wayne Dart, Wayne Green
1 Mar–18 Oct	Wayne Grey and Wayne Javelin
15–30 July	Gaffey Blue: security operation
10 Sept–4 Jan	Wayne Boulder, Wayne Breaker and Wayne Rock
11 Nov–30 Dec	Spragins White: security operation

2D BRIGADE ACROSS KONTUM AND BINH DINH PROVINCES

31 Jan–16 June	Putnam Panther: clear and search with 3d Brigade
16 Apr–22 Sept	Putnam Tiger: clear and search with 3d Brigade
21 Sept–28 Oct	Putnam Cougar: clear and search in Binh Dinh province
20 Oct–19 Nov	Hodges Black: security across Pleiku Province
1 Nov–18 Jan	Putnam Wildcat: clear and search in Binh Dinh province
2 Dec–5 Jan	Hughes Black: security across Binh Dinh

3D BRIGADE ACROSS PLEIKU, DARLAC AND KONTUM PROVINCES

31 Jan–2 April	Greene Blue, Greene Storm, Greene Cyclone, Greene Thunder, Greene Tornado, Greene Typhoon and Greene Hurricane
1 Feb–14 May	Greene Queen and Greene Lion
14 Apr–4 Aug	Greene Orange, Greene Basket, Greene Gallop, Greene Ax and Greene Jack
4 Aug–16 Oct	Greene Ace
16 Oct–30 Jan	Greene Bear and Greene Bullet

14 Oct–24 Nov	Hartle Green: security across Binh Dinh and Pleiku Provinces
16 Oct–30 Jan	Kramer White and Waldron Blue: security across Pleiku Province
11 Nov–30 Dec	Spragins White: security across Darlac Province

1970

DIVISIONAL CONTROL OF UNITS ON SECURITY OPERATIONS ACROSS PLEIKU PROVINCE

1 Mar–17 Nov	Park Silver/Hancock Dragon
14 May–28 June	Cheadle Blue, Robertson White, Wright Blue and Clemens Green
2 July–12 Oct	Brandeis Blue and Murray Blue

1ST BRIGADE ACROSS BINH DINH PROVINCE

4 Jan–16 Mar	Wayne Thrust and Wayne Stab
11 Mar–30 Apr	Earhart White and Eichelberger Black: security sweeps
4–16 May	Tame the West (Binh Tay I): invasion of the Fishhook and Parrot's Beak areas of Cambodia
15 May–14 July	Wayne Jump, Wayne Hurdle and Wayne Fast
16 July–27 Aug	Wayne Span and Wayne Pierce
28 Aug–17 Nov	Wayne Forge and Wayne Sabre
Nov and Dec	Keystone Robin (Bravo): increment V redeployment from Vietnam

2D BRIGADE ACROSS KONTUM AND BINH DINH PROVINCES

18 Jan–7 Feb	Putnam Power
30 Jan–11 Mar	Putnam Shark
11 Mar–30 Apr	Earhart White and Eichelberger Black: security sweeps
30 Apr–4 May	Plateau and Baird Silver: combat operations in Binh Dinh province
4–16 May	Tame the West (Binh Tay I): invasion of the Fishhook and Parrot's Beak areas of Cambodia
18–30 May	Fredenhall Gold: security and combat operation
18 May–12 Oct	Putnam Paragon
12–24 Oct	Putnam Valley
Nov and Dec	Keystone Robin (Bravo): increment V redeployment from Vietnam

3D BRIGADE IN PLEIKU PROVINCE

| 30 Jan–17 Mar | Greene Deuce |
| Apr | Keystone Blue Jay: Increment III redeployment |

Many items have been wrapped in plastic while haversacks have to be carried to keep them dry as a patrol wades across a stream during Operation Francis Marion. (111-CC-44503)

9th Infantry Division insignia.

9TH INFANTRY DIVISION

1ST BRIGADE DEPLOYMENTS

January 1967 arrived at Bear Cat

February 1968 moved to Dong Tam

June 1968 moved to Tan An

November 1968 returned to Dong Tam

August 1969 left Vietnam

1ST BRIGADE UNITS

2/39th Infantry: full tour

3/39th Infantry: from March 1969

4/39th Infantry: to January 1968, returned December 1968

6/31st Infantry: July 1968 to May 1970

2/47th Infantry (Mechanized): June 1967 to May 1968

2/60th Infantry: April to November 1968

2D BRIGADE DEPLOYMENTS

January 1967 arrived at Phu My

Provided the combat troops for the Mobile Riverine Force and moved to Dong Tam in May 1967

July 1969 left Vietnam

2D BRIGADE UNITS

2/47th Infantry (Mechanized): until May 1967 returned June and July 1968

3/47th Infantry (Riverine): full tour

4/47th Infantry (Riverine): full tour

3/60th Infantry (Riverine): from March 1967

3D BRIGADE DEPLOYMENT

December 1966 arrived at Bear Cat

January 1967 to Tan An and My Tho

November 1968 moved to Rach Kien

Remained behind when 9th Division left Vietnam in August 1969, joining 25th Division at Binh Phuoc

Entered Cambodia in May and June 1970 then returned to Binh Phuoc

Left Vietnam in Oct 1970

3D BRIGADE UNITS

5/60th Infantry (Mech): full tour (dismounted in September 1968)

3/60th Infantry: to February 1967

2/60th Infantry: to March 1968

3/39th Infantry: to February 1969

6/31st Infantry: April 1968 to June 1968

4/39th Infantry: February 1968 to November 1968

2/47th Infantry (Mech): from August 1968

2/60th Infantry: from December 1968

BRIGADE ARTILLERY

2d Battalion, 4th Artillery (105mm): 2d Brigade full tour

1st Battalion, 11th Artillery (105mm): 2d Brigade

3d Battalion, 34th Artillery (105mm) (Riverine): 3d Brigade until it became Riverine

Divisional Artillery: 1st Battalion, 84th Artillery (155mm) and Battery H, 29th Artillery (Searchlight)

OPERATIONS

1966

18 Oct–1 Feb	Duck: deployment from Vung Tau to Bear Cat

1967

1ST BRIGADE

29 Jan–15 Apr	Big Spring, Pittsburg and Junction City: engaged in War Zone D
20 Apr–21 Mar	Kittyhawk: securing 11th Armored Cavalry Regiment's Camp
13–18 May	Ahina: combined operation in War Zone C
5–7 Jun	Rocket: search and destroy in Bien Hoa province
9–29 Jun	Akron II: with 11th Armored Cavalry east of Saigon
3 Jul–18 Sept	Riley I and II: clearing Bien Hoa and Phuoc Tuy provinces
1 Sept	Operation Strike began in Bien Hoa province
26 Sept–21 Oct	Akron III: with 11th Armored Cavalry in Bien Hoa province
17 Nov	Operations Strike and Uniontown were consolidated

During the immediate aftermath of the Tet Offensive, a grunt watches as helicopter gunships target a surrounded Viet Cong position near Long Binh. (111-CC-45845)

17 Dec–17 Feb	Manchester: continuation of Operation Strike/Uniontown
17–20 Oct	Don Ched I: search and destroy operation in Bien Hoa province
20 Oct –7 Apr	Narasuan: search and destroy in Bien Hoa province

2D BRIGADE – MOBILE RIVERINE FORCE IN THE MEKONG DELTA

6 Jan–1 Jun	Palm Beach I and II: secure the area around Dong Tam base camp
1 Jun–7 Feb	Hoptac: search and destroy across Dinh Tuong province
Jun 1967– July 1968	Coronado I-XI: Riverine operations across the Mekong Delta to secure villages, rivers, canals and open Route 4
Jun–Dec	Tiger Coronado I-XI: Riverine operations across Rung Sat Special Zone
13–20 June	Great Bend: clearing the Long Tau shipping channel
19 June	Concordia began: clearing Soi Rap River in Long An province
21 July–14 Sept	Emporia I to IV: securing Long Khanh province
16–24 Nov	Kien Giang 9-1: clearing the Kien Giang river

3D BRIGADE

6 Jan–1 June	Palm Beach I and II: operations in Rung Sat Special Zone
7–19 Jan	Silver Lake: clearing Hat Dich Special Zone in Long An province
Feb	Bunker Hill and Brandywine: operations in Dinh Tuong province
13 Feb	Enterprise: start of twelve months of operations around Rach Kien
16 Feb–20 Mar	River Raider I: checking canals in the Rung Sat Special Zone
6–14 July	Paddington: search and destroy operation
16–24 Nov	Kien Giang 9-1: operations across Dinh Truong province

1968

11–21 Jan	Akron V: 1st Brigade cleared Binh Son rubber plantation
Feb	Tet Offensive: Viet Cong attacked targets across IV Corps

1ST AND 2D BRIGADES

After restoring order the two brigades worked alongside the ARVN People's Road operations in Dinh Tuong and Kien Tuong provinces

An Armored Troop Carrier beaches along the My Tho River during an operation by the Mobile Riverine Force. (111-CC-43673)

1 Mar–3 Aug	Truong Cong Dinh: secured Route 4
17 Mar–30 Jul	Duong Cua Dan: security for engineers repairing the roads
17 Jul–4 Mar	Quyet Chien: security along the roads
1 May–16 Dec	Kudzu I and II: continued security around Dong Tam base
1 Dec	Speedy Express started: security of Dinh Tuong and Kien Hoa provinces

3D BRIGADE

10 Mar–8 Apr	Resolve to Win (Quyet Thang): clearing around Saigon after Tet
7 Apr–31 May	Complete Victory (Toan Thang): securing the provinces around Saigon
1 Jun	Toan Thang becomes Toan Thang II

1969
1ST BRIGADE

| 31 May | Speedy Express ended and the brigade prepared to withdraw |

2D BRIGADE

| 1 Jan–31 Aug | Rice Farmer: security with the ARVN across the Delta |

3D BRIGADE

| 16 Feb–31 Oct | Toan Thang III: security in the provinces north of Saigon |
| 1 Jul–31 Aug | Keystone Eagle: 1st and 2d Brigades left Vietnam while 3d Brigade joined 25th Infantry Division, west of Saigon |

1970

| 1 Jul–15 Oct | Keystone Robin (Alpha), Increment IV redeployment of 3d Brigade |

23D INFANTRY DIVISION (AMERICAL)

The division was organized in Vietnam in September 1967 by the amalgamation of 11th, 198th and 199th Infantry Brigades. It was based at Chu Lai in the southern part of I Corps, covering Quang Tin and Quang Ngai Provinces. 196th Brigade continued to serve as an independent brigade when the division was inactivated in Nov 1971.

11TH BRIGADE DEPLOYMENTS
Joined the Division at Duc Pho
July 1971 moved to Chu Lai
Inactivated in November 1971

11TH BRIGADE UNITS
3/1st Infantry: full tour
1/20th Infantry: full tour
4/21st Infantry: to June 1971
4/3d Infantry: to July 1971
1/52d Infantry: from August 1971
6th Battalion, 11th Artillery, 105mm towed howitzers

196TH BRIGADE DEPLOYMENTS
Joined at Chu Lai
May 1971 moved to Da Nang
Became independent in October 1971
Left Vietnam in June 1972

196TH BRIGADE UNITS
2/1st Infantry: full tour
3/21st Infantry: full tour
4/31st Infantry: full tour
1/46th Infantry: from August 1971
1/6th Infantry: from November 1971
1st Battalion, 14th Artillery, 105mm towed howitzers

198TH BRIGADE DEPLOYMENTS
October 1967 arrived at Duc Pho and
  moved to Chu Lai and Tam Ky in
  December
Inactivated in November 1971

198TH BRIGADE UNITS
1/6th Infantry: to October 1971
1/46th Infantry: to July 1971
1/52d Infantry: to July 1971
4/3d Infantry: from August 1971
5/46th Infantry: from March 1968
1st Battalion, 14th Artillery, 105mm towed howitzers

23d Infantry Division (Americal) insignia.

DIVISIONAL ARTILLERY
3d Battalion, 18th Artillery, with 175mm and 8in self-propelled howitzers joined in February 1968. 1st Battalion, 82d Artillery and 3d Battalion, 16th Artillery, joined six months later; both were armed with 155mm towed and 8in self-propelled howitzers.

OPERATIONS

1967
4 Oct	Wallowa began: 196th Brigade with 1st Cavalry Division in Quang Nam and Quang Tin Provinces. 11th and 198th brigades arrived soon after and the three formed 23d Americal Division
11 Nov	Operation Wallowa was consolidated with Operation Wheeler, the start of twelve months of sweeps across the southern half of I Corps
18 Dec–10 Jun	Muscatine: search and destroy operation in Quang Ngai province

1968
28 Feb–29 Sept	Napoleon/Saline: keeping the road open to Dong Ha port
8 Mar–17 May	Carentan I and II: Quang Tri and Thua Thien provinces
16 Mar	Men of 11th Brigade committed the My Lai massacre near Quang Ngai
4 Apr–11 Nov	Burlington Trail: sweeps along the Quang Tin and Quang Nam border
10–12 May	Golden Valley: the relief of Kham Duc Special Forces Camp
5 July–3 Aug	Pocahontas Forest: across Quang Nam and Quang Tri Provinces
14 Dec–28 Feb	Fayette Canyon: 196th Brigade sweep across Quang Nam Province

1969
12 Jan–21 Jul	Bold Mariner/Russell Beach: Task Force Cooksey blocked the southern end of Batangan Peninsula in Quang Ngai while Marines cleared it
28 Feb	Iron Mountain: 11th Brigade began operations in Quang Ngai Province

A Chinook helicopter delivers a 105mm howitzer to a fire base. (111-CC-107287)

| 18 Mar | Frederick Hall: 196th Brigade in Quang Nam and Quang Tin Provinces |
| 16 May–13 Aug | Lamar Plain: operations southwest of Tam Ky |

1970

All year	11th Brigade continued Operation Iron Mountain
All year	196th Brigade continued Operation Frederick Hall
Feb	Nantucket Beach: 198th Brigade returned to the Batangan Peninsula
12 Jul–20 Sept	Elk Canyon I and II: 196th Brigade at Kham Duc in Quang Tri province

1971

30 Jan–6 Apr	11th Brigade supported Lam Son 719, the ARVN attack into Laos
28 Feb	Iron Mountain and Frederick Hall ended
1 Mar–1 July	Finney Hill and Middlesex Peak: Quang Tin and Quang Ngai provinces
29 Apr–1 July	Caroline Hill: operations across Quang Nam province
1 Sept–29 Nov	Keystone Oriole (Charlie): Increment IX redeployment begins; 196th Brigade remained behind as an independent brigade

1972

| 1 May–30 Jun | Keystone Pheasant: 196th Brigade left in Increment XII redeployment. |

25TH INFANTRY DIVISION

1ST BRIGADE DEPLOYMENTS

April 1966 arrived at Cu Chi
March 1968 moved to Tay Ninh
May and June 1970 in Cambodia
July 1970 returned to Tay Ninh
August 1970 moved to Dau Tieng
Left Vietnam in December 1970

1ST BRIGADE UNITS

4/9th Infantry: full tour
2/14th Infantry: until January 1970
3/22d Infantry: February to November 1970
4/23d Infantry: full tour (Mechanized by January 1967)
7th Battalion, 11th Artillery, 105mm towed howitzers

2D BRIGADE DEPLOYMENTS

Arrived at Cu Chi in January 1966

March and April 1970 at Long Thanh

May 1970 in Cambodia

June 1970 withdrew to Tay Ninh

July 1970 moved to Xuan Loc

Left Vietnam in April 1971

2D BRIGADE UNITS

1/5th Infantry (Mech): full tour

2/12th Infantry from February 1970

3/22d Infantry from December 1970

1/27th Infantry: full tour (except February to April 1970)

2/27th Infantry: to December 1970

1st Battalion, 8th Artillery, 105mm towed howitzers

25th Infantry Division insignia.

3D BRIGADE DEPLOYMENTS

Arrived at Pleiku in January 1966

Covered Duc Pho from June 1967

Moved to Cu Chi and Tay Ninh in
  August 1967

3D BRIGADE UNITS

1/14th Infantry: full period

1/35th Infantry: full period

2/35th Infantry: full period

2d Battalion, 77th Artillery, 105mm towed howitzers

In August 1967 the Brigade was exchanged with 4th Division's 3d Brigade

3D BRIGADE DEPLOYMENTS

August 1967 joined at Cu Chi

Moved to Dau Tieng in March 1968

August 1969 returned to Cu Chi

Left Vietnam in December 1970

3D BRIGADE UNITS

2/22d Infantry (Mech): full tour

2/12th Infantry: to January 1970

3/22d Infantry: to January 1970

2/14th Infantry: from February 1970

1/27th Infantry: February to April 1970

2d Battalion, 9th Artillery, 105mm towed howitzers

DIVISIONAL ARTILLERY

3d Battalion, 13th Artillery, was armed with 155mm towed and 8in self-propelled
  howitzers.

OPERATIONS

1965

23 Dec–23 Jan	Blue Light (Holokai XII): C-133s and C-141s from 60th and 61st USAF Military Airlift Wings flew 3d Brigade from Hawaii to Pleiku

1966

1ST BRIGADE AROUND CU CHI IN HAU NGHIA PROVINCE

6–7 Mar	Fort Smith: search and destroy and pacification along Highway 1
16–27 May	Wahiawa: Boi Loi woods, Ho Bo woods and the Filhol plantation
6–9 Jun	Joliet, Fargo, Helemano: search and destroy operations around Cu Chi
2–31 Jul	Kahana I and II: Long Khanh and Binh Tuy provinces
5 Aug–5 Nov	Akron: search and destroy north of Cu Chi
1–31 Aug	Oahu: search and destroy in Tay Ninh Province
31 Aug–12 Sept	Kipapa: search and destroy in Filhol Plantation
14 Sept	Lanikai: start of a six-month pacification operation in Long An province
15 Sept–14 Nov	Kalihi and Kamuela: Boi Loi woods, Filhol and Ben Cui plantations
24 Oct–12 Feb	Thayer II: search and destroy on the coast of Binh Dinh province
30 Nov	Fairfax: battalion joins the ARVN to improve security around Saigon
1 Dec	Ala Moana: start of a six-month operation to secure the rice producing areas west of Saigon
12–13 Dec	Asheville: search and destroy operation around Cu Chi

2D BRIGADE ARRIVED IN JANUARY AND STARTED SEARCH AND DESTROY OPERATIONS AROUND CU CHI

Feb	Bobcat Tracker, Taro Leaf, Paddy Bridge, Clean Sweep and Kolchak I
Mar	Waikiki, Honolulu and Kamehameha
28 Mar–5 Apr	Circle Pines: sweep of Ho Bo woods and Filhol plantation
6 Apr–12 May	Kahuku, Makaha, Kaena, Kalamazoo, Kahala and Maili
2–12 May	Lihue: secured Routes 1 and 22 from Cu Chi to Tay Ninh
16–27 May	Wahiawa: operations in Boi Loi and Ho Bo woods, and Filhol plantation
3 Jun–4 July	Maikiki, Mexacali, Santa Fe and Coco Palms: Boi Loi woods
2–31 Jul	Kahana I and II Long Khanh and Binh Tuy provinces
8 Jul–6 Aug	Ewa, Fresno, Mokuliea and Coco Head: across Hau Nghia province
7 Aug–1 Sept	Aiea and Lahaina: operations around Cu Chi
1 Sept–14 Nov	Sunset Beach and Kailua: operations around Cu Chi
24 Oct–12 Feb	Thayer II: search and destroy on the coast of Binh Dinh province

3D BRIGADE ACROSS DARLAC. PLEIKU AND PHU BON PROVINCES WITH 1ST CAVALRY DIVISION

20 Jan–21 Feb	Kamehameha and Taylor: secured the roads around Kontum and Pleiku
25 Feb–24 Mar	Garfield: search and destroy in Darlac province
Mar 25–17 Apr	Lincoln (I, II and III / Mosby I): search and destroy across the Chu Pong and the Ia Drang River on the Cambodian border
14 Mar–5 May	Wyatt Earp and Buchanan: along Highway 19 from Qhi Nhon to Pleiku
13 Apr–1 May	Longfellow: opening Highway 14 from Dak To to Dak Pek
10 May–31 Jul	Paul Revere: reinforced Plei Me Special Force camp
1–25 Aug	Paul Revere II: Chu Pong War Zone

Troops run to establish a firing position along the tree line moments after their helicopter has touched down during Operation Wahiwa. (111-CC-34612)

Gas masks protect these men while they wait to see if CS gas causes any Viet Cong to break cover during Operation Tra Hung Doa. (111-CC-46675)

26 Aug–10 Oct	Paul Revere III: Chu Pong and Ia Drang area
10 Oct–31 Dec	Paul Revere IV: reinforced by 1st Cavalry Division
24 Oct–12 Feb	Thayer II: search and destroy on the coast of Binh Dinh province
1–25 Nov	Attleboro: in War Zone C

1967

WHOLE DIVISION

5–27 Jan	Niagara or Cedar Falls: formed the anvil along the Saigon River during sweeping operations through the Iron Triangle
1–20 Feb	Gadsen: search and destroy operation in War Zone C
21 Feb–14 May	Junction City: sweep through War Zone C, Tay Ninh Province

A platoon returns fire following an ambush in heavy undergrowth in War Zone C. (111-CC-39092)

1ST BRIGADE IN TAY NINH AND BINH DUONG PROVINCES

18 Mar–21 Apr	Makalapa I and II: search and destroy operations
23 Apr–7 June	Manhattan: Boi Loi woods and Long Nguyen forest
13–18 May	Ahina: combined search and destroy operation in War Zone C
19 May–24 Aug	Barking Sands, Waimea, Kunia , Kawala and Akumu: Ho Bo woods, Bui Loi woods, Fillhol plantation and the Iron Triangle
14 Sept–13 Feb	Lanikai: pacification of Long An province

2D BRIGADE IN HAU NGHIA, TAY NINH, AND BINH DUONG PROVINCES, III CORPS

7 Mar–8 Apr	Waialua: search and destroy operation along the border
23 Apr–7 June	Manhattan: Boi Loi woods and Long Nguyen forest
13 May–7 Dec	Kole Kole: search and destroy operation along the border
18 Nov–23 Dec	Atlanta: search and destroy across Binh Duong and Hau Nghia
7 Dec–24 Feb	Yellowstone and Saratoga: search and destroy in War Zone C, Tay Ninh
16–31 Dec	Camden: search and destroy operation

3D BRIGADE IN PLEIKU AND KONTUM PROVINCES

1 Jan–5 Apr	Sam Houston: search and destroy and border surveillance operation
7–22 Apr	Lejune: with the 1st Cavalry Division and Marines in Quang Ngai
17 May–7 Dec	Diamond Head: search and destroy in War Zone C
18 Nov–23 Dec	Atlanta: search and destroy across Binh Duong and Hau Nghia
7 Dec–24 Feb	Yellowstone and Saratoga: search and destroy in War Zone C, Tay Ninh

1968

8 Mar–7 Apr	Wilderness: 1st Brigade search and destroy in Tay Ninh province
10 Mar–7 Apr	2d and 3d Brigades joined Operation Resolve to Win (Quyet Thang), securing the provinces around Saigon
7 Apr–31 May	Complete Victory (Toan Thang): securing the area around Saigon
1 Jun	Toan Thang II began: securing provinces around Saigon
24–30 Nov	Piedmont Swift: 2d Brigade in Hau Nghia province

1969

5–17 Jan	Big Muddy: 3rd Brigade along the Saigon river
22 Jan–3 Feb	Wheeler Place: 2d Brigade in Binh Duong
16 Feb	Toan Thang II became Toan Thang III
1 Nov	Toan Thang III became Toan Thang IV
21 Oct–11 Jan	Cliff Dweller I to IV: 1st Brigade on Black Virgin Mountain, Tay Ninh

1970

CAMBODIAN INVASIONS

14–17 Apr	Toan Thang 41: 3d Brigade advanced into the Angel's Wing
4 May–28 Jun	Bold Lancer I and II: 1st Brigade advanced into Cambodia
6–14 May	Toan Thang 44: 2d Brigade crossed the border from Tay Ninh
16 Oct–31 Dec	Keystone Robin (Bravo): redeployment (Increment V)

1971

1 Jan–30 Apr	Keystone Robin (Charlie): 2d Brigade redeployment (Increment VI)

101st AIRBORNE DIVISION (AIRMOBILE)
THE SCREAMING EAGLES

1st Brigade arrived in July 1965; the rest of the division deployed in November 1967. The Division reorganized from an Airborne to an Airmobile formation in the summer of 1968 to increase its operating range.

1ST BRIGADE DEPLOYMENTS

July 1965 arrived at Qui Nhon
October 1965 moved to Cam Ranh Bay
November 1965 moved to Bien Hoa
December 1965 moved to Phan Rang and Duc Pho
January 1968 engaged at Song Be
February moved to Hue and Phu Bai
November returned to Bien Hoa
It returned to the Hue and Phu Bai area
  in December 1969
Left Vietnam in October 1971

1ST BRIGADE UNITS

2/502d Infantry: full tour
1/327th Infantry: until November 1971
2/327th Infantry: until December 1971
3/506th Infantry: October 1967 to April 1968
3/506th Infantry: from September 1970
2d Battalion, 320th Artillery, 105mm
  towed howitzers

2D BRIGADE DEPLOYMENTS

December 1967 arrived at Cu Chi
February 1968 engaged in Hue
March 1968 engaged in Quang Tri province
Moved to Bien Hoa and Van Xa in November
Moved to Phu Bai in April 1970
Left Vietnam in January 1972

2D BRIGADE UNITS

1/501st Infantry: full tour
2/501st Infantry: to October 1971
1/502d Infantry: full tour
1st Battalion, 321st Artillery, 105mm
  towed howitzers

3D BRIGADE DEPLOYMENTS

Arrived at Phuoc Vinh in December 1967
Moved to Bien Hoa in November 1968
Based in the A Shau Valley in August 1969
Moved to Bien Hoa in September 1969
Relocated to Phong Dien in December 1969
Moved to Hue and Phu Bai in September 1970

3D BRIGADE UNITS

3/187th Infantry: full tour
1/506th Infantry: full tour
2/506th Infantry: full tour
2d Battalion, 319th Artillery 105mm
  towed howitzers

101st Airborne (Airmobile) Division insignia.

Based at Camp Carroll in March and April 1971
May 1971 moved to Hue and Phu Bai
Left Vietnam in December 1971

DIVISIONAL ARTILLERY
2d Battalion, 11th Artillery and its 155mm towed howitzers
was assigned in June 1968

OPERATIONS

1965
1ST BRIGADE
19–22 Aug	Cutlass: cooperated with Special Forces south of Nha Trang
25 Aug–1 Oct	Ramrod and Highland: opened Route 19 from Qui Nhon and An Khe
18–23 Sept	Gibraltar: search and destroy northeast of An Khe
18 Sept–19 Oct	Good Friend I: secured Cam Ranh Bay area
28 Sept–13 Nov	Good Friend II (Sayonara): secured Qui Nhon area
28 Nov–16 Dec	Checkerboard II and Bushmaster III: cleared Binh Duong province

1966
1ST BRIGADE
3–17 Jan	Hang Over, Quick Hop and Tyler: operations in Binh Thuan province
17 Jan–20 Feb	Van Buren: rice harvest security south of Tuy Hoa in Phu Yen Province
21 Feb–24 Mar	Harrison (or Reconstruction): search and destroy in the same area
25 Mar–12 Apr	Fillmore: continuation of Operation Harrison
12 Apr–18 May	Austin I to IV: operations astride the border between II and III Corps
1–21 Jun	Hawthorne: relief of Tou Morong Special Forces camp in Kontum
24 Jun–15 Jul	Beauregard: border watch in the western highlands around Dak To
20 Jun–2 Jul	Nathan Hale: operation north of Tuy Hoa in Phu Yen province

Troopers return fire from abandoned Viet Cong trenches during Operation Hawthorne. (111-CC-35684)

2–30 Jul	Henry Clay: follow-up to Nathan Hale
4 Sept–25 Oct	Seward: search and destroy across Phu Yen province
26 Oct–3 Mar	Adams: protecting the rice harvest around Tuy Hoa and Tuy An
30 Oct–4 Dec	Geronimo I: search and destroy operation
6 Dec–19 Jan	Pickett: search and destroy operation in Kontum province

1967

26 Jan–23 Mar	Farragut, Gatling I and II: search and destroy operations across Ninh Thuan, Lam Dong, Binh Thuan and Binh Tuy provinces
29 Mar–29 Apr	Summerall I, II and III: search and destroy operations across Phu Yen, Darlac and Khanh Hoa provinces
May	Joined Task Force Oregon and moved north into I Corps
10 May–2 Aug	Malheur I and II: clearing Highway 1 across Quang Ngai province
6 Jul–11 Sept	Lake, Hood River, Benton and Cook: operations across Quang Ngai and Quang Tin provinces
11 Sept–25 Nov	Wheeler: search and destroy
Nov	Eagle Thrust: start of deployment of 101st Airborne to South Vietnam, completed in December
11–30 Nov	Rose: search and destroy operation Binh Thuan, Ninh Thuan provinces
1 Dec–8 Jan	Start of Klamath Falls: Binh Thuan, Lam Dong, and Binh Tuy provinces
17 Dec	Manchester replaced Uniontown: search and destroy north of the Dong Nai River across Bien Hoa, Binh Duong, Long Khanh and Phuoc Long provinces

1968

12 Jan–7 Feb	Manchester: secured the area north of the Dong Nai river
15 Jan–9 Feb	San Angelo: 1st Brigade in Quang Duc and Phuoc Long provinces
21–27 Jan	Attalla: 2d Brigade operation in Binh Long province

A helicopter collects supplies from the congested Fire Base Berchtesgaden. (111-CC-50499)

1ST AND 2D BRIGADES MOVED NORTH TO QUANG TRI AND THUA THIEN PROVINCES IN I CORPS

21 Jan–31 Mar	Jeb Stuart: combined operation between Quang Tri and Hue
26 Feb–30 Apr	Houston and Mingo: 1st Brigade with the Marines in Thua Thien
8 Mar–17 May	Carentan I and II: combined in Quang Tri and Thua Thien provinces
18 Apr–17 May	Delaware/Lam Son 216: Quang Tri and Thua Thien, A Shau Valley
7–18 Jun	Banjo Royce: Lam Dong and Tuyen Duc provinces
4–20 Aug	Somerset Plain / Lam Son 246: Thua Thien province, A Shau Valley
10–20 Sept	Vinh Loc: pacification of Thua Thien province
20 Sept–9 Jan	Phu Vang I to IV: operations across Thua Thien province

The unacceptable face of search and destroy missions; a trooper sets fire to a Viet Cong store house during Operation Van Buren. (111-CC-33189)

3D BRIGADE OPERATED WITH 199TH BRIGADE AND 11TH ARMORED REGIMENT UNTIL SEPTEMBER

31 Jan–Mar	Units engaged in securing Saigon after the Tet Offensive
Mar	Harrisburg, Valley Forge and Box Springs: operations north of Saigon
23 Mar–7 Apr	Clarksville and Los Banos: security operations in Bien Hoa province
24 May–12 Jun	Mathews: combined operation in Kontum province
1 Jun	Start of Toan Thang II, clearing provinces north of Saigon
16 Sept–19 Oct	Golden Sword: moved north to I Corps
16–24 Dec	Rawlings Valley: Thua Thien province

1969

1ST BRIGADE

20 Feb–15 May	Spokane Rapids, Platte Canyon and Bristol Boots: clearing the Ruong Ruong Valley on the border of Thua Thien and Quang Nam provinces.
16 May–13 Aug	Lamar Plain: clearing southwest of Tam Ky in Quang Tin province
18 Aug–28 Sept	Cumberland Thunder: operations across Thua Thien province
29 Sept–6 Dec	Republic Square: Quang Tri and Thau Thien provinces

2D BRIGADE

25 Jan–9 Feb	Sherman Peak: operation in Thua Thien province
28 Feb–8 May	Massachusetts Striker: operations in the A Shau Valley
23 Jun–1 Jul	Tennessee Pride: operations in Thua Thien province
12 Jul–15 Aug	Campbell Steamer: operations in Quang Nam and Thua Thien
15 Aug–28 Sept	Claiborne Chute: securing the rice harvest around Hue
28 Sept–6 Dec	Republic Square: continuation of Claiborne Chute

3D BRIGADE

24–28 Jan	Ohio Rapids: reconnaissance across Thua Thien province
28 Feb–15 Aug	Kentucky Jumper: operations across Thua Thien province
10 May–7 Jun	Apache Snow: operations around A Shau Valley including the battle for Ap Bia Mountain which became known as Hamburger Hill
7 Jun–14 Aug	Montgomerey Rendezvous: continuation of operations in A Shau Valley

14 Aug–28 Sept	Carolina Blaster, Louisiana Lee and Richland Square: operations in the A Shau and Da Krong valleys
28 Sept–6 Dec	Republic Square: continuation of the A Shau Valley operations
29 Sept–8 Nov	Norton Falls: screened the deployment of the 4th Marines
6 Dec–31 Mar	Randolph Glen: securing the populated areas around A Shau Valley
5 Oct–4 Dec	Saturate

1970

1 Apr	Texas Star: continuation of Randolph Glen
Jul–Aug	Clinch Valley, Chicago Peak and Comeback Ridge: 3rd Brigade
5 Sept	Jefferson Glenn began: continuation of Operation Texas Star

1971

30 Jan–6 Mar	Dewey Canyon II: operations across Quang Tri Province to draw attention from the ARVN's invasion of southern Laos (Lam Son 719)
10 Aug	Jefferson Glenn ended, the last major American offensive
Aug	Lam Son 720: handed over to the ARVN in Quang Tri and Thua Thien
1 Dec–31 Jan	Keystone Mallard: withdrew as part of Increment X

1ST MARINE DIVISION

Combat units had been landing in the southern part of I Corps since August 1965 and 7th Marine Regiment was the first complete Regiment to come ashore. Divisional Headquarters arrived at Chu Lai in February 1966 to take command of 1st, 5th and 7th Marine Regiments and in November 1966 it moved to Da Nang. Battalions started redeploying in September 1970 and by April 1971 the 1st Marine Division had left Vietnam.

1ST MARINE REGIMENT

DEPLOYMENTS

Arrived at Chu Lai in January 1966
Moved north to Da Nang in June 1966
Moved to Quang Tri in October 1967
Engaged in Hue in February and
 March 1968
Relieved Khe Sanh in April 1968
Moved to Da Nang in September 1968
Left Vietnam in May 1971

UNITS

1st Battalion from August 1965 to May 1971
2d Battalion from November 1965 to May 1971
3d Battalion from January 1966 to May 1971

5TH MARINE REGIMENT

DEPLOYMENTS

HQ arrived at Chu Lai in May 1966
Moved to Da Nang in June 1967
At Hoi An in January 1968
Engaged in Hue in February and
 Phu Loc in March 1968
Returned to Da Nang in August 1968
Left Vietnam in April 1971

UNITS

1st Battalion from May 1966 to April 1971
2d Battalion from April 1966 to March 1971
3d Battalion from May 1966 to March 1971

An assistant gunner calls for more ammunition for his M60 during a fire-fight. (127-GVC-A371714)

7TH MARINE REGIMENT

DEPLOYMENTS

Arrived at Chu Lai in August 1965

Moved to Da Nang in May 1967

Left Vietnam in October 1970

UNITS

1st Battalion from August 1965 to September 1970

2d Battalion from August 1965 to October 1970

3d Battalion from September 1965 to October 1970

Two Regiments were attached from the newly formed 5th Marine Division. 26th was attached in April 1967 and 27th Marine Regiment reinforced 1st Marine Division in the aftermath of the Tet Offensive.

26TH MARINE REGIMENT

DEPLOYMENTS

HQ arrived at Da Nang in April 1967

Moved north to Dong Ha in June 1967

Moved to Khe Sanh in December 1967

Beseiged at Khe Sanh for 86 days

Moved to Hoi An in May 1968

August 1968 moved to Phu Loc

South to Da Nang in November 1968

Left Vietnam in March 1970

UNITS

1st Battalion from September 1966 to March 1970

2d Battalion from August 1966 to March 1970

3d Battalion from August 1966 to March 1970

27TH MARINE REGIMENT

DEPLOYMENTS

HQ arrived at Da Nang in February 1968

Left Vietnam in September 1968

UNITS

1st Battalion: full tour

2d Battalion: full tour

3d Battalion: full tour

ARTILLERY: 1st, 2d, 3d and 4th Battalions, 11th Artillery Regiment, and 1st and 2d Battalions, 13th Artillery Regiment (from 5th Marine Division), armed with 105mm howitzers

1st 8in Howitzer Battery, 1st and 5th 155mm Gun Batteries

A quick pull from a buddy helps this Marine out of the mud as a patrol crosses a paddy field. (127-GVC-A370496)

OPERATIONS

1965

17–24 Aug	Starlite: first regimental-sized battle on the Van Tuong Peninsula
7 Sept	Piranha: operation on the Batangan Peninsula
25 Sept	Dagger Thrust: start of many amphibious raids along I Corps' coast
2–4 Oct	Quick Draw: search and destroy in Quang Ngai province
18–19 Oct	Triple Play: search and destroy in Quang Tin province
3–5 Nov	Black Ferret: search and destroy in Quang Ngai province
10–18 Nov	Blue Marlin I and II: amphibious landing north of Chu Lai
5 Dec	Dagger Thrust V: landing 30 miles north of Qui Nhon
8–15 Dec	Harvest Moon: Phuoc Ha Valley between Da Nang-and Chu Lai

1966

3–8 Jan	Long Lance: search and destroy in Quang Nam province
28 Jan–28 Feb	Double Eagle: landing south of Du Pho and search and destroy
27 Feb–3 Mar	New York: Phu Thu Peninsula near Phu Bai
Mar	Utah, Oregon, Texas and Indiana: operations across Quang Ngai
26 Mar–7 Apr	Jackstay: clearing Long Tau shipping channel in Rung Sat Special Zone
8–30 Apr	Nevada and Wyoming: Quang Tin Province and Cape Batangan
17 Apr–1 May	Virginia: search and destroy around Khe Sanh
21–23 Apr	Hot Springs: northwest of Quang Ngai
27 Apr–2 May	Osage: rice harvest protection in Thua Thien province
5–27 May	Yuma, Montgomery and Morgan: operations in Quang Ngai province
Jun	Operations Apache, Dodge, Jay and Oakland in Quang Tri province
18–27 Jun	Deckhouse I: amphibious landing south of Qui Nhon
25 Jun–2 Jul	Jay: operation northwest of Hue
6–14 Jul	Washington: reconnaissance across Quang Ngai province
7 Jul–4 Aug	Hastings: large operation across Quang Tri province
16–30 Jul	Deckhouse II: amphibious landing in support of Operation Hastings

26–29 Jul	Franklin: search and destroy operation in Quang Ngai province
2–8 Aug	Bucks: search and destroy south of Da Nang
16–29 Aug	Deckhouse III: landing in Binh Tuy province, east of Saigon
1–15 Sept	Troy, El Paso and Napa: operations in Quang Tin and Quang Nam
8–16 Sept	Fresno: search and destroy in Quang Ngai province
15–18 Sept	Deckhouse IV: landing between the DMZ and Cua Viet river
17–27 Sept	Golden Fleece: rice harvest protection in Quang Ngai province
28 Sept–3 Oct	Monterey: search and destroy in Quang Tin province
18–30 Oct	Kent and Dover: operation in Quang Ngai and Quang Tin provinces
5–27 Nov	Shasta I and Rico Blanco: search and destroy in Quang Nam province
30 Nov–6 Dec	Sutter: operation in Quang Tin province
6–21 Dec	Trinidad, Glenn and Shasta II: search and destroy in Quang Nam
12 Dec–21 Jan	Sierra: search and destroy in Quang Ngai province

1967

Jan	County Fair: security operations across Quang Nam province
23–28 Jan	Tuscaloosa: search and destroy in Quang Nam province
26 Jan–7 Apr	Desoto: operations southeast of Quang Ngai city
30 Jan–9 Feb	Trinity and Searcy: search and destroy in Quang Ngai province
31 Jan–3 Feb	Clay: search and destroy in Quang Tri province
12–28 Feb	Stone, Lanoke and Pulaski: search and destroy in Quang Nam province
17–22 Feb	Rio Grande: search and destroy in Quang Ngai province
16 Feb–3 Mar	Deckhouse VI: operation southeast of Quang Ngai city
Feb	Lafayette: search and destroy across Quang Nam province
13–18 Mar	Tippecanoe: search and destroy in Quang Ngai province
10 Mar–17 Apr	Yuba, New Castle and Humboldt: operations in Quang Nam
4–21 Apr	Big Horn II: search and destroy operation in Thua Thien province
28 Apr–14 May	Beaver Cage: landing northwest of Tam Ky
20 Apr–6 Jun	Union and Duval: operations in Quang Nam and Quang Tin provinces
15–28 May	Hickory/Beau Charger: search and destroy in Quang Tri province
6–11 Jun	Colgate: search and destroy operation in Thua Thien province

A squad wades across a stream during a routine patrol. (127-GVC-A800539)

The Bravo Bushmasters board a CH-53 helicopter so it can take them back to An Hoa base. (127-GVC-A372102)

13–22 Jun	Arizona: search and destroy in Quang Nam province
15 Jun–1 Jul	Adair and Calhoun: Quang Nam and Quang Tin provinces
16 Jul–31 Oct	Kingfisher and Ardmore: search and destroy in Quang Tri province
20–26 Jul	Bear Chain and Pecos: operations on the coast at Quang Tri and Hue
21–30 Jul	Beacon Guide: operation southeast of Hue
27 Aug–5 Sept	Yazoo: search and destroy in Happy Valley
4–28 Sept	Shelbyville and Swift: search and destroy operation in Quang Nam
11–20 Oct	Bastion Hill/Medina: Hai Long Forests in southern Quang Tri province
20 Oct–16 Feb	Osceola: continuation of Operation Medina
25 Oct–6 Nov	Granite: operation in Thua Thien province
1 Nov–31 Mar	Scotland: holding Khe Sanh and the surrounding hills
1 Nov–20 Jan	Lancaster I: search and destroy operation in Quang Tri province
4 Nov–28 Feb	Napoleon: keeping the supply line to Dong Ha open
6–17 Nov	Essex: search and destroy operation in Quang Nam province
17–21 Nov	Cove: operation in Thua Thien province
5–23 Dec	Pitt and Citrus: operation in Quang Nam province
26 Dec–1 Feb	Badger Tooth: Quang Tri and Thua Thien provinces
28 Dec–3 Jan	Auburn: security of Da Nang rocket belt

1968

23 Jan–28 Feb	Badger Catch and Saline: search and destroy in Quang Tri province
31 Jan–25 Feb	Tet Offensive and the battle to recapture Hue
26 Feb–26 Mar	Tampa and Worth: operation in Quang Nam province
26 Feb–12 Sept	Houston: operation along the Thua Thien and Quang Nam border
2–26 Mar	Mingo, Rock, Ford and Worth: Quang Nam and Thua Thien provinces
10–14 Apr	Jasper Square: search and destroy in Quang Nam province
14 Apr–28 Feb	Scotland II: clear and search around Khe Sanh
19–26 Apr	Baxter Garden: sweep through Thua Thien province

4 May–24 Aug   Allen Brook: clearing Go Noi Island and south of Da Nang

18 May–23 Oct   Mameluke Thrust: operation in Quang Nam and Thua Thien
                 provinces

5 Jul–3 Aug   Pocahontas forest: clear and search operation in Hiep Duc Valley

8–16 Aug   Dodge Valley: clear and search operation in Quang Nam province

11–28 Aug   Cochise: search and destroy in Quang Nam and Quang Tin provinces

29 Aug–9 Sept   Sussex Bay: clear and search operation in Quang Nam province

25 Sept–14 Oct   Owen Mesa: clear and search operation in Quang Nam and Thua
                  Thien

30 Sept–5 Oct   Talladega Canyon: clear and search operation in Quang Nam
                 province

5–19 Oct   Maui Peak: operation in Quang Nam province

23 Oct–6 Dec   Henderson Hill, Garrad Bay, Sabine Draw, Nicoliet Bay and Meade
                River: search and clear operations in Quang Nam province

6 Dec–8 Mar   Taylor Common: clear and search operation in Quang Nam
               province

1969

13 Jan–21 Jul   Bold Mariner and Russell Beach: operations on Batangan Peninsula

27 Jan–7 Feb   Linn River: clear and search operation in Quang Nam province

1 Mar–29 May   Oklahoma Hills: operation southwest of Da Nang

10 Mar–2 May   Maine Crag: reconnaissance along the Quang Tri and Laotian border

31 Mar–29 May   Oklahoma Hills: 7th Marines south of Da Nang

6–20 Apr   Muskogee Meadow: clear and search operation in Quang Nam
            province

17 Apr–17 May   Rice: combat operation in Quang Tri and Thua Thien provinces

25 May–7 Nov   Pipestone Canyon: operation south of Da Nang, in Quang Nam
                province

30 Jun–3 Jul   Forsythe Grove: clear and search operation in Quang Nam

20 Jul–13 Aug   Durham Peak: search and clear across Quang Nam and Quang Tin

1970

19 Feb–1 Mar   Double Eagle II: search and destroy operation in Quang Tin Province

5–9 May   Cavalier Beach: transfer of I Corps command from III Marine
           Amphibious Force to XXIV Corps

27 Jul–24 Aug   Lyon Valley: land clearing operation

15 Jul–24 Aug   Pickens Forest: clear and search in Song Thu Bon valley, Quang Nam

24 Jul–11 Aug   Chicago Peak: combined operation as part of Operation Texas Star
                 in Thua Thien province

24–26 Jul   Barren Green

13–31 Aug   Ripley Center: Quang Nam province

1 Sept–12 May   Imperial Lake started: search and clear in Quang Nam province

5–8 Sept   Nebraska Rapids: combined operation

10–19 Sept   Ballard Valley/ Dubois Square: operations around Da Nang

18–19 Sept   Catawba Falls

2–27 Oct   Tolare Falls I and II: Quang Nam province

22 Oct–3 Nov   Noble Canyon: Quang Nam province

17 Dec–19 Jan   Hoang Dieu 101: operation with Koreans and ARVN

1971

11 Jan–29 Mar   Upsur Stream: Quang Nam province

3–10 Feb   Hoang Dieu 103: operation around Danang

3D MARINE DIVISION

Battalion Landing Teams belonging to 3d and 9th Regiments began landing on the beaches near Da Nang in March 1965, the first major combat units to be deployed, and the Divisional Headquarters arrived in the city on 6 May 1965. It transferred to Hue in October 1966 and in March 1968 moved to Quang Tri to retake control of the area south of the Demilitarized Zone. The division moved to Dong Ha in June 1968 and twelve months later combat units began to redeploy; the divisional headquarters finally returned to Da Nang in November 1969 just before its departure from Vietnam.

3D MARINE REGIMENT

DEPLOYED

Arrived at Da Nang in April 1965
Moved to Hue in December 1966
Relocated to Dong Ha in May 1967
After spending January 1968 at
 Camp Carroll it returned to Dong Ha
Moved to Cam Lo in August 1968
December 1968 returned to Dong Ha
June 69 moved to Khe Sanh
Left Vietnam in September 1969

UNITS

1st Battalion from March 1965 to October 1969
2d Battalion from April 1965 to November 1969
3d Battalion from May 1965 to October 1969

4TH MARINE REGIMENT

DEPLOYED

May 1965 arrived at Hue
January 1968 based at Phong Dien
February 1968 moved to Camp Carroll
Relocated to Khe Sanh in July 1968
Moved to Cam Lo in December 1968
Left Vietnam in November 1969

UNITS

1st Battalion from May 1965 to November 1969
2d Battalion from May 1965 to November 1969
3d Battalion from April 1965 to October 1969

A clash of cultures as Marines commandeer villagers to carry them across a flooded paddy field in their sampans. (127-GVC-A188926)

9TH MARINE REGIMENT

DEPLOYED
Arrived at Da Nang in July 1965
Moved to Dong Ha in May 1967
Based at Con Thien in February 1968
Relocated to Cam Lo in May 1968
November 1968 moved to Khe Sanh
November 1968 moved to Khe Sanh
Left Vietnam in August 1969

UNITS
1st Battalion from June 1965 to July 1969
2d Battalion from July 1965 to August 1969
3d Battalion from March 1965 to August 1969

ARTILLERY
1st, 2nd, 3d and 4th Battalions, 12th Artillery Regiment, armed with 105mm howitzers
3d 8in Howitzer Battery and 3d 155mm Gun Battery

OPERATIONS

1965
17–24 Aug	Starlite: first regimental-sized battle on the Van Tuong Peninsula
Sept	Golden Fleece: protecting the rice harvest south of Da Nang
25 Sept	Dagger Thrust: start of many amphibious raids along I Corps' coast
18–24 Oct	Trail Blazer: reconnaissance operation in Quang Nam province
22–25 Oct	Red Snapper: search and destroy operation in Thua Thien province
10–12 Nov	Blue Marlin: amphibious landing north of Chu Lai
8–15 Dec	Harvest Moon: Phuoc Ha Valley between Da Nang and Chu Lai

1966
11–17 Jan	Mallard: search and destroy operation in Quang Nam province
28 Jan–28 Feb	Double Eagle: landing south of Du Pho and search and destroy
7–16 Feb	Taut Bow: reconnaissance operation in Happy Valley
20–23 Mar	Oregon: area north of Hue
1–11 Apr	Orange: search and destroy operation south west of Da Nang
21 Apr–10 May	Georgia: search and destroy operation south of Da Nang
4–12 May	Cherokee and Wayne: operation in Thua Thien province
Jun	Athens, Reno, Beaver, Florida, Dodge and Jay operations south of Hue
7–30 Jun	Liberty: sweep and clear operation around Da Nang
4 Jul–20 Oct	Macon: securing An Hoa industrial zone, southwest of Da Nang
7 Jul–4 Aug	Hastings: large operation across Quang Tri province
3 Aug–31 Jan	Prairie I: follow on from Operation Hastings in Quang Tri province
13–29 Aug	Suwanee and Allegheny: search and destroy in Quang Nam province
26 Aug–14 Sept	Pawnee I and II: search and destroy in Thua Thien province
1–25 Oct	Kern: search and destroy operation in Quang Ngai province
8 Nov–16 Dec	Arcadia, Mississippi and Sterling: search and destroy in Quang Nam
19 Dec–4 Apr	Chinook: blocking Viet Cong access from the mountains to the coast

1967
1–16 Jan	Deckhouse V: landing in Thunh Phu Secret Zone in the Mekong Delta
6 Jan–7 Feb	Cimarron: operation across Quang Tri province
25–28 Jan	Maryland: search and destroy in Thua Thien province
31 Jan–18 Mar	Prairie II: Con Thien and Gio Ling areas of Quang Tri province

A squad leader searches the horizon through his binoculars before ordering his men forward. (127-GVC-A191306)

12–22 Feb	Stone: search and destroy in Quang Nam province
18 Mar–31 May	Prairie III, IV and V: continuing operations across Quang Tri province
20–31 Mar	Beacon Hill: search and destroy north east of Dong Ha
23–24 Mar	Early: search and destroy operation in Quang Nam province
31 Mar–7 Apr	Boone: search and destroy operation in Quang Ngai province
5–10 Apr	Canyon and Dixie: operations in Quang Nam and Quang Tri
21–25 Apr	Grand: search and destroy operation in Quang Nam province
22 Apr–21 May	Shawnee: operation in Thua Thien province
24 Apr–13 May	Capture of Hills 861 and Hill 881 north and south of Khe Sanh
22 Apr–12 May	Beacon Star: along the O Lau River to Khe Sanh
3–7 May	Gulf: search and destroy operation, Quang Nam province
15–28 May	Hickory/Beau Charger: search and destroy in Quang Tri province
13 May–16 July	Crockett: search and destroy operation in Quang Tri province
19–25 May	Duval: search and destroy operation in Quang Nam province
20–23 May	Belt Tight: search and destroy south of the Ben Hai river
22 May–9 Jul	Choctaw: continuation of Operation Shawnee
2–25 Jun	Bear Bite, Butler and Brown: operations in Quang Nam
3 Jun–15 Sept	Cumberland: operation across Thua Thien province
17 Jun–1 Jul	Beacon Torch, Beacon Guide and Calhoun: Quang Nam province
2–16 Jul	Buffalo, Beaver Track, Gem and Hickory II: attack on Con Thien and sweeps south of the DMZ
16 Jul–31 Oct	Kingfisher: continuation of Hickory II
17 Jul–31 Oct	Ardmore: search and destroy operation in Quang Tri province
10 Jul–31 Oct	Fremont: search and destroy in Quang Tri and Thua Thien provinces
Jul–Oct	Con Thien was constantly under attack
1–22 Aug	Pike, Rush Colorado and Beacon Gate: Quang Nam, Quang Tin and Thua Thien provinces
27 Aug–6 Sept	Belt Drive: along the Nhung River south of Quang Tri City
1–3 Sept	Beacon Point: land and amphibious sweep of Street without Joy area
16–22 Sept	Ballistic Charge: Dai Loc District in Quang Nam province

17–24 Oct	Formation Leader: sea and air assault
20 Oct–16 Feb	Osceola I and II: search and destroy in Quang Tri and Thua Thien
1 Nov–31 Mar	Scotland: holding Khe Sanh and the surrounding hills
1 Nov–24 Jan	Neosho: search and destroy operation in Thua Thien province
1 Nov	Start of Kentucky: clear and destroy around Con Thien
4 Nov–28 Feb	Napoleon: keeping the supply line to Dong Ha open
13–30 Nov	Foster and Badger Hunt: operations in Quang Nam province
24–27 Nov	Ballistic Arch: air and sea assault in Quang Tri province
5–24 Dec	Pitt, Citrus and Fortress Ridge: operations in Quang Nam province

The control tower at Khe Sanh fire base, the focus of attention during the long siege. (127-GVC-A189984)

1968

21 Jan–8 Apr	Siege of Khe Sanh in Quang Tri province
20 Jan–23 Nov	Lancaster II: search and destroy operation across Quang Tri province
1–15 Apr	Pegasus: relief of Khe Sanh
14 Apr–28 Feb	Scotland II: clearing the hills in the Khe Sanh area and heavy fighting along the DMZ
28 Feb	Napoleon/Saline I and II: keep the supply line open to Dong Ha port
28 Nov–26 Jan	Dawson River: clear and search operation around Khe Sanh

A mortar team watch as a helicopter hovers in to pick them up. (127-GVC-A193487)

1969

22 Jan–18 Mar	Dewey Canyon: clearing Da Krong and A Shau Valleys
23 Feb–8 May	Purple Martin: clear and search operation northwest of Khe Sanh
15 Mar–2 May	Maine Crag: operation south of Khe Sanh
22 Mar–3 Apr	Montana Mauler: reconnaissance in Force in Quang Tri province
18 Feb	End of Kentucky around Con Thien
1 May–16 Jul	Virginia Ridge: operation north of the Rockpile
1 May–16 Jul	Herkimer Mountain: clear and search in Quang Tin province
10 May–7 Jun	Apache Snow: operation southwest of Hue
29 May–23 June	Cameron Falls: operation southwest of Quang Tri
12 Jun–9 Jul	Utah Mesa: operation northwest of Khe Sanh
3 Jul–21 Sept	Arlington Canyon: securing Vandegrift base rocket belt
6 Jul–25 Sept	Georgia Tar: clear and search northeast of Khe Sanh
12–29 Jul	Williams Glade: operation in Quang Tri province

INDEPENDENT BRIGADES

1ST BRIGADE, 5TH INFANTRY DIVISION (MECHANIZED)

Following the acceptance of the value of mechanized formations in Vietnam, the Brigade was reorganized at Fort Carson in March 1968. It reached Vietnam in July 1968 and deployed in Quang Tri province, just south of the DMZ in I Corps in October.

1st Brigade, 5th Mechanized Division insignia.

BRIGADE DEPLOYMENT	BRIGADE UNITS (ALL FULL TOUR)
Arrived at Cam Lo in July 1968	1/77th Armored Regiment with M48A3 tanks
October moved to Quang Tri and served at Dong Ha in November	1/11th Infantry Battalion
	1/61st Infantry Battalion
Engaged at Khe Sanh in April 1971	75th Support Battalion (Mechanized)
Left Vietnam in August 1971	5/4th Artillery Regiment with 155mm SP howitzers

An M48 tank deploys for roadside security. (111-CC-44716)

OPERATIONS

1968

July joined Operation Kentucky around Con Thien and Operation Napoleon/Saline keeping the lines of communication open to Dong Ha port

10 Sept–15 Nov	Comanche Falls I, II and III: with 1st Cavalry Division
13 Sept–25 Oct	Sullivan, Pioneer and Rich in Quang Tri province
25 Oct–28 Feb	Vernon Lake I and II: operations west of Quang Ngai city
9 Dec	Napoleon/Saline II ended and Marshall Mountain started

1969

28 Feb	Kentucky, Marshall Mountain, Vernon Lake I and II all end
10 Mar–2 May	Maine Crag: reconnaissance on the Laotian border west of Khe Sanh
16 Mar–29 Apr	Task Force Remagen: reconnaissance in force in Quang Tri province
22 Mar–3 Apr	Montana Mauler: clear and search with 1st Marine Division
23 Apr–15 June	Massachusetts Bay: rice denial in Quang Tri province
30 Apr–16 July	Virginia Ridge: clear and search on the DMZ with the 3d Marine Division
11 Jun–9 Jul	Utah Mesa: with 1st Marine Division around Khe Sanh
15 Jun–25 Sept	Iroquois Grove: clear and search operation with 3d Marine Division
12–29 Jul	Williams Glade: with 3d Marine Division
22 Oct–18 Jan	Fulton Square: clear around bases and rice denial operations

1970

19 Jan–22 Jul	Green River and York Market: clear and search, reconnaissance in force
10 Feb–29 Mar	Dakota Clint: west of Quang Tri City
22 Jul–30 Jan	Wolfe Mountain: Quang Tri province
5 Sept	Jefferson Glenn: patrolling Thua Thien and Quang Tri provinces

1971

30 Jan–6 Mar	Dewey Canyon II: cleared down Route 9 and secured Khe Sanh while the ARVN invaded Laos (Lam Son 719)
8 Apr–11 July	Montana Mustang: Quang Tri province
23 Jul–5 Aug	Keystone Oriole (Bravo): redeployment from Vietnam

3D BRIGADE, 82D AIRBORNE DIVISION

Following the Tet offensive in February 1968, there was an immediate need to reinforce I Corps. The Brigade was airlifted from Fort Bragg to Chu Lai by 135 C-141 and six C-133 aircraft and it landed on the 18th, immediately joining 101st Airborne Division as it battled for Hue.

3d Brigade, 82d Airborne Division insignia.

BRIGADE DEPLOYMENT	BRIGADE UNITS
February 1968 arrived at Hue	1/505th Infantry (Airborne): full tour
April covering Hue and Phu Bai	2/505th Infantry (Airborne): full tour
September moved south to secure the west	1/508th Infantry (Airborne): full tour
side of Saigon and the Tan Son Nhut complex	2/321st Artillery (Airborne) Regiment,
Left Vietnam by December 1969	105mm towed howitzers

OPERATIONS

1968

17–24 Feb	The Brigade arrived in I Corps and reinforced 101st Airborne Division by deploying around Hue
8 Mar–17 May	Carentan I and II: in Quang Tri and Thua Thien provinces
17 May	Nevada Eagle began: securing the rice harvest across Thua Thien province
Sept	Golden Sword: moved south to III Corps and came under Capital Assistance Command, securing the west side of Saigon and Tan Son Nhut air base

1969

18 Sept–15 Dec	Keystone Cardinal: Increment II withdrawal from Vietnam

173D AIRBORNE BRIGADE

BRIGADE DEPLOYMENT	BRIGADE UNITS
Arrived at Bien Hoa in May 1965	1/503d Infantry (Airborne): full tour
November 1967 moved to An Khe	2/503d Infantry (Airborne) : full tour
May 1969 moved to Bong Son	3/503d Infantry (Airborne) : full tour
Left Vietnam in August 1971	4/503d Infantry (Airborne) : full tour
	3d Battalion, 319th (Airborne) Artillery,
	105mm towed howitzers

OPERATIONS

1965

7 May–9 Jul	Operation Order (Op Ord) 5-17-65: operation in War Zone D
7 Jun–2 Aug	Fragmentary Order (Frag Order) 1-11-65: Bien Hoa area
28 Jul–2 Aug	Op Order 19-65: operation in Rung Sat Special Zone
7–11 Aug	Frag Order 12-65: operation in Phuoc Thanh province
10 Aug–5 Sept	Pleiku: relief of Du Co Special Forces Camp near Pleiku
7 Sept–8 Oct	Big Red: Ben Cat, Puoc Ving, Di An, Phu Loc
19–28 Sept	Order 24-65: search and destroy in War Zone D
4–6 Oct	X-Ray One and Frag Order 15-65: operations in War Zone D
8–14 Oct	Order 25-65: operation in the Iron Triangle

173d Airborne Brigade insignia.

The crew of an M60 machine gun keep watch on the perimeter of their fire base. (111-CC-70744)

21–27 Oct	New One: cleared an area for 1st Division around Di An and Phu Loi
5–9 Nov	Hump: operation in War Zone D
21 Nov–17 Dec	New Life: La Nga River Valley rice security
17–23 Dec	Smash: Courtenay Rubber Plantation

1966

1–8 Jan	Marauder: along the Oriental River in the Plain of Reeds
8–14 Jan	Crimp: combined operation in the Ho Bo Woods, Binh Buong province
17–21 Jan	On Guard and Retriever: operations around Di An and Phu Loi
4–16 Feb	Roundhouse and Entrée: search and destroy in War Zone D
26 Feb–1 Mar	Phoenix: operations across Binh Duong and Bien Hoa province
9–22 Mar	Silver City: along the Song Be River in War Zone D
30 Mar–15 Apr	Abilene: Phuc Tuy and Long Khanh provinces
9–25 Apr	Denver: operation around Song Be in Phuoc Long province
4–6 May	Dexter: Tan Uyen in Bien Hoa province
16 May–8 Jun	Hardihood: covering 1st Australian Task Force's move
8–18 Jun	Hollandia: search and destroy on Long Hai Peninsula
23 Jun–8 Jul	Yorktown: Long Khanh province
9 Jul–3 Aug	Aurora I and II: Long Khanh province
10 Aug–7 Sept	Toledo: May Tao Secret Zone on the Vung Tau Peninsula
13–22 Sept	Atlantic City: Dau Ting Airfield security
14–25 Sept	Attleboro: large search and destroy operation in War Zone C
26 Sept–9 Oct	Sioux City: search and destroy northwest of Xam Cat
8 Oct–4 Dec	Winchester: 4/503d Battalion with 3d Marine Division near Da Nang
10–17 Oct	Robin: covered 4th Division's move Vung Tau to Bear Cat
25 Nov–2 Dec	Waco: securing the Bien Hoa Area
8 Oct–4 Dec	Winchester: 4/503d Infantry at Da Nang
7 Dec–5 Jan	Canary and Duck: convoy protection along Route 15

1967

5–25 Jan	Niagara/ Cedar Falls: clearing the Cau Dinh Jungle and the Iron Triangle
30 Jan–16 Feb	Big Springs: operation in War Zone D
22 Feb–15 Mar	Junction City: parachute jump into War Zone C
20 Mar–13 Apr	Junction City II: setting up fire bases along Route 13, east of An Loc
18 Apr–4 May	Newark and Fort Wayne: operations in War Zone D
5–17 May	Dayton: Phuoc Tay province
17–23 May	Cincinnati: operation around Bien Hoa and Long Binh
23 May–18 Jun	Winchester and Francis Marion: operations around Pleiku
18–22 Jun	Stilwell and Greeley: Dak To and Kontum
19 Sept–31 Jan	Bolling: Tuy Hoa and Phu Hiep
1 Nov–14 Dec	MacArthur: Dak To and Kontum

1968

16 Jan	Walker started: twelve-month operation around An Khe
30 Mar	Cochise: operations along the coast near Bong Son

1969

31 Jan	Cochise Green, McClain, Walker, Bolling and MacArthur ended
1 Jan–15 Apr	Skysweep and Darby Crest I, II and III: 1/503d Airborne Infantry in Binh Dinh province

A patrol waits for a helicopter to take their prisoners away for interrogation during Operation Cedar Falls in the Iron Triangle. (111-CC-38314)

31 Jan–6 Mar	Darby March I, II and III: 4/503d Airborne Infantry in Phu Yen province
31 Jan–7 Apr	Hancock Knight I, II and III: 3/503d Airborne Infantry around Lam Dong
3 Feb–15 Apr	Darby Trail I, II and III: 2/503d Airborne Infantry in the Bong Son area
6 Mar–24 May	Sting Ray and Darby Punch II: operations in the An Khe area
15 Apr	Washington Green began: pacification of An Loa Valley in Binh Dinh

1970

All year	Washington Green
12 Mar–21 Apr	Darby Talon: Phu Yen
2–24 Dec	Darby Swing: security in Binh Dinh

1971

1 Jan–21 Apr	Greene Lightning, Greene Storm and Greene Sure: Binh Dinh province
1 Jul–31 Aug	Keystone Oriole (Bravo): withdrawal from Vietnam

196TH INFANTRY BRIGADE

The brigade deployed in August 1966 and served as an independent formation until it joined the 23d Americal Division in September 1967.

BRIGADE DEPLOYMENTS

August 1966 arrived at Vung Tau

Moved to Chu Lai and Tam Ky in April 1967
 with Task Force Oregon

September 1967 joined 23d Division

BRIGADE UNITS

2/1st Infantry: full tour

3/21st Infantry: full tour

4/31st Infantry: full tour

3d Battalion, 82d Artillery (105mm)

196th Brigade insignia.

OPERATIONS

1966

30 Aug–29 Sept	Blue Jay: deployment from Vung Tau to Tay Ninh province
1–7 Sept	Alice: security in War Zone C
14 Sept–25 Nov	Attleboro: search and destroy operation in War Zone C
20–24 Oct	Bethlehem: operation in Binh Duong province
25 Nov–8 Apr	Fitchburg: clearing a deployment area around the Iron Triangle

1967

1–27 Jan	Niagara–Cedar Falls: search and destroy operation in the Iron Triangle
1–20 Feb	Gadsen: search and destroy operation in War Zone C
21 Feb–15 Apr	Junction City: blocking position on the west side of War Zone C
17–23 Apr	Lawrence and Golden Fleece: 2/1st Battalion search and destroy operations in Quang Ngai province
May	The rest of the brigade joined Task Force Oregon and moved north into Quang Ngai province to join 2/1st Battalion
10 May–2 Aug	Malheur I and II: clearing Highway 1
2–10 Sept	Cook: search and destroy operation in Quang Ngai province
25 Sept	The brigade joined 23d Americal Division

199TH (LIGHT) INFANTRY BRIGADE

Served as an independent brigade throughout its tour in Vietnam.

BRIGADE DEPLOYMENT	BRIGADE UNITS
December 1966 arrived at Long Binh	2/3d Infantry: full tour
Jan 1968 moved to Bien Hoa	3/7th Infantry: full tour
May returned to Long Binh	4/12th Infantry: full tour
Moved to Xuan Loc in August 1969	5/12th Infantry: from April 1968
July 1970 returned to Long Binh	2d Battalion, 40th Artillery, 105mm
Left Vietnam in October 1970	towed howitzers

OPERATIONS

1966

11 Oct	Uniontown: engaged in War Zone C
20 Nov	Start of Fairfax: one battalion joined the year-long operation to secure Saigon and the surrounding area
28 Nov–1 Jan	Canary: road security from Vung Tau to Saigon and Long Binh
16–26 Dec	Initiator: search and destroy operation in Long Binh province
27–31 Dec	Wiggins: search and destroy operation in Bien Hoa province

1967

8–27 Jan	Niagara – Cedar Falls: part of the anvil along the Saigon River during the clearing of the Iron Triangle
13 Feb	Enterprise: year-long operation to clear Long An province
17 Nov–17 Dec	Operations Strike and Uniontown combined to clear Bien Hoa province
18–23 Dec	Warm Springs: a continuation of Strike and Uniontown
14 Dec	Fairfax ended
17 Dec–17 Feb	Manchester: search and destroy north of the Dong Nai River

1968

13–23 Jan	Altoona: search and destroy operation in Bien Hoa province
13 Jan–18 Feb	Haverford: operations across Gia Dinh and Long An provinces
31 Jan–7 Mar	Engaged in Saigon during the Tet offensive
5 Feb–8 Mar	Tran Hung Dao I and II: clearing up operation across Saigon
7–28 Mar	Harrisburg, Valley Forge and Box Springs: engaged in War Zone D
8 Mar–7 Apr	Wilderness: Engaged in War Zone C

199th Brigade insignia.

199th Brigade swept the villages around Saigon as part of Operation Toan Thang following the Tet Offensive. (111-CC-51628)

10 Mar–8 Apr	Resolve to Win (Quyet Thang): securing the area around Saigon
7 Apr–31 May	Complete Victory (Toan Thang): continued to clear around Saigon
1 Jun	Toan Thang II started

1969

4–16 Feb	Strangler I and II: clearing Gia Dinh province
16 Feb	Toan Thang II became Toan Thang III
29 Aug–30 Sept	Burnham: land clearing in Phuoc Tuy province
1 Nov	Toan Thang III became Toan Thang IV
24–28 Nov	Ransom Raider: long Khanh province

1970

6 May–27 Jun	Toan Thang 45: Cambodian invasion from Phuoc Long province
1 Jul–15 Oct	Keystone Robin (Alpha): Increment IV withdrawal from Vietnam

11th Armored Cavalry insignia.

11TH ARMORED CAVALRY REGIMENT

3d Squadron arrived in August 1966; 1st and 2d Squadrons arrived in September. Although the three squadrons were usually based with the Headquarters, they often served other units.

The Regiment was based at Bien Hoa until November 1966 and Long Binh until February 1967. It was then based at Black Horse Camp at Xuan Loc until January 1969, helping to secure large areas of III Corps. After a brief stay at Long Giao, the regiment moved to Bien Hoa; it relocated to Di An in July 1970 and left Vietnam in March 1971.

1st Squadron served with the Headquarters until March 1969 and then with 1st Cavalry Division until June 1970, joining the invasion of Cambodia. It reported to II Field Force in July and August 1970 and to 25th Infantry Division in October and November 1970. The squadron's final assignment was with II Field Force; it left Vietnam in March 1971.

One of 11th Armored Cavalry's Mobile Advisory Team's questions villagers about recent Viet Cong activity. (111-CC-42857)

2d Squadron was based with the headquarters until March 1969, joining Task Force Oregon at Chu Lai between May to September 1967. It then served 1st Cavalry Division until March 1971, joining the invasion of Cambodia in June 1970. After serving with Third Regional Assistance Command and Hau Nghia Province Command from its base at Long Binh, the squadron briefly served 25th ARVN Division at the end of 1971. Its final assignment was with 3d Brigade, 1st Cavalry Division; it left Vietnam in April 1972.

3d Squadron was based with the headquarters until March 1969, with 1st Infantry Division until June 1969 and with 199th Infantry Brigade until August 1969. After a second period with 1st Infantry Division, at Lai Khe and Bien Hoa, it served with 1st Cavalry Division at Bien Hoa from January to June 1970, joining the invasion of Cambodia. The squadron then served alongside 1st Squadron until it left Vietnam in March 1971.

OPERATIONS

1966

5–29 Sept	Meadowlark: deployed from Vung Tau to Long Binh
14 Sept–25 Nov	Attleboro: combined operation in War Zone C, Tay Ninh province
6–15 Oct	Hickory: 3d Squadron operation across Bien Hoa province
11 Oct	Uniontown: joined the defense of Long Binh
20 Oct–8 Dec	Atlanta: search and destroy in the Iron Triangle
16 Nov–12 Jan	Dan Tam 81: rice harvest security in Long Khanh and Binh Tuy

1967

8–27 Jan	Cedar Falls: combined operation in Iron Triangle
21 Feb–14 May	Junction City: combined operation in War Zone C
20 Apr	Kittyhawk starts: security for the Regiment's Black Horse Camp
23 Apr–7 Jun	Manhattan: operations in Boi Loi Woods and Long Nguyen forest
17–26 May	Dallas: 1st Squadron search and destroy in War Zone D
9 Jun–14 Jul	Akron, Rhino, Lion and Paddington: Phuoc Tuy and Bien Hoa provinces
21 Jul–14 Sept	Emporia I to IV and Valdosta: 9th Division in Long Khanh province
11 Sept–25 Nov	Wheeler: 2d Squadron in Quang Tin province with Task Force Oregon
18 Sept–9 Oct	Arkansas City I and II: search and destroy across Phuoc Tuy province
22–28 Sept	Richmond: 3d Squadron in Long Khanh province
2 Nov–5 Jan	Santa Fe: road clearing across Long Khanh and Binh Tuy provinces
17 Nov	Uniontown and Strike combine around Long Binh and Bien Hoa
14–21 Dec	Quicksilver: security of highway between Ben Cat and Phuoc Vinh
21 Dec–21 Jan	Fargo: road clearing between An Loc and Loc Ninh
23 Dec	Uniontown and Strike are renamed Warm Springs

1968

20–27 Jan	Attalla and Casey: search and destroy in Binh Long province
31 Jan–7 Mar	Tet Offensive in Saigon: fighting in the city ended in the Cholon area
31 Jan–8 Mar	Adairsville: the defense of Long Binh
7–16 Mar	Valley Forge: 2d Squadron across Long Khanh province
10 Mar–8 Apr	Quyet Thang (Resolve to Win): securing the provinces around Saigon
21 Mar	Kittyhawk: the security of Black Horse Camp ends
21 Mar–6 Apr	Alcorn Grove: security across Long Khanh province
7 Apr–31 May	Toan Thang (Complete Victory): extended security around Saigon
15–26 Apr	Clifton Corral: armored cavalry raid into War Zone D
1 Jun–15 Feb	Toan Thang II: securing the provinces south, west and north of Saigon

1969

16 Feb	Toan Thang III: continued security around Saigon
18 Mar–10 Apr	Atlas Wedge and Atlas Power: clearing Michelin Rubber Plantation
12 Apr–14 May	Montana Raider: in War Zones C and D with 1st Cavalry Division
22 Jun–31 Jan	Kentucky Cougar: across Tay Ninh and Binh Long provinces
Aug	Battle of Binh Long
24–27 Nov	Texas Traveler: 3d Squadron in War Zone C
5–26 Dec	Long Reach: Binh Long province

1970

29 Jan–30 Apr	Fresh Start: land clearing operation in War Zone C
29 Apr–7 July	Toan Thang 42: into Cambodia, the Fishhook area north of Kien Tuong
1 May–30 June	Toan Thang 43: into Cambodia, the Fishhook area west of Tay Ninh

1971

5 Mar	1st and 3d Squadron left Vietnam
27 Sept–2 Oct	Katum: 2d Squadron in Tay Ninh province

1972

6 Apr	2d Squadron left Vietnam

A cavalryman cools off on blocks of ice while he reads his Christmas cards. (111-CC-64243)

Left to right:

*Military Assistance Advisory
  Group – Vietnam.*
*Military Assistance Command,
  Vietnam.*
US Army, Vietnam (USARV).
I Field Force, Vietnam.

Left to right:

II Field Force, Vietnam.
XXIV Corps.
1st Cavalry Division.
1st Infantry Division.

Left to right:

4th Infantry Division.
5th Infantry Division.
9th Infantry Division.
23d Infantry Division.

Left to right:

25th Infantry Division.
82d Airborne Division.
101st Airborne Division.
11th Cavalry Regiment.

Left to right:

11th Infantry Brigade.
173d Airborne Brigade.
196th Infantry Brigade.
198th Infantry Brigade.
199th Infantry Brigade.

CHAPTER 10

THE SOLDIER

RANKS

Officers displayed their rank on their epaulets while the enlisted men wore sleeve insignia. Officers and men were sometimes referred to by their pay grades; O for officers and E for enlisted men.

OFFICER RANKS	PAY	SHOULDER INSIGNIA	TYPICAL COMMAND
General		Four silver stars	Commander or Deputy
Lieutenant-General	O-9	Three silver stars	Field Force
Major-General	O-8	Two silver stars	Division
Brigadier-General	O-7	One silver star	Brigade
Colonel	O-6	Gold eagle	Brigade or division staff
Lieutenant-Colonel	O-5	Silver oak leaf	Battalion
Major	O-4	Gold oak leaf	Battalion staff
Captain	O-3	Two silver bars	Company
First lieutenant	O-2	Silver bar	Company staff or platoon
Second lieutenant	O-1	Gold bar	Platoon

ENLISTED RANKS	PAY	SLEEVE INSIGNIA
Command Sergeant Major	E-9	Three chevrons, three rockers below, wreathed star
Sergeant Major	E-9	Three chevrons, three rockers below, star in center
First Sergeant	E-8	Three chevrons, three rockers below, diamond in center
Master Sergeant	E-8	Three chevrons and three rockers below
Platoon Sergeant	E-7	Three chevrons and two rockers below
Sergeant First Class	E-7	Three chevrons and two rockers below
Specialist 7 (Spec 7)	E-7	Three arches over an eagle
Staff sergeant	E-6	Three chevrons with a rocker below
Specialist 6 (Spec 6)	E-6	Two arched bars over an eagle
Sergeant	E-5	Three chevrons
Specialist 5 (Spec 5)	E-5	Arched bar over an eagle
Corporal	E-4	Two chevrons
Specialist 4 (Spec 4)	E-4	Eagle
Private First Class (PFC)	E-3	Single point up chevron, rocker added in 1968
Private 2	E-2	No marking, single point up chevron added in 1968
Private 1	E-1	No sleeve marking then given a single point up chevron

TYPICAL ENLISTED OCCUPATIONS

Command Sergeant Major: Senior battalion NCO

Sergeant Major: Division and higher staffs

First Sergeants: Senior company NCO

Master Sergeant: Battalion and brigade staffs

Platoon Sergeant: Senior platoon NCO

Sergeant First Class: Battalion and brigade staffs

Staff Sergeant: Section leaders, rifle and weapons squad leaders, armored vehicle commanders

Specialist 6: Medical assistants, supply sergeants

Sergeant: Assistant squad leaders, fire team and mortar squad leaders

Specialist 5: Senior radar operators, communications chiefs, Forward Observers, armored vehicle drivers and gunners, senior vehicle mechanics, senior medical aidmen and first cooks

Corporal: Machine gunners, automatic rifleman, grenadiers and mortar gunner

Specialist 4: Clerks, armorers, radio operators and mechanics

PFC: Riflemen, assistant gunners, observers, ammunition bearers and tank loaders

MILITARY PAY

Pay was on the last Friday of the month and the company commander wore a loaded .45-caliber pistol as he paid the men in cash. Before deductions, the basic pay for men with less than two years' service was $137.70. Additions of $65 were added as combat pay and another $16 for serving overseas; paratroopers received $55 jump pay (even if they did not make parachute jumps). Married men without children were given a basic allowance of $55.20 and a $30 separation allowance for serving overseas. There were no income tax deductions in Vietnam but men had Social Security deductions taken; they could also make optional Savings Bonds contributions. Most men deposited the bulk of their money in a bank account or sent it home by postal money order.

The American military authorities were aware of the adverse impact the flood of US dollars would have on the fragile Vietnamese economy. American dollars had to be exchanged for Military Payment Certificates which were legal tender on military installations while men could exchange a limited amount into piasters for use outside the base. MACV Ration Cards limited the sale of liquor, cigarettes and electrical goods to curtail the amount of items ending up on the black market.

A rifle platoon of the 1st Cavalry Division receives new orders from their commander as he circles overhead in a helicopter. (111-CC-41848)

New arrivals exchange dollars for Military Payment Certificates at Long Binh before they are posted to their units. (111-CC-67742)

STATESIDE UNIFORMS AND EQUIPMENT

It was stylish to have long hair during the late 1960s but the Army immediately made its mark on the soldier with a severe haircut. Every man had ¼in of hair left on top and nothing around the nape of the neck and the the ears; they had to shave every day.

Next came the issue of uniforms: after stripping down to underwear (civilian clothes were mailed home), the men were measured and given the following items to store inside their duffel bags:

Four sets of olive green utility uniforms, three tan shirts and two short-sleeve khaki shirts
Summer and winter weight uniforms in Army green
Olive-drab helmet (weighing nearly 3½lb) and helmet liners
Two field caps, two garrison (envelope style) caps and one service cap (baseball style)
Five sets of white shorts, undershirts, and handkerchiefs
Two pairs of black leather combat boots with five pairs of black duty socks
One pair of black low-top dress shoes with three pairs of black dress socks
One pair of black leather gloves with two pairs of olive-drab wool inserts
Field jacket (either M1951 or M1965 pattern) and two black web belts
Army green overcoat and a taupe raincoat

The utility uniform was known as fatigues and the loose-fitting shirt was worn with sleeves down was and tucked into the trousers; trousers were also tucked into the boots. The drill sergeants and camp staff wore immaculately starched and pressed fatigues to differentiate them from the trainees in their unpressed and unstarched utilities. Men had to replace damaged and lost equipment at the Quartermaster Clothing Sales Store.

The men were no longer individuals as they paraded for the first time with their new haircut and uniform and everyone was expected to dress the same or expect to be punished. Their only visible form of identification was an olive drab nametape displaying their name in bold black letters sewn above the right pocket on their fatigue shirts; a similar black nametape above the opposite pocket displayed the words US ARMY in gold. A plastic nameplate was worn on the field jacket. Recruits wore no other form of insignia.

Two recruits need to wear their field jackets as they practice mine sweeping techniques at Fort Richardson, Alaska. (111-SC-17195)

Men had to carry two stainless steel identity tags, known as dog tags, listing their name (the letters NMI indicated no middle initial), serial number, blood group and religion. Plastic tubing and frames were used to stop the chains making a noise on maneuvers. If a man was killed in action, one tag was handed in with the casualty report while the other remained with the body.

Each man had a unique seven-digit Army number (Social Security numbers were used after January 1968) preceded by a two digit code:

RA - Regular Army three-year volunteers
ER – Enlisted Reserve
NG - National Guard
US - United States (conscripts)

Enlisted men who gained a commission were issued with a new serial number preceded by the letter O.

The new recruit was issued with a footlocker filled with his personnel equipment. He was expected to learn how to care for it, keeping everything in good condition, ready to be inspected at any time.

The soldier could carry all his equipment on a series of belts and straps, known as the M1956 pattern webbing, fastened around the waist and chest. The heavy-duty belt carried a pair of ammunition pouches and a small first-aid pouch, containing a field dressing, on the front; a quart-sized plastic canteen and cup were always carried on the right hip. The soldier could also fasten a folding entrenching tool and bayonet scabbard on his left hip and a small pack, carrying a raincoat and spare socks, on the back of the belt. A pair of braces attached to the belt transferred the weight of the equipment to the man's shoulders. Two ammunition pouches, each carrying two 20-round magazines, could be attached to the braces. Finally, each soldier was issued with an M14 semi-automatic rifle.

VIETNAM UNIFORMS AND EQUIPMENT

The terrain, the climate and a difference in attitude could drastically alter a soldier's appearance once he had spent some time in Vietnam. The khakis and fatigues were changed for three sets of tropical combat uniforms and jungle fatigues which were loose-fitting, lightweight and fast drying, ideal for the hot, humid climate. They also had a lot more pockets that the Stateside uniforms. Each man was also issued with five sets of olive-green undershirts and shorts and two olive-green towels.

Each soldier was issued with two pairs of lightweight tropical combat boots. They were canvas-topped and while the drainage eyelets allowed moisture out, the cleated soles gave some protection against punji stakes. Every man was issued with a steel helmet and a tropical hat; virtually everyone acquired the preferred baseball cap.

Every man carried the following items in his wallet:

Armed Force Identification Card and the Geneva Conventions Card
Payment certificates, ration cards and driving licenses, both military and Stateside

Two strips were sewn above the breast pockets, US Army on the left and the soldier's name on the right. Before 1968 uniform insignia included color unit patches on the shoulder and rank insignia on the arm; color skill badges

were also displayed. After 1968 subdued unit patches and skill badges were introduced, and while the shape and layout remained the same, the colors were replaced by olive drab and black. Rank insignia were replaced with small black collar pin badges at the same time. Between 1968 and 1970 there was a mixture of color and subdued insignia across a unit while uniforms were recirculated and replaced. Out in the field uniforms often did not display a name tag or insignia because they had to be exchanged at the laundry on a regular basis.

A heavily laden radio operator takes a break during Operation Kole Kole. (111-CC-41022)

IN THE FIELD

The men could ditch their equipment on the base and many preferred to go shirtless or wear undershirts during the day; mosquitoes made sure that everyone wore their shirts after sunset. Before long the terrain and climate took their toll on the men's uniforms and they became smeared in mud, faded and starched with sweat and torn or patched. Personal appearance also changed as the months passed and standards varied considerably between units as leaders set their own rules, but they were generally more relaxed in the field than at the large installations. Many men grew their hair and sideburns or sprouted moustaches to follow the current fashion in the United States; most acquired an assortment of bracelets, beads, necklaces and lucky charms.

On operations the men had to find a compromise between personal comfort and practicality so they could move quickly and quietly on the long patrols while weighed down with weapons and ammunition. Anyone carrying too much equipment would soon grow exhausted in the oppresive heat and experienced platoon sergeants and squad leaders soon taught new arrivals what to take on operations and what to leave behind. The style of operation and the number of times helicopters would be able to bring out supplies often dictated what was needed. Ponchos were essential during wet weather.

Many of the pockets were difficult to access and most personal items were carried inside plastic bags in the haversack or tucked in an elastic camouflage band around the helmet to keep them dry. The M1956 cotton webbing quickly disintegrated the humid climate and a nylon version had started to replace it by 1967. Personal items, including dry socks and toiletries, were carried in the butt pack but many soldiers acquired a lightweight rucksack at the first opportunity to ease their load; a tropical rucksack appeared in later years.

Soldiers took as many rifle magazines and canteens filled with water as possible, carrying them in their uniform pouches or claymore mine bags on their belts. Extra ammunition for the M60 machine gun was distributed around the squad members and each man carried a claymore mine and a few sandbags if the squad was staying out in the field overnight. Entrenching tools, poncho liners, mosquito nets and air mattresses were often shared between two men so they could make their shared foxhole more comfortable.

A small number of C-Rations were also taken but appetites were suppressed on the long patrols and many preferred to wait until the resupply helicopter arrived in the evening before eating. The men also carried a number of field dressings in case there were casualties.

Sleeves were often rolled down to guard against abrasions, insects and leeches while trousers were taped up to protect the legs. Towels were then hung around the neck to absorb sweat. Parachute cord was sometimes used to replace rotting bootlaces and many soldiers tied their dog tags to their boot laces so they would be secure.

HELMETS AND FLAK JACKETS

Virtually everyone wore their steel helmet with the green side of the camouflage cover displayed, although out in the field a few preferred to wear their boonie hat.

Soldiers were issued with body armor to protect their torso from bullets and fragments. They were unpopular with the men operating in the field due to their weight and, although it was frowned upon, some opted to accept the risk of not wearing their flak vest and left them back at base.

The Army issue M1952 Fragmentation Protective Body Armor was a nylon fabric vest with a front zipper fastener and elasticated side tapes so it fitted all sizes. There were three pockets, two protecting the chest and one covering the back, for the protective panels that were made from layers of ballistic nylon cloth encased in plastic film. A pair of side pockets was added to carry personal equipment or ammunition while cloth tapes sewn on to the front of each shoulder could secure grenades. The vest was updated in 1969 with stitched interior panels and a protective collar to protect the neck. It was named the M69 Fragmentation Protective Body Armor and weighed 8½lb.

The Marine Corps M1955 Armored Vest was a sleeveless nylon jacket with a flexible protective pad sewn in to cover the upper chest and shoulders;

US Air Force troops man a bunker during an attack on Tan Son Nhut air base; the man on the left has chosen the cartoon character Snoopy to decorate his flak jacket. (111-CC-48595)

overlapping Doron plates protected the lower torso. Equipment could be clipped to a waist band or carried in a breast pocket. The Marine version weighed 10lb 3oz. A small raised ridge was later added to the shoulder to secure the Marine's rifle on the march; a protective collar was also stitched on. Helmet covers, boonie hats and flak vests were usually covered in graffiti such as:

Rank insignia, unit badges and unit slogans or nicknames
The soldier's nickname, his home town or state and a girl friend's name
Phrases, sometimes aggressive statements, sometimes reflective sayings
Peace symbols and anti-war slogans became popular during the later years

THE RULES OF ENGAGEMENT

The following two leaflets, detailing the special skills needed to operate in Vietnam, were issued when personnel arrived. The first was issued to all ranks:

Ten Rules for Personnel of US Military Assistance Command, Vietnam
1. *The Vietnamese have paid a heavy price in suffering for their long fight against Communists. We military men are in Vietnam now because their government has asked us to help its soldiers and people in winning their struggle. The Viet Cong will attempt to turn the Vietnamese people against you. You can defeat them at every turn by the strength, understanding, and generosity you display with the people. Here are nine simple rules:*
2. *Remember we are guests here: We make no demands and seek no special treatment.*
3. *Join with the people! Understand their life, use phrases from their language, and honor their customs and law.*
4. *Treat women with politeness and respect.*
5. *Make personal friends among the soldiers and common people.*
6. *Always give the Vietnamese the right of way.*

A platoon commander issues orders to his squads in the jungles of Binh Dinh Province. (111-CC-41411)

7. *Be alert to security and ready to react with your military skill.*
8. *Don't attract attention by loud, rude or unusual behaviour.*
9. *Avoid separating yourself from the people by a display of wealth or privilege.*
10. *Above all else, you are members of the US Military Forces on a difficult mission, responsible for all your official and personal actions. Reflect honor upon yourself and the United States of America.*

Officers were also issued with the following leaflet outlining the basic rules for commanding men effectively:

Guidance for Officers in Vietnam
1. *Make the welfare of your men your primary concern with special attention to mess, mail and medical care.*
2. *Give priority emphasis to matters of intelligence, counterintelligence, and timely and accurate reporting.*
3. *Gear your command for sustained operations: keep constant pressure on the enemy.*
4. *React rapidly with all force available to opportunities to destroy the enemy; disrupt enemy bases, capturing or destroying supply caches.*
5. *Open up methodically and use roads, waterways, and the railroad; be alert and prepared to ambush the ambusher.*
6. *Harass enemy lines of communication by raids and ambushes.*
7. *Use firepower with care and discrimination, particularly in populated areas.*
8. *Capitalize on psywar [psychological warfare] opportunities.*

9. *Assist in 'revolutionary development' with emphasis on priority areas and on civic action wherever feasible.*
10. *Encourage and help Vietnamese military and paramilitary units; involve them in your operations at every opportunity.*
11. *Be smarter and more skilful than the enemy; stimulate professionalism, alertness, and tactical ingenuity; seize every opportunity to enhance training of men and units.*
12. *Keep your officers and men well informed, aware of the nine rules for personnel of MACV, and mindful of the techniques of Communist insurgency and the role of Free World Forces in Vietnam.*

RATIONS IN VIETNAM

The base camp canteens went out of their way to provide high-calorie meals of a standard expected at a Stateside barracks. Soldiers feasted on a variety of hot meals and cold drinks, something they could not get in the field. To begin with soldiers were fed B-Rations, a mixture of canned, dehydrated, and preserved foods packaged in one-gallon cans. As soon as a base had cold storage facilities and bakeries they were replaced by fresh and frozen foodstuffs including meat,

A weary GI heats up his tin of C-Rations at the end of a day's patrol. (111-CC-49003)

fish, fresh fruit, vegetables and dairy products; otherwise known as A-Rations. Off base the men could try their luck in one of the many Vietnamese bars and restaurants in the towns and cities. Hygiene standards varied enormously and some senior officers discouraged eating out.

The grunts despised the fact that the large numbers of men based at the huge logistics and supply depots could eat well every day while they had to get by with the universally detested C-rations or C-Rats (the official title was Meal, Combat, Individual). Men usually only carried a small number on patrol, anticipating regular deliveries by the daily resupply helicopter; they went hungry if it could not land.

The prepacked meals were sealed in three tins and packaged in small carton complete with a foil packet containing coffee and creamer, four cigarettes and matches, sugar and salt, gum and toilet paper and a plastic spoon. Wise soldiers hung a C-Ration tin opener on their dog tag chain. The B-Units came in three types and the varied contents produced twelve kinds of meals, all containing 1,200 calories.

B-1 Unit: Small can of meat, a large can of fruit and a small can of crackers and candy spread.

B-2 Unit: Large can of meat, a small dessert can and a small can of crackers and savoury spread.

B-3 Unit: Small can of meat, a small can of bread and a small can with cocoa powder, cookies and jelly or fruit

The cans of the meat contained either chicken, turkey, beef, ham, or meat loaf, and soldiers argued over who would have what when they discovered the contents of their pack; ham and lima beans was detested by almost everyone. Dessert cans had fruit cake, pecan roll, or pound cake; fruit cans contained apple sauce, fruit cocktail, peaches, or pears.

GALLANTRY AWARDS

MEDAL OF HONOR

The Medal of Honor was the highest award for gallantry and 246 were awarded during the Vietnam conflict, around 60 per cent posthumously. They had to be nominated by an officer and then submitted and approved at each level of command. The medal was often sometimes referred to as the Congressional Medal of Honor because the President presents the award 'in the name of the Congress'. Each branch had a different design based on a five-pointed gold star and while a new Air Force design was introduced in 1965, both the Marine Corps and the Coast Guard used the Navy medal. The Army medal had a gold star surrounded by a wreath, topped by an eagle above a bar inscribed 'Valor.' The medal is attached by a hook to a light blue silk and it is worn around the neck.

SILVER STAR

The Silver Star was awarded for gallantry in action. It has a gold star with a circular wreath in the center surrounding a silver star and the reverse has the inscription 'FOR GALLANTRY IN ACTION'. It is accompanied by a red, white and blue striped ribbon.

Men of the 101st Airborne Division receive gallantry awards from their general as they prepare to leave Vietnam. (111-CC-80040)

LEGION OF MERIT

The Legion of Merit was awarded for exceptionally meritorious service rather than valor. It has a five-pointed white and purple cross pattee mounted on a laurel and a gold rose; the blue center is covered by stars. The award is attached by a hook to a white-edged purple sash and worn around the neck.

DISTINGUISHED FLYING CROSS

The Cross was awarded for heroism or extraordinary achievements carried out during an aerial flight; medals awarded for bravery had an attached V-device. The bronze cross pattee, with rays between the arms of the cross, is suspended on a bar. The obverse has a propeller of four blades while name and rank are inscribed on the rear. It is worn with a red, white and blue ribbon.

BRONZE STAR

The Star could be awarded for valor or for meritorious conduct. It is a bronze star with a second smaller star in the center; an attached V-device identified the medal as one awarded for gallantry.

The reverse is inscribed with the words 'HEROIC OR MERITORIOUS ACHIEVEMENT' and the name of the recipient. It is suspended from a scarlet, white and blue ribbon by a rectangular loop.

ARMY COMMENDATION MEDAL

The medal was awarded for overall service; officers usually received the Bronze Star Medal.

PURPLE HEART

Men who were wounded or killed in action were awarded the Purple Heart and the largest number awarded to one man was eight. It is gold-edged, purple heart-shaped medal with the profile of George Washington in the center below the Washington coat of arms. The reverse has a raised bronze heart with the words 'FOR MILITARY MERIT'.

Further awards of the Silver Star, the Distinguished Flying Cross, the Bronze Star and the Purple Heart were recognized by oak-leaf clusters in the Army and Air Force and award stars in the Navy.

COMBAT INFANTRYMAN'S BADGE
The badge was awarded to men who served under fire for at least thirty days, to distinguish them from those who served at the bases.

AIR MEDAL
Anyone who distinguished themselves by meritorious achievement on regular aerial flights was awarded the Air Medal, medals awarded for bravery had an attached V-device. It has a bronze compass rose with an eagle carrying lightning flashes in its talons in the center; the ribbon is blue and gold.

MERITORIOUS SERVICE MEDAL
This medal was introduced in January 1969 as a non-combat service award comparable to the Bronze Star. Six rays and part of a five-pointed star rise above an eagle with outstretched wings and the obverse of this bronze medal reads 'UNITED STATES OF AMERICA' and 'MERITORIOUS SERVICE'. It is accompanied by a crimson and white ribbon.

SERVICE MEDALS

VIETNAM SERVICE MEDAL
Originally men and women serving overseas were awarded the Armed Forces Expeditionary Medal. It was replaced in 1965 by the Vietnam Service Medal which was awarded to anyone with more than thirty consecutive or sixty non-consecutive days service in Vietnam, including personnel stationed on ships supporting operations. Servicemen also received a service star for each campaign they served in. The periods covered were from 15 November 1961 to 28 March 1973 and the 29 and 30 April 1975, covering the final evacuation of Saigon. Servicemen and women could replace their Armed Forces Expeditionary Medal with the Vietnam Service Medal.

NATIONAL DEFENSE SERVICE MEDAL
The medal was awarded to anyone on active duty, including those stationed in the United States, between 1 January 1961 and 14 August 1974.

MORALE DECLINES

Morale declined rapidly after 1971 as the number of combat operations was reduced, leaving many men bored and frustrated. The high turnover of drafted men and the shortage of experienced officers and NCOs meant that discipline problems arose. Peer pressures, based on social class, race and drug culture, also created their problems as worldwide protests left many feeling that they were involved in a lost cause.

Men occasionally refused to carry out orders, either individually or as a group. New officers were often viewed with suspicion, especially regular officers who were seen to be working to improve their status. Disgruntled men could vent their anger by throwing a grenade into an officer's bunker, either as a warning or in an attempt to kill him. Fragging incidents also increased as frustrations and dissent grew. They were usually directed against a junior officer or a staff sergeant and warnings were sometimes given by using smoke or CS grenades; occasionally a fragmentation grenade with the pin still in was used.

While racial problems were isolated in combat units where men faced danger and relied on each other to survive, there were many problems in support units. Combat units confined to bases during the latter stages of the withdrawal developed problems as men were drawn to others of their own social background, usually divided along racial lines. Many found comradeship with men who had common ideals or interests, similar to groups found in high schools.

Drug abuse was a problem inherent in 1960s America and it slowly spread into the Armed Services; increasing with the disaffection with the war and the withdrawal of troops from Vietnam. Drugs, ranging from marijuana through barbiturates and amphetamines to heroin and opium, were far easier to buy in Vietnam where prices were much cheaper than in the United States. It meant that many bored soldiers were introduced to drugs for the first time while a few made a living out of selling them to others. Over half of enlisted men tried marijuana while one in six had experimented with opium; the numbers of officers involved were lower. Problems were far greater in the support units stationed at the large bases where it was easier to get access to dealers. The men in the field had neither the time nor the inclination to become involved in hard drugs. Self-preservation was far more important.

The Armed Services recognized the problem and tried several ways, ranging from educational material and talks from ex-addicts to buddy programs and amnesty schemes to help those in trouble. Men were also encouraged to approach their commanding officer, the chaplain, or the unit surgeon for assistance. However, the American press saw this as a soft option and called for men to be imprisoned or discharged. The Armed Services disagreed and after a short hospital stay and counseling men returned to duties.

THE MY LAI MASSACRE

While the American Armed Forces and Civic Agencies were trying to win the hearts and minds of the people, isolated incidents, some accidental, others intentional, could turn the population against them. The nature of the conflict in Vietnam brought the soldiers into close contact with the population as they repeatedly searched their villages and questioned them about the Viet Cong's whereabouts, and frustration could lead to angry exchanges or violence, especially if a unit had recently suffered casualties. Although incidents resulted in investigations which could lead to disciplinary proceedings, the accidental killing or injuring of civilians during fire-fights or fire support missions, and the mistreatment of villagers during search operations did occur.

The worst case happened in March 1969 at My Lai village in Quang Ngai Province. 11th Brigade had suffered a large number of casualties from snipers and booby traps, when confusing orders were issued to sweep the village where it was believed that a Viet Cong unit was hiding. Within hours of landing two platoons had rounded up and killed around 200 elderly men, women and children before killing the livestock and burning the hamlet to the ground; several prisoners were later tortured. There were no US casualties from enemy fire.

After the massacre, every level of command in 23d Americal Division took steps to cover up the incident and during the subsequent trial the unit commander, Lieutenant William Calley, was convicted of murder. Although

Heavily armed GIs keep their fingers on the triggers of their weapons while Viet Cong suspects are interrogated in front of their terrified families. (111-CC-33238)

he was sentenced to life in prison, he was eventually only held under house arrest for several years. It took eight months for the story to reach the press where the news that US servicemen could commit such atrocities was met with worldwide revulsion. In some people's eyes that single morning in My Lai tarnished the work carried out by every serviceman and woman during eight years of conflict. How many more My Lais were committed, or smaller, equally violent encounters took place, will never be known.

THE REAL WORLD

As the serviceman's year-long tour came to an end they became known as 'short-timers' and some officers withdrew their 'short-timers' from the field so they could pass on their skills to new arrivals; others felt that they had an adverse effect on unit effectiveness due to their caution. As the DEROS (Date Eligible for Return from Over Seas) date drew nearer, those serving in the field flew to the divisional base before heading on to Bien Hoa Air Base. 90th Replacement Battalion, based at Long Binh Army Base, carried out the necessary administration before the men were taken to Tan Son Nhut Airport where they boarded the 'Freedom Bird' to the United States. The announcement that the plane had left Vietnamese airspace was greeted by cheers as the men settled down for the long flight across the Pacific. They had survived their tour of duty.

Further administration followed for the soldier at the US Army Personnel Centers in Oakland, California, or Fort Lewis, Washington. Troops had to carry Public Health Service cards for two weeks, notifying doctors that they may have been in contact with several contagious diseases. Returning troops were segregated from those heading out to Vietnam and those with less than five months remaining service were immediately processed for discharge. Following a physical, further administration where they learnt that they were in the Standby Reserve, briefings on benefits, including the GI Bill which gave assistance for college education and low-interest home loans, they also received due pay and a new uniform. Often within less than 24 hours of landing on American soil, they were on a flight home.

A stewardess greets servicemen at Bien Hoa Air Base as they board their Freedom Bird back to the United States, referred to by many as 'The World'. (111-CC-43521)

A member of the Lai Khe Service Club hands out gifts during a party for the local children. (111-CC-65062)

WOMEN IN VIETNAM

More than 7,500 women served in the military in Vietnam, the majority as Army, Navy and Air Force nurses or medical specialists. Most were young and inexperienced, but all were volunteers, working alongside their male counterparts in emergency rooms, operating rooms, intensive care units, surgical wards and convalescent centers, administering aid and comfort to the injured, the sick and dying. More than 1,200 female soldiers served in various branches of the military, working in a variety of roles including clerks, typists, translators, intelligence officers and flight controllers.

Red Cross workers, both male and female, worked with the 'Service to Military Hospitals' service, looking after patients and carrying out social work and recreation therapy. Others served with the 'Service to Military Installations', dealing with family crises, including births, deaths, and emergencies. Those who worked with the 'Supplemental Recreational Activities Overseas', known to the men as the Donut Dollies, served drinks, and arranged entertainment at the bases, bringing a glimpse of home comforts in Vietnam.

Many civilians served with the Special Services range of organizations, including service clubs, libraries, entertainment, sports, and movies. Others worked with the Humanitarian Workers US Agency for International Development and the range of initiatives designed to help the thousands of war orphans.

CHAPTER 11

WEAPONS

SMALL ARMS WEAPONS

M1911A1 .45-CALIBER AUTOMATIC PISTOL

The pistol had been adopted in 1911 and it was designated the M1911A1 following minor changes in 1926. It was considered surplus after the Second World War but they were still used in Vietnam and were the preferred weapon of the Tunnel Rats. The pistol had a seven-round magazine and an effective range of 50m; it weighed 2.5lb.

M1 .30 CALIBER RIFLE AND M2 .30 CALIBER CARBINE

The M1 and M2 were issued to the South Vietnamese Army until assault rifles were available. They were the standard weapons of the Regional Forces, Popular Forces and CIDG troops. The M1 rifle was a single-shot weapon using an eight-round clip and it could fire 10 rounds a minute to an effective range of 460m. It was 43.6in long and weighed 9.5lb. The M2 rifle could fire 60 rounds a minute from 30-round cartridges, but it only had an effective range of 250m. It was 35.5in and only weighed 5.5lb.

Pump-action shotguns were sometimes used for close protection in thick undergrowth. (111-CC-38705)

A Marine keeps a lookout during a sweep of Rung Sat Special Zone. (USN-K-36424)

M3A1 .45-CALIBER SUBMACHINE GUN

This blowback automatic submachine gun only had an effective range of 100m but it could fire 60 rounds a minute from 30-round magazines. Although it had been superseded by the assault rifle this modified version of the 1942 M3 weapon was still used by Special Forces troops and armored vehicle crew. It was 22.8in long with the stock retracted and weighed 9lb.

XM177E2 5.56MM COMMANDO SUBMACHINE GUN

This gas-operated semi-automatic weapon could only fire up to 15 rounds a minute from 20-round magazines but the effective range was 460m. It was 28in with the butt extended and weighed 7.1lb.

M14, 7.62MM RIFLE

Studies had shown that men rarely took aimed shots during combat and sustained fire was usually the deciding factor. The M14 was adopted as a semi-automatic version of the M1 rifle and it was introduced to Vietnam as early as 1957. A gas-operated rotating bolt fired bullets from the detachable 20-round box magazines giving it a sustained rate of fire of 20 rounds per minute and an effective range of 460m. It was 1,118mm (44.1in) long and weighed 5.1kg when it had a full magazine. The M14A1 variant was fitted with a pistol grip and a folding forehand grip while the folding bipod allowed it to be used as a light machine gun, increasing the range to 700m. A compensator on the muzzle aided accuracy.

The M14 National Match (Accurised) was introduced for snipers in 1969 (it was unofficially called the M21) and a velocity-reducing suppressor fitted to the muzzle reduced the noise of the rifle shot. It was equipped with an adjustable ranging telescope which could be ranged from 300–900m.

Over 1.3 million M14s were made before it was superseded by the M16.

M16A1 5.56MM RIFLE

The AR-15 rifle was licensed to the Colt Manufacturing Company in 1959 and after successful trials with the US Air Force, it was designated the M16 three years later. The Army purchased its first consignment for trials in 1963 and they were soon being issued to advisors and Special Forces personnel in Vietnam.

A rifleman fires a short burst with his M-16 during Operation Cook. (111-CC-43086)

Plastic was used to reduce the weight to 7.6lb and the smaller 5.56mm round allowed men to carry extra ammunition in the field. The operator could flip the selector between automatic and semi-automatic fire, firing from twenty or thirty-round magazines to an effective range of 460m; it was 39in long.

The original weapon was found to be unreliable and liable to jam in the field. A number of modifications were made in 1966, which eliminated many problems. However, some soldiers did not like the 'toy-like' appearance of the M16 and kept their sturdier M14 for as long as possible. The M16 eventually became the standard rifle in Vietnam.

KNIVES AND BAYONETS

The M3 Fighting Knife had a 6.5in long steel blade with a protective black coating to prevent light reflection. The leading edge was sharpened along its full length while the back had 3.5in sharpened. The handle was made with compressed leather discs topped by a steel pommel. The M4 Bayonet, with its compressed leather handle, fitted the M1 Carbine. It was 11.8in long with a 6.5in-long blade; the leading edge and the back of the tip were sharpened. The M6 Bayonet, with its checkered grip plastic handle, replaced the M4 bayonet. The M7 was introduced for the M16 rifle and it was the same as the M6 except for a 3in-long sharp edge on the rear of the blade. It was carried in an olive-drab fiberglass scabbard complete with a steel throat and drag.

GRENADES

A wide variety of grenades were issued in Vietnam, giving the soldier a short-range indirect defensive capability. The majority were explosive designs, called fragmentation or frag grenades and the smooth lemon shaped body contained composition B-explosive cased inside a liner. The heavier 1.7lb versions measured 2.5in in diameter while the lighter 0.9lb versions measured 2.25in in diameter. After pulling the arming pin, the fuse detonated after four or five seconds on delay grenades while impact grenades would explode immediately if they hit ground sooner. Later models had a safety clip that had to be turned to release the arming lever; they were also ball shaped to improve the spread of fragments. Most grenades could be thrown up to 40m and they had an effective radius of 15m.

GRENADE TYPE	LEMON	BALL
1.7lb delay fragmentation grenade	M26A1	M61
1.7lb impact fragmentation grenade	M26A2	M57
0.9lb delay fragmentation grenade	M33	M67
0.9lb impact fragmentation grenade	M59	M68

The cylindrical Mk3A2 Offensive Grenade covered a 25m radius when it exploded; it weighed 15.6oz and had a diameter of 5.3in.

The M7 Riot Grenade produced a cloud of CS gas lasting up to sixty seconds. The gas induced nausea and vomiting and it was often used in bunkers and tunnels. The infantry would don gas masks before entering. The grenade weighed 1.1lb and the cylinder had a diameter of 5.7in.

Only the strongest men could fire the M60 machine gun from the shoulder as this Marine is doing during Operation No Name 97 south of Da Nang. (127-GVC-A370625)

Smoke grenades could be used to mark targets and landing zones or provide a temporary protective screen while troops moved to a new location. The M8 grenade produced white smoke lasting around 2 minutes while the M18 grenade could be issued in a variety of colors. Both kinds weighed 1.5lb and the cylinder had a diameter of 5.7in.

White phosphorous grenades burned at a high temperature and produced a chemical smoke when they exploded, and incendiary grenades could be used to start fires. Both were issued in an assortment of shapes and sizes.

SUPPORT WEAPONS

MACHINE GUNS

M60 7.62MM CALIBER GENERAL PURPOSE MACHINE GUN (GPMG)

This was the standard fire support weapon of the infantry squad but many were mounted on vehicles and helicopters. The gas-operated automatic recoil system was limited to 200 rounds per minute by the 100-round belts and the barrels were susceptible to overheating; the crew was issued with heat-resistant mittens to change them. They needed constant attention in the field despite modifications made in 1970 to alleviate problems. The two-man crew could only carry about 900 rounds, an insufficient amount for prolonged combat. The rest of the squad usually carried extra belts of ammunition.

This radio operator has strapped a number of smoke grenades to his pack during an operation near Cu Chi. (111-CC-49435)

Effective range: 500m with the integral folding bipod, 1,100m mounted on a tripod
Length: 42.4in (107.70cm)
Weight: 18.75lb (8.51 kg)

The M60 could fire M80 balls and M62 ammunition and the usual mix was one tracer to four balls to aid accuracy. M61 Armor-piercing ammunition was also available.

M2 .50-CALIBER MACHINE GUN
A vehicle-mounted weapon with a short automatic recoil system feeding the ammunition belt.
Length: 66in
Weight: 126lb

M1919A6 .30-CALIBER MACHINE GUN
Another vehicle-mounted machine gun with a maximum rate of fire of 75 rounds per minute
Effective range: 1,100m
Length: 32.5in
Weight: 33lb

GRENADE LAUNCHERS

M79 GRENADE LAUNCHER
This single-shot, shoulder-fired weapon was introduced in 1961 to cover the gap between the throwing distance of a hand grenade and a mortar's minimum range. The 'Thumper' or 'Blooper', as it was nicknamed, resembled a large bore, single barrel, sawn-off shotgun and the 40mm diameter grenade was loaded into the break-action breech. An experienced grenadier could fire half a dozen aimed shots a minute using the flip up back sight and the leaf foresight.
Range: maximum 400m and a safe minimum range of 30m
Length: 737mm with 355mm barrel
Weight: 6.2lb

The M406 high explosive grenade had a muzzle velocity of 75m/second and a blast area covering 5m. Smoke, CS gas and flare grenades were also available; an experimental flechette round armed with darts was soon replaced by a buckshot-filled round.

M203 GRENADE LAUNCHER
The M16 rifle and the M79 grenade launcher were combined into one weapon to increase the squad's firepower. The launcher was slung beneath the rifle barrel.
Length: 15.67in
Weight: 11lb
Ranges: maximum 400m and a safe minimum range was 30m

A Marine prepares to fire his M79 grenade launcher as his squad pursues fleeing Viet Cong during Operation Independence. (127-GVC-A369981)

A solider prepares to fire an experimental version of the combined M16 and grenade launcher, commonly known as the 'Over and Under' during Operation Cook. (111-CC-43120)

MORTARS

The deployment of mortars in the field was very limited in Vietnam and they were usually kept at the fire bases due to the weight of the weapon and its ammunition. They were further restricted in thick jungle where the tree canopy prematurely detonated shells. They could fire high-explosive, smoke or illumination rounds.

M19 60MM MORTAR
This lightweight weapon could fire up to 30 rounds per minute.
Ranges: 2,000m maximum and 50m minimum
Length: 32.25in
Weight: 45.2lb

M29 81MM MORTAR
Infantry companies had three 81mm mortars grouped in a section.
Effective range: 3,650m
Length: 45.5in
Weight: 132lb

The crew of an 81mm mortar fire their weapon during the Marines' defense of Khe Shan in March 1968. (Marine-A374591)

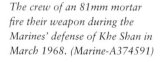

M30 4.2IN MORTAR
Each division had a chemical company armed with 4.2in mortars. The M106 variant of the M113 armored personnel carrier also held a 4.2in mortar.
Effective range: 5,500m
Length: 60in
Weight: 672lb

M4 PHOUGAS
This short-range device consisted of partially buried steel drums filled with napalm. The blasting cap or fuse ignited the incendiary burster so it showered an area with burning liquid. A 5gal container had a range of 35m while a 55gal drum could reach 85m.

ROCKET LAUNCHERS

M72 66MM LIGHT ANTI-TANK WEAPON (LAW)

This single shot smooth bore rocket launcher had been designed as the squad's anti-tank gun, however, in Vietnam it was used against emplacements and bunkers. It could be carried by one man and would be discarded after firing; squads could carry several into action. The LAW was carried in the closed position, with the watertight end covers locked in position. The operator removed the locking pins and slid out the telescopic inner tube to prime the weapon.

The trigger ignited the 66mm HEAT rocket, creating a small back blast, and propelled it towards the target guided by six spring-loaded fins.

Ranges: maximum 1,000m but only effective to 250m
Length: 630mm (24.8in) closed, 880mm (34.7in) extended, a 508mm (20in) long rocket
Weight: 2.3kg (5.1lb) launcher and a 1.0kg (2.2lb) rocket

M20 3.5IN ROCKET LAUNCHER

The M-20 had virtually been replaced by the LAW by 1965 but some launchers were deployed to Vietnam. The two-man crew could fire around five HEAT rockets a minute to an effective range of 1,200m but the rockets created a dangerous back blast. The long tube was folded in half when it was being carried and while the launcher weighed 5.5kg the hollow-charge rocket was 4kg.

The one-shot LAW rocket launcher is being carried in the closed position by this soldier of the 1st Cavalry Division. (111-CC-47352)

RECOILLESS RIFLES

These single-shot weapons had been designed to engage armored vehicles and bunkers but in Vietnam they were often deployed around military installations or on vehicles. The crew opened the hinged breech to load a shell and the case was ejected from the rear of the breech when the rifle was fired. The mechanism had been designed to reduce the recoil to a minimum.

M67 90MM RECOILLESS RIFLE
The M67 fired a 9.5lb HEAT round and it could either be mounted on the ground or fired from the shoulder. It had a three-man crew; a gunner, an assistant and an ammunition carrier. Although it was sighted to 800m the effective range was often half that. It was 1,346mm (53in) long and weighed 16kg (35lb).

M40A1 106MM RECOILLESS RIFLE
The M40 was armed with a .50-caliber machine gun so the crew could fire tracer rounds to aim the gun; it had an effective range of 700–1,000m. It was 134in long and weighed 460lb.

FLAMETHROWERS

Each infantry company had an assault platoon armed with twelve M2A1-7 flamethrowers. They were gas propelled and while fuel could only be sprayed up to 20m, adding thickener more than doubled the range. They were rarely taken out on operations due to their excessive weight (42.5lb) and the limited amount of fuel which could be carried by the four-man team.

MINES

M18A1 CLAYMORE ANTI-PERSONNEL MINE
This portable mine had a plastic box filled with 700 steel balls and 1.5lb (0.68kg) of C-4 explosive detonated by a No. 2 electric blasting cap. It was 216mm wide, 35mm thick and 86mm high (8.5in x 1.4in x 3.3in) and weighed 3.5lb (1.6kg). It was set up on four pronged legs and then aimed with a sight and the words

The crew of a jeep-mounted 106mm recoilless rifle patrol the base camp of 3d Brigade, 82d Airborne Division. (111-CC-48220)

'Front – Towards Enemy' made sure that the soldier pointed it in the right direction.

The claymore mine was detonated by a manually-operated trigger device, or a trip wire, and sprayed the steel balls out to a range of over 50m and across a 60-degree arc. Fragments would also be thrown backwards by the blast and troops used sandbags to absorb them.

Claymores were often arranged around a night defense position and they could be retrieved if they had not been fired. Many mines were positioned around fire support bases and were often linked to trip wires and flares.

M14 ANTI-PERSONNEL MINE

This tiny device was 2in thick and 2in in diameter, while the 2oz of plastic explosive was packed in a plastic case so it could not be located by metallic mine detectors.

M16 ANTI-PERSONNEL MINE

The Bouncing Betty was triggered when a man stood on the pressure pull fuse. A small charge threw the mine into the air where it exploded with maximum effect. It weighed 8lb.

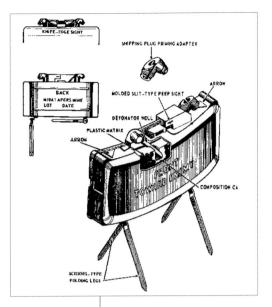

Diagram of the Claymore mine.

ARTILLERY

TOWED HOWITZERS

M101A1 105MM HOWITZER

This Second World War era howitzer had been modified to improve its mobility and reliability. It weighed 2,220kg (4,980lb) and could either be towed by a 2½-ton truck or airlifted by a CH-47 Chinook helicopter. The howitzer could be ready for action in a few minutes and the eight-man crew was able to fire up to 10 rounds per minute for short bursts to a maximum range of 11,000m. Three rounds per minute were typical for sustained fire and a battery had a reserve of 200 rounds per weapon.

M102 105MM HOWITZER

This lighter version was first deployed to Vietnam in March 1966 and by 1970 it had replaced the M101. The howitzer had a full traverse and the silhouette was much lower than the M101. It weighed only 1,470kg (3,017lb) and Chinook helicopters could carry extra ammunition using a double sling; it could also be towed by the smaller ¾-ton truck. The howitzer was also able to fire the Beehive flechette round needed to defend a base perimeter. Its maximum range was 11,000m.

M114A1 155MM HOWITZER

This Second World War era howitzer had been modified to improve its mobility and its limited traverse was improved by a number of field improvisations. It weighed 5,800kg (12,950lb) and could be towed by a 5-ton truck or airlifted by a CH-54 Tarhe helicopter. The gun could fire (to a maximum range of 14,600m) up to 3 rounds a minute for short periods, reducing to 1 per minute on lengthy fire missions; a battalion carried 150 rounds per weapon.

The crew of a 105mm howitzer fire their weapon in support of a 25th Division operation. (111-CC-40145)

SELF-PROPELLED HOWITZERS

M108 105MM HOWITZER

This cumbersome weapon weighed 22,452kg (46,221lb) and the two battalions sent to Vietnam were usually deployed on static missions. It had a limited range of 11,500m.

M109 155MM HOWITZER

This version deployed with 1st Brigade, 5th Mechanized Division. It weighed 20,500kg (52,461lb) and had a maximum range of 14,600m. A battalion carried around 275 rounds per weapon and a fused 155mm shell weighed 95lb while the charge added another 9lb.

This gun pit at Bien Hoa is lined with shells for the 155mm howitzer. (111-CC-31568)

M110A2 SELF-PROPELLED HOWITZER

A hydraulically operated stabilizing spade fixed the howitzer while the twelve-man crew loaded the shell and elevated the barrel. It could be fitted with two barrels, the M107 175mm for long-range area fire and the M110 8in for accurate short-range missions; they could be exchanged in a few hours. Batteries could deploy a mixture of guns at the same time and battalions usually carried around 100 rounds of each type of shell for each howitzer.

To begin with barrels had to be changed after only 300 rounds but an improved version could fire over 1,000 rounds before it had to be exchanged; it also took less time to fit. The howitzer weighed 58,500lb when it was fitted with the 8in gun while the 175mm barrel increased the weight to 62,100lb.

The 175mm gun fired on a low trajectory up to 32,700m and the shell had a large impact radius of 500m. The 8in gun fired on a high trajectory only up to 16,800m but it was far more accurate and often used to hit small targets.

SHELL TYPES

High-explosive: Jagged metal fragments are sent in all directions when the shell explodes. The burst areas for different shells are as follows:

105mm howitzer: 15m deep x 50m wide

155mm howitzer: 18m deep x 60m wide

8in gun: 20m deep x 80m wide

Base-Ejection Smoke: Hexachlorethane produced a cloud of smoke along the ground. It took up to 60 seconds to create an effective screen and it lasted for 2 or 3 minutes; rain increased the effect. The smoke charge ejected just before impact to stop it burying itself in the ground.

The crew of this M110 howitzer are setting their weapon with the rear-mounted spade before firing another 175mm shell. (111-CC-72858)

Illuminating Shells: Shells burned for about a minute and a 155mm shell illuminated an area over half a mile in diameter. Gun crews fired every 2 minutes, exploding shells in pairs to reduce shadows.

White Phosphorous (WP or Willie-Peter): Shells showered an area with burning fragments and sent a plume of smoke into the air when they exploded; it was a useful shell for marking targets as well as causing damage.

Beehive: The shell was an anti-personnel weapon that covered the immediate area with thousands of tiny darts when it exploded.

Improved Conventional Munitions: An ICM round produced similar results to an Air Force Cluster Bomb Unit.

A static quad machine opens fire at targets near the perimeter of a fire support base. (111-CC-64224)

FUSES

Quick Fuse: The fuse detonated when the shell hit a hard surface.

Mechanical or Powder-Train Timer Fuse: The fuse detonated after a fixed time, usually used as an air burst above a target.

VT or Proximity Fuse: A radio signal detected when the shell was close to a hard surface and detonated the fuse; it was developed to increase the accuracy of the timing of air bursts.

Delay Fuse: The fuse detonated after the shell had buried itself in the ground; it increased the explosive power of a shell against underground structures.

HEAVY WEAPONS

A number of weapons designed for anti-aircraft purposes were often used to protect installations or convoys.

M42A1 DUSTER

Twin 40mm M2A1 cannon turrets, complete with a .30-caliber machine gun, had been fitted on to the M41 Bulldog chassis in the 1950s and used as escorts for tank columns. Some of the obsolete weapons were deployed to Vietnam as ground support vehicles and on base defense; each cannon could fire 120 shells a minute. They had a six-man crew.

M55.50 QUAD MACHINE GUN

Several battalions armed with ninety-six quad machine guns were deployed to Vietnam. They were either mounted on armored personnel carriers or carried on trucks as convoy protection. Others were fixed in static positions around bases and could be towed by a 2½-ton truck. They could fire up to 600 ball, tracer and armor-piercing rounds a minute to a range of 1,825m.

XM 741 VULCAN

This anti-aircraft weapon could fire 3,000 rounds a minute at aerial targets but it was deployed in a ground role in Vietnam, often around military installations, where its rate of fire was reduced to 1,000 rounds per minute. Ball, tracer and armor-piercing rounds were available and it had a range of 3,000m. Towed and self-propelled versions were deployed.

CHAPTER 12

EQUIPMENT

ARMORED PERSONNEL CARRIERS

The M113, and its variants, was a lightweight aluminum armored personnel carrier and its low ground pressure allowed the carrier to operate in many areas of South Vietnam, even during the monsoon season. It was able to cross paddy dikes and small streams, while crews were trained to recover their vehicles with winches, cables and beams. The M113s gave squads greater mobility while the armor protected anyone inside from small arms fire and shell fragments. However, the carriers were vulnerable to mines and men often preferred to sit on top of their vehicle rather than sweat it out inside. Some squads stacked sandbags inside to absorb an explosion but the added weight reduced speed and range.

The commander of an M113 receives new orders as it breaks through the undergrowth during one of 4th Division's operations in the Central Highlands. (111-CC-59146)

The standard M113 was armed with a 12.7mm machine gun and a 7.62mm machine gun and it could carry up to 2,000 rounds of ammunition. It was 4.46m long, 2.33m wide, 2.16m high and weighed nearly 11.5 tons. The gas (petrol) engine in the A1 version had a maximum speed of 40mph but they were vulnerable to enemy fire and most M113s in Vietnam were the A2 variant fitted with a diesel engine.

Several M113 variants were deployed and the body of the M577 command variant was higher to allow the staff inside to work at map tables and operate their communications equipment while the M114A1 reconnaissance version was smaller and only weighed 7.5 tons; the unarmed M548 cargo carrier could carry up to 6 tons of equipment or ammunition for the rest of the platoon. Two variants carried mortars for providing indirect support. The M125A1 variant was armed with a 81mm mortar and it had an effective range of 3,650m. The M106A1 was armed with the heavier 107mm (4.2in) mortar with an effective range of 5,500m. A variety of field modifications were made to the M113 to suit the conditions in Vietnam, including a portable scissor bridge and fire-fighting equipment.

UPGRADING THE M113

Once it became clear that the M113 was as effective fighting vehicles, upgrade kits were deployed to armored cavalry units. Gun shields, pintle mounts and hatch armor gave the crew extra protection. Kit A allowed a .50in machine gun to be fitted to the commander's cupola and two 7.62mm machine guns either side of the troop compartment. Modified versions allowed miniguns, recoilless rifles or grenade launchers to be fitted above the commander's cupola. Kit B fitted a .50mm machine gun mounting to the mortar variants.

BATTLE TANKS

M48 COMBAT TANK

The M48 was the main battle tank used in Vietnam and despite initial concerns that deployment would be restricted by the terrain, it proved to be a versatile infantry support weapon. Over 350 had been deployed by the summer of 1969. The earlier A1 and A2 variants had gas (petrol) engines but they had been replaced by the A3 diesel variant by 1968 with a top speed of 30mph. The gunner could aim the 90mm main gun with the stereoscopic range finder while the loader used the mechanical ammunition selection system to choose between high explosive, HEAT, canister, beehive or white phosphorous ammunition.

Many tank commanders sighted the main gun by eye while their gunner sat on the tank's rear deck armed with an M16 for close protection. A powerful xenon searchlight and infrared fire-control equipment were fitted for fighting at night. The crew also had a .05in machine gun and a .03in machine gun.

The M48 was 6.88m long, 3.63m wide, 3.10m high and weighed 52 tons. The four-man crew often used steel planking, spare track and sandbags to increase protection against rocket propelled grenades.

M551 ARMORED RECONNAISSANCE VEHICLE (SHERIDAN)

The M551 was a high-speed, yet heavily armed, armored reconnaissance vehicle capable of operating in swampy areas. It was developed to replace the heavy M48 tanks operating with the divisional and regimental cavalry squadrons

An M48 Patton tank moves through thick jungle during Operation Pershing, 1st Cavalry Division's sweep of Binh Dinh Province. (111-CC-40380)

The crew of an M551 Sheridan keep watch during a land-clearing operation. (111-CC-75949)

(11th Armored Cavalry continued to use their M48). The main weapon, a 152mm M81 gun/missile launcher, was equipped with advanced night-vision equipment; the tank also had a .50in machine gun and a 7.62mm machine gun. The tank had a four-man crew and the diesel engine had a maximum speed of 43mph. It was 6.30m long, 2.79m wide, 2.95m high and weighed 16.7 tons.

The first Sheridans were delivered to 3rd Squadron, 4th Cavalry and the 1st Squadron, 11th Armored Cavalry Regiment in 1969 but confidence in the new tank was undermined when a mine ruptured the hull and detonated the ammunition inside one. There were reliability issues with the missile electronics and the caseless ammunition but the combination of the night sight and the 152mm canister round proved to be effective. Over 200 Sheridans were in action by the end of 1970.

M41 WALKER BULLDOG LIGHT TANK

The lightweight M41 served with the South Vietnamese Army. It was too small to act as an infantry support weapon and had a limited operating range of only 100 miles. The four-man crew operated the 76mm main gun, and the .30in and .50in machine guns.

SPECIALIST TANKS

M728 COMBAT ENGINEER VEHICLE

The M728 was a variant of the M60A1 battle tank developed for combat engineering units. While the 165mm gun could blast apart fortifications, the hydraulically operated bulldozer blade could clear obstacles. The four-man crew could lift items with the turret mounted winch and boom and they relied on the .50in and 7.62mm machine guns for protection.

M60A1 TANK CHASSIS WITH AVLB LAUNCHER

The Armored Vehicle Launched Bridge could launch and retrieve its scissor type class 60 bridge, bridging a watercourse up to 18m wide (60ft). The bridge could be left in place until other vehicles had crossed and then retrieved from either end. It took the two-man crew less than 5 minutes to place or pick up the bridge but the time was doubled if they had to work from inside the hull. It was not armed. The Armored Vehicle Launched Bridge could also be mounted on an M48A3.

M88 MEDIUM RECOVERY VEHICLE

The M88 was an armored recovery vehicle armed with a large winch for towing disabled tanks and a front spade, giving extra leverage for extracting vehicles from soft ground. The rigid tow bar and towing pintle were used for long journeys. The four-man crew could also use the boom to lift engines for repair while they relied on the .05in machine gun for protection. The M88 also acted as a mobile workshop, carrying tools, spare parts and welding equipment.

An M88 recovery vehicle uses its spade to dig foxholes for armored personnel carriers as the men prepare to set up a night defensive position during Operation Cedar Falls. (111-CC-38101)

OTHER ARMORED VEHICLES

M56 SCORPION SELF-PROPELLED ANTI-TANK GUN
This tracked anti-tank weapon had been developed to support airborne troops. It had a crew of four and had a top speed of 28mph. It was 4.55m long, 2.57m wide, 2.03m high and weighed 7.75 tons.

M50 SELF-PROPELLED MULTIPLE 106MM RIFLE
This light anti-tank vehicle had six 106mm recoilless rifles mounted in threes either side of the turret. Four rifles had .50-caliber rifles attached so the three-man crew could fire spotting rounds while a single .30in machine gun was carried for self-defense. The Ontos (Greek for 'the Thing') was only deployed by the Marine Corps as a fire support vehicle and it was effective at clearing jungle areas with its beehive rounds. The Marine units were deactivated in 1969, but some continued to serve with Army units until 1970; a few turrets were mounted in fixed positions.

XM-706 COMMANDO VEHICLE (V-100)
The V-100 was developed as a lightweight, high-speed armored car for security duties and the military police often used it for convoy protection, patrolling and base security. It had a range of 600 miles and top speed of 62mph while the multiple axles allowed it to travel off-road. The closed version had a turret armed with two .30 machine guns and gun ports; an open-topped version was also deployed.

The Ontos, with its six recoilless rifles, was used as a close support weapon by the Marines. (127-GVC-A370992)

Transport included this tiny Mule, working for 1st Cavalry Division during Operation Pegasus. (111-CC-48842)

TRACKED PERSONNEL LANDING VEHICLES

The Marine Corps Amphibious Ready Group used a variety of armored amphibious vehicles to conduct landings on the beaches of South Vietnam. The Mark 5 had a three-man crew and it could carry thirty-four men on land and twenty-five in the water; a cupola-mounted .30in machine gun was used for self defense. It was 9.04m long, 3.56m wide, 3.05m high and weighed nearly 44 tons. Top speed on land was 30mph and it could travel at 7mph in the water.

A command version equipped with communications equipment had a ten-man crew. The Mark H6 was armed with a 105mm howitzer, a .50in and a .30in machine gun; it was operated by a seven-man crew. A recovery version equipped with a winch and a boom had a three-man crew. The V-shaped bow improved its speed in the water while the tracks were protected by a return channel. A1 versions had improved air intakes and exhaust systems.

TRUCKS

A variety of cargo trucks transferred supplies, ammunition and personnel on supply convoys around and between bases. The 8-ton M520 truck, a diesel-powered 4x4, weighed over 20 tons and had a top speed of 30mph. The 5-ton 6x6 M54A2 truck, weighed over 10 tons and had a maximum speed of 54mph while the 2½-ton M35A2 truck weighed 6.7 tons and had a maximum speed of 56mph. Both the M54 and the M35 could be powered by diesel or gas (petrol) engines.

Two 1¼-ton trucks were available. The M715 gas- (petrol-) powered version and the heavier M561 diesel model; both had top speeds of around 55mph. The petrol powered M151 ¼-ton Utility Truck, only weighed 1.8 tons and it had a maximum speed of 65mph. The M-274 ½-ton Mechanical Mule was a 4x4 truck developed for airmobile and airborne units and although it only weighed 870lb it could carry a similar weight over dirt roads. The driver removed the seat and steering column before it was slung beneath a helicopter and it could be dropped by parachute; soldiers turned it upright if it landed the wrong way up.

Right: An Amtrack carries out amphibious landings along the coast. (127-GVC-A191204)

Below: An 18-ton GOER wrecker truck ploughs through the mud in the Central Highlands. (111-CC-41243)

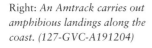

US Air Force F-4C Phantoms head towards their target in North Vietnam. (342B-VN-95077)

Diesel wrecker powered trucks were equipped to recover damaged or disabled vehicles. The 5-ton M816 6x6 version weighed 18 tons while the 10-ton M553 4x4 version weighed over 23.5 tons. The M559 4x4 fuel truck carried 2,500 gallons and was often used to service armored units.

The smaller M718 ¼-ton ambulance had a gas (petrol) engine while the larger M792 1¼-ton ambulance was powered by a diesel engine.

FIXED WING AIRCRAFT

FIGHTER AIRCRAFT

MCDONNELL F-4 PHANTOM

Numerous variants of the versatile two-seater Phantom served throughout the conflict, carrying out raids across Vietnam, Laos and Cambodia. They were engaged in aerial dog fights, shooting down over 130 MiGs, attacked ground targets and prepared targets for B-52s by dropping bundles of radar-reflecting metallic fibers, known as chaff.

The first US Air Force squadrons of F-4C Phantoms arrived in April 1965 as escorts for F-105 Thunderchiefs but they were soon carrying out their own missions. The F-4D appeared in December 1965 and the F-4E took to the skies eighteen months later but C variants continued to operate as reconnaissance planes. The US Navy deployed shipboard versions of the Phantom (F-4Bs and F-4Js) and they flew over North Vietnam from Seventh fleet's carriers in the South China Sea.

Size: 8.38m with wings folded and 11.71m with wings extended, 17.73m long, 5.03m high
Loaded Weight: US Air Force variants, 58,000lb and US Navy variants, 44,600lb
Speed: 1,400mph maximum; 590mph cruising
Armament: ip to 16,000lb ordnance and a variety of rockets, missiles or 20mm cannon

Ground crewmen push a South Vietnamese Air Force F-5 Freedom Fighter into its stall at Bien Hoa Air Base. (342B-VN-93323)

NORTHROP F-5A/E FREEDOM FIGHTER

The F-5A single-seater fighter was tested in combat in 1966 and 1967 under the 'Skoshi Tiger' program. A modified Variant E, known as the Tiger II, had a more powerful engine but the planes only served briefly with the US Air Force before they were handed over to the South Vietnamese Air Force in 1967. Many Tiger II's were captured by the North Vietnamese in 1975.

Size: 7.87m wingspan, 14.38m long, 4.14m high
Loaded weight: 20,576lb
Speed: maximum 925mph; cruising 575mph
Armament: two 20mm cannons, rockets, missiles and 5,500lb of external bombs

VOUGHT F-8E/J CRUSADER

The single-seater F-8 fighter plane had been operational since 1955 and four Crusaders from aircraft carrier USS *Ticonderoga* sunk a North Vietnamese vessel during the Gulf of Tonkin incident in August 1964. The F-8E was capable of flying in all weathers, invaluable during the monsoon season, and many had been modified and updated to F-8J's by 1966; they were superseded by Phantoms and had been phased out by 1969.

Size: 10.87m wingspan, 16.53m long and 4.80m high
Max take-off weight: 34,000lb (15,422kg)
Speed: 1,120mph (1,802km/h)
Armament: four 20mm cannons and it could carry 5,000lb (2,267kg) under the wings

NORTH AMERICAN F-100F SUPER SABRE

The single-seater variant D of the F-100 fighter (nicknamed the Hun) made its first flight in 1956 and a two-seater training version appeared in 1957. Super Sabres were deployed to Vietnam in 1964 and carried out ground support missions to begin with. They later targeted surface to air missile batteries in Operation Iron Hand while others were deployed as high-speed Forward Air Controllers known as Misty FAC. They were withdrawn in 1971 having completed over 300,000 missions.

Size: 11.81m wingspan, 15.24m long and 4.95m high
Weight: 21,000lb (9,526kg) empty and 34,832lb (15,800kg) maximum take off
Maximum speed: 864mph at 36,000ft (1,390km/h at 10,973m)
Variant E armament: four 20mm cannons, two missiles and 7,500lb (3,400kg) ordnance
Variant F Armament: two 20mm cannons and up to 5,000lb ordnance

LOCKHEED F-104 STARFIGHTER

F-104-A single- and F-104-B two-seater trainers had been in service since 1955. Most of the Starfighters deployed to Vietnam after April 1965 were C variants, a fighter-bomber version. They were phased out in 1967.

Size: 6.62m wingspan, 16.66m long and 4.11m high
Weight: 12,760lb (5,788kg) with a 15, 903lb (6,846kg) payload
Maximum speed: 1,150mph (1,85lkm/h)
Load-armament: one 20mm cannon and 2,000lb (907kg) ordnance

REPUBLIC F-105 THUNDERCHIEF

The single-seater Thunderchief, an all-weather attack aircraft, carried out over three-quarters of all bombing missions in 1965. They were vulnerable when loaded and Phantoms had to act as escorts. A two-seater variant, the F-105-G Wild Weasel, was later introduced to locate surface-to-air batteries.

Size: 10.64m wingspan, 19.58m long and 5.99m high
Weight: 27,500lb (12,474kg) with a 25,046lb (11,361kg) payload
Speed: maximum 1,372mph; cruising 596mph
Armament: one 20mm cannon and 14,000lb (6,350kg) ordnance

FIGHTER ATTACK PLANES

DOUGLAS B-26K (LATER THE A-26A) – COUNTER INVADER

This low-speed, two-seater plane had been withdrawn in 1958 but a few were deployed as tactical bombers during the advisory period. Variants reappeared as A-26's fighter attack planes in 1966; they had been withdrawn by 1969.

Size: 21.79m wing span, 15.72m long and 5.79m high fuselage
Weight: 38,314lb maximum
Maximum speed: 323mph
Armament: eight .50-caliber machine guns, 12,000lb ordnance

An F-100 Super Sabre dives towards its target in South Vietnam. (342B-VN-97645)

An A-1 Skyraider loaded with two 1,000lb and twelve 250lb bombs flies towards its target. (342B-VN-96080)

DOUGLAS A-1 SKYRAIDER

The Skyraider was the last piston engine combat plane to fly over Vietnam. Despite its low speed, it was sturdy, heavily armed and capable of operating in all weathers. Single-seater A-1Hs and two-seater A-1Es were deployed. They were withdrawn in April 1968, having flown over 100,000 missions.

Size: 15.24m wingspan, 11.83m long and 4.77m high
Weight: 11,968lb (5,429kg) empty
Speed: 325mph maximum and 240mph cruising
Armament: four 20mm cannons and 7,960lb (3,630kg) ordnance

DOUGLAS A-4 SKYHAWK

The Skyhawk was introduced as a jet replacement for the A-1 Skyraider and it eventually carried over half of the US Navy and US Marine Corps missions flown over Vietnam:

Size: 8.38m wingspan, 12.27m long and 4.57m high
Weight: 10,000lb (4,535kg) empty
Armament: two 20mm cannons and 10,000lb (4,500kg) ordnance
Speed: 675mph maximum

GRUMMAN A-6 INTRUDER

The first two-seater Intruders flew over Vietnam in October 1962 and their advanced electronic equipment enabled crews to spot small targets in all weathers. It often escorted A-4 Skyhawks and the improved A-6E became the standard variant after 1972; the EA-6B had larger cabin space for its electronic equipment.

Size: 16.15m wingspan, 16.64m long and 4.75m high
Weight: 25,684lb (11,650kg)
Armament: 15,000lb (6,804kg) ordnance
Maximum speed: 685mph (1,102km/h)

VOUGHT A-7 CORSAIR II

The single-seater A-7A Corsair was deployed by the Marines at the end of 1967. The electronic navigation and weapons systems proved to be so effective that the Air Force began using variant D in 1972 while the Marines upgraded to variants B and E.

Size: 11.79m wingspan, 14.05m long and 4.90m high
Weight: 19,781lb (8,972kg) empty
Armament: one 20mm cannon and 15,000lb ordnance
Speed: 663mph maximum and 545mph cruising

Above: *An A-6 Intruder loaded with twenty-two 500lb bombs takes off. (127-GVC-A422128)*

Left: *A Marine A-4 Skyhawk prepares to take off. (127-GVC-A421746)*

A-37 DRAGONFLY

Following heavy losses of A-1 Skyraiders, the Air Force decided to test modified twin-engine Cessna T-37 aircraft in combat and twenty-five reached Vietnam in August 1967 where they were evaluated under the Combat Dragon program with their new designation, the A-37A Dragonfly (many pilots called it the Super Tweet). Model Bs rectified design problems and over 250 were delivered to the South Vietnamese Air Force; many were captured by the North Vietnamese in 1975.

Size: 10.93m wingspan, 8.92m long and 2.70m high
Weight: 5,440kg (12,000lb) including 2,130kg (2,700lb) ordnance
Speed: 478mph (769km/h) maximum and 425mph cruising

C-47 DAKOTA

This Second World War vintage plane was converted for several uses in Vietnam and the AC-47D gunship version was armed with three 7.62mm miniguns on portside so it could circle over targets or provide fire support for bases under attack. This model had also been given an improved fuel capacity so it could remain in the air for longer. Other versions of the C-47 were fitted with photographic reconnaissance and electronic warfare equipment.

Size: 29.41m wingspan, 19.43m long and 5.18m high
Weight: 31,000lb and it could carry 6,000lb of cargo
Cruising Speed: 160mph

Above: *A C-47 Dakota drops thousands of propaganda leaflets during a psyops mission. (342B-VN-93123)*

Left: *Vietnamese A-37s peel off to attack a target. (342B-VN-105934)*

AC-119G SHADOW GUNSHIP

The Shadow was a converted twin-engined C-119 Flying Boxcar taken from Air Force Reserve units across America. They were armed with four multi-barrelled Gatling guns but when the first ones were deployed in December 1968, it soon became clear that they needed to operate close to their maximum weight, compromising performance.

Size: 33.30m wingspan, 26.37m long and 8.13m high.

Speeds: a cruising speed of 180 knots and a combat speed of 130 knots

AC-119K STINGER GUNSHIP

The Stinger was introduced in 1969 as an improvement on the Shadow, and with its two jet engines and two 20mm Gatling cannons, it was used to attack truck convoys on the Ho Chi Minh Trail. Flares and a 1.5-million candlepower illuminator could be used to light up targets.

Size: 33.30m wingspan, 26.37m long and 8.13m wide.

Combat speed: 180 knots

BOMBERS

B-52 STRATOFORTRESS

The B-52 had been designed after the Second World War to carry nuclear bombs on long-range, high-altitude missions over the Soviet Union. In June 1965 Strategic Air Command started using the aircraft for low-altitude tactical missions across Vietnam and the modified versions could carry around 60,000lb of conventional bombs. B-52s flew over 125,000 sorties over Southeast Asia.

Crew: aircraft commander, pilot, radar navigator, navigator and electronic warfare officer

Size: 56.41m wingspan, 48.56m long and 12.40m high

Speed: 638mph maximum and 526mph cruising

Armament: four .50-caliber machine guns in the tail

A B-52 Stratofortress flies over the coast of South Vietnam en route to its target.
(342B-VN-95230)

OBSERVATION AIRCRAFT

Small, slow-moving observation aircraft were used for a variety of reconnaissance and observation missions, including artillery spotting, communication relays and medical evacuation.

CESSNA O-1 BIRD DOG (FORMERLY L-19A)
This single-engine, unarmed, two-seater reconnaissance plane was used by Forward Air Controllers.
Size: 10.97m wingspan, 7.87m long and 2.79m high
Weight: 1,614lb (732kg) and a maximum take-off weight of 2,400lb (1,090kg)
Cruising speed: 86 knots for 4 hours

CESSNA O-2A SKYMASTER
The first twin engine O-2 was deployed in March 1967. O-2As were used by Forward Air Controllers while the O-2B was equipped with loudspeakers and leaflet dispensers for psychological warfare. The two-seater O-2 could be armed with a 7.62mm minigun and two rocket pods. It was equipped with enhanced navigation aids and communications equipment.
Size: 11.58m wingspan, 8.89m long and 2.87m high
Weight: 4,900lb loaded
Cruising speed: 144mph

Top: *O-1 Bird Dog observation planes are checked over at Phu Bai Air Base before take-off. (111-CC-68447)*

Above: *This OV-1B Mohawk is equipped with the Side Looking Airborne Radar (SLAR) for checking targets. (111-CC-42978)*

OV-1 MOHAWK
The three variants of this two-seater plane had a maximum speed of 255 knots and a cruising airspeed of 185 knots:
A Model – Photographic reconnaissance
Size: 12.8m wingspan, 12.52m long. Basic weight: 9,781lb and 5,239lb payload
B Model – Electronic surveillance using Side Looking Airborne Radar (SLAR)
Size: 14.63m wingspan, 13.39m long. Basic weight: 11,217lb and 5,426lb payload
C model – Infrared (IR) Reconnaissance
Size: 14.63m wingspan, 12.52m long. Basic weight: 10,379lb and 4,923lb payload

OV-10A NORTH AMERICAN BRONCO
This armed twin-engine two-seater plane was deployed by the US Marine Corps and the US Air Force in July 1968. The rear compartment could carry five men or 3,200lb of cargo.
Size: 12.19m wingspan, 12.12m long and 4.62m high
Weight: 7,190lb (3,260kg) empty and a 7,254lb (3,290kg) payload
Armament: four 7.62mm machine guns and 3,600lb of mixed ordnance or external gun pods
Speed: 281mph maximum; 223mph cruising

CARGO AIRCRAFT

Cargo aircraft carried men, cargo and equipment from the main air bases to forward airfields around the country.

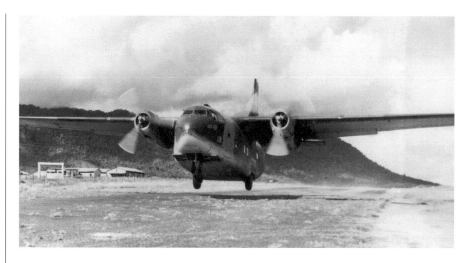

A C-123 Provider takes off from a temporary airfield made from perforated steel planking. (342B-VN-98353)

C-123B AND C-123K FAIRCHILD PROVIDER

The twin-engine C-123B often kept the isolated Special Forces camps supplied while modified versions carried out low-level defoliant spraying missions. By 1969 nearly 200 C-123Bs had been converted to C-123Ks by adding two J-85 jet engines.

Size: 32.53m wing span, 23.24m long and 10.52m high
Weight: maximum 60,000lb
Cruising speed: 170mph

C-2B DE HAVILLAND CARIBOU (LATER C-7A)

The twin-engine Caribou could carry twenty-six troops, twenty litters or over 3 tons of cargo. In January 1967 the US Air Force took over fixed-wing tactical transports and they were redesignated the C-7A.

Size: 29.16m wing span, 22.12m long and 9.68m high
Basic weight: 18,576lb and a 9,924lb payload
Cruising Speed: 150 knots

UTILITY PLANES

These small utility transport planes carried personnel and cargo across Vietnam.

U-1A OTTER

Size: 17.68m wingspan, 12.75m long and 3.84m high
Weight: 4,900lb and ten passengers or a 3,100lb payload
Cruising Speed: 104 knots

U-6A BEAVER

Size: 14.63m wing span, 9.27m long and 3.18m high
Weight: 3,310lb and five passengers or a 1,790lb payload
Cruising Speed: 105 knots

U-8 SEMINOLE

D Model size: 13.79m wing span, 9.63m long and 3.51m high
D Model weight: 4,978lb with a 2,322lb payload, including over 400lb of cargo
F Model size: 14.00m wingspan and 10.16m long
F Model weight: 5,282lb with a 2,418lb payload, including over 800lb of cargo
Cruising Speed: 155 knots

Above: *A U-21 Ute used by 1st Signal Brigade as a communications relay and to carry personnel. (111-CC-67806)*

Left: *A C-7A Caribou aircraft flies along the coast of South Vietnam. (342B-VN-100452)*

U-21A UTE

A heavier utility plane that was used for command and control missions, administration and transferring patients between hospitals; it could carry up to ten passengers.

Size: 14m wing span, 10.82m long and 4.34m high
Weight: 5,500lb with a 4,100lb payload
Cruising Speed: 164 knots for 4 hours and 30 minutes

HELICOPTERS

ATTACK HELICOPTERS (AH)

AH-1G HUEY COBRA

The tandem-seated Cobra was the first purpose-designed gunship and the first delivery of six helicopters was assigned to the 1st Aviation Brigade in September 1967 for training purposes they were in action two months later and their first test came during the Tet Offensive the following February.

Size: 16.13m long with a rotor diameter of 13.41m
Weight: 5,783lb with a 1,993lb payload
Airspeed: cruise at 130 knots and a maximum of 190 knots (219mph)
Armament: chin-mounted 40mm grenade launcher and minigun, up to seventy-six 2.75in rockets on its stub wings

The crew of a Cobra helicopter scan the ground for targets. (111-CC-54847)

Above: *A CH-3 Jolly Green Giant helicopter heads out on a rescue mission.* (127-GVC-A191573)

Right: *A CH-47 Chinook helicopter delivers a load of supplies to an isolated firebase.* (111-CC-65953)

CARGO HELICOPTERS (CH)

SIKORSKY CH-3E

The USAF had started operating the Navy's Sikorsky S-61 transport helicopter as early as 1962, renaming them CH-3A/Bs. CH-3Cs appeared the following year and the CH-3E was adopted in 1966. Fifty CH-3Es were modified for rescue missions and designated HH-3Es with the nickname Jolly Green Giant. They were fitted with two .50-caliber machine guns, armor and self-sealing fuel tanks, while the three-man crew was trained to operate a rescue hoist; they could also refuel in-flight.

Size: 22.25m long, 5.51m high and a main rotor diameter of 18.90m
Weight: 11 tons when loaded
Speed: maximum 177mph; 154mph cruising

CH-34C CHOCTAW - SIKORSKY

The CH-34 had been in service with the US Army since 1955 but it had been replaced by the Huey and the Chinook by 1965. It was used by the ARVN and could carry eighteen men. The Marines used their version, the UH-34D Seahorse, as their main utility and assault helicopter but it could not carry weapons like the UH-1 Huey; the high cockpit was an obvious target for snipers.

Size: 14.25m long with a main rotor diameter of 17.07m
Basic weight: 7,800lb with a payload of 2,175lb and an external cargo of 3,000lb
Speed: maximum 123mph; 98mph cruising

CH-47A CHINOOK

The first tandem-rotor Chinooks reached Vietnam in 1962 and over the next eleven years three models served as medium transport helicopters. They could carry thirty-four troops or heavy loads of cargo, including a 105mm howitzer

A CH-54 Flying Crane helicopter helps an artillery crew from 4th Division relocate to a new firebase. (111-CC-65959)

complete with ammunition and crew and the three-man crew became adept at slinging large loads beneath the helicopter.

MODEL A

Size: 29.95m long and a 18.01m diameter main rotor
Basic weight: 18,500lb with a 14,916lb payload or 16,000lb of external cargo
Speed: cruise at 140k (110 knots); maximum 165k

MODEL B

This model, with improved rotors, a strengthened airframe and stronger engines, was introduced in May 1967 to increase the external payload to 20,000lb. However, it could only stay airborne for one hour and was quickly superseded by the Model C.

MODEL C

This model could fly for two hours and it became the mainstay helicopter for cargo transport. Eleven CH-47A sorties could move an 105mm howitzer battery and ammunition to a new position in a short time.
Size: length 30.18m and a 18.29m diameter main rotor
Weight: 19,772lb with a 19,772lb payload or 26,228lb of external cargo
Cruising speed: 120 knots

The Chinook could be armed with two side-facing M60 machine guns, mounted on the doors, and a rear facing M60 machine gun mounted on the cargo ramp; some were equipped to drop riot control gas or napalm tanks from the ramp. It could also be fitted with a powerful hoist and cargo hook for recovery missions and Chinooks rescued over 12,000 damaged aircraft and helicopters.

The crew of an OH-58 Kiowa helicopter fires its minigun. (111-CC-63939)

SIKORSKY CH-54 TARHE 'SKY CRANE' OR 'FLYING CRANE'

The Sky Crane was used to lift heavy loads of cargo and the Army deployed nearly 100 between 1964 and 1972. The helicopter had a minimum 'backbone' airframe design and the pilot sat in a rear-facing seat so he could direct the hoist. A detachable pod capable of carrying over forty men, a command post or a workshop was available. Other pods were equipped as Mobile Army Surgical Hospitals complete with a theater, X-Ray equipment and blood bank. The Sky Cranes were used to move supplies or vehicles and they could airlift 155mm towed howitzers; they also recovered nearly 400 downed aircraft. They could carryn huge 10,000lb cratering bombs which were used to create instant landing zones. The Model B, with its improved engine, was introduced later.

Size: 20.41m long with a 7.73m diameter six-bladed main rotor
Basic weight: 20,700lb with a 15,400lb payload or 20,760lb external load
Speed: 128mph maximum; 111mph cruising

OBSERVATION HELICOPTERS

Observation helicopters were used for reconnaissance and target acquisition missions while commanders became increasingly reliant on them for watching their area of operations.

OH-6A CAYUSE - LOACH

The two-seater Cayuse could be armed with 7.62mm machine guns or a minigun to attack targets.

Size: 7.16m long and an 8.03m diameter main rotor
Weight: 1,163lb and a 1,163lb payload
Cruising speed: 100 knots

OH-58A KIOWA

The two-seater Kiowa could be armed with a minigun.

Size: 9.86m long and a 10.77m diameter main rotor
Weight: 1,583lb and a 760lb payload
Cruising speed: 100 knots

UTILITY HELICOPTERS

UH-1 IROQUOIS

The UH-1 or Huey helicopter became an iconic symbol of the Vietnam War and they became the lifeline for the men in the field, flying troops into battle,

An OH-6 Loach Helicopter takes off for a reconnaissance mission near the Cambodian border. (111-CC-45973)

A UH-1D helicopter carries ARVN troops to their next landing zone. (111-CC-70778)

delivering cargo to fire bases and evacuating the wounded to safety. Pilots were able to fly at low altitudes and high speeds, landing on tiny landing zones carved out of the jungle, often under heavy fire, gaining the admiration of everyone, in particular the men at the sharp end.

The first model, the XH-40, was tested in 1956 and it had soon proved that its powerful turbine engine was reliable and easy to maintain under the most extreme of conditions. The Model A had been superseded by the time the Huey was deployed to Vietnam but many were still kept in service in the United States as transport and training helicopters. By June 1963 most helicopter companies had been issued with the Model B with its more powerful engine and higher cruising speed; it had also been modified to carry machine guns.

By the end of 1966 over 3,000 Hueys had been ordered from Bell Helicopters and the machine was being used in many roles:

Air Assault: the Huey placed men on landing zones at the start of an operation and then moved them around the area of operations.
Gunships: Hueys were modified into gun ships and they could provide protection during an air assault, give close support fire or act as convoy escorts.
Cargo Carrier: the UH-1D and UH-1H became the mainstay of cargo delivery.
Medevac: between 1965 and 1969, over 378,000 casualties were evacuated by helicopter.

MODEL B

Size: 13.03m long and a 13.41m diameter main rotor
Weight: 4,600lb and a 3,900lb payload or eight passengers
Crew: pilot and co-pilot; a crew chief and a door gunner could also fly with the helicopter
Cruising speed: 90 knots

MODEL C

The Model C had an increased cruising speed of 110 knots, a longer range and a higher carrying capacity. It could also be fitted with grenade launchers, 2.75in rockets or miniguns.
Size: 13.00m long and a 13.41m diameter main rotor
Weight: 4,830lb and a 4,670lb payload

The Model D and Model H were introduced to incorporate improvements developed for Vietnam. They both had a 12.78m long fuselage, a 14.63m diameter main rotor and weighed 4,900lb; the Model D had a 4,561lb payload while the Model H had a 4,100lb payload.

HELICOPTER WEAPONRY

Early operations by the South Vietnamese Army proved to their American advisors that the helicopter could also be used as a flying gun platform. Over the years that followed there was an increasing tendency to add machine guns, miniguns, rockets, cannons and grenade launchers to helicopters. Eventually, a purpose-built attack helicopter, the AH-1G Huey Cobra, was introduced.

OH-6A CAYUSE AND OH-58 KIOWA OBSERVATION HELICOPTERS
An M27 minigun carrying 2,000 rounds of ammunition could be mounted. An XM8 mounting allowed the helicopters to carry an M129 40mm grenade launcher armed with 150 rounds.

OH-13 SIOUX AND OH-23 RAVEN OBSERVATION HELICOPTERS
Twin .30-caliber (XM1) or twin 7.62mm (M2) machine guns could be mounted on the skids. The XM1 had 500 rounds per gun, the M2 had 650 per gun. A joystick was used to move the weapons up or down.

UH-1 HUEY HELICOPTERS

Temporary supports were used to arm the helicopter with machine guns and rocket launchers in the early days, but they were soon replaced by specially designed mountings. Over the years that followed Hueys were armed with a variety of weapons systems:

M60 7.62MM MACHINE GUNS
M23: The door pintle-mounted machine gun was armed with 550 rounds of ammunition and they were dispensed into a bag to prevent damage to the engine and the rotors. The XM29 was an improved door pintle mount
M6: Two forward-facing machine guns were mounted on each side of the helicopter. They were aimed by the pilot or the co-pilot and each gun was armed with 1,500 rounds

2.75IN ROCKETS
XM3/M3: 24-tube launchers were fitted in pairs, one on each side of the helicopter

SIDE-MOUNTED COMBINED WEAPONS SYSTEMS
M16: Two forward facing 7.62mm machine guns and a seven-tube 2.75in rocket launcher were mounted on each side of the helicopter
M21: An M134 minigun replaced the pair of machine guns

SIDE-MOUNTED CANNONS
XM30: 30mm guns were armed with 600 rounds of ammunition
XM31: Twin 20mm cannons were armed with 600 rounds of ammunition

CHIN-MOUNTED 40MM GRENADE LAUNCHER
M5: A pod carried a M75 grenade launcher armed with 150 or 300 grenades

SIDE-MOUNTED MISSILE LAUNCHERS
The M22 launcher fired XAGM-22B anti-tank guided missiles
The X26 mounting carried wire-guided TOW missiles in three-round pods. The experimental program was stopped in March 1968 but the appearance of tanks during the NVA's 1972 offensive saw them mounted on Hueys

OTHER WEAPON SYSTEMS
XM18: Twin six-tube launchers mounted on the back of the helicopter and armed with flares, munitions or CS grenades; two strapped together made an XM15 dispenser
XM19: 24 tubes armed with 2 million candle power flares for lighting targets
XM47: Four anti-personnel mines were held in a pod until released by the pilot

CH-47A CHINOOK
The transport version of the Chinook helicopter could be armed with 7.62mm machine guns using side-facing M24 door mounts or a rear-facing M41 ramp mount; each gun had 200 rounds. The armed ACH-47A Chinook was used for close support fire missions. It had twin .50-caliber or twin 7.62mm machine guns fixed on XM32 mounts or twin 20mm cannons fixed on XM34 mount-fitted to the sides. Rear-facing .50-caliber or a 7.62mm machine gun could be fitted with the XM33 ramp mount.

AH-1G 'HUEY' COBRA
The purpose-built attack helicopter could have an M134 7.62mm electrically driven minigun mounted in an M18 gun pod. The preferred weapon arrangement was the M28 twin-mounted chin turret. The pilot could move

the turret from side to side to aim and it was either armed with two miniguns or two M75 or M129 40mm grenade launchers. It was, however, usually mounted with one of each to reduce jamming. The miniguns had 4,000 rounds of ammunition while the grenade launchers had 400 rounds each. The Cobra could also have an M35 mount, with a M195 six-barrel 20mm automatic gun, fitted to the port side; the gun carried 1,900 rounds.

THE PEOPLE SNIFFER

A personnel detector, otherwise known as the People Sniffer, was introduced in 1968 in an attempt to locate hidden personnel. While some were carried by infantry squads, the majority were mounted on UH-1 helicopters. The electronic equipment was capable of analyzing carbon, ammonia, and compound sigma air samples gathered in an air scoop. Positive readings indicated the possibility that there were humans hiding in the undergrowth beneath the helicopter.

Numerous tests showed that the equipment had a good success rate and an experienced operator could tell if the reading was a residual scent, an animal or a discarded pile of human excrement. Unfortunately, a high turnover of staff gave inconsistent results and many viewed the equipment with suspicion, preferring to rely on established forms of intelligence.

People Sniffer helicopters flew in pairs to confirm their results and the command helicopter dropped CS canister clusters when a positive reading was reported. They then hovered low to blow the undergrowth aside with the rotor wash while two observation helicopters kept a lookout; any sign of movement and a pair of waiting Cobras swooped down to engage the target.

People Sniffers successfully served with 9th Division where the flat open spaces of the Mekong Delta proved to be ideal. By 1969 over half of positive readings resulted in finding a target; a third of all the division's contacts.

NIGHT HAWK KITS

Kits were developed to allow sniper teams to work from the Huey helicopter at night. They had a night observation device and small searchlights (pink for moonlit nights and white for dark nights) and two Night Hawk kits were fitted to each helicopter in case one jammed. Snipers searched for targets as the pilots flew low over suspect areas and they were able to use their minigun if they came under fire.

Two Cobras flew close by in case the snipers spotted the large target. The kits could easily be removed so the Huey could fly transport missions during the day.

RIVER AND SHALLOW WATER VESSELS

PATROL LAUNCH
The launch patrolled the shallow coastal waters, stopping and searching suspicious craft.
Crew: 6 men
Mark I size: 15.27m long and 3.99m wide
Mark II size: 15.65m long and 4.14m wide

Left: *A patrol boat moves at high speed along a river near Saigon. (111-CC-76655)*

Below: *A monitor patrols the Quan Cong Tyon River near My Tho. (111-CC-477728)*

The following boats were operated by the Mobile Riverine Force, mainly in the Mekong Delta. Many were protected by armored plate and iron bar lattices to counter rocket-propelled grenades.

50FT ASSAULT SUPPORT PATROL BOAT - ALPHA BOAT
Two Alpha boats usually led a riverine flotilla while a third boat guarded the rear; its operating speed was around 14 knots. The five-man crew could use their vessels as a tug or patrol the riverine bases.
Size: 15.29m long and 4.65m wide

LANDING CRAFT MEDIUM CONVERSIONS
These four variants were either 18.36m or 17.12m long, 5.21m wide and they typically sailed at around 8 knots.

Command and Communications Boat: The Charlie Boat carried the assault squadron and ground force commanders and their communications equipment. It had a crew of eleven.

Armored Troop Carrier: The Tango Boat could carry forty troops, one M113 APC, one 105mm howitzer and truck or 12 tons of supplies. It was armed with .30 and .50-caliber machine guns, rapid fire grenade launchers and 20mm cannons and was manned by a crew of seven.

The crew of an Air Cushion Vehicle prepare to move to their next objective during Operation Troung Cong Dinh. (111-CC-49561)

Monitor: The monitor provided fire support while the squadron was on the move and for the ground troops during operations. The eleven-man crew was able to fire .50-caliber, 40 and 20mm gun mounts, 40mm grenade launchers or an 81mm mortar. In 1969 some monitors were fitted with a 105mm howitzer, while others, nicknamed Zippos, were fitted with flamethrowers.

Armored Troop Carrier Refueler: The craft could carry 1,200 gallons of gasoline and 300 gallons of lube oil for the rest of the flotilla; it had a crew of seven.

31FT PATROL RIVER BOAT MARK I

This high-speed fiberglass reinforced plastic boat patrolled rivers and canals at speeds up to 25 knots, and the four-man crew searched suspicious craft or engaged the enemy on the shore. It was 9.45m long, 3.23m wide and equipped with two PRC-25 radios and a radar unit. The boat was armed with twin .50-caliber machine guns mounted in a forward rotating turret (they could be replaced by a 20mm cannon) and a 7.62mm machine gun mounted at the rear. The crew also carried a shotgun, a grenade launcher and their M16s. Ceramic armor protected the pilot's position and the machine gun positions.

The Mark II was slightly larger and faster while the body had been strengthened and the new jet engines were less likely to get fouled by reeds. A .50-caliber machine gun and a second grenade launcher were also added.

AIR CUSHIONED VEHICLE (ACV) SK-5

This hovercraft was able to skim across water and land on a cushion of air, while rubber canvas skirts allowed it to pass over rice paddy dikes, streams and grassland. The first navy ACVs reached Vietnam in 1966 and three larger Army variants arrived two years later, forming the Airboat Platoon. They served as 39th Cavalry Platoon during the summer of 1970 under 9th Division's 3d Brigade. It was crewed by an operator and a radar man and they could carry up to twelve men; they generally worked in pairs with a helicopter guiding them.

Size: 11.84m long and 7.24m wide
Speed: 40mph over land and 70mph on water

CHAPTER 13

TOUR OF DUTY

NEW ARRIVALS

Those destined to serve in the north of South Vietnam collected at Fort Lewis, Washington, so they could be taken to McChord Air Force Base and flown to Cam Rahn Bay. Men heading for the south gathered at Oakland Army Terminal, California (it was known as Oakland Army Base after June 1966) so they could be flown from Travis Air Force Base to Tan Son Nhut Airport near Saigon.

The day they climbed aboard the civilian airliner bound for South Vietnam was the start of their year-long tour and men immediately began counting down the 365 days until their Date Eligible for Return from Over Seas (DEROS). Once the plane touched down the first thing the new arrivals noticed as they were hustled on to waiting buses was the oppressive heat and the smell; many were surprised to see Vietnamese working on the base.

Men were introduced to service life, Vietnam style, during a week of lectures, inoculations and kit issues. In 1966 new courses covered patrols, ambushes, booby traps and refresher courses on their weapons. New arrivals stood out in their new uniforms and they were often referred to as 'Cherries' or FNGs (f**king new guys).

22d Replacement Battalion processed new arrivals at Cam Ranh Bay while 90th Replacement Battalion worked at Long Binh. Everyone was issued with a Geneva Conventions Card and a Next of Kin notification form to be used if they were killed, seriously injured, reported missing or taken prisoner. At the end of their induction men were assigned and taken either by convoy, transport plane or helicopter to their unit.

Another round of instructions and advice was given as they moved from division, to brigade and then to battalion headquarters but before long they were being helicoptered to their unit's fire base.

On arrival, the new guy was escorted to the command post (CP) and given a final few words of advice before he was assigned to a squad. Few acknowledged his arrival, they had seen many come and go before, but they all had faded uniforms compared to the new arrival's fatigues. It would be some time before the Cherry fitted in.

PLATOON LIFE

The officers and men had known little about Vietnam and many would have taken taken little interest in the news reports on the war until they had been drafted. As sons of the Second World War and Korean War veterans, most believed in the values of conservatism, anti-communism and the God-given rights of any average middle-American.

Above: *New arrivals receive the first of many instructions on how to conduct themselves in Vietnam. (111-CC-70011)*

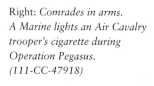

Right: *Comrades in arms. A Marine lights an Air Cavalry trooper's cigarette during Operation Pegasus. (111-CC-47918)*

The relationship between the platoon officers (the LT) and their men was often down to individual management styles but some company commanders demanded certain standards. Successful officers usually maintained a friendly and fair approach while keeping a professional distance. Some tried to be too friendly while others were unapproachable and problems soon occurred, particularly during the later years. If they were seen to be too easy-going, unfair or too strict, poor discipline emerged, storing up problems for the platoon when it was out on patrol.

The platoon officers lived in a separate bunker and they were kept busy with administrative and operational duties, often leaving the platoon sergeant to deal with the men. They endured the same hardships as the men on operations and they were constantly aware that their decisions could cost lives.

The enlisted men would be a mixture of economic and social backgrounds, some white, black, some Hispanic, but they all had one thing in common; they were counting the days until they left Vietnam. They were close on one level, teasing each other with jokes and stories, usually calling each other by nicknames. Few knew little about their buddies' backgrounds in the United States, referred to by many as 'The World'. Colonel Hal Moore (later Lieutenant-General), the commander of 1/7th Cavalry, summarized the feelings of the American soldier under fire following the Battle of the Ia Drang Valley in November 1965: 'American soldiers in battle don't fight for what some president says on TV, they don't fight for mom, apple pie, the American flag . . . They fight for one another.'

FIRE SUPPORT BASES

The fire support base or fire base was home to many American troops when they were out in the field. They were built as safe havens, securing artillery positions so batteries could cover a unit's area of operations. Typically an average sized fire base was home to a company of infantry protecting a battery of 105mm howitzers with the help of a platoon of engineers and sections of support services troops.

Fire bases were often a simple ring of bunkers surrounded by barbed wire, but some became semi-permanent positions with trenches, tunnels, bunkers and helipads, protected by a complex network of mines, trip flares, sensors and searchlights. They became refuges for the soldiers, where they could eat, shower and rest after the stresses of operating in the field. Commanders had to make sure their men were kept active so they did not develop 'fire-base psychosis' and become reluctant to leave. They also had to make sure that the number of troops allocated to base administration and defense did not become too excessive.

A typical fire base was 250yd in diameter with an 800yd perimeter and it could have any of the following features:

Infantry tactical operations center (TOC), the base command post
Artillery fire direction center (FDC)
Logistics, communications, medical and mess facilities
Howitzer positions and ammunition storage
Helicopter pads

CONSTRUCTING A FIRE BASE

Fire bases differed in size and shape, according their function and the terrain. The main concern was to build a defensible perimeter as quickly as possible and by 1969 many procedures and equipment had been standardized.

Artillery and infantry commanders had to agree on the location of the fire support base with both wanting to cover the allocated area of operations. The infantry wanted a tight perimeter that could be defended and they were often on high ground, where they were difficult to target with rockets and mortars; hilltops were often chosen in I Corps and the Central Highlands. The artillery needed space and suitable ground to deploy their howitzers. Helicopters also had to be able to supply the base.

A mortar team build their bunker during 1st Division's Operation Bluefield. (111-CC-403-62)

An air cavalry aerorifle platoon landed first (by rappel in difficult terrain) and set up a perimeter while engineers began work clearing undergrowth and cutting down trees. As soon as a helicopter could land, engineer equipment was delivereded followed by extra infantry so the perimeter could be extended. Air cavalry scouts and gunships patrolled the immediate area at all times.

Once the area had been cleared, the engineers hammered a stake in at the center and scribed out the bunker line with a 40m-long rope. Twenty-four stakes were placed at 5m intervals, one for each bunker, while helicopters dropped a bundle at each one. Each bundle contained a demolition charge, two sheets of steel planking and empty sandbags (twenty-five CH47 Chinooks carried an entire fire base kit). The infantry used the charge to start the excavation, using the planks and sandbags to cover it. The hole could be extended when the perimeter was secure.

Out on the perimeter, another circle was marked 75m from the bunker line and covered by a triple layer of concertina wire. The area between the wire and the bunkers was covered by claymore mines and trip wires linked to flares.

As the infantry prepared the perimeter, the engineers completed the rest of the base. Small bulldozers, flown in by Chinook and Tahre helicopters, excavated holes for the command posts, mortar positions and the howitzer battery. They would also shape low bunds between the infantry bunkers. A Chinook positioned a 6m high observation tower in the center to complete the new fire base. The time taken to complete the basic fire base varied depending on the terrain but the perimeter defenses and the bunker line had to be complete before nightfall.

Napalm was used to burn off undergrowth while 750lb Daisy Cutter bombs, timed to detonate just above the ground, were dropped into jungle areas, clearing foliage and trees without making a crater. The 10,000lb Instant LZ bombs, codenamed Commando Vault, appeared in March 1969 to give the engineers a head start on clearing an area; they were also used to create emergency landing zones. Once the perimeter was secure, work could start on the command bunkers. Many were built from prefabricated timber beams, while some had two bunker modules made from steel CONEX containers placed side by side. The troops sometimes slept under steel half-culvert sections, covered by earth and sandbags.

1st Cavalry Division covered an enormous area of operations in the Central Highlands and its units became adept at opening and closing fire bases on a regular basis. A platoon of engineers supervised the closing stage, helping the infantry to salvage everything while bulldozers leveled the area.

FIRE BASE LIFE

Life on the main bases consisted of endless work details to keep the GIs busy around the clock. Security of the base was of uppermost importance; patrols continually checked the immediate area and guards watched the perimeter while details improved the perimeter fences and minefields. Observation towers kept a watch on the surrounding countryside during the day while listening posts, some outside the perimeter, were occupied at night. The endless number of radios, radars and sensors also had to be monitored.

The daily deliveries of ammunition, food and equipment had to be unloaded from the supply helicopters and the men spent hours extending and repairing their bunkers. In the monsoon season there was always a need for extra drainage ditches as the base turned into a quagmire. The worst task was cleaning the latrines, using diesel, and the smell of burning human waste often filled the air.

Meals marked the passing of time and the men usually had B-rations for breakfast and dinner, and the smaller C-rations at lunchtime. When possible traditional food was served on Thanksgiving Day and Christmas Day; the Fourth of July was usually celebrated with a mad minute of weapons fired on automatic. Post was delivered as often as possible by the resupply helicopters while chaplains held regular religious services for all denominations.

Keeping watch along the perimeter of Long Binh base; netting has been hung around the bunker to stop grenades and satchel charge attacks. (111-CC-82836)

DEFENDING A FIRE BASE

Each fire base had a coordinator to make sure that everyone and every weapon, both on and off the base contributed to the defense, while defensive plans had to be regularly updated. Everyone knew that they were under observation both day and night, and the occasional probe tested the base's perimeter. Base commanders sometimes held practice alerts to check the men's reactions.

Outside the base, patrols kept the Viet Cong observers at a distance, often following up intelligence leads. Established bases knew where the danger areas were and ambushes, listening posts and radars kept them under surveillance. Random harassment and interdiction artillery missions were often used to shell suspect areas while the Air Cavalry's helicopters and the Forward Air Controller's observation planes made wide-ranging searches.

The perimeter of the base was surrounded by an open area covered with barbed wire, claymore mines, CS grenades, fougasse and trip flares. The men kept a watch on the perimeter throughout the night, taking it in turns to stand guard with their night observation devices.

If enemy sappers got inside the wire, the Americans were vulnerable as artillery and helicopter support became impossible and illumination helped friend and foe alike. The enemy fired indiscriminately, throwing satchel charges into the bunkers for maximum effect before withdrawing. Barbed-wire barriers split the base into defensive compartments and fighting holes and trenches between bunkers allowed the men to move around without exposing themselves.

FORWARD BASES

Conditions at the divisional and brigade base camps were an improvement on the fire base, but the men still lived under canvas, alternately plagued by dust and mud as the seasons changed, spending long hours in their underground bunkers when they were under attack. There was limited lighting in the billets as generators worked at full capacity to keep the base functioning; clean water had to be delivered. Urinals were pipes or plastic mortar round tubes set in a gravel bed; DDT powder was sprinkled over the area as a disinfectant. The latrines were wooden outhouses with toilet seats over a cut-down oil drum, but the waste still had to be burnt with diesel.

INTO ACTION

PLANNING AN OPERATION

The division allocated its limited aviation units to the brigades in turn and when the Assault Helicopter Company and Air Cavalry Troop arrived it was time to choose several targets. The operations and intelligence staff studied photographs and maps, trying to identify enemy positions, using information

Huey helicopters fly to their next landing zone during 25th Division's Operation Wahiawa. (111-CC-34624)

gleaned from agents and Viet Cong prisoners. Long-range reconnaissance patrols watched overnight aided by radars while helicopters armed with Side Looking Airborne Radar and Red Haze infrared equipment circled overhead.

Brigade headquarters staff arranged artillery missions while Chinooks and Tarhes repositioned batteries and flew in ammunition; helicopter refueling and rearming points also had to be set up. While fire zones were cleared with the government officials, requests for air strikes and naval gunfire were made.

By morning the night surveillance and interrogation reports would have been assessed, the amount of fire support decided and orders could be issued to the waiting assault companies.

AIRMOBILE OPERATIONS

At the flight briefing, pilots were told how to approach the landing zone (LZ), but wind, ground fire, and even the sun, could cause the pilot to land at the wrong angle. Platoon leaders were assigned sectors around the perimeter and the critical moment of the assault was the first few moments after landing as squad leaders orientated themselves and ran to their assembly points while the noise of helicopters and support fire drowned out their commands. Indecision could cause the men to go to ground on the landing zone, jeopardizing the mission.

The pilot indicated the direction of the objective over the intercom during the final approach so the crew chiefs could mark up an orientation card and hand it to the squad leader. Later versions were marked with a compass and the objective so the squad leaders could check their bearings at the first opportunity.

Company commanders briefed their platoon commanders while the men checked their weapons and equipment and collected their ammunition, water and C-rations. Squad leaders were then briefed on what to expect before assembling their men alongside the helipads. Men often had to wait for hours while the helicopters shuttled men and ammunition to the landing zones; they sometimes had to unload wounded men from returning helicopters.

PREPARING THE LANDING ZONE

As the troops loaded on to the helicopters, preparations were underway to hit the landing zone with suppressive fire. Artillery targeted specific areas while planes dropped bombs and napalm before using their cannons to fire at tree lines and other likely hiding places. The fire plan made sure that the planes did not cross the artillery zone and the Forward Air Controller guided pilots on to their correct approaches. The gunships came next, firing their machine guns, miniguns and rockets at the immediate area around the landing zone. By the time the transport helicopters (slicks) came in for their final approach, the landing zone was obscured by smoke and flames.

It was soon realized that preparation by fire was not always the correct approach. A complex fire plan, taking several days to coordinate, was needed while the incoming fire alerted the enemy and consumed large amounts of ammunition. In many operations preparatory fire was included at the combat commander's request. The gunships accompanying the transport helicopters were usually enough and air cavalry gunships could engage anyone seen escaping. Air strikes and the artillery could be saved for observed fire missions at lucrative targets later in the operation.

HITTING THE LANDING ZONE

A flight of slicks and their armed escorts flew in V-formation at around 1,500ft en route to the landing zone to avoid ground fire; subsequent flights varied their routes to confuse the enemy. On the final approach the pilots dived down to fly low and fast, following the contours of the ground, a technique known as 'Nap of the Earth' flying. The troops were forced to hold on during the last minute's exhilarating ride above the tree-tops.

The flight slowed as it came in above the landing zone when the pilots flared (effectively braked) their machines almost to a standstill. They came into a low hover together to stop the enemy concentrating their fire on one machine, but did not touch down until the landing zone had been cleared of mines and obstacles. Men stepped or jumped off the helicopter skids and followed their squad leader

A door gunner fires at the landing zone as the helicopters make their final approach. (111-CC-71495)

Gunships prepare the landing zone with smoke rockets. (111-CC-60794)

219

1st Cavalry Division slicks take off from a landing zone in An Lao while the squads head for the perimeter and shells explode on the hills. (111-CC-41854)

to their allocated sector of the perimeter while the helicopter door gunners gave covering fire. Defended landing zones were rare (they were known as 'Hot'). If there was too much fire the flight could be ordered to an alternative. landing zone. To begin with landing zones were chosen up to 1,000m from the objective to minimize the amount of fire on the helicopters. However, the men were often exhausted by the time they had forced their way through the jungle or rice paddies, and the element of surprise had been lost. If there were a few .50-caliber machine guns in the area, the distance could be reduced to 300m, the effective range of light machine guns. In some areas pilots would land on top of an objective, having learnt that the Viet Cong usually fled or hid; the few that opened fire were dealt with by the circling gunships.

JITTERBUGGING

When the Viet Cong started to disperse, it was time to reorganize the Assault Helicopter Companies and small teams of five slicks were dispatched at short notice to check sightings. Each team could make up to a dozen insertions a day; reserves were on standby if a significant contact was made. The enemy unit's escape routes were cut off one by one as units landed around the position and once the cordon was complete it was time to pile-on. Artillery, air strikes and helicopter gunships pounded the enemy position. The infantry made sure no one escaped and psyops teams attempted to encourage the trapped Viet Cong to surrender. The operation continued until everyone had surrendered or had been killed.

The Viet Cong soon responded to what they called the Hawk Tactic. Ambush squads, armed with a machine gun, a claymore mine and a number of AK47s, waited in hiding for the jitterbug team. A sniper would target the helicopters and the squad leader while the rest of the squad opened fire as they landed, detonating the claymore mine to complete the ambush. The American response was to stop reconnoitering landing zones, using People Sniffers to check if the area was clear.

BUSHMASTER OPERATIONS

If a strongly held area was discovered, an infantry company inserted its platoons nearby at dusk. The men then set up prearranged ambushes covering the trails leading to the enemy position and attacked the Viet Cong and when they moved. At first light the company could call on fire support to hit the surrounded position while helicopters watched for enemy reinforcements.

CHECKERBOARD OPERATIONS

Attacks on weakly held areas were made during the day by lightly armed companies equipped with extra radios. Squads landed in a checkerboard formation, at 500m intervals, and search the squares hoping to flush out any Viet Cong. Once contact was established, the rest of the company could move in to form a cordon while artillery and helicopter gunships targeted the area. Fifteen squads could cover 3 sq km in two days.

NIGHT OPERATIONS

The Viet Cong often moved at night and Night Hunter Teams were organized ready to pounce. Networks of AN/TPS-25 ground surveillance radars were monitored and when a large group was spotted, air cavalry gunships scrambled, while slicks carried infantry to blocking positions. As the gunships flew in low, artillery fired both high explosive and illuminating rounds to light up the target. The gunships arrived moments later, raking the lit area with their weaponry. The infantry then moved in to round up survivors.

The Night Hunter Teams were successful but they tied up a lot of troops as they were soon replaced by the Night Search Teams. A command helicopter flew low over an area while a spotter or sniper looked for targets with a starlight scope; artillery flares provided artificial light on cloudy nights. When contact was made, bursts of tracer fire directed two gunships down to the target. The command helicopter watched for men fleeing the area as Cobra attack helicopters dived down to engage targets. The tactic was used extensively against the Viet Cong's supply routes.

Some Viet Cong units preferred to disperse during the day and gather together at night to plan raids. Night Raid ambushes were often used to target known gathering places. Two slicks, each carrying a dozen men, flew towards the target while artillery flares lit up the area and Cobra gunships strafed the surrounding area. The command helicopter marked the target with a flare as the team came in to land and snatch prisoners before the Viet Cong could react. Within minutes of landing the Night Raid team was on its way back to base with its prisoners.

AMBUSHES

The Viet Cong spent the hours of darkness on the move and disruption of these night-time communication routes reduced their ability to operate. Special Forces, Long-Range Patrols and later Ranger teams identified well-used trails so radars and sensors could be set up to monitor the enemy's movements. Ambushes were often set around base areas, limiting the Viet Cong's night-time activities, and they could protect hamlets and villages, sources of food for the Viet Cong. They were also set to capture known political or military leaders as part of the Phoenix program.

Ambushes could also form part of search-and-clear operations, set covertly before the main force arrived to try to drive the Viet Cong into them in what were known as fire and flush or rabbit hunt operations. Teams were sometimes left behind following an operation, targeting anyone emerging from their hiding places or returned to retrieve weapons and the dead.

THE PLANNED AMBUSH

A successful ambush could reap high rewards, but there were many difficulties organizing one, particularly for inexperienced troops. The assault group would set up the ambush, aiming to cover the killing area with its weapons, while a support group covered any escape routes with machine guns and mines. A security element was posted on lookout while a search party was detailed to search the area when it was over.

Setting ambushes secretly was always a problem as the Viet Cong questioned villagers for information on passing patrols. If the number of men coming back

A squad waits for new orders during a patrol along a stream bed. (111-CC-41412)

from the patrol was smaller than the number setting out, an ambush had been set. Units often kept ambush teams out in the field, exchanging them every few days, to keep the patrol numbers constant. If a patrol leader suspected he was being watched, the ambush party would return to base.

Ambushes were laid along roads, trails and waterways, between known Viet Cong sanctuaries, and natural obstacles, including streams and embankments, were used to channel the enemy into a killing zone. The men formed interlocking fields of fire and it was advisable to reconnoiter the site in daylight, setting aiming stakes to sight their weapons. They had to be well trained in camouflage and everyone had to maintain strict silence as they waited. Men took it in turns to man the infrared and starlite night sights, alerting the team if they spotted movement on the trail.

Claymore mines were set to trigger the ambush and the men raked the area with fire while machine guns covered the head and tail of the killing zone. A sniper armed with a night sight often triggered the ambush by targeting the enemy's leader.

Flares would light up the area as the ambush reached a crescendo as claymores, rifle fire, machine-gun bursts and shouts filled the night air. Once it was over, the search group would search the bodies for weapons and documents while the rest of the team assembled and prepared to withdraw before the enemy returned with larger numbers.

When an American unit moved into an area, intelligence was limited and troops had to be ready to react if they stumbled on enemy trails, and they had to be trained to set up ambushes immediately. The head of the patrol set up the ambush, while the second and third platoons moved left and right to cover escape routes and the fourth platoon guarded the command post.

The Viet Cong often entered hamlets at night to get food and shelter. Scouts would watch the trails and the main ambush would be set inside the perimeter while the locals were kept under curfew. Machine guns and mines covered the escape routes and the trap was sprung when the Viet Cong entered the hamlet.

SNIPING

The Army Marksmanship Unit started a sniper program at Fort Benning in January 1968, teaching men to use upgraded M14 rifles with sniper-scopes and improved ammunition, meanwhile divisions set up their own schools at their base camps. By the end of the year each battalion was supposed to have six snipers but company commanders often deployed them as riflemen to begin with. The problem was rectified by allocating the snipers to battalion headquarters so they could be assigned to suitable missions.

At night they worked in pairs and while one looked for targets with a starlight scope, the other had his rifle ready, reducing eye fatigue. Pink filtered searchlights were used on dark or cloudy nights. Two riflemen guarded the sniper team and their radio. Six-man teams were sometimes deployed along trails during daylight hours.

LOCATING AND DESTROYING THE SANCTUARIES

During the early days of the conflict the Viet Cong Main used the jungles and plantations as hiding places for men and supplies. Well-known sanctuaries surrounding Saigon were the Iron Triangle, Rung Sat Special Zone and War Zones C and D. American troops staged large operations in these areas, deploying several battalions at a time to sweep the areas.

Companies worked their way through the area, driving the Viet Cong while others waited to stop them escaping, a tactic known as the Hammer and Anvil. Smaller reconnaissance patrols would then sweep back and forth across the area searching for isolated groups.

Villages were often fortified with bunkers, entrenchments and tunnels, and after evacuating the civilians to refugee camps they were razed to the ground. This scorched earth policy proved to be controversial and the press began to associate the term Search and Destroy with wholesale destruction of the villages.

Operations became smaller and fragmented following the Tet Offensive, as the Viet Cong scattered across the countryside and company-sized operations became

Above: *A patrol destroys a Viet Cong shelter and supply cache before moving on during a search and destroy operation.* (111-CC-37609)

Right: *Viet Cong suspects are hurried towards a waiting helicopter so it can take them to brigade headquarters for questioning.* (111-CC-38-407)

commonplace. The term Search and Destroy was eventually phased out in favor of less contentious terms to differentiate between different types of operation including reconnaissance, security, clear and search, cordon and search.

Finding and eliminating the Viet Cong and NVA base camps was a major objective of the American Armed Forces during the early stages of the conflict and the staff at the Combined Intelligence Center discovered that patterns could be detected. In the mountains they were often built in valleys near watercourses with bunkers covering the high ground. In the paddy fields of the Mekong Delta they had to be situated on high ground to remain dry during the monsoon season. Elsewhere they were often near roads or trails, protected by bunkers and booby traps. Possible base locations and trails were marked on maps. A combination of visual and photographic reconnaissance, sightings by Special

Forces and Rangers patrols, agent's reports, radar readings and interrogations confirmed a location. Helicopters armed with People Sniffers could detect movement on the ground while defoliant missions stripped away the tree canopy to reveal camps and trails. Once the sanctuary had been located it was time to plan how to destroy it.

A large number of combat troops were needed to deal with a big camp and the men knew there was a good chance they would encounter the enemy and numerous booby traps. It took time to search a base thoroughly, several days with larger complexes, and the infantry sometimes withdrew while air and artillery strikes were called in. The infantry often called in the Tunnel Rats to conduct a detailed search.

Tank 'dozers and Rome Plows were sometimes used to cut swathes through the jungle, starting with a cut ring around a base before cutting paths into the center. The combat troops and engineers then moved in to search each area while 'dozers plowed bunkers into the ground.

No matter how hard the American engineers tried to obliterate a base, there was always something left hidden and the Viet Cong returned to retrieve it as soon as the US troops left.

Australian troops run to their helicopter as it hovers, waiting to extract them. (111-CC-70571)

SEARCHING AND DESTROYING THE TUNNELS

The Viet Minh had used tunnels during their battle with the French and the Viet Cong spent the years that followed extending the systems so they could hide from their enemies, secretly move troops quickly and store supplies and

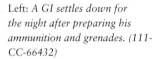

Left: A GI settles down for the night after preparing his ammunition and grenades. (111-CC-66432)

Below: A squad hits the dirt behind a paddy dike after coming under fire from a bunker. (111-CC-33496)

GIs and Vietnamese police search fish baskets for arms or ammunition during 1st Cavalry Division's Operation Pershing. (111-CC-40240)

A fire team radios for assistance after spotting a potential sniper disappearing into a tunnel. (111-CC-33502)

ammunition underground. (See Chapter 18 for details of Viet Cong tunnel construction and life underground).

If soldiers stumbled on a tunnel entrance during a firefight and there was no time to explore, they used CS and fragmentation grenades to stop it being used as a fighting position. If time permitted, Mity Mite Portable Blowers were used to fill the system with smoke or CS gas. The fumes would drive the Viet Cong into the deeper levels or suffocate them and other entrances were sometimes revealed by plumes of smoke. CS powder was scattered around the entrances but the soldiers knew that the Viet Cong would return and the tunnels would soon be repaired.

Exploring the tunnels was dangerous and time-consuming, and a large number of troops had to secure the area while specialist search teams headed deep underground. It took a special kind of bravery to enter a tunnel and a new type of elite unit known as the Tunnel Rats emerged with innovative skills developed by trial and error.

Once a tunnel entrance had been discovered the infantry secured the immediate area and formed a perimeter while the tunnel team moved in. Each Tunnel Rat chose his own personal equipment, but it usually included a pistol and bayonet, a flashlight, a protective mask, insect repellent and a compass. Pistols had to be small caliber or fitted with silencers so they did not burst the man's eardrums or cause a section of tunnel to collapse. The team brought probing rods and entrenching tools, colored smoke grenades, CS grenades and powdered CS; it also had a telephone for communications.

After checking the entrance for booby traps, two Tunnel Rats entered, one searching in front while the second followed with the communications wire. Once underground they faced a host of terrors as they crawled through the cramped tunnels. The Viet Cong were experts at placing hidden booby traps while snakes, spiders and insects, many of them poisonous, lurked in the darkness. Some sections were filled with lethal carbon monoxide and there was always the chance that the enemy, one who knew every twist and turn, was trapped below.

The Tunnel Rat teams crawled forward slowly, probing with bayonets for traps and hidden entrances, as they explored the maze of tunnels. They soon became experts at mapping and found new exits with colored smoke grenades.

Once the ground commander was convinced that the Tunnel Rats had gone as far as they could, it was time to destroy the complex. Captured items were recovered and turned over to the infantry while the Tunnel Rats advised the engineers on how to destroy the tunnels. Many different combinations of explosives were tried but the damage was minimal. Shallow tunnels could be sealed and pumped full of acetylene gas and oxygen before charges were detonated while lower levels could be flooded with water. The most effective and least time-consuming way was to wire together 40lb cratering charges, linking in sacks of powdered CS. The explosions collapsed sections while the powder made the tunnel uninhabitable for several weeks.

A soldier cautiously looks for signs of life in a tunnel discovered in the Iron triangle during Operation Cedar Falls. (111-CC-38203)

SEARCHING THE VILLAGES

While the NVA and Main Force Viet Cong units preferred to hide in the mountains or jungle, the local Viet Cong mingled with the population, using villages and hamlets as cover for their operations. They would tunnel beneath the buildings, hiding their weapons and ammunition in and around the houses. Villagers provided shelter and food, sometimes under duress. Patrols had to routinely visit the villages and hamlets, looking for suspects or hidden caches.

A cordon had to be established quickly around the village and helicopters were the perfect form of transport for inserting troops. Otherwise troops had to approach quickly from several directions, forcing the Viet Cong either to stand and fight, or withdraw into the cordon as it closed.

Guards were placed on all the roads ready to search anyone attempting to leave the village and stop anyone wishing to enter until the operation was complete. The guards had to be able to cover every part of the cordon with fire and they needed to watch for men breaking cover from a hidden tunnel entrance. Reserves, either an airmobile Eagle Flight or mechanized infantry mounted on M113s, were always kept on standby in case anyone tried to escape or counterattack. Machine gun and mortar teams usually waited outside the village.

Once the cordon had been established, the assault force moved in slowly to secure a second cordon around the perimeter of the village, well aware that a trapped force could try and fight its way out. The Reconnaissance Team entered the village first, and interpreters looked to secure the cooperation of the government official or the village elder. The Civilian Control Team gathered the civilians together and escorted them to a safe area to be questioned while the search teams began work. Everyone had to carry papers and outsiders needed to explain their reason for being away from home; anyone who did not satisfy the interrogation team had to be evacuated for further interrogation.

Searching for supply caches was time-consuming and frustrating for the GIs and although they were ordered to treat the villagers with respect, it was degrading for them to stand by and watch as their homes were thoroughly investigated. The GI had to probe carefully for clues while avoiding booby traps; mine detectors and scout dogs were also used. Schools were eventually set up to teach the soldiers how to spot hiding places. Flocks of birds often gave away the location of large rice caches and the Americans either distributed the cache to the

Above: *A family looks on anxiously while a soldier searches their storage tunnel during 1st Division's Operation Silver Springs.*

Right: *GIs prepare to escort villagers to a safe area before they start searching their village during 1st Cavalry Division's Operation Masher. (111-CC-33493)*

local population or destroyed it. Captured medical supplies were forwarded to Intelligence so the suppliers could be located and prevented from selling them.

When it became clear that the Viet Cong were using villages as hideouts, each discovery was noted and used to train new troops in search techniques. A thorough cordon-and-search operation could have dramatic results, especially when specialized equipment was available. It was monotonous but dangerous work and a quiet search could quickly erupt into fierce fighting if the patrol cornered anyone inside their hiding place.

The Viet Cong were experts at disappearing when the American troops approached. Lookouts gave the alarm and while some hid in spider holes or underground rooms, others crawled under houses, shrines, refuse heaps or latrines; some were even buried alive by the villagers and used a hollow reed to breath. Entrances were often hidden in gardens and animal pens, where it was natural to dig. Tunnel entrances were sometimes hidden away from the hamlet beneath haystacks, under bushes and in river banks. In river areas, men submerged themselves under water, or burrowed into the soft mud on the banks, and used bamboo as a breathing tube.

The Viet Cong only had limited stocks of equipment and every man guarded his weapon carefully. Ingenuity knew no bounds and items could be buried in gardens or animal pens, hidden under floors, behind walls or in false roofs and even tied to treetops. Weapons were often wrapped in sheets of plastic and buried in mud while munitions had to be kept dry and were often hidden under haystacks. If a weapon or souvenir was discovered, particularly if it had been left in an obvious place, the probing GI had to make sure that it was not booby trapped.

Everywhere, including walls, ceilings and floors had to be searched, and it could take hours to probe an area by hand. Mine detectors were treasured items as they could quickly find buried weapons, ammunition or booby traps while causing the minimum disturbance; the AN/PRC-3 was particularly useful for detecting large underground voids. Scout Dog teams were used to speed up a search and they were far more thorough than the men at finding tunnels and buried equipment in dry conditions.

As the Search Team went to work, moving from house to house, the rest of the platoon waited on standby, ready to give covering fire if anyone broke cover. The search had to be systematic, leaving no stone unturned, to be successful. From time to time the GIs were put to the test as frightened civilians emerged from their hiding places; the members of the Search Team only had a split second to decide if a suspect was Viet Cong or not.

Prisoners were handed over to the Prisoner of War Team which worked on the five S principle; Seize, Search, Segregate, Silence and Speed in evacuation. Tunnels were searched if time permitted but the Search Team often used white phosphorous grenades to clear an underground chamber; engineer teams then used explosives to destroy it.

Once the search had been completed the villagers were released as the GIs withdrew to their outer perimeter. It was a vulnerable time and the Viet Cong often counterattacked as the platoon prepared to move to the next village.

CONVOY OPERATIONS

OPENING THE ROADS

Roads were the lifelines for moving supplies and the Armored Cavalry played a constant game of cat and mouse with the Viet Cong as they fought to keep them open and keep the supply convoys moving. The 11th Armored Cavalry, the Blackhorse Regiment, saw extensive action across III Corps and quickly developed defensive strategies and offensive tactics to counter ambushes.

The Viet Cong controlled many main roads to begin with, confining the population to their villages, and securing a road fell into distinct phases. Heavily armed units continually patrolled, locating the Viet Cong's ambushes so the artillery could cover likely points with harassment and interdiction missions. The engineers and planes flying defoliant missions then cleared the undergrowth either side of the road to limit their effectiveness.

Outposts were built at bridges and choke points, keeping ambush points under constant observation, often employing searchlights at night. The engineers then swept the road for mines every day, looking to establish patterns so the artillery could sweep trouble areas at night. Finally, road construction gangs would move in to asphalt the road, making it virtually impossible to plant mines without them being noticed.

Local traffic increased as the roads became safer, allowing the local population to resume trading. It was found that a safe road network not only improved living conditions, it also increased the government's status in the eyes of the people.

CONVOYS

While a road was being secured, convoys had to run the gauntlet of ambushes and mines and in some areas the crews added armor and guns to their vehicles, turning them into Gun Trucks. Fire support was soon registered on prearranged targets along the route. Helicopter gunships flying overhead

A convoy carefully negotiates a destroyed bridge as it carries supplies to a forward base. (111-CC-51935)

targeted ambush parties while Forward Air Controllers called in artillery fire from nearby fire bases. The Armored Cavalry kept a reaction force on standby at a nearby fire base in case a convoy came under attack.

The order of vehicles in a convoy was chosen to provide maximum protection for the supply trucks. A small one was typically led by a tank and two M113s; another M113 followed while a tank brought up the rear.

Vehicles sometimes fired into the trees either side of the road hoping to prematurely spring an ambush, but the tactic was used sparingly because vehicles could only carry enough ammunition for 10 minutes sustained firing. When the column came under fire, odd-numbered vehicles fired to one side while even-numbered vehicles fired to the other, until it was clear where the ambush parties were. While the .50-caliber and M60 gunners covered the area around the vehicles, grenades were used to keep the enemy at bay. The commander's vehicle kept moving, directing fire and distributing ammunition while his men replaced wounded crew members.

The column tried to keep moving but they sometimes stopped and vehicles turned alternately left and right into a herringbone formation. Helicopter gunships and artillery targeted the ambush site while the relief force moved up. Two platoons could sometimes leapfrog each other along a dangerous stretch, taking it in turns to take up firing positions while the other moved through their herringbone.

BOOBY TRAPS

Over half of booby traps were made from Chinese Chicom grenades, a third were made from locally made materials while the rest were made from recovered US munitions.

The Viet Cong could place their traps anywhere but studies showed that one in three were located along trails and rice paddy dikes in the hope of catching a patrol on the move. Another third were arranged around bunkers, caches and rest camps while the remaining third were scattered randomly. Fortunately, the Viet Cong rarely kept watch over their booby traps, but the stress of having to look for them, knowing that each step could result in a fatal explosion, was a constant burden for the grunt on patrol.

The most common type of booby trap encountered involved taking a grenade and removing the safety pin, inserting it into a tin can to trap the level in place. A wire was then stretched across a trail, ready to pull the grenade free if it was snagged. If a grenade-type booby trap was spotted the patrol would either neutralize it or detonate it from a safe distance using a drag device to pull the wire; heavy objects were sometimes thrown at it to dislodge the grenade.

AVOIDING BOOBY TRAPS AND MINES

Patrolling involved forcing a way through the thick undergrowth (hacking the undergrowth aside was too noisy) and the leader, known as the point man, had to edge forward slowly looking for booby traps. It was tiring work and he had to be changed at regular intervals while the rest of the squad followed slowly, keeping a watch on their surroundings. The platoon leader had to make sure that his men spread out to reduce the chance of multiple casualties and the ideal was 20–30m. It also gave the impression that the unit was larger but control was much more difficult. A report from one experienced platoon leader summed up how a platoon should operate: 'Remember, keep the VC guessing as to where you are going and how you plan to get there. Never think the VC do not know you are out there, they do, and when they learn how, when, and where you are going, they will most often have a reception of some sort planned for you.' Caution, alertness and common sense were the men's greatest assets.

Platoons had to stay off trails, footpaths and tracks whenever possible, often zigzagging either side of a well-trodden route. Units also had to be wary of reacting too quickly to a chance sighting in the distance in case they were scouts trying to lure the patrols into a booby-trapped area

The Viet Cong often warned the local population about booby trapped areas and discreet questioning or bribery could extract information. Alternatively, close observation of where the villagers avoided gave clues.

An Air Cavalry trooper probes carefully with his knife for booby traps before a convoy uses the road. (111-CC-41875)

Mine-detecting equipment was usually left at the landing zone but units took it along if they were entering a notorious area. Ideally every man had been trained how to operate it.

When a soldier spotted anything suspicious, it could be the start of his unit's troubles as it often meant they had strayed into a booby-trapped or mined area. There was also a possibility that a Viet Cong patrol could be watching and waiting for an opportune moment to open fire.

If no one had been injured or killed, the men went carefully prone while the platoon leader reported the situation to his company headquarters. The men then cautiously probed to determine the extent of the booby-trapped area and it could take many hours of patient and nerve-wracking work before they could move on. Helicopters had to extract a unit from such an area by hovering overhead with a rope ladder.

If a man had been wounded by a booby trap, there was the added problem of getting him to hospital as soon as possible. While the nearest men probed their way forward to administer first aid, the rest of his unit checked their areas ready to prepare a landing zone as the squad leader called for a medevac helicopter.

This check list reminded GIs about the dangers of booby traps:

REMEMBER!
Be alert
Utilize the expertise of the Tiger Scouts
Don't walk on trails and rice paddy dikes if you can help it
Probe jungle foliage carefully
Watch where you step
Change point men often when you are tired
Use artificial drag lines
Don't bunch up
And when the above don't work and you hear a booby trap 'pop', holler 'HIT IT' and
*   hit the ground*

GI's were also issued with a wallet-sized card giving warnings about mines and booby traps:

TIPS ON VC/NVA MINES AND BOOBY TRAPS

BE ALERT --- STAY ALIVE

Mines and booby traps can kill so be alert - stay alive
If possible, don't be in too much of a hurry
Never take anything for granted, it might look harmless but it might be a killer
Evidence of old camouflage may indicate mines and booby traps
Suspect all objects that appear loose or out of place
Always look for trip wires
Never bunch up and become a good target for command detonated mines
Destroy mines and booby traps in place or mark, report and leave them alone

Before cutting trip wires, check both ends for booby traps
Objects should not be disturbed without checking for booby traps
Only the enemy's imagination limits his use of mines and booby traps - remember that
Be especially careful in areas where you are expected to slow down, bunch up or become a good target.
You can learn a lot from the local people; seek their help in locating mines and booby traps
Trails and roads should be suspected. Check refilled holes, areas covered with straw or grass, littered with dung, pavement repairs, and other suspicious spots
Report mines and booby traps immediately
Always check your area for evidence of mines and booby traps when you set up your defense
Probe gingerly when mines are suspected; don't depend solely on mine detectors
Since there was nothing in the area yesterday, don't assume there is nothing there today

Knowledge inspires confidence

Remember

Mines and booby traps are favorite devices of the VC/NVA. Grenades, spike traps, AP and AT mines and a variety of other means are employed to harass, slow down, confuse and kill friendly forces. The forms of these weapons are limited only by the imagination of the designer. Your best defense against mines and booby traps is . . .

Alertness & Caution

Booby traps maimed soldiers and civilians alike. This medevac helicopter has been called to evacuate two injured Vietnamese farmers.

MILITARY INSTALLATIONS

Many servicemen and women who went to Vietnam spent their twelve months working at the military installations, air bases, ports, logistics areas and divisional base camps. Thousands were employed as administrators, nurses, technicians, storemen and cooks while others operated machinery, vehicles and communications equipment. Their experiences were often completely different to the men serving in the field.

BASE LIFE

The Army, Marine Corps, Navy and Air Force engineers built huge military installations across South Vietnam and they had barracks, mess halls, administrative offices, communications centers and clinics. Huge depots, motor pools and maintenance workshops, were soon joined by recreation faciliites including clubs, PXs, post offices, and outdoor movie theaters to make base life as comfortable as possible. They were, however, vulnerable to attack by sappers, rockets and mortars, and the soldiers lived behind a defensive perimeter, ready to run for cover bunkers when the alarm sounded.

CONSTRUCTION STANDARDS

To begin with there were no set standards on what a base had to provide. Army and Marine Corps combat and support troops were trained to operate with minimum facilities in the field but living standards quickly improved, often inconsistently, as each division and brigade extended their bases. Before long semi-permanent billets and offices of all shapes, sizes and standards were appearing and soldiers could expect a higher standard of living than during any other war if they were stationed at a major base.

Limits were eventually imposed to stop units spending too much time and money on their facilities, but it took time to enforce them and acquire the standard building units required. Temporary Standard was applied if the base was needed for more than four years and the troops lived in one- or two-storey wooden barrack blocks connected by paved roads while the mess hall and dispensary were housed in wooden or corrugated steel structures. The men could expect piped water and sewage systems while most areas were linked up to central electricity systems. By the time work was completed the main bases looked similar to Stateside facilities, if a little more basic.

The Intermediate Standard was applied to outlying bases established for combat operations. Men were housed in temporary billets, comprising a mixture of tents and timber huts built on wooden or concrete floors. Main roads, motor pools and maintenance facilities were often paved but the rest of the facilities were connected by dusty dirt roads that became quagmires in the monsoon season. Generators were needed to cope with power surges during busy periods and billets were often without electricity. Maintaining an adequate supply was always a problem as military hardware took precedence and an electrical distribution system was installed as quickly as possible to remove the reliance on generators. Cold storage facilities for food storage were also a high priority and while everyone wanted air conditioning, it could only be installed in important areas (it was often needed to cool down electronic equipment) due to the amount of electricity it consumed. Water had to be collected from stand pipes and the latrines were dealt with by a consolidated treatment plant.

Living conditions at the main bases varied considerably – the engineers based at Vung Tau compared their accommodation with a well-known motel chain. (111-CC-81073)

An outpost returns fire against snipers during an attack on Long Binh at the height of the Tet Offensive in February 1968. (111-CC-46018)

Shanty towns soon appeared alongside the military bases and some civilians worked on the base, after their background had been checked, carrying out menial tasks, including cleaning, washing and laboring. Others made their money by running bars and massage parlors, or shops (some sold black market items); prostitution was a lucrative trade for some.

Service exchanges (PXs) sold many household items and the men could buy from mail-order houses or ask for items to be posted from home. Before long billets were filled with kitchen equipment, television sets and electric fans, placing a huge burden on the overloaded electrical system.

MAJOR BASES ACROSS SOUTH VIETNAM

I Corps: In the north Phu Bai had 6,500 billets and Da Nang had 5,500 while Chu Lai in the south had 11,900.

II Corps, North: Pleiku and Camp Enari in the Central Highlands had over 10,000 billets each while 1st Cavalry Division's camp at An Khe had space for 14,000 men. The largest camp in the area was at Qui Nhon on the coast with 22,900 billets while Tuy Hoa port had another 7,800.

II Corps, South: Nha Trang had 8,400 billets while the large base at Cam Ranh Bay could house 18,700.

III Corps: MACV Saigon had accommodation for 34,100 men while Long Binh to the northeast could house 42,800 and nearby Bien Hoa another 9,200. Three bases surrounded the Iron Triangle and while 25th Division's base at Cu Chi was the largest with 14,100 billets, Lai Khe and Phu Loi could house 4,200 and 6,700 respectively. Bear Cat to the east of the capital had 8,600 billets while the port of Phan Rang had accommodation for 4,700 men and Vung Tau could house 8,500.

IV Corps: 9th Division's base at Dong Tam could accommodate 12,200 men; there were smaller bases at Vinh Long and Can Tho.

DEFENDING A MAJOR BASE

The number of mortar and rocket attacks increased in number towards the end of the American involvement, and a great deal of planning was put into trying to stop them. Each base had a nominated commander and an operations center dedicated to coordinating field units, nearby artillery batteries, helicopter gunship and tactical aerial support.

Personnel shelters protected with sandbags were dug at regular intervals across the base and regular drills using sirens and PA systems were given to test the men's reactions. Buildings and equipment were also surrounded by layers of sandbags, while aircraft, helicopters and vehicles were parked at intervals behind revetments.

Some of the bases relied heavily on local labor to carry out menial tasks and it was important to check the background of all the workers, carrying out daily checks on their identification. It was important to assess intelligence and log suspicious events to try and outwit the Viet Cong; unidentified Vietnamese seen observing the base had to be checked. Close cooperation with the local population could turn up useful intelligence and civic action programs helped to improve civilian cooperation.

As much of the surrounding countryside as possible was kept under direct observation and observation posts equipped with binoculars and battery commander scopes were manned at all times. The observers used starlight scopes, capable of spotting targets up to a mile away, at night.

Radars were used to watch the area surrounding the base. The AN/TPS-33 had a range of over 18,000m and it could be relied on to spot personnel up to 6,000m away; weather conditions and thick jungle canopies reduced its range considerably. It was difficult to maintain and required a lot of power to run. The AN/TPS-25 had a shorter range (12,000m under ideal conditions), it was easier to maintain and only took 3 hours to set up. They were usually set on observation towers to improve their range.

Short-range radars were available to cover the perimeter of the base. They could also be set in dead ground, to track patrols, both friendly and enemy. The AN/PPS-6 covered a 1,500m radius while the heavier AN/PPS-5 had four times the range. The AN/MPQ-4A counter-mortar radar only had a small scan sector and the Viet Cong learnt to monitor the radar dish's movements; screens had to be used to hide the dish.

A large area surrounding the base (a 122mm rocket had a range of 11km), called the rocket belt, was searched for likely launch sites by helicopters before ground patrols and ambushes watched suspicious areas. Villages and dead ground (areas hidden by hills or gullies) outside the range of radars and observation posts had to be regularly patrolled. Some areas were also sprayed to strip away the vegetation.

From the moment the first shell or rocket was fired, to the time the crews scattered was rarely longer than 20 minutes and it was a race against time to call down fire or scramble helicopters to intercept them. Observation posts reported their bearings and distance to the flashes so the operations center could calculate the position of the launch site. To begin with each attack was plotted as it happened but before long predetermined grids were used, reducing the response time to a few seconds.

Artillery was the fastest to respond to an alert. Likely targets were registered and cleared in advance, and nightly curfews were arranged so that free-fire zones could be extended. Pre-plotted targets were fixed in seconds and clearances followed a minute or two later. The observation post then adjusted the fall of shot. Indirect fire had a low success rate and observed fire support from helicopter gunships or planes was preferable so bases tried to maintain round-the-clock aerial cover. AC-47 Spookys, armed with flares and three miniguns, often flew night patrols and could be over the base within minutes. On some bases, gunships were kept on standby and their crews could be in the air in minutes. The larger bases sometimes had an infantry company on alert in a barracks next to the helipads, ready to fly to the launch site.

Trained teams studied the launch site and impact points for clues following an attack, reporting useful intelligence to the base defense coordinator.

RELAXATION

ENTERTAINMENT

Wherever they were, the men were often bored when they were off duty and while some played baseball or football others passed the time reading books, writing letters home, or playing cards. Some read the *Stars and Stripes* newspaper and *Army Digest* magazine but the divisional newspaper, with its local information, tended to have a wider circulation. Many preferred to hang out, drinking beer or smoking, while they discussed cars, girls, politics or what they intended to do when their tour was over and they returned to The World.

Men soak up the sun on the beach at Vung Tau Rest and Recuperation Center. (111-CC-46-516)

The new music cassette tapes were starting to appear and while some men preferred contemporary blues or folk, others listened to country and western or rock. The late 1960s was a time for anti-war music as the hippy generation spread their message in the States and a lot of it was found playing at the bases across South Vietnam. The tapes could also used be used to record messages, replacing letters as a way of keeping in touch with loved ones.

Movies were sometimes shown at the larger bases while the Armed Forces Radio and Television Service (AFRTS) showed reruns of popular television shows, interspersed with weather reports and warning announcements. If they were lucky, the men were able to attend one of the United Service Organization (USO) shows which were sometimes headlined by famous acts from the States.

REST AND RECREATION

Servicemen were allotted a five- or six-day vacation that could be taken after they had served at least four months in Vietnam. These Rest and Recreation (R&R) breaks were non-chargeable to annual leave and came with free airfare tickets. Soldiers often did not know when they were due for their R&R and they could be transported from a fire base and be on a plane to an exotic destination in a matter of hours. The culture shock was immense and many men took the opportunity to relax on the beach and spend their money on drinking, eating, gambling and women, knowing full well that they would soon be back in the jungle. Soldiers were granted thirty days' leave back in the States and a second R&R if they extended their tour for another six months.

Rest and Recreation locations included:

Bangkok in Thailand and Taipei in Taiwan
Manila in the Philippines and Kuala Lumpar in Malaysia
Honolulu in Hawaii and Sydney in Australia
Tokyo, Hong Kong and Singapore

Each soldier was also allowed to take a three-day break at the two in-country R&R centers at China Beach and Vung Tau.

A soldier would be allowed thirty days' compassionate leave and flights back to the States if there was a death in his immediate family.

CHAPTER 14

NAVAL COMMAND IN SOUTHEAST ASIA

The Commander in Chief, Pacific, commanded all American forces in Asia but as the war intensified General Westmoreland's Military Assistance Command, Vietnam, took control of the war across South Vietnam. Meanwhile, the Commander in Chief's staff concentrated on the bombing campaign in North Vietnam and Laos and other military activities across the Far East. They also coordinated the logistics chain across the Pacific Ocean.

Pacific Command's naval component, the US Pacific Fleet, controlled Seventh Fleet which, in turn, had several Task Forces operating in the South China Sea:

Attack Carrier Striking Force, Task Force 77, conducted the air war over Laos and North Vietnam
Various Task Forces composed of cruisers and destroyers shelled coastal targets
Amphibious Force, Task Force 76, supported landings along the coast by Marine units
Mobile Logistic Support Force, Task Force 73, kept the fleet supplied and maintained

THE CARRIER FORCE

Seventh Fleet stationed an Attack Carrier Strike Force, known as Task Force 77, at Yankee Station in the South China Sea for over twelve years while ships were deployed at Dixie Station in 1965 and 1966. Typically, there were two or three carrier groups deployed at a time, increasing to three or four in the summer of 1966, and they rotated every few months for maintenance and repairs.

The carriers ranged in size from the huge Enterprise and Forrestal-class ships down to the smaller Essex-class and the number of planes varied on each ship from seventy to one hundred. Each carrier had a wing organized into two-fighter and three-fighter attack squadrons. At first fighter squadrons were equipped with a mixture of F-4 Phantoms and F-8 Crusaders but by 1970 the Crusader had been phased out. Their squadron numbers began with the letters VF.

The fighter attack squadrons flew piston-engined A-1 Skyraiders and jet powered A-4 Skyhawks or A-6 Intruders when they first deployed to the South China Sea. A-7 Corsairs started to appear in November 1967 and the A-1 Skyraiders had been phased out by April 1968; the last A-4 Skyhawks were withdrawn from the South China Sea in May 1969. Their squadron numbers began with the letters VA.

Carriers also had detachments of planes armed with electronic equipment for reconnaissance missions and detachments of helicopters for rescue and transport duties.

Above left: *A flight crew guides a Phantom on to the deck of USS* Enterprise. *(USN K-107506)*

Above right: *Pilots start their engines at the start of another raid on North Vietnam. (USN K-37800)*

Several destroyers kept a watch for approaching vessels or aircraft; they would also guide friendly planes to the carriers.

The planes carried out all types of missions ranging from reconnaissance and bombing missions over North Vietnam and Laos to ground support for combat operations in South Vietnam. The types of planes and their roles are listed below:

STRIKE OPERATIONS: A-4 Skyhawk, A-1 Skyraider, A-7 Corsair II and all-weather, day-night Grumman A-6 Intruder

ATTACK: F-4 Phantom II, also flew fighter escort, as did the F-8 Crusader

RECONNAISSANCE: RA-5 Vigilante, RA-3B Skywarrior, reconfigured Crusaders and Phantoms

ELECTRONIC COUNTER-MEASURES (ECM): Intruder, Skyraider, and Skywarrior variants

Grumman E-2 Hawkeyes detected approaching enemy MiGs, guided aircraft to and from their targets and provided airborne communications support.

The attack aircraft used general-purpose bombs, ranging from 250lb to 2,000lb, napalm bombs, magnetic mines, and both 5in and 2.75in rockets. They could also be loaded with Bullpup air-to-ground weapons, Shrike anti-radar missiles and the new Walleye TV-guided bomb. Fighters were armed with Sidewinder and Sparrow air-to-air missiles and 20mm machine guns.

A number of helicopters were also stationed on each carrier. The Sikorsky SH-3 Sea King rescued downed fliers from the sea while the Kaman UH-2 Sea Sprite was equipped for land-based rescue operations. Around half of shot-down pilots were rescued. Utility helicopters were also used for transferring ammunition and supplies from logistics ships on to the carriers.

AIRCRAFT CARRIERS

USS *America* (CVA-66)
Displacement: 60,300 tons   Length: 1,047ft   Beam: 129ft
Complement: 4,580 men and 100 Aircraft   Speed: 34 knots

USS *Bon Homme Richard* (CV-31)
Displacement: 27,100 tons   Length: 872ft   Beam: 93ft
Complement: 3,448 men and 82 aircraft   Speed: 34 knots

USS *Coral Sea* (CVA-43)
Displacement: 45,000 tons   Length: 968ft   Beam: 113ft to 136ft at the flight deck
Complement: 4,104 men and 137 aircraft   Speed: 33 knots

USS *Enterprise* (CVA-65)
The world's first nuclear-powered aircraft carrier and the largest warship ever built when it was launched.
Displacement: 89,600 tons   Length: 1,101ft   Beam: 133ft
Complement: 5,800 men and over 90 aircraft   Speed: over 30 knots

USS *Forrestal* (CVA-59)
On 20 July 1967 a rocket ignited and set off a chain reaction of explosions; the fire killed 135 and injured sixty-three; fifty-two planes were lost or damaged. The carrier was immediately withdrawn.
Displacement: 79,300 tons   Length: 1,101ft   Beam: 129ft, 252ft at flight deck
Complement: over 4,000 men and 100 aircraft   Speed: 33 knots

USS *Franklin D. Roosevelt* (CVA-42)
Specifications were the same as the USS *Coral Sea*.

USS *Intrepid* (CVS-11)
Specifications were the same as the USS *Bon Homme Richard*.

USS *Oriskany* (CV-34):
Displacement 30,800 tons   Length: 904ft   Beam: 129ft
Complement: 3,460 men and 82 aircraft   Speed: 33 knots

USS *Kitty Hawk* (CVA-63)
The first aircraft carrier deployed for combat.
Displacement: 60,100 tons   Length: 1,047ft   Beam: 129ft
Complement: 4,580 and over 100 aircraft   Speed: 34 knots

The congested hangar deck on USS Enterprise *where planes are stored, repaired and armed. (USN K-36520)*

The pilot's view of an aircraft carrier's deck as he comes into land. (USN K-31301)

Coming into land on USS Constellation. *(USN K-32742)*

USS *Midway* (CVA-41)
The first aircraft carrier to be deployed to the Western Pacific in 1964.
Displacement: 45,000 tons   Length: 968ft   Beam: 113ft
Complement: 4,680 men and 137 aircraft   Speed: 33 Knots

USS *Ranger* (CVA-61) – **Forrestal Class**
The flagship of the fleet.
Displacement: 56,000 tons   Length: 1,039ft   Beam: 129ft
Complement: 4,280 men and 100 aircraft   Speed: 33 Knots

USS *Ticonderoga* (CVA-14) – **Class**
Displacement: 27,100 Tons   Length: 888ft   Beam: 93ft
Complement: 3,448 men and 82 aircraft   Speed: 33 knots

NAVAL GUNFIRE SUPPORT

US Seventh Fleet's Cruiser/Destroyer Group, Task Group 70.8, could give fire support, aided by spotting teams along the coast. The Group usually had one cruiser, four destroyers, one inshore fire support ship and two medium rocket landing ships, but it could be much larger, and twenty-two ships joined the gun line during the Tet Offensive, firing over 800 shells a day.

MACV issued its requirements for support and the Group commander deployed his ships under the direction of the Naval Gunfire Support Unit (Task Unit 70.8.9). Task Force 115 would also deploy any Coast Guard cutters it could spare from Operation Market Time.

Ships usually cruised at low speed around 4,000m from the coast to avoid drawing fire, sailing with low navigation lights at night. Sometimes the Group was asked to send ships into river estuaries, especially next to the Rung Sat Special Zone east of Saigon. Captains had to plot routes so their vessels could make a quick escape and damage control teams were always kept on standby.

The Naval Gunfire Liaison Officer was the point of contact for requesting naval support. The Marines had Naval Gunfire Teams down to battalion level and while Marine officers acted as Forward Observers, naval officers carried out liaison duties. There was a Naval Gunfire Liaison Officer with each US Field Force and their equivalent ARVN headquarters while extra Liaison Officers joined combat units operating along the coast, advising on the feasibility of support requests. Spotter teams requested support via the naval office based at MACV headquarters and then adjusted fire directly with the ships.

Field Force Headquarters requested naval support and if MACV agreed, ships sailed into range. The group commander would report his capabilities and ammunition when he was on station and requests from combat units had to be matched with what was available. The Liaison Officer had to arrange clearances and Forward Observers before putting in his request, giving at least forty-eight hours' notice. Non-scheduled missions could be requested via a flash message to the ship if there was an emergency, but clearances still had to be obtained. Ammunition was limited and the ship's gunnery officer selected the smallest gun possible to conserve his stock of shells.

The Group was particularly useful for shelling sizeable targets, including enemy bases and infiltration points along the coast, it often responded when sensors reported large troop concentrations in inaccessible areas.

The destroyer USS Orleck *fires her 5in guns at Viet Cong positions near Vung Tau. (USN K-36776)*

SHIP ARMAMENTS AND AMMUNITION

The type of target determined the size of gun and type of ammunition to use:

TARGET	PREFERRED GUN AND AMMUNITION
Concrete fortifications	8in to 6in armor-piercing
Log bunkers and masonry buildings	8in high explosive, 6in armor-piercing
Light buildings	8in to 5in high explosive (HE)
Dispersed targets in the open	8in to 5in HE, proximity fuse or airburst

5in guns could use Rocket Assisted Projectile (RAP) ammunition which had a longer range and a larger spread of fragments, however, accuracy was lower.

As the Time-on-Target drew near, final communications and radar checks were made and while the bridge rechecked its position and the bearings to the target, the crew loaded their guns. ORESTES voice nets were used for sending messages from ship to shore.

CRUISERS: CA Class Heavy Cruiser's main armament was its nine 8in guns while the CLG Class Guided Missile Light Cruiser had six 6in guns; both carried 5in and 3in secondary guns. Guns were effective up to 70 per cent of the maximum ranges listed below; reduced charges could be used to lower the minimum range by 25 per cent.

GUN	RANGE	AMMUNITION CARRIED	RATE OF FIRE
8in/55	15.6 miles	1,450	10
6in/47	12.0 miles	1,700	10
5in/38	9.4 miles	5,800	15
3in/50	7.3 miles	8,000	50

Although armor-piercing rounds were available, ships mainly carried high-explosive rounds; 5in/38 guns could also fire illumination and white phosphorous rounds.

DESTROYERS: Classes were armed with the following guns:

DD Class - Destroyer armed with two 5in/38 guns
DDG Class - Guided Missile Destroyer armed with two 5in/54 guns

DE Class: Escort Ship armed with 5in/38 or 3in/50 guns
DEG Class: Guided Missile Escort Ship armed with one 5in/38 gun
DER Class: Radar Picket Escort Ship armed with one 5in/38 gun
DLG Class: Guided Missile Frigate armed with one 5in/54 gun

The 5in/54 gun's maximum range was 13.5 miles and while the automatic loading system increased the rate of fire, it took time to change ammunition type. Coast Guard cutters were armed with a single 5in/38 gun.

Shallow-draft inland fire ships and landing ships were armed with the short-range guns and rocket launchers which could fire 380 5in rockets a minute up to a range of 10,000yd.

At the allotted time the crews opened fire, hitting targets several miles away inland. Although the gun crews had no idea if they had destroyed the target, the bridge was able to guide a remote-controlled drone equipped with camera equipment over the target. The QH-50 helicopters, nicknamed Snoopy, were flown high over targets and then guided into a low hover and while the cruisers could receive pictures, only some of the destroyers were able to receive signals.

The ships and their onshore spotters were in continuous communicationand while the spotters reported damage, the bridge reported when the ship would next be in a position to fire and what its ammunition stocks were.

The explosive power of naval guns could be devastating and constant checks on the ships position in relation to targets and friendly troops had to be made to prevent accidents. Request forms had to be filled out accurately by personnel conversant with naval gunnery terminology and ambiguities were clarified while two stations cross-checked coordinates. Although the ground troops' fire coordination center had responsibility for obtaining clearances, the ship's gunnery officer had the final say. The naval spotter issued information to the aviation agencies in his area on Savaplane forms, while the ship's radar teams kept a constant check on aircraft movements during fire missions.

NAVIGATION DUTIES

The coast of South Vietnam had long straight beaches fronting marshland and rice paddies and there were few terrain features to refer to. Aerial spotters could radio coordinates of reference points to the ship as they flew over so the fire control radar could keep track as the ship sailed along the coast. AN/UPN-32 radar beacons were used to fix the ship's position but on many occasions buoys equipped with radar reflectors had to be anchored as reference points.

THE US COAST GUARD

Sea and river travel had always been important in South Vietnam and there were an estimated 60,000 junks, sampans and trawlers on its coastal waters, rivers and canals. US Navy's Vietnam Patrol Force, Task Force 71, was organized in March 1965 to stop the Viet Cong ferrying supplies on the sea and along rivers. Operation Market Time coordinated US Navy and US Coast Guard movements with the South Vietnamese Navy Junk Force, controlling operations on land, sea and air along 1,200 miles of coastline.

Coast Guard Squadron One (Ron One) arrived in July 1965 with seventeen 82ft patrol boats and two support boats crewed by officers and men trained in coastal surveillance techniques. It was split into two divisions and while Division 12 covered the east coast from Da Nang, Division 11 patrolled the west coast from An Thoi in the Gulf of Thailand. Task Force 71 was renamed Coastal Surveillance Force, Task Force 115, at the same time and it set up five Coastal Surveillance Centers at Da Nang, Qui Nhon, Nha Trang, Vung Tau, and An Thoi. Minesweeper and destroyer escorts assisted with offshore navigation while Vietnamese junks monitored the shallow waters; Special Forces teams often accompanied patrols.

Naval forces operating in the shallow coast waters and along the rivers across South Vietnam were controlled by the Commander Naval Forces, Vietnam, after April 1966 and Task Forces were divided as follows:

Task Force 115: Coastal Surveillance Force covered the shallow waters along the coast
Task Force 116: River Patrol Force carried out routine patrols of waterways
Task Force 117: Riverine Assault Force was equipped to undertake offensive operations

The Commander was also responsible for Naval Support Activity, Saigon, supplying naval forces across the country (III Marine Amphibious Force controlled the Naval Support Activity covering I Corps from Da Nang) and both the Seebees and civilian contractors working on naval construction projects.

PATROLLING THE COASTAL WATERS

Task Force 115 split the coast into nine sectors, each with three observation zones:

Air Surveillance Zone: Planes identified and photographed targets up to 150 miles from the coast and reported them to the Coastal Surveillance Centers.
Deep Water Zone: US Navy and Vietnamese destroyers and minesweepers patrolled a 40-mile zone, searching trawlers.
Shallow Water Zone: US Navy Coast Guard patrol boats and South Vietnamese junks patrolled out to a 12-mile limit, searching trading and fishing vessels.

Market Time's priorities were to search craft in the following order:

Vessels passing through an area
Junks fishing or operating in local areas
Anchored fishing boats
Working fishing boats

Squadron One searched over 65,000 craft during the first twelve months, seizing over 100 tons of supplies and arresting dozens of suspects. The patrol boats also aided craft in distress, rescued downed pilots and seamen from the water, guided lost craft and escorted survey boats along the coast and rivers; they also covered many of the Navy's patrols during the monsoon season.

Another nine patrol boats arrived in February 1966 and they formed Division 13. It was based at Cat Lo and patrolled the Mekong Delta and the Rung Sat Special Zone. After August 1966 the patrol boats also started visiting inhabited islands off the coast to search for Viet Cong bases. During their visits they handed out government literature, administered medical treatment and promoted building projects. Cam Ranh Bay became the center of coastal air patrol operations in April 1967 with the establishment of the US

Naval Air Facility with its P-2 Neptune and P-3 Orion patrol aircraft. Coastal Surveillance Force staff moved to the base a few months later and while the Naval Communications Station improved control of Operation Market Time, a new pontoon dock was built for repairing coastal patrol vessels.

The patrol boats were not designed for extended patrols and they only had a restricted range with a limited capacity for ammunition and supplies; living conditions were also austere, particularly on high seas. Five high-endurance cutters arrived in May 1967 to improve the patrols' effectiveness and they formed Coast Guard Squadron Three. Ron Three, as it was known, patrolled the Gulf of Thailand from Song Ong Doc. Royal Australian Navy craft also joined Market Time in 1967.

One of the cutters was assigned as logistical support for Squadron One. The crew quarters were used as a rest center, allowing crews to work in shifts, while the patrol boats were supplied with stores delivered by passing ships. An onboard medical officer dealt with injuries and sickness for ships in the area. Ron Three also surveyed the coastline and charted the shallow waters.

Modern cutters with improved gunfire control and crew quarters arrived in October 1969 and a flight deck allowed helicopters to deliver fuel, supplies and personnel. Vietnamization began at the beginning of 1969 when the Vietnamese Navy started training with the Squadrons and the last of the cutters were handed over at the end of 1971.

The Viet Cong's seaborne supply routes had been virtually brought to a standstill by 1967 and attempts to revive them in 1969 failed. Over 8,000 Coast Guardsmen served in Vietnam and their craft covered over 5.5 million miles. Over 900,000 vessels had been reported and over 250,000 had been boarded or inspected. The Coast Guard also detained over 10,000 suspects and killed or wounded nearly 2,000 Viet Cong in fire-fights.

AMPHIBIOUS LANDINGS

Numerous amphibious landings were made on the coast of Vietnam by the Marine Corps's Amphibious Ready Group and the Special Landing Force. The Group had an assault ship with twenty-four UH-34 helicopters, a tank landing ship carrying over forty amphibious landing vehicles (LVTs), a dock landing ship and a transport dock; other vessels were often attached during

Marines wade ashore on the banks of the Con Thien River. (USN K-35643)

operations. The Force, a Marine Battalion Landing Team, was based on the ships and they could land either by helicopter or LVT.

Transport submarines sometimes landed SEAL units and demolitions teams ahead of the assault to clear the beach of obstacles. At other times they swam or rowed rubber rafts ashore to carry out reconnaissance missions.

Operation Starlite was the first amphibious operation and Marines landed on the shore south of Da Nang while a cruiser and two destroyers shelled the Viet Cong's assembly area; Operation Piranha soon followed. The battalion landing team was constantly probing the coast and a second Amphibious Ready Group and Special Landing Force arrived in April 1967; the two were divided into Alpha and Bravo.

A patrol boat cruises at high speed along the rivers of the Mekong Delta. (USN K-51404)

NAVIGATION AIDS

The coast of South Vietnam could be treacherous and the outdated charts were of little use to the crews of the transport ships bringing supplies to the ports. A tender set buoys for offloading fuel at the four main ports in the spring of 1966 before marking safe passages through the coral reefs and sandbars. It also worked with the dredgers, marking channels and moorings with the help of a landing craft.

The Coast Guard took over in May 1967, surveying sea channels and setting off-shore firing range boards for aviation and naval units. It also established the Long-range Aid to Navigation system (or LORAN) so sailors and pilots could safely navigate over the sea during bad weather.

PORT SECURITY AND SAFETY

Coast Guard Merchant Marine Details were organized in December 1966 to take over control of discipline at the ports, establishing law and order on the dockside. They handed over to the United States Consular

Missions when the ports were scaled down. Thousands of tons of ammunition were delivered to the US ports along the coast and trained Port Security and Explosives Loading Detachments taught US Army and Vietnamese stevedores how to unload and store their dangerous cargo. They also regulated the delivery of ammunition to inland bases by landing craft.

PATROLLING THE RIVERS

River Patrol Force (Task Force 116) was formed in December 1965. It was soon patrolling rivers across the country, the majority of them in the Mekong Delta, with small river patrol boats (PBRs). Thousands of craft were searched during Operation Game Warden and by August 1968 it had grown to include five river divisions, each with two ten-boat sections. They were deployed as follows:

River Division 51: Can Tho and Binh Thuy
River Division 52: Sa Dec (later Vinh Long)
River Division 53: My Tho
River Division 54: Nha Be River
River Division 55: Da Nang

Landing craft, converted to carry two armed UH-1B helicopters, supported each PBR section. The helicopters were able to give aerial fire support, reconnoiter river banks and evacuate wounded men.

Three Patrol Air Cushion Vehicles (PACVs – small hovercrafts) operated in the Mekong Delta throughout 1966 and 1967 and then in the Da Nang area. Although they were extremely fast over water and paddy fields, they were noisy and difficult to maintain.

THE SEALORDS CAMPAIGN

A concerted attack on the river traffic ferrying supplies along the waterways of the Mekong Delta, known as the Southeast Asia Lake, Ocean, River, and Delta Strategy, or SEALORDS, began in October 1968, replacing Operations Game Warden and Market Time. The combined resources of the US and South Vietnamese Navies were formed into Task Force 194 and it worked with ground troops and the River Assault Force's monitors and transports to cut the flow of ammunition and equipment from Cambodia. The US Navy's Coastal Surveillance Force deployed over 140 vessels, including Swift boats and Coast Guard craft, while the River Patrol Force operated over 250 patrol boats and minesweepers. The Vietnamese Navy added over 650 ships, assault craft, patrol boats and other vessels to the Task Force. Five SEAL platoons accompanied many patrols while a squadron of OV-10 Bronco observation aircraft and another of helicopter gunships kept watch overhead.

The first phase involved laying a screen of electronic sensor devices along the Cambodian border to monitor river traffic. Around-the-clock patrolling began on the waterways in November 1968 and by early 1969 the Viet Cong supply vessels had to cross a series of electronic barriers stretching from Tay Ninh to the Gulf of Siam:

Operation Search Turn: Vinh Te Canal between the Bassac River and the Gulf of Siam
Operation Foul Deck: From the Gulf along the upper reaches of the Bassac River

Operation Giant Slingshot: Along the Vam Co Dong and Vam Co Tay Rivers
Operation Barrier Reef: Covering the canals from the Vam Co Tay to the Mekong River

A heavily camouflaged member of a SEAL team silently keeps watch on a stream. (USN K-74900)

SEALS

Missions carried out by the navy's elite commando units were coordinated by the River Patrol Force. Platoons, each with fourteen men organized into two squads, were deployed in Rung Sat Special Zone, along the rivers around Da Nang and in the Mekong Delta.

The six-man squads had their own SEAL team assault boats (STABs), but they could also operate from landing craft, armored trimarans, patrol boats, sampans or helicopters. They were extremely versatile and able to carry out all types of missions ranging from raids and ambushes to reconnaissance and intelligence-gathering operations.

US NAVY CONSTRUCTION FORCES

Personnel serving with the Navy Construction Battalions were known as Seabees and Amphibious Construction Battalion 1 had been engaged in building refugee camps across Vietnam since 1954. They turned their attentions to Special Forces camps in 1962 and built many along the border over the next three years. The first Naval Mobile Construction Battalions

landed at Da Nang in May 1965 to support III Marine Amphibious Force and began work on Chu Lai and Phu Bai bases in I Corps; each battalion had 24 officers and 738 men. 3d Naval Construction Brigade was responsible for planning and coordinating construction projects, while 30th and 32d Naval Construction Regiments supervised the Battalions. The Seabees built everything from bases and storage facilities to roads and ports; twenty-one Battalions eventually served in Vietnam, each one controlling a number of teams.

*Navy Seabees work on
a timber bridge near Chu Lai.
(USN K-40935)*

VIETNAMIZATION AND WITHDRAWAL

A Naval Advisory Group started to work with the South Vietnamese Navy at the beginning of 1969 and before long Vietnamese sailors were training alongside American crews. By March 1970 Operation SEALORDS was handed over and the biggest test of how well the handover was progressing came two months later when a combined Vietnamese-American naval task force sailed up the Mekong River and into Cambodia. While the American vessels only traveled part of the way to Phnom Penh, the Vietnamese continued into the capital and over the weeks that followed they evacuated over 80,000 ethnic Vietnamese.

One by one the naval patrols along South Vietnam's coastal waters and rivers were handed over and by April 1971 the Advisory Group's Accelerated Turnover to the Vietnamese, or ACTOV, was complete. South Vietnam's Navy had grown to over 42,000 personnel operating 1,200 modern vessels and 240 junks organized into two Task Fleets:

Task Fleet 21: Covering the SEALORDS Operations with eight task forces
Task Fleet 22: General surveillance with nine task forces

As the final Navy units withdrew from South Vietnam, there was one remaining task to carry out: the removal of mines laid in North Vietnamese waters. Task Force 78, Seventh Fleet's Mine Countermeasures Force, started Operation End Sweep in February 1973 and over the next six months minesweepers and destroyers swept the coast while amphibious ships and salvage boats cleared the rivers. Minesweeping gear was also handed over and American sailors trained their North Vietnamese counterparts to carry on operations after they withdrew the following July.

Successful patrolling of South Vietnam's coastal waters and rivers continued until US financial support was drastically cut in 1975, resulting in over 600 vessels being laid up to conserve fuel and ammunition. The resultant fall in the number of patrols came just as the North Vietnamese were planning their final offensive on South Vietnam.

CHAPTER 15

THE AIR WAR

United States Air Force planes played an increasing role in the war against the Viet Cong and the North Vietnamese Army. Planes, ranging from the huge B-52 bombers to small tactical attack fighters, took part in a wide range of bombing and close-support missions while cargo planes delivered large quantities of supplies to outlying bases. Other support missions were as diverse as reconnaissance, forward air control and jungle defoliation.

AIR BASES

Air supply was essential during the early days of the conflict when the Viet Cong had many roads under their control, and the isolated Special Forces bases were dependent on regular air supply for their survival. South Vietnam only had three main air bases in 1965, and many outlying air strips were little more than grass runways. Da Nang was in the north while Bien Hoa and Tan Son Nhut were the civil and military airfields north of Saigon. An enormous amount of construction work was started in 1966, much of it carried out by the Navy and Air Force engineers working alongside civilian contractors, and by 1967 five new major air terminals capable of handling jet fighter aircraft and heavy cargo planes had been built.

F-102 Delta Daggers taxi out of their protective revetments towards the runway. (342B-VN-95011)

A C-123 Provider taxis to a standstill on the forward airstrip at Plei Djerang Air Base. (342B-VN-100038)

Seventh Air Force organized Prime Base Engineer Emergency Force construction (Prime Beef) specialized units to help the Army engineers. A Prime Beef unit had sixty American engineers and up to 300 Vietnamese laborers. Heavy Repair Civil Engineering Squadrons were expanded into Rapid Engineer Deployable Heavy Operational Repair Squadron, Engineering (Red Horse Squadrons) in 1966. The squadrons in South Vietnam had 400 US engineers supervising up to 1,000 Vietnamese workers while 566th Squadron employed over 3,000 Thais at U-Tapao (Sattahip):

A 3,500ft-long jet airfield complete with arresting gear was built at Chu Lai to support Marine operations across I Corps but the runway had soon been extended to 8,000ft with a parallel taxiway and a large parking apron. A 10,000ft long runway complete with taxiway, high-speed turnoffs and large aprons was built at Cam Ranh Bay, while a second 10,000ft-long runway and airfield complex was built at Phan Rang nearby. Contractors also built a 9,000ft runway, taxiway and 165,000 sq yd of apron at Tuy Hoa, on the coast east of Saigon. Fuel was stored in a system of rubber bladders, each holding 300,000 gallons, until welded steel tanks were built. Fuel pipelines were installed on jetties so that tankers could pump their cargo directly into the tanks.

FORWARD AIRFIELDS

As the number of units and operations across Vietnam grew, so did the need for additional supplies; it was estimated that up to 200 daily aircraft sorties, delivering 100 tons of supplies, were required during large operations. General Westmoreland also wanted a network of airbases across the country, until everywhere was within 25km of a landing strip. Existing air strips were upgraded to accept C-123 Provider and C-130 Hercules transport planes while dozens of new ones were added, increasing the number across South Vietnam to over 100.

Once a suitable location had been chosen, infantry secured the area while engineers cleared the runway and approach areas of obstructions. Earth - moving equipment shaped the runway area and covered it in crushed stone so a new rubberized fabric, known as T17 membrane, could be laid and covered with skid-proofing. The membrane was waterproof, dustproof and easy to install, but it lacked durability and airfields were eventually covered by steel or aluminum matting. Pierced steel plank (PSP) and M8A1 solid steel planks formed truck parks and roads. The planks were also used for jet fighter plane landing strips. MX19 aluminum panels arrived in 1966 but they too were replaced by concrete runways on busy airfields.

Standard airfields had a 3,500ft-long runway that was 60ft wide and it had parking for three C-130 aircraft; earth mounds, called berms, protected the ammunition and fuel stores. Runways used by jet planes needed to be built to higher specifications due to the huge amounts of drag and thrust created during landing and take-off and the engineers were kept busy carrying out repairs.

By 1968 the Viet Cong and NVA had improved their rocket and mortar tactics to such an extent that fighter aircraft were being damaged at an unacceptable rate. The Air Force Prime Beef teams started the Hardened Shelter Program to counter the threat, building shelters to protect them. Large corrugated steel arches were linked together and covered in concrete to form open-ended bunkers measuring 72ft long, 48ft wide and 24ft high.

AIRCRAFT GROUP AND WING LOCATIONS

I CORPS

1st Marine Aircraft Wing headquarters was established at Da Nang in May 1965 and it controlled air support across I Corps for the next six years. It controlled three fixed-wing and three helicopter groups, with around 250 fixed-wing and 225 helicopters, at its height. Although squadrons constantly rotated the Wing's structure remained the same from 1966 to 1969.

The three Fixed Wing Groups operated F-4B Phantom and F-8E Crusader fighters as well as A-4 Skyhawk and A-6 Intruders fighter bombers. Marine fixed-wing squadrons were designated VM in front of the aircraft type and they had 11 to 15 operational aircraft. Aircraft Group 11 was based at Da Nang from July 1965 but it moved to Chu Lai in August 1970 ready to withdraw. Aircraft Group 12 was based at Chu Lai from June 1965 to February 1970 while Aircraft Group 13 was based at the same air base from September 1966 to September 1970.

The three Helicopter Groups operated light and observation squadrons with UH-1E helicopters and medium squadrons equipped with both CH-46A and CH-53A helicopters; Cobra attack helicopters arrived in April 1969. Observation squadrons started with twenty-three UH-1H helicopters but they were replaced by fixed-wing OV-10 Broncos in the summer of 1968. Helicopter Squadrons were designated HM before their helicopter type and each one had around twenty-two operational helicopters.

Aircraft Group 16 arrived at Da Nang in March 1965 and moved to nearby Marble Mountain to take over Phu Bai the following August; it withdrew in June 1971. Aircraft Group 36 was based at Chu Lai from September 1965 and moved to Phu Bai in October 1967; it left Vietnam in November 1969. Aircraft Group 39 was based at Quang Tri from March 1968 to December 1969.

An F-105 Thunderchief fires a volley of rockets at a target in North Vietnam. (342B-VN-95571)

DA NANG AIR BASE

United States forces took over the French-built air base in the early 1960s and it quickly grew into a huge installation for USAF, US Marine and South Vietnamese air units. Military Airlift Command also flew C-141 Starlifter and C-5 Galaxy cargo planes into the base. Da Nang was also used as an emergency airfield for planes returning from missions over North Vietnam.

A radar station was installed at Da Nang in September 1961 and the following June, Tactical Air Force Transport Provisional Squadron 2 started delivering supplies to Special Forces camps with C-123 Providers under the code name Mule Train. In 1962 American pilots started flying Vietnamese AD-6 Skyraiders as part of Project Farm Gate and 777th Troop Carrier Squadron started flying C-123s out of the base in April 1963. The following United States Air Force units served at Da Nang:

23d Air Base Group from June 1962 to July 1965
6252d Tactical Wing from July 1965 to April 1966
35th Tactical Fighter Wing from April to October 1966
366th Tactical Fighter Wing from October 1966 to June 1972

II CORPS: NORTH

PLEIKU AIR BASE
A simple airstrip was improved in 1965 and 21st Tactical Air Support Squadron flew O-1 Observation planes across the Central Highlands. 633d Special Operations Wing was based at the airfield from July 1968 to March 1970.

PHU CAT AIR BASE
37th Tactical Fighter Wing from March 1967 to April 1970
12th Tactical Fighter Wing from April to November 1970
6259th Air Base Squadron from November 1970 to December 1971

TUY HOA AIR BASE
31st Tactical Fighter Wing from December 1966 to September 1970

II CORPS: SOUTH

NHA TRANG AIR BASE
14th Air Commando (later Special Operations) Wing, March 1966 to September 1971

CAM RAHN BAY
12th Tactical Fighter Wing from November 1965 to March 1970.
Cam Rahn Bay was also a huge entry point for cargo and personnel. Personnel and cargo were flown into and out of South Vietnam by C-141 Starlifter and C-5 Galaxy aircraft, while C-130 Hercules and C-7 Caribou squadrons transported them across country. 834th Air Division carried over one million passengers and 100,000 tons of cargo a year; it was split into 463d and 483d Wings.

483d Tactical Airlift Wing took over Caribou transport squadrons from the Army
463d Tactical Airlift Wing flew the C-130 Hercules

PHAN RANG AIR BASE
366th Tactical Fighter Wing from March to October 1966
35th Tactical Fighter Wing from October 1966 to May 1971
315th Air Commando Troop Carrier (later Special Operations and then Tactical Airlift) Wing from June 1967 to March 1972
14th Special Operations Wing from October 1969 to September 1971

III CORPS

BIEN HOA AIR BASE
Bien Hoa had been a Vietnamese air base since 1955 and 4400th Combat Crew Training Squadron, nicknamed 'Jungle Jim', was the first USAF unit to arrive in Vietnam in October 1961 and it trained Vietnamese personnel while flying covert missions, codenamed Operation Farm Gate. The following units later controlled operations at Bien Hoa:

34th Tactical Group from July 1963 to November 1965
6251st Tactical Fighter Wing from July to November 1965
3d Tactical Fighter Wing from November 1965 to March 1971

TAN SON NHUT AIR BASE

507th Tactical Control Group, arrived in September 1961 to install radars for monitoring South Vietnam's air space. Four RF-101s soon began flying reconnaissance missions, building up a photographic library of the country, and before long they were joined by 67th Tactical Reconnaissance Wing and 45th Tactical Reconnaissance Squadron.

Twelve C-123 transports reached Vietnam in January 1962 and while two based themselves at Da Nang, the rest flew out of Tan Son Nhut on Operation Mule Train, taking supplies to the isolated Special Forces Camps along the border. Thirty pilots, nicknamed the Dirty Thirty, flew C-47 transport planes for the Vietnamese Air Force. 315th Troop Carrier Group (Combat Cargo) and 8th Aerial Port Squadron took over transport operations in December 1962.

505th Tactical Air Control Group took control of South Vietnam's airspace in April 1964, making sure that fast moving fighters did not enter the same airspace as slow-moving cargo planes. The operators also coordinated the Forward Air Controllers. The following units arrived as the American presence increased:

33d Tactical Group from July 1963 to July 1965
6250th Combat Support Group from July 1965 to April 1966
460th Tactical Reconnaissance Wing from February 1966 to August 1971

In April 1966 834th Air Division took command of all USAF units at the base:

315th Air Commando Wing, Troop Carrier, from March 1966 to June 1967
377th Air Base Wing from April 1966 to March 1973

IV CORPS

BINH THUY AIR BASE

22d Tactical Air Support Squadron flew observation planes from May 1965 to January 1971.

These F-4 Phantoms have been guided to their target by radar. (342B-VN-95128)

TACTICAL AIR SUPPORT (TACAIR)

The lack of enemy air defenses gave the Allied Air Force pilots command of the skies, and the troops on the ground knew that they could usually rely on immediate tactical air support. Seventh Air Force eventually coordinated the tactical air support missions as well as coordinating an extensive interdiction campaign against the Viet Cong and NVA base areas and lines of communications. It was a complex task, involving an extensive communications system and dedicated personnel; at the height of the conflict over 400 tactical air missions were being flown every day.

As well as its own assets, Seventh Air Force also issued orders to 1st Marine Air Wing, covering I Corps and the Royal Australian Air Force. It also issued a list of targets to the US Navy so that it could deploy squadrons based with the carrier fleet. Seventh Air Force had to work closely with the Vietnamese Air Force and liaison officers at the joint Tactical Air Control Center at Tan Son Nhut Air Base.

The nature of the conflict in Vietnam called for new doctrines, tactics and weapons systems but the extensive communications system allowed pilots to accurately deliver a variety of munitions close to friendly troops, guided by aerial Forward Observers in contact with the ground commander. Although there were instances of 'friendly fire', they were extremely rare and the men on the ground came to rely on tactical air support (sometimes too often) to deal with the enemy.

An Air Operations Control Center was set up at Tan Son Nhut in January 1962 to run two Air Support Operations Centers to coordinate air operations over Vietnam. The system was later expanded to four Direct Air Support Centers, controlling American and Vietnamese Air Liaison Officers (ALOs) and Forward Air Controllers (FACs):

I Corps Center under Marine Corps control at Da Nang
II Corps Center at Pleiku
III Corps Center at Tan Son Nhut
IV Corps Center at Binh Thuy; it was exclusively Vietnamese

While the Control Center received and prioritized requests on the Air Operations Order, the Support Centers had control over operations and could change priorities to meet changing requirements.

Viet Cong structures disappear beneath sheets of flames. (342B-VN-95010)

An F-100 Super Sabre releases two high-drag bombs over a suspected Viet Cong camp. (342B-VN-102577)

TACAIR CONTROL SYSTEM

TACAIR coordinated all forms of air support, including missions directed by Strategic Air Command. The centralized control of mission requests and the decentralized control of operations meant that most requests could be dealt with quickly. If an Air Liaison Officer on the ground or a Forward Air Controller flying overhead called for assistance the combat troops could usually expect air support within 45 minutes.

The direction of a large number of aircraft and helicopters needed an extensive radar system. South Vietnam was split into two sectors, each covered by a central radar station and booster stations. The four Direct Air Support Control Centers had to coordinate the tactical aircraft providing close air support and a host of other fixed-wing aircraft and helicopters flying at different altitudes:

Slow-moving reconnaissance aircraft on all kinds of low-level missions
Transport helicopters and aircraft delivering supplies and ammunition
Air Cavalry helicopters on patrol, search and destroy or convoy escort missions
Utility helicopters and their gunships carrying troops to and from their landing zones
High altitude B-52 aircraft flying Arc-Lite missions
Emergency airlift aircraft, rescuing endangered Special Forces and Ranger teams
Helicopters and planes on psyops missions
Low-level aircraft flying defoliant missions
Rescue aircraft, locating downed pilots

The decision to use a close air support mission usually started with the Battalion Commander or his Air Liaison Officer. The Brigade Air Liaison Officer flew over targets to assess priorities and the Brigade commander forwarded a list of targets to the division, which in turn forwarded them to the Field Force headquarters and then MACV.

MACV's Joint Air-Ground Operations System had to prioritize targets and obtain clearances, before the Tactical Air Control Center could decide how to deploy its squadrons. The Strike Plans Branch then issued orders to the fighter wing headquarters so planes could be armed and flight paths planned. The types of squadrons available were as follows:

This Forward Air Controller has written a list of possible targets on the window of his cockpit. (111-CC-72645)

Fighter aircraft: F-4 Phantoms, F-8 Crusaders and F-100 Super Sabres
Attack aircraft: A-1 Skyraiders, A-4 Skyhawks, A-6 Intruders and A-37 Dragonflies

The Tactical Air Control Center also notified the four Direct Air Support Centers so they could alert their Air Liaison Officers and Forward Air Controllers.

Combat units sometimes needed immediate air support when they were in a difficult situation and the battalion commander would ask the Brigade Air Liaison Officer to put in a radio request to the Direct Air Support Center. The request would be approved by the Field Force or Corps headquarters while the air liaison staff at MACV headquarters monitored the radio; they would only step in if they knew an alternative form of support was available.

If a preplanned mission in flight was diverted to the troubled unit, the Forward Air Controller only had a few minutes to collect target information before the aircraft appeared. Sometimes the Tactical Air Control Center scrambled aircraft or diverted aircraft from another Corps.

FORWARD AIR CONTROLLERS (FACS)

Close contact had to be maintained between the troops on the ground and the pilots flying the close support mission to prevent a potentially disastrous misguided air strike. Forward Air Controllers had the responsibility for liaising between the two. They were experienced pilots and although a few worked with the troops on the ground, the majority flew overhead in an observation plane or helicopter. Pilots were allocated an operating area so they became familiar with the territory, and they were often the first to spot enemy activity.

To begin with the highly maneuverable Cessna O-1 Bird Dog was used because it could operate from short runways and fly for long periods at low speeds. The pilot used three radio sets to keep in contact with everyone:

A VHF link with the Tactical Air Control Party to make new requests and relay results
An FM link with the Air Liaison Officer attached to the combat troops on the ground
An UHF link with the incoming fighter aircraft

The Army later used the Cessna O-2 Skymaster, with improved communications and navigation aids; it also had two engines, making it less vulnerable to mechanical failure. The Marine Corps used the faster North American OV-10 Bronco which could also operate over Laos and North Vietnam. Many of the O-1s were transferred to the South Vietnamese Air Force.

DAY OF THE MISSION

On the day of the mission the Forward Air Controller flew over the target area and made contact with the Tactical Air Controller and the Air Liaison Officer, collecting information on artillery fire and combat troops in the target area so he could plan safe approaches for the aircraft.

Meanwhile, the aircraft had left their base or aircraft carrier and were on their way to the target, following in-flight advice on air traffic. The Forward Air Controller contacted the pilot, directing him to a rendezvous point as he briefed him on the target area. He also gave the pilot a clear approach and break-off headings to avoid anti-aircraft fire.

As soon as the Forward Air Controller had visual contact with the aircraft he marked the target with smoke or white phosphorous rockets (sometimes

The pilot of a Vietnamese A-1 Skyraider banks away quickly as white phosphorous bombs explode beneath his plane. (342B-VN-94740)

a ground commander marked the target from his command helicopter), meanwhile the troops on the ground used smoke to outline their perimeter.

Each aircraft had to be given clearance to attack and pilots sometimes made trial runs without firing (known as dry runs), returning to drop their ordnance (known as a wet run) when they were satisfied. The Forward Air Controller noted the impact point so he could adjust the next plane's pass.

When the pilots had finished, they circled high above the area while the Forward Air Controller made a low pass over the target to carry out a Bomb Damage Assessment. The pilots could then head for home. Radars relayed vectors to the nearest base, or in the case of a damaged plane, to a safe bail-out area. The radar personnel would also alert a rescue team. After landing the pilots had to be debriefed before they could relax and prepare for the next mission.

CLOSE AIR SUPPORT AT NIGHT

The majority of Viet Cong and NVA attacks against bases took place at night and the Air Force responded by converting the Second World War vintage transport planes into flying gun platforms. The AC-47s were armed with three 7.62 miniguns, each capable of firing up to 6,000 rounds per minute, in one side of the fuselage; several tons of ammunition were also loaded on board. The planes could circle a base when it was under attack, illuminating the target area with 2-million candlepower flares. It would stay overhead until the base's own helicopters were in the air and able to take over. They were known as Spooky, but the GIs christened it Puff the Magic Dragon after a well-known song because the thousands of tracer bullets made it look like the plane was breathing fire.

The AC-119 Shadow and AC-119 Stinger were introduced at a later date. The Stinger was also armed with two 20mm multi-barrel guns capable of firing up to 2,500 high explosive incendiary rounds per minute while a 2-billion candlepower searchlight lit up targets.

ORDNANCE

The following types of ordnance could be delivered by aircraft:

High explosive bombs, known as 'iron bombs' were a popular all-round choice
General purpose bombs could be used to penetrate bunkers or caves
CBU weapons were used against troops in the open, particularly linear targets
BLU anti-personnel weapons were very accurate and used close to friendly forces
2.75in rockets were used against personnel hiding in the undergrowth
20mm cannons were an accurate weapon with a high rate of fire
7.62mm miniguns could fire several thousand rounds a minute
.50-caliber machine guns could penetrate buildings and bunkers

DIRECT AIR SUPPORT

Seventh Air Force's interdiction campaign aimed to hit the enemy base camps and their supply chain, targeting trails, roads, bridges, truck parks and storage areas. Where possible a concentrated effort was made to totally disrupt the enemy's activities in an area, delaying him by weeks or months.

Forward Air Controllers were given sectors to watch and they were often the first to spot signs of enemy activity. Alternatively information came from intelligence sources, including aerial photography, ground sensors, captured documents or prisoner interrogations. However, targets had to be confirmed from several sources before an air strike was ordered, and the Special Forces teams or Long-Range Patrols (renamed the Rangers in 1969) were used to confirm targets.

Once confirmed, clearances had to be obtained so attacks could begin. Regular Bomb Damage Assessments by the Forward Air Controllers were needed to make sure that the target was destroyed before operations were suspended.

GROUND-CONTROLLED RADAR BOMBING

Rain and mist (and there were prolonged periods during the monsoon season) made flying hazardous, particularly in mountainous areas. The Air Force's MSQ-77 Skyspot system and the Marine Corps' TPQ-10 system were ground-controlled radars capable of safely guiding pilots to their target; the systems could also operate at night.

The controlling Direct Air Support Center forwarded the target data to the radar station so it could compute the optimum flight path. After takeoff the pilot logged on to the nearby station and followed the route to the bomb release point. Although everything was computed for the pilot, leaving him little to do expcept follow the radar station's instructions, it took nerves of steel to fly blind through mountainous areas.

B-52S AND ARC-LITE STRIKES

The B-52 bomber had been designed with nuclear capability as part of the United States Cold War strategy, however, the deteriorating situation in Vietnam mean that Strategic Air Command had to consider deploying its bomber force based on Guam in a conventional role. In June 1965 B-52F bombers from 7th and 320th Bomb Wings flew from Andersen Air Force Base in Guam to attack targets north of Saigon. Many bombs missed the target and two planes were lost in a mid-air collision, leaving the Air Force commanders questioning the validity of using strategic bombers to attack small tactical targets. However, the ground commanders thought they were perfect for striking isolated targets and, with General Westmoreland's support, Strategic Air Command's B-52s started out a systematic program of saturation bombing against targets along the border; over 3,700 missions were flown in the first twelve months. It was the start of a controversial bombing campaign, one that grew in intensity when President Richard Nixon took a personal interest and ordered top-secret attacks against the NVA's bases in Cambodia.

By February 1966 B-52Ds, with larger bomb bays modified under the Big Belly program, were in use and three months later they began striking targets in North Vietnam. The modified bombers could carry up to 108 500lb bombs, some internally and some externally, however, various combinations of 500, 750, and 1000lb bombs could be loaded up to a maximum weight of 27 tons. Typically 36,000lb of 'iron bombs' armed with a variety of close proximity, impact and delay fuses were used. Wings were also based at U Tapao Airfield in Thailand and Kadena Air Base.

The planes flew at a high ceiling, out of earshot from the ground, and the enemy had no warning prior to an Arc-Lite strike; anything in the blast area was destroyed. The number of Arc Light sorties was limited to around fifty a day and targets could be requested either by the Field Force Headquarters, Corps Headquarters, their ARVN equivalents, or based on information gathered by Special Forces missions. Military Assistance Command, Vietnam, put together the list of targets and General Westmoreland often dealt personally with requests from field commanders. Seventh Air Force also had to coordinate missions with the Vietnamese Aviation Agency so airspace could be allocated. Although missions usually had to be requested 24 hours in advance, they could be diverted at a few hours notice if a lucrative target was reported and six planes were always kept on standby.

B-52s played an important part in keeping the NVA at bay during the siege of Khe Sanh base at the start of 1968, with 90 per cent of missions flown hitting targets near the DMZ as part of Operation Niagara. By the time the operation ended on 31 March, they had dropped 76,000 tons of ordnance around the Marine base. At its height the bombers were flying over the base every 90 minutes, dropping bombs within a few hundred meters of the perimeter. About 20,000 sorties were flown throughout the year, with each plane carrying an average of 26 tons of explosives.

The number of missions over South Vietnam had started to decrease by 1970 but when it became clear that the NVA was building extensive bases in neutral Cambodia, President Nixon decided it was time to divert B-52s across the border. It was a highly controversial policy, one that could have triggered an international incident if news leaked out. To keep the bombing campaign secret, special technology had to be used so that even the bomber crews did not know that they were attacking a neutral country.

The crews headed for what they thought was a target inside South Vietnam, but when the pilot put his plane on to autopilot during the final bombing run, the target coordinates were reprogrammed without his knowledge. Planes were guided over the border, usually only a few miles and a matter of seconds from the planned target, to drop their load of bombs. By the time the pilot resumed control, the radar had guided the plane back into South Vietnamese airspace.

The North Vietnamese Easter Offensive in 1972 was followed by air raids on Hanoi and Haiphong and Operations Linebacker I and Linebacker II at

Saturation bombing by B-52s devastated this area of War Zone D. (342B-VN-95286)

the end of the year included many Arc Light missions. The last mission was flown on 15 August 1973. The following statistics illustrate the importance of the B52:

B-52 aircrews flew over 12,000 sorties
B-52s dropped over 2.5 million tons of bombs, costing over $800 per ton
55 per cent of the sorties were flown over South Vietnam
31 B-52s were lost; 18 shot down by SAM missiles, the rest following operation problems

AERIAL RECONNAISSANCE

Aerial reconnaissance was combined with military intelligence to plan operations. Tactical reconnaissance planes used a variety of methods to search for new targets or check existing targets. The Air Liaison Officer discussed the feasibility of a reconnaissance mission with Air Force Reconnaissance Officers who in turn forwarded the request up through the levels of command. The final decision lay with MACV's Operations Air Officer who had to consider requests from all sources and allocate his resources to maximize results. His orders were issued by the Reconnaissance Operations Branch. Specialized units were able to cover large areas with photographic or infrared cameras while smaller-scale missions could involve one or more of the following methods:

Visual Reconnaissance: A quick way to confirm a ground target, often carried out by Forward Air Controllers.
Photographic Cameras: A variety of patterns could be taken and flares were often used to light up areas at night; both black-and-white and color film were used.

Photographic film was processed at a central laboratory and while one copy was flown direct to the nearest combat unit, a second copy was forwarded to a specialist detachment at Corps Headquarters so trained staff could study the

A tanker loads a C-123 Provider with Agent Orange on the runway at Operation Ranch Hand's base in Nha Trang. (342B-VN-105726)

photographs. The two opinions were compared to determine what action had to be taken:

Immediate action: either a tactical air strike, artillery mission or a B-52 Arc-Lite mission

Plan further action: either by ground troops, artillery or air strikes

Further surveillance: either more aerial reconnaissance, special operations or by agents

The following reconnaissance methods gave instant results and could be acted on immediately:

Electronic Sensors: recorded electromagnetic radiation
Infrared Cameras: able to pinpoint anything emitting heat at night
SLAR Radars: used to locate fixed or moving targets on trails, rivers and canals

DEFOLIATION

The Viet Cong and NVA often used jungle areas for their sanctuaries and in 1961 a combined US and Vietnamese counterinsurgency center started investigating using herbicide to defoliate the hiding places. The herbicide was codenamed Agent Orange and the spraying of large areas from the air became one of the most controversial campaigns of the war. The chemicals killed off undergrowth and foliage, leaving tinder-dry areas of dead vegetation tinted pink. Operation Ranch Hand began in January 1962 with the clearance of vegetation along the highways north of Saigon.

Early experiments were less successful than expected, but once the spray equipment had been modified, crews were soon spraying the Viet Cong bases and their rice fields. The pilots had to fly straight and level at around 150ft over their targets to begin with, often drawing ground fire, but as the crews' experience grew, they were soon spraying mountainous areas.

Attempts to start forest fires by dropping concentrations of fuel (known as Operation Inferno and then Operation Banish Beach) proved economically expensive but the dropping of incendiary bombs on defoliated areas was more successful and Operation Pink Rose continued until Ranch Hand came to an end.

There had been suspicions that Agent Orange was carcinogenic and in 1969 the National Cancer Institute announced the chemical was linked to serious health problems. There was a public outcry and it intensified when it was claimed that the chemical had been sprayed over Cambodian territory. Operation Ranch Hand was soon phased out and although the last mission was flown in January 1971, the effects would be felt by many for the rest of their lives.

SURFACE-TO-AIR MISSILE SUPPRESSION

As the surface-to-air missile threat increased over North Vietnam (most downed US planes were hit by SAMs) plans were underway to counter the threat. Operation Iron Hand was launched at the beginning of 1966, pairing up F-100 Wild Weasels equipped with electronic equipment with F-105D's and the Wild Weasel crews located the SAM sites for the fighters to attack.

The Weasels had no range estimation capability to begin with and the F-105D's pilots needed to see the target to aim their free-fall bombs and unguided rockets. Better location equipment and the introduction of the guided AGM-45A Shrike missile improved the success rate; a new vector warning system in the F-105 aircraft was able to warn against approaching missiles and enemy planes.

AERIAL OPERATIONS

The US Air Force and Navy squadrons worked alongside on many operations during the air war. At the end of 1961 three air operations, disguised as training missions, began:

OPERATION ABLE MABLE
In October 1961 four RF-101 Voodoo jets landed at Tan Son Nhut allegedly to take part in South Vietnamese National Day celebrations. They never returned to Okinawa and were soon flying low-level reconnaissance missions, taking aerial photographs of the terrain. Four more RF-101s joined them a month later.

OPERATION FARM GATE
In November 1961 4400th Combat Crew Training Squadron began flying missions out of Bien Hoa. The Jungle Jim Squadron was supposed to be

F-100 Super Sabres head towards their next target. (342B-VN-94896)

training South Vietnamese pilots but it was also flying support missions for Special Forces teams.

PROJECT MULE TRAIN

In December 1961 sixteen C-123 Providers, piloted by the Dirty Thirty, flew to Vietnam to train South Vietnamese pilots. The planes displayed Vietnamese Air Force markings and they were allowed to carry out combat missions if there was a Vietnamese national on the pretext that he was being given combat training.

All three missions continued until US combat troops were deployed in 1965, expanding as the months passed and new aircraft replaced the aging Vietnamese planes. By 1963 American pilots were flying over 80 per cent of missions in support of US Special Forces and the South Vietnamese Army.

The deception ended in 1965 when US Air Force markings replaced the South Vietnamese insignia on aircraft and the requirement to carry South Vietnamese personnel on board was lifted. Later in the year Operation Able Mable and Project Mule Train came to an end as USAF and Navy planes took over combat, supply and reconnaissance missions. Planes continued to fly Operation Farm Gate missions until 1967.

A bombing raid has devastated this Viet Cong base camp. (342B-VN-94954)

AIR ATTACKS AGAINST NORTH VIETNAM

FLAMING DART I AND FLAMING DART II: FEBRUARY 1965

Operation Flaming Dart was ordered in retaliation for mortar attacks on Camp Holloway at Qui Nhon and Pleiku airfield on 7 February 1965 and planes bombed installations at Dong Hoi in North Vietnam for the first time. Operation Flaming Dart II followed two days later after the Viet Cong attacked Qui Nhon base. The two raids were precursors to Operation Rolling Thunder.

OPERATION ROLLING THUNDER: 2 MARCH 1965 TO 31 OCTOBER 1968

A third Viet Cong attack on Pleiku airfield in February 1965 had enormous consequences for both Vietnams and the United Sates. President Johnson ordered the deployment of 50,000 US ground troops to South Vietnam to protect the air bases and restore stability across the country. He also instigated Operation Rolling Thunder, a 3½-year bombing campaign against North Vietnam, and while Navy squadrons flew from the aircraft carriers based at Yankee and Dixie Stations in the South China Sea, US Air Force planes flew from air bases in Thailand.

The objective was to force the North Vietnamese to the negotiating table and, although targets were restricted to areas just north of the Demilitarized Zone to begin with, new target areas were added as the months passed until only the following areas were off limits:

A 25-mile- (40km-) wide strip along the Chinese border
North of Vinh where many North Vietnamese fighters and SAM missiles were based
A 10-mile radius around Hanoi and a 4-mile radius around Haiphong port

Washington placed a number of restrictions on the targets and while SAM missile sites could only be attacked in self-defense, North Vietnamese air bases were placed off-limits because Soviet technicians were known to be working on them. Frustrated by the ban, the USAF devised a plan, codenamed Operation Bolo, to lure the North Vietnamese Air Force into the air.

Above: *A fuel depot near Hanoi burns out of control after an airstrike. (342B-VN-96167)*

Right: *A flight of F-105 Thunderchiefs heads towards targets in North Vietnam. (342B-VN-95082)*

Twenty-eight Phantoms from 8th Tactical Fighter Wing flew slowly towards targets on 2 January 1967 (a similar number from 366th Tactical Fighter Wing were turned back by bad weather), pretending to be F-105 Thunderchiefs on a bombing mission. The F-105s were no match for the MiGs and the pilots were soon scrambled looking for an easy kill but once they were airborne they found the Phantom pilots waiting for them. Seven MiG-21s were shot down in 15 minutes in the largest aerial dogfight of the conflict. Washington lifted the restrictions on attacking air bases three months later.

A seven-day halt was called in May, codenamed Mayflower, while attempts were made to open negotiations with Hanoi but they all failed and bombing resumed. Attacks escalated over the next six months and a second month-long break in the bombing campaign over the Christmas period again failed to entice the North Vietnamese to the negotiating table. If anything it stiffened their resolve to carry on and when the American pilots resumed their missions, they found damaged targets had been rebuilt while new ones had appeared. Rolling Thunder eventually ended on 31 October 1968 after 3½ years of sustained bombing:

304,000 fighter-bomber and 2,380 B-52 sorties
634,000 tons of bombs dropped for a loss of 922 aircraft

OPERATIONS LINEBACKER I AND LINEBACKER II:
10 MAY – 29 DECEMBER 1972
On 10 May 1972 President Nixon ordered the renewal of air strikes against North Vietnam, in the hope of forcing a decision at the Paris peace talks. It started with attacks against lines of communication into the country and while the ports were sown with mines, roads and railways leading into China were cut; Long Bien Bridge and the Yen Vien railroad yard in Hanoi were two principal targets. New laser-guided bombs and electro-optically guided bombs meant that targets close to civilian structures could be hit for the first time and the raids cut North Vietnamese imports in half.

After crippling North Vietnam's power supply by hitting petroleum storage facilities and power generating plants, the bombers turned their attentions to training camps, military barracks and air defense facilities. President Nixon had given the military the freedom to choose their targets, unlike President Johnson and the combined effects of the attacks cut the North Vietnamese supply lines, forcing troops to withdraw across the border.

With progress being made in Paris, the raids were curtailed on 23 October and planes returned to attacking targets in Hanoi and Haiphong and south of the 20th Parallel. The peace talks ended on December 13 when the North Vietnamese delegation withdrew from the negotiations having achieved nothing except to allow the people of North Vietnam time to repair the damage.

President Nixon gave the North Vietnamese 72 hours to return to the negotiating table and when they did not, he ordered the Air Force to resume bombing. Only selected planes could fly in the winter conditions but starting on 18 December B-52s, F-111 fighter-bombers, and A-6 Intruders once again attacked the capital and sowed mines in Haiphong Harbor.

Planes flew in huge formations in scenes reminiscent of the saturation bombing raids over Germany in the Second World War, but losses were high; three B-52s were lost on the first night and more were shot down on the second night as SAM missiles found their targets. Despite attempts to avoid civilian targets, over 1,500 were killed and thousands were injured. Over the next few days planes targeted the air defense system and the attacks culminated in the largest raid of the war on 26 December. After F-105 and F-4 fighter bombers had knocked out many of the SAM sites and their guidance radars around Hanoi, waves of B-52s attacked ten targets across the defenseless city over a 15-minute period. Although two planes were shot down, the ferocity of the attacks forced the North Vietnamese to return to the negotiating table.

On 29 December President Nixon once again limited the bombing to below the 20th Parallel, bringing Operation Linebacker II to an end. Over 15,000 tons of bombs had been dropped, hitting over 1,600 military structures and ten airfields; they had also severely damaged the North Vietnamese railway system, destroyed many electricity plants and decimated their fuel stocks.

On 1 January 1973 negotiations resumed and twenty-two days later a cease-fire agreement was finally drawn up.

A MiG goes into an uncontrollable dive after being hit by the cannon of this F-105 Thunderchief. (342B-VN-101259)

SUPPORTING THE SOUTH VIETNAMESE ARMY

OPERATION FREEDOM TRAIN: APRIL 1972

US Air Force planes flew support missions for the ARVN during the North Vietnamese Easter Offensive. The US planes inflicted grievous losses on the NVA and although the South Vietnamese eventually halted the offensive, it illustrated how reliant they were on American firepower.

AIR ATTACKS AGAINST LAOS

The US Air Force started flying reconnaissance missions over Laos as early as May 1964 and President Johnson ordered a retaliatory air strike when a plane was shot down a month later; it was the start of a nine-year aerial campaign over Laos by the US Navy and Air Force planes. Washington selected targets but differences between the two services combined with frequent bad weather resulted in few successes and inflated damage reports gave the impression that the North Vietnamese were suffering heavy losses. Below are listed the long-term aerial campaigns:

OPERATION BARREL ROLL

Support for the Laotian Pathet Lao and the CIA-trained Hmong irregular forces in the Plain of Jars area of northern Laos lasted from June 1964 to April 1973.

OPERATION YANKEE TEAM

Reconnaissance of the Ho Chi Minh Trail began in September 1964.

OPERATION STEEL TIGER

Reconnaissance and air strikes against the Ho Chi Minh Trail below the 17th Parallel began in December 1964.

OPERATION TIGER HOUND

In December 1965 air missions across Laos were split into two areas. Tiger Hound concentrated on targets along the Ho Chi Minh Trail selected by Special Force teams working on Operation Shining Brass. The teams also controlled the air strikes from the ground and then assessed bomb damage in a concept codenamed SLAM; Seeking, Locating, Annihilating and Monitoring targets. Steel Tiger missions covered the rest of the country but they were still chosen by Washington.

OPERATION COMMANDO HUNT

Raids were scaled down in October 1968 and Steel Tiger and Tiger Hound were combined in November 1968 as the Special Forces missions were renamed Operation Prairie Fire. Anti-aircraft activity along the Trail increased to such an extent that daylight raids were limited to the Tchepone area and although defoliation missions stripped away the jungle to expose huge truck parks and storage areas, the bombing raids that followed rarely stopped the flow of traffic for long.

Commando Hunt ended in April 1972 when planes were diverted to attack targets in North Vietnam, however, missions continued for another twelve months.

AIR ATTACKS AGAINST CAMBODIA

OPERATION FREEDOM DEAL

When the Nixon administration took over one of its first acts was to authorize the top secret bombing of NVA and VC sanctuaries in Cambodia. The first mission took place on March 18 and a series of raids called Breakfast, Supper, Lunch, Dessert, and Snack (collectively known as Operation Menu), which continued over the next seventeen months. Only a few government officials knew of the deception until the New York Times newspaper exposed the story on 15 August 1970.

More than 100,000 tons of bombs were dropped on Cambodia and the news was leaked to the public in 1973 to further discredit the troubled Nixon administration.

OPERATION PATIO

In April and May 1970 US planes were able openly to carry out air strikes in support of the invasion of Cambodia.

CHAPTER 16

FREE WORLD ALLIES

Early discussions with the members of the Southeast Asia Treaty Organization in 1961 considered multilateral aid and troop deployments to Southeast Asia. A small Australian advisory team arrived in the north of the country the following year to train ARVN units in case the war in Laos threatened the border. The situation was temporarily settled by the 1962 Geneva Accords and attentions turned to South Vietnam when the political situation deteriorated as Viet Cong activity increased. The assassination of President Diem increased worries and following President Lyndon B. Johnson's public call for 'more flags' in April 1964, Australia increased its commitment to the country while New Zealand, Thailand, Korea and the Philippines deployed military and civil teams.

Following the arrival of large numbers of US combat troops in March 1965, Korea, Australia and New Zealand sent military task forces; Thailand followed two years later. Each country served under different terms and while the two Korean divisions were deployed around the ports and military installations along the coast, the rest of the Allies operated in the provinces around Saigon.

AUSTRALIA

The Australian Armed Forces had a history of fighting guerillas in jungles and swamps, during the Second World War in Borneo against the Japanese and then in Malaya alongside the British. In July 1962 a team of thirty advisors specializing in jungle warfare, known as the Australian Army Training Team, Vietnam (AATTV), deployed to South Vietnam and began working alongside US advisors in the north of the country. The Australian contingent increased in 1964 when a detachment of six Caribou aircraft began providing support for Vietnamese units. An engineer civic action team and the first of several surgical teams also started work.

Arrangements for the deployment of a reinforced battalion and 100 jungle warfare advisors were discussed following the commitment of US ground troops and in May 1965 1st Battalion Royal Australian Regiment (RAR) and a logistics support company reinforced 173d Airborne Brigade. To begin with Australian troops were restricted to the defense and patrolling of the area around at Bien Hoa air base but the restriction was removed in August. The following month a 105mm howitzer battery, an engineer troop, an armored personnel carrier troop, a signal troop and an air reconnaissance flight joined the new Headquarters, Australian Army Force, Vietnam.

In March 1966 a second battalion arrived with extra support, bringing the strength of the Australian contingent to over 4,500. 1st Australian Task Force, as it was known, covered the eastern half of the Rung Sat Special

Zone for II Field Force, from its base in Phuoc Tuy Province. Headquarters, Australian Forces, Vietnam, coordinated operations with the US headquarters in Saigon.

The Task Force secured Highway 15 and occasionally ran into strong opposition; a company of 6th Battalion fought off over 1,500 North Vietnamese and Viet Cong in Binh Ba rubber plantation on 18 August 1966. The Australian Army Training Team eventually joined the Task Force and its advisors would continue to work with ARVN troops until it left in December 1972; four men were awared the Victoria Cross, the highest award for bravery.

In the spring of 1967 the arrival of a Royal Australian Air Force Canberra Squadron and a Royal Australian Navy guided missile destroyer completed Australia's tri-service commitment. Elite Special Air Service Squadrons were also deployed for the first time. Although the government planned to send a third infantry battalion, deployment was delayed until the end of 1967 by political opposition. A company joined two New Zealand companies, forming the ANZAC Battalion, at the same time. The arrival of a medium-tank squadron armed with fifteen Centurion tanks, a cavalry troop an engineer construction troop, eight extra helicopters and extra headquarters staff, increased the Australian contingent to over 8,000 men.

Protests against Australian involvement in South Vietnam had begun in 1968 and as they continued to increase, the government considered withdrawing troops in line with the American redeployment. The Australian Army Assistance Group, Vietnam, was organized to train ARVN units in Phuoc Tuy Province as part of the Vietnamization process and in November 1969 the first withdrawal took place. Combat and support troops left in stages throughout 1971 and the last infantry battalion left in October. The Task Force and Headquarters staff followed in March 1972 but the Assistance Group remained behind until January 1973.

A soldier of the 2nd Royal Australian Regiment keeps watch on a trail with his M-60 machine gun. (111-CC-70221)

DEPLOYMENT OF COMBAT UNITS

In contrast to the US practice of rotating individual personnel, Australian units were usually rotated at the end of a year-long tour.

Members of an Australian assault pioneer platoon work on a community well, while the villagers watch. (111-CC-39083)

INFANTRY	FIRST TOUR	SECOND TOUR
1st Battalion:	May 1965 to June 1966	January 1968 to February 1969
2d Battalion:	March 1967 to June 1968	April 1970 to June 1971
3d Battalion:	December 1967 to December 1968	February 1971 to October 1971
4th Battalion:	January 1968 to 30 May 1969	May 1971 to March 1972
5th Battalion:	April 1966 to July 1967	January 1969 to March 1970
6th Battalion:	April 1966 to July 1967	May 1969 to May 1970
7th Battalion:	March 1967 to April 1968	February 1970 to March 1971
8th Battalion:	November 1969 to November 1970	
9th Battalion:	November 1968 to December 1969	

CAVALRY	
1st Armored Personnel Carrier Troop:	September 1965 to April 1966
1st Armored Personnel Carrier Squadron:	April 1966 to January 1967
A Squadron, 3d Cavalry Regiment:	January 1967 to May 1969
B Squadron, 3d Cavalry Regiment:	May 1969 to January 1971
A Squadron, 3d Cavalry Regiment:	January 1971 to March 1972

ARMOR	
C Squadron, 1st Armored Regiment:	January 1968 to February 1969
B Squadron, 1st Armored Regiment:	February 1969 to December 1969
A Squadron, 1st Armored Regiment:	December 1969 to December 1970
C Squadron, 1st Armored Regiment:	December 1970 to September 1971

ARTILLERY

105th Field Artillery Battery:	September 1965 to March 1966
1st Field Artillery Regiment:	April 1966 to July 1967
4th Field Artillery Regiment:	March 1967 to May 1968
12th Field Artillery Regiment:	January 1968 to March 1969
1st Field Artillery Regiment:	February 1969 to May 1970
4th Field Artillery Regiment:	February 1970 to March 1971
12th Field Artillery Regiment:	January 1971 to December 1971
104th Field Artillery Battery:	May 1971 to December 1971

SPECIAL AIR SERVICE SQUADRON

	FIRST TOUR	SECOND TOUR
1st Squadron:	March 1967 to February 1968	February 1970 to February 1971
2d Squadron:	January 1968 to March 1969	February 1971 to October 1971
3d Squadron:	April 1966 to July 1967	February 1969 to February 1970

NEW ZEALAND

Although the New Zealand government did not want to get deeply involved in Vietnam for political reasons, the military was anxious to gain experience in combat operations. An engineer platoon and surgical team arrived in July 1964. They were joined by 161st Artillery Battery armed with 105mm howitzers a year later; it served with the Australian task force in Phuoc Tuy Province.

General Westmoreland requested a battalion of infantry so he could form a three-battalion ANZAC brigade but political difficulties and elections in New Zealand reduced the offer to two extra howitzers and extra men for the surgical team. Eventually V Company, Royal New Zealand Infantry Regiment, deployed in May 1967 and it was joined seven months later by W Company. Each company had 150 officers and men and they were organized as an ANZAC battalion with a third Australian company. Number 4 Troop of New Zealand Special Air Services, numbering twenty-six men, also arrived in December 1967 and they joined a similar Australian unit on long-range patrols and reconnaissance. They increased the New Zealand troop strength to more than 500 men.

The New Zealand government announced the start of troop withdrawals in August 1970 and three months later, W Company was replaced by a training team. The artillery battery left in March 1971 and V Company followed at the end of the year.

KOREA

As early as 1954 Korea had offered to send a Korean Army element to Vietnam but the offer was turned down. Ten years later a Survey (Liaison) Team arrived in August 1964 to give asssistance with civic action programs while discussions about Korea's future involvement took place.

Its first contribution was the Republic of Korea Military Assistance Group, which arrived at Bien Hoa in February 1965 and started work on civic action projects, helping in areas affected by heavy flooding during recent monsoons. The force, nicknamed the Dove Unit, numbered over 2,400 and it was organized as follows:

A squad leader of the ROK Tiger Division keeps in contact with his men during an operation in the Central Highlands. (111-CC-62889)

Construction support group
Marine Corps engineer company
Navy landing craft
Korean Army security company

Troops worked on bridges, schools and dispensaries and while operating under special rules of engagement that only allowed them to return fire, they relied on the ARVN for assistance if they came under sustained attack.

Following high-level talks between President Johnson and President Park in May 1965 the decision was taken to deploy the equivalent of a division, supported by an F-86 fighter squadron. However, there were conditions. The Korean government announced that its troops must be under US control as a separate and distinct force as a matter of pride. Although they wanted to display support for a neighbouring country they did not want Korean soldiers acting like paid mercenaries; they had to be operating independently under US military control. They also wanted full US logistical support and a large amount of financial aid.

Military Assistance Command, Vietnam, wanted to prevent competitiveness between Korean and South Vietnamese units and it chose the coastal areas surrounding their logistics bases for their deployment. The Capital Division, known as the Tigers, began to arrive in the area west of Qui Nhon in September 1965 and over the next six months it helped to take control of Binh Dinh Province.

CAPITAL DIVISION

Headquarters and Headquarters Company
Cavalry Regiment, 1st and 26th Infantry Regiments, each with three battalions
Headquarters and Headquarters Battery, Artillery Division
10th, 60th and 61st 105mm Field Artillery Battalions
628th 155mm Field Artillery Battalion
Armor Company, Reconnaissance Company and Aviation Section

Combat support was supplied by an engineer battalion, a signal company and a military police company. Support and Service troops included a medical company, an ordnance company and a quartermaster company.

The 2d Marine Corps Brigade, known as the Blue Dragons, deployed at the same time around Cam Rahn Bay but it soon had to move to secure the Tuy Hoa area. In August 1966 it moved to the Bong Son area, north of Qui Nhon.

2D MARINE CORPS BRIGADE

1st, 2d and 3d Battalions; 5th Battalion joined in 1967

9th (White Horse) Infantry Division deployed along II Corps' southern coast in September 1966 where it took over responsibility for the area around Cam Rahn Bay, Tuy Hoa and Ninh Hoa.

9TH INFANTRY DIVISION

Headquarters and Headquarters Company
28th Regiment, 29th and 30th Infantry Regiments, each with three battalions
Headquarters and Headquarters Battery, Artillery Division
30th, 51st and 52d 105mm Field Artillery Battalions
966th 155mm Field Artillery Battalion

It had the same combat support and service troops as the Capital Division.

The arrival of this second division brought the strength of the Korean forces in Vietnam to around 45,000, and the Republic of Korea Military Assistance Group was increased in size so it could operate as a corps headquarters. It was based in Nha Trang and reported to II Field Force while working alongside II Corps.

2d Marine Brigade left Vietnam between December 1971 and February 1972. The rest of the Korean troops were some of the last to withdraw, leaving the country during the first three months of 1973.

THAILAND

As neighbors to Cambodia, Thailand was concerned that they would be the next target for the Communists. Prime Minister Thanom wanted his country to take an active part in the defense of Southeast Asia while modernizing the Armed Forces. A small number of pilots started flying South Vietnamese cargo aircraft in September 1964 and they came under the control of the Royal Thai Military Assistance Group, Vietnam, when it formed in February 1966.

After the Bangkok press announced that a battalion combat team would be deploying to South Vietnam, thousands volunteered for the Armed Forces,

A patrol of the Queen's Cobra Regiment pauses during a patrol while the men scan the undergrowth. (111-CC-45863)

allowing the Thai contribution to be increased to a regimental combat team. In September 1967 the Royal Thai Army Volunteer Regiment, an elite unit known as the Queen's Cobras, arrived at Bear Cat where it was stationed for twelve months with 9th Division. The Thais were issued with modern US equipment, however, the infantry had to be issued with a mixture of M16s assault rifles and M2 carbines due to material shortages.

Further negotiations led to the Thai contribution being increased to a division assisted by US combat support and financial aid. The Royal Thai Army's Expeditionary Division (known as the Black Panthers) started to deploy in July 1968 and it was joined by the Headquarters, 2d Brigade and two artillery battalions in December, bringing the number of troops deployed to over 11,000. 3d Brigade replaced 1st Brigade the following summer.

ROYAL THAI ARMY EXPEDITIONARY DIVISION

Division Headquarters
1st Brigade: 1st, 2d, 3d Infantry Battalions
2d Brigade: 1st, 2d, 3d Infantry Battalions
3d Brigade: 1st, 2d, 3d Infantry Battalions
105mm towed howitzers: 1st, 2d and 3d Artillery Battalions
155mm towed howitzers: 1st Battalion
1st Armored Cavalry Squadron and 1st Long-Range Reconnaissance Troop

The division was supported by a combat engineer battalion, a signal battalion, a military police company and an aviation company.

In August 1970 the Black Panthers Division became the Royal Thai Army Volunteer Force and twelve months later, the number of Thai troops was scaled down in line with US withdrawals. 2d Brigade replaced 1st Brigade in September 1971 and it too withdrew five months later.

The Thai Navy had also deployed two ships to South Vietnam and they worked alongside US Navy vessels on Operation Market Time.

A team of the Philippine Civic Action Group distributes medicine in Tay Ninh Province. (111-CC-51508)

Thailand was also used as a base by many US units. The US Army based 9th Logistical Command at Khorat while the US Air Force used numerous air bases across Thailand to stage their bombing raids over North Vietnam, Laos and Cambodia. Reconnaissance and fighter planes used the bases to strike at targets along the Ho Chi Minh Trail.

Ubon:	8th Tactical Fighter Wing
Nakhon Phanom:	58th Air Commando Wing
U Tapao:	307th Strategic Wing
Ta Khli:	355th and 366th Tactical Fighter Wings
Khorat:	388th Tactical Fighter Wing and 553d Reconnaissance Wing
Udorn:	432d Tactical Reconnaissance Wing
Hakhon Phanom:	633d Special Operations Wing

THE PHILIPPINES

A small medical group had been working in Vietnam since 1953 and additional medical groups served in Vietnam between 1964 and 1966 while Philippine Army officers advised on psychological warfare and civil affairs in III Corps' area.

President Macapagal had wanted to send a force of around 2,500 but he faced government opposition and when President Marcos was elected in the fall of 1965 he refused to send military aid. He did, however, agree to dispatch the Philippine Civic Action Group in return for US financial aid. It arrived in the Thanh Dien Forest area of Tay Ninh Province in September 1966 with an infantry battalion supported by artillery, engineer and medical battalions. It returned to the Philippines at the end of 1969.

CHAPTER 17

SOUTH VIETNAM'S ARMED FORCES

GOVERNMENT CONTROL

Central government was run from Saigon with delegates acting on behalf of the four regions, North, Center, South and the Highlands. The countryside was divided into forty-four provinces ranging from 500 to 10,000 sq km and the government officials were responsible for as few as 33,000 inhabitants to as many as 850,000; six city provinces covered the heavily populated areas of Hue and Da Nang in the north, Da Lat, Cam Ranh and Vung Tau in the south and Saigon. Provinces were also sub-divided into a small number of districts (236 countrywide) led by district chiefs drawn from the population. The American liaison officers had to work closely with the chiefs to gain approval for operations and they needed their assistance accurately to assess intelligence, both political and military. Each district controlled a number of villages led by Village Administrative Committees. There were larger villages (or villes) but in isolated areas they were usually a scattered group of straw and mud houses grouped into hamlets. Each hamlet had a hamlet chief on the Village Citizens' Council. The Americans usually adopted the Vietnamese name of villages (although names were bastardized into something pronounceable) and numbered each hamlet.

A large crowd of demonstrators gather in July 1964, on the tenth anniversary of the signing of the agreement at Geneva which split Vietnam in two. (111-CC-26827)

Province chiefs controlled all the services in their area, using the Regional Forces for security, and liaised with the Regular Army during operations. District chiefs controlled the Popular Forces, guarding the villages against Viet Cong infiltration. American advisors were attached to the province, and later district, offices to improve communications but it took time to build up a good working relationship. Leaders often operated their own rules and while some gave their full support, others were indifferent or unwilling to cooperate.

HEARTS AND MINDS CAMPAIGNS

The United States involvement in Vietnam had many objectives but it was clear that defeating the North Vietnamese Army and the Viet Cong would not be sufficient; the people had to be convinced that the government had their interests at heart. While military operations could temporarily drive the Viet Cong away from the populated areas, civil programs had to be implemented to give the people security, shelter and the chance to trade their goods.

THE STRATEGIC HAMLET PROGRAM

The first attempt at winning hearts and minds was to move the people away from contested areas into new villages with improved facilities where they could be protected. A pilot Strategic Hamlet program called Operation Sunrise moved villagers out of War Zone D early in 1962 and the plan was to build 11,000 new hamlets over the next two years.

The Program received American approval by presenting visible evidence that money was being invested wisely but in reality it was a fiasco. Conditions in Ben Tuong, the main hamlet, were terrible and people were soon returning to their homes; the Communists compared them to concentration camps. In October 1963 Diem declared that over 10 million people had been moved into strategic hamlets but the truth was that the program had collapsed. The Viet Cong had overrun Ben Tuong two months earlier and work on Strategic Hamlets had been stopped.

Moving the people to sanctuaries was not the answer. The American and Vietnamese Armed Forces would have to drive the Viet Cong away from the villages so that Government control could be restored.

AMERICAN PACIFICATION BEGINS

In order to bring stability back to South Vietnam, the American military and civil authorities had to work with the Vietnamese authorities to restore security and then develop the nation before the government could take over. Integrated programs of political, economic and social developments were needed to get the support of the people and give them self-sufficiency if pacification was to succeed. In 1965 General Westmoreland visited Malaya to see how the British had restored government control following the Communist insurgency in the 1950s and it was clear that the provinces and their districts had to be involved.

The Province Chiefs were responsible to the President on two counts; maintaining security and administering government services. It was a difficult role and often presented the chief with conflicting targets as he implemented government programs while cooperating with the military and their American advisors.

Villagers construct a new dispensary. (111-CC-44029)

By 1965 eighty construction teams were being trained to supervise work in the field and the projects were called a variety of names including Pacification, Rural Reconstruction, Rural Construction and eventually Revolutionary Development. The Americans also had teams from the US Public Affairs Office, the US Agency for International Development and the Office of the Special Assistant working on projects but they were usually undermanned and coordination between agencies was often poor. The Office of Civil Operations was formed in November 1966 to coordinate the activities while MACV's Revolutionary Development Support Division stepped up military support of pacification. Although progress was being made, there was still some way to go before the province chiefs had the advisors they needed.

CORDS OPERATIONS

New changes were made when Ellsworth Bunker took over as the US Ambassador at Saigon in April 1967. The Revolutionary Development program was taken over by MACV while Presidential Assistant Robert W Komer joined General Westmoreland's headquarters as deputy for the new Civil Operations and Rural Development Support. CORDS operations coordinated civil and military activities and they were run by Regional Directors with each Vietnamese corps and advisors with each Province Chief. District advisory teams were absorbed into the CORDS system while extra Army and Marine staff improved the military contribution. For the first time it was possible to plan operations with the ultimate objective in mind; the pacification of South Vietnam.

THE ONE WAR CONCEPT

The various military and civil agencies were all working towards the same objectives but a lack of coordination meant that the varied initiatives, programs and operations were often contradictory. In an attempt to draw together military, pacification and government activities, General Abrams introduced the One War Concept.

Military operations were planned to push the Viet Cong away from populated areas so that the Regional and Popular Force garrisons could take over local security. Revolutionary Development Programs followed, aiming to convince the people that the government had their interests at heart. Attempts were made to assess the needs of each village using the Hamlet Evaluation System but results were sometimes biased by political motives and the American assessors did not always appreciate what the Vietnamese wanted. Divisions produced weekly operational review and analysis maps charting military operations, civic action programs and hamlet evaluations. Eventually, the Accelerated Pacification Campaign was introduced to make sure that military and civil operations complemented each other, targeting key areas so that the South Vietnamese territorial forces and civil affairs programs could start work.

The political sway of the population was an effective tool for monitoring the mood of the people but it was difficult to assess. Hamlet Evaluation Survey Reports were published every month, detailing key security and civic action issues. Welfare, health, educational, and economic development were also graded, enabling all agencies to focus on trouble spots.

It took careful cooperation to gain successful results, but a single destructive act, such as an accidental friendly fire incident, or a deliberate violent incident, like the massacre at My Lai in March 1968, could undo months of hard work.

PSYCHOLOGICAL OPERATIONS

The Viet Cong was constantly targeted by propaganda campaigns, aiming to get disillusioned men to lay down their arms and surrender. It was hoped that some could be persuaded to work for Allies as *Chieu Hois* or scouts. Many methods were used, including radio broadcasts, helicopter loudspeakers, hand-held megaphones, and dropped propaganda leaflets. Results were mixed and while scattered Viet Cong units produced many *Chieu Hois*, it was difficult to get men to rally from intact units.

When available, Kit Carson or Tiger Scouts accompanied each infantry platoon or squad, and used cards printed in English and Vietnamese to call out to the Viet Cong, however, poor translation meant mistakes were made and results were sometimes disappointing.

Psychological operations also targeted the civilians, and many attempts were made to win over their hearts and minds. Soldiers were taught Vietnamese customs so they would not offend villagers and they were encouraged to play games with the children and hand out leaflets and T-shirts, government officials held raffles and gave speeches and bands provided musical entertainment.

CIVIC ACTION PROGRAMS

Civic Action Programs were designed to give aid that would ultimately give the Vietnamese the motivation to help themselves and three Civil Affairs Companies coordinated activities with the Vietnamese province and district leaders. Combat troops were often involved in Civic Action Programs and while some constructed churches, dispensaries, marketplaces and dwellings, others delivered building materials for the Vietnamese to use.

Soldiers often gave their own time to help with construction projects or donated money to help build orphanages, churches and shelters for the physically handicapped. They also distributed food, water and clothing provided by the programs. Medical units worked their way from village to village, often with infantry protection, to administer aid and train the Vietnamese in basic medical skills. Educational help was given to schools either by donating learning material or by teaching English.

Rebuilding the road network was important for opening contact with the government agencies and reestablishing trade across the country. While the American engineers worked on the major roads, surplus engineering equipment was donated to the district so that Vietnamese engineers could work on the secondary roads. In many cases a minimum amount of effort opened a road for local transport, much of which depended on bicycles, oxcarts and motorbikes.

A civil affairs team hand out leaflets. (111-SC-34474)

TRAINING THE ARMED FORCES

The South Vietnamese Armed Forces were hindered by a variety of problems, many of them stemming back many years. The coup following President Diem's assassination in 1963 found many military leaders in government posts, but while officers were often politically motivated, a general lack of urgency and aggressiveness had spread across the Armed Forces. The rapid expansion of the Army had also led to many officers commanding beyond their capacity and a lack of experienced officers and NCOs.

The South Vietnamese Army (ARVN) was under strength in 1965 and although thousands of new recruits had been called up in October 1964, many immediately left, confident that the authorities did not have the resources to track them down. Amnesties, and harsher punishments for deserters, did little to stem the number of men going absent and many joined their local Popular Forces unit so they could stay at home. Over 200,000 youths evaded military service and although further recruiting campaigns had little effect, the South Vietnamese Government did not lay down plans for a partial mobilization until the end of 1967.

Military Assistance Command, Vietnam, helped to instigate many programs and actions to overcome the problems. Pay increases, new awards and enhanced systems of promotions and leave improved motivation while improved rations and living standards for the soldiers made life more bearable. However, corruption was a constant problem and many supplies ended up on the black market.

Many problems started at the training schools where recruits were often taught by incompetent teachers working from an outdated curriculum and while lectures filled a lot of the time, there was limited practical training. Once in the field unit, commanders failed to promote unit training or refresher courses and the men were often allowed to rest between operations.

Military Assistance Command, Vietnam, tried to impose American training regimes on the ARVN to improve efficiency but language difficulties and cultural differences often prevented progress. The training curriculums were updated for new recruits while Small Unit Leaders' Guides were issued to officers and NCOs in the field. New training centers across the country were supposed to give practical experience with new tactics and weapons but a shortage of instructors and poor management meant that the men learnt very little.

By 1967 the Vietnamese Military Academy had been turned from a two-year to a four-year institution patterned after West Point and graduates initially went to combat units before rotating between different posts to gain a broader range of skills. To make up for the shortage in officers, experienced enlisted men could attend the Special Officer Candidate Training Courses while battlefield promotions were introduced for NCOs.

Technical posts posed a greater problem as men who had grown up in an undeveloped country struggled to come to terms with modern equipment

A US advisor watches while ARVN recruits practice infiltration techniques. (111-CC-67737)

made in another country. Some candidates were sent to overseas schools to learn their skills while others worked side by side in programs such as 1st Logistical Command's Operation Buddy. Pilots had the added problem of becoming proficient in English before they could serve as apprentices in American squadrons; only then could they start to learn to fly.

COMBINED OPERATIONS

The most efficient way of training ARVN units was allowing American and South Vietnamese troops to work together on operations. The Army had tried local schemes since 1965 but the largest was conducted by III Marine Amphibious Force in I Corps. Its Combined Action Program had Marine rifle squads working alongside Popular Forces platoons until they were competent to defend their own village. Three Combined Actions Battalions were formed in October 1967 and although the program was effective, it required too many men to implement across the rest of the country.

The Army's first large-scale pairing program, Operation Fairfax, began at the end of 1966 when American and Vietnamese infantry battalions worked side by side in key districts around Saigon. Early coordination and control problems were soon resolved as the ARVN units' confidence grew and after twelve months the US troops were able to leave the paramilitary forces in control.

The number of programs increased after the Tet offensive and in I Corps area, XXIV Corps began integrating all its US and Vietnamese Army tactical operations, deploying a mixture of battalions led by dual command posts. II Corps instigated the 'Pair-Off' program where American and Vietnamese worked in tandem while 1st Cavalry Division worked closely with Vietnamese airborne regiments, giving hands-on experience of airmobile operations. American units handed over sectors on a unit-for-unit basis when the time came for them to withdraw.

III Corps' corps-wide program, known as 'Progress Together' (Dong Tien) started in June 1969 and US combat units paired up with ARVN units so they could learn from each other. While the Americans taught the South Vietnamese how to conduct operations, they exchanged intelligence information, gleaning local information from the Regional and Popular Forces, a previously untapped source.

A senior US advisor discusses the day's operations with the province chief in his command and control helicopter. (111-CC-70097)

To begin with, US aviation units flew ARVN troops into battle but before long Vietnamese helicopters were introduced. As successes were chalked up, the ARVN unit's performance increased and the US unit was eventually able to withdraw. By the end of the year the number of ARVN operations across South Vietnam had risen from 50 per cent to 80 per cent.

As Vietnamization gathered momentum, attempts were made to hand over control of fire support to the Vietnamese, but they continued to rely heavily on American artillery, helicopter gunships and aircraft. Vietnamese commanders were prone to ignore the available fire support or requested inappropriate support and Combined Fire Support Coordination Centers had to be set up improve operational procedures. The Centers assessed requests from the

ARVN and Regional Forces and allocated fire support from suitably positioned artillery; either US or Vietnamese. Interpreters working at the Centers removed the language barrier and although they improved fire support coordination, Vietnamese officers often felt the Americans had too much control over their operations. The reliance on American fire support left the ARVN vulnerable after 1973; it was a mistake that would cost South Vietnam dear two years later.

SOUTH VIETNAM'S ARMED FORCES

After it had recovered from the shock of the Tet Offensive in 1968, the ARVN emerged with new confidence and responsibility. Many Viet Cong and NVA attacks had been stopped in their tracks and despite prolonged fighting in some areas, they were driven back to their sanctuaries.

The Government responded by lowering the draft age, recalling reservists and it finally took steps to control desertion. In June general mobilization came into force, increasing the size of the Armed Forces, in particular the air force and navy, as they were restructured. A new People's Self-Defense Force was also organized for the young and old; it would eventually recruit over 4 million part-time militiamen.

The tremendous growth of South Vietnam's Armed Forces is charted below:

	ARMY	AIR FORCE	NAVY	MARINES	TOTAL
1964	220,000	11,000	12,000	7,000	250,000
1968	380,000	19,000	19,000	9,000	427,000
1972	410,000	50,000	42,000	14,000	516,000

SOUTH VIETNAM'S ARMY – ARVN

The last four brigades of US ground troops withdrew during the first half of 1972 leaving the defense of South Vietnam to its own armed forces. Each infantry division had three regiments (1st and 23d Divisions had four), three 105mm and one 155mm artillery battalions and an armored cavalry squadron. Corps headquarters artillery also controlled a number of battalions and there were 176 two-gun platoons, armed with 105mm howitzers, stationed at military installations across the country.

I Corps Headquarters was based at Da Nang supported by the 1st Armor Brigade and the 1st Ranger Group. 3d Division covered Quang Tri Province, 1st Division protected the capital, Hue, and 2d Division was based in Quang Nai Province.

II Corps Headquarters was based at Pleiku in the Central Highlands and it was supported by the 2d Armor Brigade and the 2d Ranger Group. 22d Division protected Route 19 through the mountains while 23d Division guarded Ban Me Thuot and Route 21 in the south.

III Corps Headquarters was at Bien Hoa and it had 3d Armor Brigade and 81st Ranger Group in support. 25th Division was to the west at Duc Hoa, 5th Division was to the north at Lai Khe and 18th Division was to the east at Xuan Loc. 3d Ranger Command was also based at Bien Hoa with three Ranger Groups while the elite Parachute and Marine Divisions protected Saigon. 4th Ranger Group and 4th Armor Brigade were based at Chi Long covering 44th Special Tactical Zone, an area used by the VC for staging attacks on the capital.

IV Corps Corps Headquarters was at Can Tho with 7th Division based close by at the US Riverine Base of Dong Tam. 9th Division was at Rach Gia on the west coast of the Ca Mau Peninsula while 21st Division was at Bac Lieu on the east coast.

Twenty-two Ranger Battalions were organized into mobile reserve Groups while another thirty-three battalions (over 14,000 men) were based in the Special Forces camps along the border. The Marine Division stationed at Saigon had three Regiments while four Armored Brigades and forty engineer battalions gave the infantry armored and engineering support.

Vietnamese paratroopers go on the counterattack during an attack on Tan Son Nhut Air Base. (111-SC-48583)

VIETNAMESE SPECIAL FORCES

Poor results during early operations left the Vietnamese Special Forces with a bad reputation but confidence began to grow following successes in 1966 and 1967. US detachments had soon started to hand over responsibilities and 5th Special Forces Group starting withdrawing personnel in April 1970; it left Vietnam twelve months later.

The Special Forces Group detachments were organized along the same lines as their American counterparts. There were four C-detachments, one in each corps' tactical zone, twelve B-detachments, and seventy-three A-detachments supported by a signal company and a headquarters and service company; an airborne Ranger battalion was on standby to reinforce detachments under threat. The Group also ran its own Project Delta to conduct long-range reconnaissance missions.

REGIONAL AND POPULAR FORCES

South Vietnam's volunteer paramilitary forces constituted around half of the country's armed forces. They were divided into locally recruited Popular Forces, with squads and platoons providing security for their village or hamlet, and Regional Force units which could be deployed to troubled areas by the province. Both suffered from poor leadership and they were armed with obsolete weapons to begin with.

During the advisory period, assistance was needed to restore order and confidence in the isolated rural areas where Viet Cong support was widespread. The paramilitary forces needed assistance to help them protect their villages and throughout 1964 and 1965 five-man advisory teams were allocated to each district where they were often the only American representatives. Special Force A-detachments were posted to outlying districts, where Viet Cong activity was high. Progress was slow to begin with due to inconsistent government control but before long there were improvements as districts began to coordinate their defensive efforts.

By 1966 there were over 5,300 advisors working across the country, supported by dedicated helicopters; psychological operations advisors, civil affairs advisors or engineer advisors were dispatched to give specialist assistance. The program was expanded in 1967 with the addition of advisory teams to the ARVN security detachments being deployed across the country. At the end of the year Military Assistance Command, Military Assistance, was organized to control all the advisory efforts.

A Popular Force squad displays its new weapons as it stands guard over its village. (111-CC-60697)

Although both the Regional and Popular Forces had their own separate command structure, they were controlled by corps and divisions in their sectors, a troubled arrangement that often caused confusion. It was changed in 1967 when they were placed under their local sector and sub-sector commanders and both the US and ARVN combat units began to involve them in their operations.

The growth of the Territorial Forces is shown below:

	REGIONAL FORCES	POPULAR FORCES	TOTAL
1964	96,000	168,000	264,000
1968	220,000	173,000	393,000
1972	284,000	248,000	532,000

The National Police had also grown to 116,000 by 1972.

SOUTH VIETNAM'S AIR FORCE – SVNAF

In 1964 the South Vietnamese Air Force had four wings based at Da Nang, Pleiku, Tan Son Nhut and Can Tho, one in each of the corps' tactical zones. There were ten fixed-wing squadrons, four fighter, four observation and two transport, and three helicopter squadrons; they were all armed with obsolete aircraft and helicopters. Over the next ten years the SVNAF grew into a large modern air force as units took over American squadrons. It operated the following planes and helicopters:

Regional Forces insignia.

Fighters:	A-1 Skyraiders, A-37 Dragonflys and F-5 Freedom Fighters
Attack planes:	AC-119Ks and AC-47Ds
Reconnaissance planes:	EC-47 modified planes
Transport squadron:	C-7B Caribou planes
Utility helicopters:	UH-1H Hueys
Transport helicopters:	CH-47A Chinooks

By 1972 the Air Force could call upon over 1,000 aircraft and helicopters deployed as follows:

I Corps: 1st Air Division was based at Da Nang with 61st and 41st Tactical Fixed Wings and 51st Tactical Rotary Wing.

II Corps: 6th Air Division was based at Pleiku with 72d Tactical Wing, operating fighters and utility helicopters. 2d Air Division and 62d Tactical Fixed Wing flew out of Nha Trang. 82d Tactical Wing operated fighters and utility helicopters out of Phu Cat.

III Corps: 2d Air Division and 92d Tactical Wing operated three fighter squadrons out of Phan Rang air base. 3d Air Division controlled 23d and 63d Tactical Fixed Wings and 43d Tactical Rotary Wing at Bien Hoa. 53d Fixed Wing and 33d Tactical Wing, flying Special Air Missions, operated out of Tan Son Nhut.

IV Corps: 4th Air Division, 74th Fixed Wing and 84th Rotary Wing, flew from Binh Thuy.

Popular Forces insignia.

The crew of a Vietnamese patrol boat checks a fishing boat while their American advisor looks on. (111-CC-72867)

SOUTH VIETNAM'S NAVY

A Naval Advisory Group started to work with the South Vietnamese Navy at the beginning of 1969 and before long Vietnamese sailors were working alongside American crews as they prepared to take over.

By March 1970 the Delta patrol operations, codenamed SEALORDS, were handed over but the biggest test of how well the handover was progressing came two months later when a combined Vietnamese-American naval task force sailed up the Mekong River into Cambodia. While the American vessels were only allowed to travel part of the way to Phnom Penh, the Vietnamese boats continued into the capital and over the weeks that followed evacuated over 80,000 ethnic Vietnamese.

One by one the naval patrols along South Vietnam's coastal waters and rivers were handed over and by April 1971 the Advisory Group's Accelerated Turnover to the Vietnamese, or ACTOV, was complete. South Vietnam's Navy had grown to over 42,000 personnel operating 1,200 modern vessels and 240 junks organized into two Task Fleets:

Task Fleet 21: Covering the SEALORDS Operations with eight task forces
Task Fleet 22: General surveillance with nine task forces

Successful patrolling continued until US financial support was drastically cut in 1975, resulting in over 600 vessels being laid up to save fuel and ammunition. The resultant fall in the number of patrols came just as the North Vietnamese were planning their final offensive on South Vietnam.

Although the Americans had trained and equipped over one million men, the questions still to be answered were how well led were they, how prepared were they and how motivated were they? The North Vietnamese had consistently scored highly on all three counts; would South Vietnam's Armed Forces?

CHAPTER 18

THE VIET CONG AND THE NORTH VIETNAMESE ARMY

When American combat troops arrived in Vietnam in 1965 they were entering a struggle that had been ongoing for nearly twenty-five years. The Indochinese Communist Party (ICP) had formed the Viet Minh, or League for the Independence of Vietnam, in 1941, to oppose the French. War raged back and forth across the Pacific for the next four years, ending when the Americans dropped two atomic bombs on Hiroshima and Nagasaki in August 1945, forcing Japan to surrender unconditionally.

In the same year the Marxist Study Club replaced the ICP and six years later Ho Chi Minh reorganized the Viet Minh into the Vietnam Workers' Party, or the Vietnam Dang Lao Dong, to oppose the French. After three years of inconclusive fighting, during which the French were continually frustrated by their enemy's hit-and-run tactics, the Army decided to draw the Communists into battle at Dien Bien Phu in the mountains near the Laotian border. The French had underestimated the Viet Minh's military strength and as their troops became surrounded their outposts fell one-by-one, and the garrison eventually capitulating after a six-month siege.

Vietnam was granted its independence in June 1945 and the French signed a ceasefire with the Viet Minh a month later as the country was split into two at the 17th Parallel. The Communists had control of the north while the French still held the south, but plans were laid at the peace talks in Geneva for a general election in the south the following year.

A group of engineers display captured Communist banners. (111-CC-82923)

President Diem's new regime immediately ran into difficulties and when it became clear that a national election would not be held, the Lao Dong Party sent dissenters south of the border to organize armed opposition. As the number of American advisors aiding the South Vietnamese Army increased each year in the war against the Communists, the terrorists were given the collective name Viet Cong. The National Liberation Front of South Vietnam was formed in December 1960, but as the Viet Cong had no formal command structure, it was just a name rather than an organization.

A year later the People's Revolutionary Party took over the southern branch of the Lao Dong Party and its 300,000 members, forming a military branch called the Liberation Army of the Front (it was renamed the People's Liberation Armed Force in 1966), organizing them into main force regular units and local paramilitary units.

THE VIET CONG (VC)

The command of the Viet Cong across South Vietnam had grown into an organized structure by 1964 and most provinces had military, logistics and political systems. It was a decentralized system, where district leaders followed orders given by their regional headquarters, and they were expected to use their local knowledge to accomplish them, bringing the population under their control. Their main objective was to establish a network of camps and supply caches ready to hand over to Main Force or North Vietnamese Army (NVA) units when they arrived in the area.

The Viet Cong usually lived and fought in their own area and only moved away if the enemy presence became too great. They built a network of hidden camps and could quickly relocate if they were threatened. As the years passed, the number of camps, tunnels, supply caches and bunkers increased, with new ones appearing to replace those destroyed by the Americans or the ARVN.

Regional Units operated in their own provinces and districts, providing support, both armed and logistical, and local knowledge for the Main Force units, while training and giving assistance to the Local Militia Units. They numbered around 75,000 in 1965.

The local militias (*Dan Quan Du Kich*) used propaganda and force to persuade the population to support the People's Revolutionary Party. They had little military training and only a few weapons but they often organized local labor to help the Regional Units. Propaganda teams persuaded the population to support the Viet Cong, acting as laborers, providing rice and shelter, or paying tax. They would also try to recruit new members.

A member of the Viet Cong and a North Vietnamese soldier lie in wait for a passing patrol. (111-CC-53047)

The various types of Viet Cong units worked together to keep the villages in their area under their control. Units usually evaded the enemy unless they were cornered but a few carefully prepared attacks were made when the opportunity arose. They usually tried to draw the American patrols away from their supply caches, often towards a booby-trapped area.

The Main Force Regulars (Chu Luc-Quan) were well-armed, experienced fighters who lived in hidden camps known as sanctuaries where the government forces would not enter. They were indoctrinated in Communist ideals and while each company had a Party commissar, every platoon had a Party cell. Between 1961 and 1965 the number of regiments increased from two to five as their numbers grew to 35,000.

The Viet Cong's Code of Discipline and Code of Honour give an insight into how they aimed to secure their objectives by winning over the people. Strict discipline, personal sacrifice and a respect for the local population were the ideals but not all units followed them. Reports of executions, threats and pressure were commonplace as Viet Cong units pressurized the people to assist them in the war against the Americans and the South Vietnamese.

Four Viet Cong soldiers captured inside a tunnel complex wait to be taken away for interrogation during Operation Cedar Falls. (111-CC-38316)

THE VIET CONG CODE OF HONOR

I swear I am prepared to sacrifice all for Vietnam. I will fight to my last breath against imperialism, colonialism, Vietnamese traitors, and aggression in order to make Vietnam independent, democratic and united.

I swear to obey absolutely all orders from my commanders, executing them wholeheartedly, promptly and accurately.

I swear to fight firmly for the people without complaint and without becoming discouraged even if life is hard or dangerous. I will go forward in combat without fear, will never retreat regardless of suffering involved.

I swear to learn to fight better and swear to shape myself into a true revolutionary soldier battling the American imperialists and their servants, seeking to make Vietnam democratic, wealthy and strong.

I swear to preserve organizational secrecy, and to keep secret my unit's plans, the name of my unit commander and all secrets of other revolutionary units.

I swear if taken by the enemy I will not reveal any information even under inhumane torture. I will remain faithful to the Revolution and not be bribed by the enemy.

I swear in the name of unity to love my friends in my unit as myself, to work cooperatively with them in combat and at all other times.

I swear to maintain and protect my weapons, ensuring they are never damaged or captured by the enemy.

I swear that in my relationships with people I will do three things and eschew three things. I will respect, protect and help the people; I will not steal from, threaten, nor inconvenience the people. I will do all things to win their confidence.

I swear to indulge in self-criticism, to be a model soldier of the Revolution, and never harm either the Liberation Army or Vietnam.

THE VIET CONG CODE OF DISCIPLINE

I will obey the orders from my superiors under all circumstances.
I will never take anything from the people, not even a needle or thread.
I will not put group property to my own use.
I will return that which is borrowed, make restitution for things damaged.
I will be polite to people, respect and love them.
I will be fair and just in buying and selling.
When staying in people's houses I will treat them as I would my own house.

NVA regulars surrender near the Demilitarized Zone to a patrol of the 101st Airborne Division. (111-SC-647264)

I will follow the slogan: All things of the people and for the people.
I will keep unit secrets absolutely and will never disclose information even to closest friends or relatives.
I will encourage the people to struggle and support the Revolution.
I will be alert to spies and will report all suspicious persons to my superiors.
I will remain close to the people and maintain their affection and love.

THE PEOPLE'S ARMY OF VIETNAM (PAVN) OR NORTH VIETNAMESE ARMY

The North Vietnamese Army (NVA) had started to send advisors south to coordinate Viet Cong activity in 1960. By 1964 it had grown extensively as soldiers were recalled and the draft extended its age range from seventeen to thirty-five, increasing the number of potential recruits to over 2.5 million.

Typically one NVA regiment controlled each province with two regional force battalions and an elite provincial force battalion. Units moved every few days to avoid detection, a process described as nomading, using separate camps and trails from the Viet Cong. Battalions usually split into small units to avoid detection, reassembling near their objective. Local Force Viet Cong acted as guides, arranging shelter, food and ammunition. Following an attack they would head back into the mountains and jungles to rest and regroup at one of the fortified camps.

By 1966 the Army was training over 95,000 men per year and the length of service had been increased to cover the duration of the war. The Tet Offensive of 1968 decimated the Viet Cong, but as the number of recruits fell, the North Vietnamese Army responded by forcing men and under-age boys to join up.

By the time the majority of American combat troops had withdrawn, the Viet Cong had virtually ceased to exist, leaving the North Vietnamese Army to fight against the South Vietnamese Army. Although the 1972 offensive failed, more recruits were still being trained. Reduced American aid, political problems and military ineptness left the ARVN at the mercy of the NVA and in March and April 1975 they swept across South Vietnam, taking the capital after only seven weeks of fighting.

SUPPLYING THE NVA

The North Vietnamese Army recruited and trained in the north and its units infiltrated South Vietnam by one of three routes. In the early days many units were able to cross the Demilitarized Zone, moving south through the Central Highlands to bases near Saigon. Battalions camped in isolated areas and they were able to move freely around the country until the American deployment in 1965. Many units used the Ho Chi Minh Trail, a network of trails and paths through Laos and Cambodia, assembling in camps close to the South Vietnamese border. Others traveled by sea to Cambodia and then moved overland via the Sihanhouk Trail to the same area.

The US Marine Corps' heavy presence in I Corps and an increasing number of outposts, fortifications and sensors (the barrier was later called the McNamara Line after the American Secretary of Defense) along the Demilitarized Zone diverted most troops into Laos and Cambodia.

The Laotian coalition government had an arrangement with North Vietnamese sympathizers while the Cambodian government was pressurized into letting their Army establish bases close to the border so they could strike at Saigon. In March 1970 Marshal Lon Nol seized power but his attempts to restrict the amount of activity inside Cambodia were ignored.

The Ho Chin Minh Trail, as it became known, started as a network of jungle paths with endless lines of porters carrying everything by hand to supply dumps near the South Vietnamese border. During the early stages of the conflict supplies were broken into small packages and carried by porters, pack animals and sampans across the border into the sanctuaries near Saigon. When pressure from US operations increased, the NVA withdrew across the border into Cambodia so they could establish new base areas.

Despite covert bombing missions by the US Air Force, the movement of supplies continued unabated as engineers built roads and pipelines, and developed the rivers so they were navigable by barges. By the end of 1968 the trail had grown into a sophisticated logistics route with rest areas, supply depots, fuel and maintenance stations.

In the spring of 1970 President Nixon authorized an attack on the Cambodian sanctuaries and US and ARVN troops crossed the border at several points. During a series of operations they uncovered large base camps, complete with billets, training areas and maintenance facilities; huge stocks of ammunition and supplies were also seized.

CIVILIANS

The local population lived in constant fear as American, ARVN and Viet Cong patrols passed through, questioning them for information. Some acted as informants or spied on military installations for the Viet Cong, while others worked as paid agents for the US and ARVN.

Soldiers search through a Viet Cong supply cache during one of 25th Division's sweeps of the Michelin plantation. (111-CC-34257)

Once the men had left to fight or find work in the cities, tending the land was left to the women, children and elderly. (111-SC-60053)

Anyone seen running away or found hiding automatically fell under suspicion and most civilians stood by in silence, learning to speak only when spoken to. Most men were under suspicion of supporting one side or the other and many joined the Viet Cong after seeing their family or friends killed, injured or harassed by the Americans; others moved into the cities to escape the Viet Cong's warnings. It left the women to care for the children and the elderly as they tried to keep a roof over their head and food on the table.

The Viet Cong relied on the population for food, money and shelter, often forcing them to build fortifications, tunnels, supply caches and booby traps. They were sometimes called upon to act as observers, porters or guides.

PERSONAL WEAPONS

PISTOLS

Pistols were carried by officers and some senior NCOs; Viet Cong political officers often carried one as a sign of power. The Soviet Tokarev TT33 7.62mm and the Chinese Type-51 and Type-54 copies were semi-automatic, single-action recoil pistols with an 8-round magazine. It weighed 2.2lb (1kg) when loaded. The Makarov PM 9mm Automatic Pistol was the preferred weapon and it became the standard pistol in the North Vietnamese Army. It was lighter, weighing 1.8lb (0.8kg), and its 8-round magazine was loaded by double-action blowback. Both models had an effective range of around 50m.

RIFLES

The Viet Cong used what weapons were available and local force units were armed with a mixture of old converted French weapons, antiquated Soviet weapons and captured weapons. The most common modern rifle used was the robust and easily maintained AK-47 Assault Rifle.

The Soviet-manufactured semi-automatic AK-47 7.62mm Assault Rifle had high front sights, a wooden buttstock and a distinctive long, curved magazine holding 30 rounds. The Chinese copy, the Chicom Type-56, 7.62mm Assault

A GI of the 9th Infantry Division displays two types of automatic rifle used by the Viet Cong. (111-CC-45850)

Rifle had a folding metal stock. The gas-operated weapon could fire 40 rounds a minute up to 400m on semi-automatic; it had a higher rate fire on automatic, but the effective range was reduced.

The Simonov 7.62mm Self-Loading Rifle (SKS) was a semi-automatic carbine with a 10-round integral magazine capable of firing 30 rounds a minute to an effective range of 400m. Although it looked like a conventional bolt action rifle, there was a folding bayonet under the muzzle. It weighed 3.86kg.

The Soviet PPSh-41 7.62mm Submachine Gun was Second World War vintage. It either used a 71-round drum or a 35-round box of ammunition. The weapon's effective range was 150m and a fire-selector allowed the operator to switch between automatic and semi-automatic fire.

The PRC Type 50 Submachine Gun was similar to the PPSh-41 and the Vietnamese produced their own variant, replacing the wooden butt with a wire butt stock and wooden pistol grip. They also shortened the barrel jacket, removed the muzzle brake and moved the foresight on to the barrel. The variant was designated the K50M.

The MAT49 7.62mm Submachine Gun was a veteran of the war with the French and weapons were modified with a 7.62mm caliber barrel. The butt stock and magazine could be folded away so it could be carried on the march.

SQUAD AND PLATOON WEAPONS

MACHINE GUNS

The RPD-7.62mm General Purpose Machine Gun was the standard infantry squad support weapon and it could fire 150 rounds a minute from 100-round drums to an effective range of 800m. It was manned by a gunner and an assistant; the rest of the squad carried extra ammunition.

The Chinese-made Type-24, 7.62mm Heavy Machine Gun could be carried by its two crew members but many were mounted on wheels. They were usually placed in defensive or anti-aircraft positions near the border so they could be withdrawn if they were threatened. Helicopter gunships often singled out these lethal weapons during an air assault.

This collection of rifles, machine guns, rockets, mines and grenades was captured by ARVN soldiers during attacks on Tan Son Nhut Air Base in May 1968. (111-CC-48606)

ROCKET LAUNCHERS

Viet Cong and NVA units were often armed with 40mm rocket launchers and although they had been designed as an anti-tank weapon, they were often used against infantry and helicopters.

The RPG-2 and Chicom Type-56 launchers fired a fin-stabilized rocket-propelled grenade while the improved RPG-7 and Chicom Type-69 fired a finless projectile.

The operator could often hit stationary targets up to 500m away, but moving targets and helicopters were harder to hit. The grenade either exploded on impact or at its maximum range of 900m. It could penetrate up to 150mm of armor at short ranges and it was used to great effect against M113 armored personnel carriers.

HEAVY WEAPONS

REGIMENTAL WEAPONS COMPANIES

The Mortar Company had around ten officers and 100 men organized into three platoons. A platoon had between two and six 81/82mm mortars manned by three squads of ten men. Some platoons were armed with recoilless rifles.

The Soviet-made 82mm M-1937 and the Chicom copy Type-53 had a range of 3km and the assembled weapon weighed 123lb. They had a crew of three.

Squads were sometimes armed with 60mm mortars including the French made Stokes-Brandt 60mm, captured US M2 mortars and the Chinese Type-31: all could fire 60mm ammunition. Mortars weighed around 40lb and had a crew of two.

Machine gun companies had three platoons divided into eight to ten squads of around a dozen men. They were armed with Soviet 12.7mm machine guns, and occasionally captured .50-cal US machine guns, and they often deployed as anti-aircraft guns.

ROCKET REGIMENT

The use of rockets to strike fixed installations increased towards the end of the American deployment and rocket regiments were organized to carry out attacks. The headquarters squadron commanded three rocket battalions and a signal and reconnaissance company. Each battalion had a headquarters company and the three rocket companies were typically grouped as follows:

107mm company had twelve launchers and usually carried 24 rockets
122mm company had six launchers and usually carried 18 rockets
140mm company had sixteen launchers and usually carried 16 rockets

ARTILLERY

By 1966 medium artillery regiments armed with Soviet howitzers were being positioned along the North Vietnam border so they could shell the Marine positions across the Demilitarized Zone. 105mm batteries usually had twenty-four guns while 130mm or 152mm batteries had twelve; smaller 85mm or 100mm pieces were sometimes attached.

Batteries were scattered across large areas in camouflaged emplacements and guns were protected by 12.7mm anti-aircraft guns. They could only fire random rounds during the day and usually moved position every night.

Artillery crossed the border for the first time in the spring of 1972. Survey teams plotted gun positions and linked communications to a central control base so guns could be deployed individually to conduct surprise and opportunity fire missions. A wide variety of guns deployed, including M46 130mm field guns, D74 122mm field guns, M38 122mm howitzer, A19 122mm corps guns, M44 100mm field guns, D44 85mm field guns and ZIS3 76mm field guns.

This 37mm anti-aircraft gun was seized by men of the 1st Cavalry Division. (111-CC-49396)

BOOBY TRAPS

The Viet Cong were adept at laying booby traps and they caused over 10 per cent of American fatalities and nearly 20 per cent of injuries in South Vietnam. Explosives were in short supply but the Viet Cong had the time, patience and ingenuity to construct fiendish traps from unexploded ordnance and discarded ammunition and equipment. Tin cans, dud ammunition, pieces of metal and plastic could be turned into a booby trap as the following example illustrates:

A small piece of explosive was packed tight into an old C-ration tin can
Candle wax sealed a frictional pull fuse and a piece of string into the can
The can was placed inside a small hole and covered with a piece of discarded plastic
Twigs and leaves were used as camouflage

A simple punji booby trap made from two pieces of wood and a few rusty nails set to injure a man's ankle. (111-SC-52993)

The punji trap was the most common type of non-explosive booby trap encountered. It consisted of a small hole, large enough to trap a foot, and sharpened bamboo or metal sticking out from the bottom and sides. They could be hidden in camouflaged pits or under water. Poison or excrement was sometimes smeared on the sharpened stakes to infect the wound. Other types of explosive traps encountered were:

Homemade crossbows fired by bent branches attached to trip wires
Spiked mud balls hung from vines and triggered to swing along a trail
A balanced beam covered in spikes and set like the spiked mud ball
Tree branches studded with metal spikes
A bamboo whip covered in poisoned spikes and sprung by a tripwire

If a vehicle drove over the wooden switch of this elaborate affair, it would detonate an old 155mm shell. (111-CC-53028)

The most common type of explosive booby trap encountered was a hand grenade tied to a bush or stake and then attached to a trip wire. If an unwary soldier caught the wire with his foot the pin was pulled out of the grenade. A more sophisticated version involved taking the safety pin out and placing the grenade into a length of bamboo or a tin to hold the safety lever down. Other types of explosive traps encountered were:

Coconuts filled with explosives
A clay-encrusted grenade with the safety pin removed it exploded when disturbed
Rifle rounds set in bamboo and buried resting on a nail, known as toe poppers
Armed grenades held in bamboo or tins, attached to trip wires

The Viet Cong laid home-made mines along roads, often at bottlenecks such as bridges or culverts. Several types of mine were encountered but unexploded shells were a favorite source of explosive. The explosive stripped from a large mortar shell could be fitted with a blasting cap and buried. Rocket-propelled grenades were made by inserting a B-40 anti-tank grenade into a piece of bamboo and then aiming it down a narrow stretch of road. Both types of mine were command-detonated from a distance. A wristwatch-detonating device was devised to detonate a 5-gallon oil drum filled with explosives. Mines were sometimes stolen from the perimeter defenses of a military installation so they could be reused.

A great deal of ingenuity was also used to booby-trap landing zones in the hope of disabling a helicopter. Three types of devices encountered were:

Grenades set on posts around a clearing wired to go off simultaneously
A Claymore mine laid face up, ready to detonate
Mines set in treetops and rigged to detonate by the down force of rotors

LIFE WITH THE VIET CONG AND THE NVA

ON THE MOVE

Units moved regularly to avoid detection and a reconnaissance party set off the night before to check the route, questioning villagers about enemy troop movements along the way. A liaison team also went ahead to organize lookouts, guides, billets and supplies.

Virtually all movement was at night and routes had to be checked for ambushes before moving out and the main force cleared the camp and camouflaged their bunkers before leaving at nightfall. Scouts led the way as the rest of the battalion formed up in a column of companies, and each company moved in single file, often stretching for several miles. A rearguard and reconnaissance team made sure that no one followed. The men had to spread out even more if a unit was forced to move during the day and they often made long detours to remain hidden.

Crossing roads and canals was particularly dangerous and RPG teams covered the crossing point while a reconnaissance party crossed to check the far side was clear. The rest of the battalion followed in small groups.

CAMPS

The local Viet Cong established a network of camps and trails across their area, some small camps for their own units while others were transit camps for Main Force or NVA units. All were well camouflaged and they had tunnels, bunkers, billets, supply caches and escape routes.

When starting a new camp, the Main Force unit built a ring of bunkers inside a defended perimeter while local sympathizers kept a lookout. Plans were then coordinated with the local Viet Cong, so they could arrange lookouts, guides and provide food. The lookouts would ambush approaching enemy units, allowing the Main Force time to evacuate the camp; it could return to its supply caches at any time. The Americans soon learnt where Main Force units were likely to settle, forcing units to scatter across several smaller camps.

A typical defensive position had an outer defensive belt, and a concealed second belt, 50 to 200m inside the first. The troops would hold the outer line, using the inner line to fall back on to regroup and, if possible, counterattack.

This flexible tactic was known as 'rubber banding'. Semi-permanent base camps in the jungles often had a third line of bunkers and trenches. Bunkers were often large enough for several men and were covered by several feet of logs and earth. They had low ceilings and the firing slits served as exits.

Main Force camp areas were often hidden in dense jungle where there were limited approach routes and well-concealed escape routes. Billets, classrooms and training areas were often above ground while underground headquarters and hospitals were connected by tunnels. The camps were protected by bunkers and slit trenches linked by trenches and tunnels.

Camps were often destroyed and the local villagers resettled so the Viet Cong had to move elsewhere. Although effective, the scorched earth policy proved unpopular with the population and the American press.

Local Viet Cong units often took advantage of the US Rules of Engagement prohibiting artillery and air attacks close to inhabited areas. Villagers were placed under curfew as soon as the unit arrived and were often forced to help build the new fortifications. The outer belt was built outside of the village, covering obvious approaches, while the inner defensive belt was dug around and beneath the huts. Increasing American pressure eventually forced them to withdraw into the jungle and build camps close to the fortified base camps.

BUNKERS

The Viet Cong and the North Vietnamese Army used a mixture of natural material and discarded items to build their bunkers. Most were dug into the ground and reinforced with logs held together with a mixture of mud and cement; sandbags and tin sheeting from abandoned American positions were treasured items.

A Viet Cong soldier crouches inside his bunker, clutching an SKS rifle . . . (111-CC-53045)

Studies proved that bombs and shells had little effect on the shelters, except through concussion, and craters were easily turned into new bunkers. Napalm was ineffective against individual shelters, but it could devastate a series of connected bunkers.

The NVA and Viet Cong soldiers were experts at using natural camouflage and while shells, napalm or white phosphorous could strip away foliage, defoliants were used to expose entire base camps.

Assault trenches were shallow, measuring around 4ft (12m) deep. Approach trenches snaked across country, ending in a T-shaped trench with fighting positions. Although there were camouflaged assembly areas at regular intervals, the assault trenches were left exposed.

Long lines of small camouflaged holes were dug alongside trails for men to rest in and they were usually situated beneath trees or in undergrowth. Some L-shaped holes had both arms covered and the firing slits served as entrances and exits; others had one arm left open as a firing trench.

Hilltop observation posts were protected by tepee bunkers. A triangular shelter of logs was built inside a hole and it was then filled with earth and covered by a camouflaged layer of logs. A sloped tunnel served as an entrance and an air vent at the opposite end kept the air fresh.

Single anti-aircraft and mortar positions were dug among living areas or along supply routes while larger battery positions were situated on hilltops or ridges for increased observation. Mortar gun pits were small and shallow while aircraft gun pits were deeper and up to 30ft (10m) in diameter. Both types were connected by shallow trenches and well camouflaged while ammunition shelters were protected by thick layers of logs and earth.

. . . Meanwhile, outside, GIs try in vain to smoke him out. (111-CC-45928)

TUNNEL COMPLEXES

Tunnels had been used during the war against the French as hiding places and the old systems were expanded and deepened during the war with the Americans. Local Force units dug their complexes under their village, protecting them with a perimeter of camouflaged bunkers.

Main Force units dug underground tunnels in plantations and jungle areas and they were usually larger and better constructed than the local complexes. The Iron Triangles and War Zones C and D were used as staging areas for attacks on Saigon.

Tunnel entrances and fighting positions were heavily camouflaged. Some were covered by concrete slabs covered with dirt while others were made from dried mud reinforced by wire mesh. Wooden boxes filled with earth were often inserted into the tunnel entrance so they could not be found with probes. Several widely spaced exits were dug and construction tunnels leading to the surface were only filled with loose earth so they could be dug out in an emergency. Many entrances were booby-trapped.

The tunnel systems were split into cells, each with a maze of narrow winding passageways; many were only 2ft (0.6m) wide and 3ft (0.9m) high, too small for the average American soldier. Camouflaged trapdoors, random twists and turns, hidden side tunnels and dead-ends made sure that search teams had to take their time exploring. Occasionally larger tunnels ran through the complex so units could move quickly to their destination, but only a trusted few knew the hidden trapdoors connecting the cells. Small rooms – usually only 4ft (1.2m) wide by 6ft (2m) long and no higher than the adjoining tunnel – with shelving and seating cut into the sides, were dug at regular intervals for men to rest in.

There was always a danger of suffocation or build-ups of explosive gases and the trapdoors were designed to keep the lower levels supplied with a steady supply of fresh air. Conical air shafts were dug in the roof of the upper tunnels, each narrowing to a tiny hole that was almost impossible to locate. Water and airlocks were added to stop fire and gas spreading; they also reduced concussion from explosions.

SUPPLY CACHES

Large central caches were used to begin with but they were soon scattered and hidden in a network of small hoards. Rice was often hidden in villages, on the pretence that it was for the inhabitants, but the Americans confiscated suspicious caches. Many ingenious ways were devised for hiding weapons and ammunition, ranging from buried earthenware pots and metal containers, to anthills. Many items were hidden in the walls or beneath the roofs of the village huts, others were wrapped in plastic and buried in gardens or animal pens where it was natural to dig.

VIETCONG AND NVA TACTICS

AMBUSHES

One of the main tactics employed by the Viet Cong and the NVA was the ambush, and they could vary in size from a small, hastily sprung attack to a well-planned regimental-sized action. A small team could engage a large number of troops before melting away into the undergrowth as the patrol regrouped and tended to their casualties. The tactic was also used to threaten supply convoys, tying up large numbers of US troops to protect the road network.

PREPARING THE AMBUSH

An advance party took time to locate their ambush position, choosing hidden approach routes, observation posts, hiding places for the team, and a safe withdrawal route. A large ambush could have any of the following elements:

A command post overlooking the ambush site; a small reserve might be kept on standby

Observation posts overlooking the approach routes

Snipers to harass the patrol as it approached

Patrols for drawing the enemy into the ambush

A lead-blocking party to stop the enemy patrol in its tracks

A rear-blocking element to stop the enemy withdrawing to safety

A main assault element with heavy weapons for maximum firepower

Runners, and occasionally radios, kept the commander in touch with his men. Terrain, the size of the team, the likely enemy reaction and a host of other considerations determined what type of ambush would be laid; the following are some of the main types:

Mine Ambush: Command-detonated mines were laid along a trail and detonated from a distance. The ambush site could be strewn with booby traps to catch the enemy as they scattered for cover.

Point or Bloody Nose Ambush: A small unit prepared a series of ambush positions along a trail, withdrawing from one to another to keep the enemy disorganized.

Flank or Linear Ambush: Set up alongside a trail with booby traps laid in the undergrowth on the opposite side to catch the enemy patrol as it dived for cover.

'L' Ambush: A linear ambush with a machine gun added, ready to fire down the trail, catching the enemy patrol in a devastating crossfire.

'V' Ambush: Two teams straddled a trail to catch the enemy in a crossfire. One team fired first so the enemy patrol turned and faced, exposing its flank to the second ambush team.

'Z' Ambush: Slit trenches and log bunkers were dug along a trail with numerous interlocking fields of fire.

Maneuver Ambush: A two-part ambush set up on the inside of a bend of a trail or road. A small team stopped the head of a passing column, while the main part of the convoy was out of sight. The main party then ambushed the rear of the column, splitting the convoy's attention in two.

SPRINGING THE AMBUSH

The preferred time for springing the ambush was dusk, when the enemy patrol would be tired and looking forward to halting for the night. The approaching darkness would provide perfect cover as the ambush party disappeared into the undergrowth.

As one team engaged the head of the enemy patrol, the rest of the column stopped, scattering in front of the main assault force. A second team engaged the tail of the column, causing further confusion, as the main ambush party engaged the center of the column.

Marines dive for cover and crawl forward through thick elephant grass to try and hide after coming under fire. (Marine A370616)

WITHDRAWING AND MOPPING UP

Flares, whistles, bugles or verbal commands signaled the withdrawal, and teams retired along different routes to their rendezvous point. If the patrol had been overwhelmed the ambush team would gather up weapons and papers from the dead and escort prisoners away (or execute them).

THE HILL TRAP MANEUVER

In 1966 the NVA developed a new tactic called the Hill Trap Maneuver, designed to draw large US units towards prepared hilltop positions. The two main areas were in the A Shau and Da Krong mountains west of Hue, and west of Dak To in II Corps. An NVA division would establish a screen around the chosen hills while conscript labor fortified the hilltops. Once the position was complete the NVA troops would occupy the fortifications and wait for the Americans to find them.

The NVA had fortified the hills west of Dak To at the beginning of 1967 before they were attacked by 4th Division. Heavy fighting followed as 101st Airborne Division and 173d Airborne Brigade joined the fighting but they were hampered by the difficult terrain as they fought to clear the bunker complexes. Counterattacks from hidden tunnels engaged reserves and the Americans found it difficult to coordinate support fire as the NVA infiltrated their positions. Fighting finally drew to a close at the beginning of 1969 as the NVA slipped away across the border. General Peers, 4th Division's commanding officer, summed up the Hill Trap Maneuver with the following words: 'The enemy had prepared the battlefield well. Nearly every key terrain feature was fortified with elaborate bunker and trench complexes. He had moved vast quantities of supplies and ammunition into the area. He was prepared to stay . . .'

OFFENSIVE PLANNING

One favorite tactic was a hit-and-run attack against a fixed installation, usually carried out at night. In the early days the targets were government buildings and police outposts but the American intervention created new lucrative targets including fire bases, airfields and logistics areas. A Military Affairs Committee selected targets and, after gaining the approval of the Province Committee, delegated the planning to three staff sections.

The Military Staff dispatched reconnaissance units to study the target and the surrounding terrain. Estimates of the defenses, troop strength and weapons were calculated by long-range observation while sappers tried to infiltrate the perimeter to find out more detailed information.

The Political Staff questioned the local Viet Cong and villagers about military activity, and encouraged (often forcibly) anyone working inside the target to spy. Meanwhile, the Rear Services Staff rounded up civilians to help as laborers, porters, guides or lookouts. They also found sympathetic villagers who would provide food or hiding places for the attack force.

The Military Staff eventually submitted a detailed plan to the Military Affairs Committee for approval. Whatever the target, the NVA and VC planners used the 'One slow, four quick' principle for their attacks:

Slow Plan: The attack force rehearsed using sand tables and models of the target while the local Viet Cong stockpiled supplies in hidden caches. Many attacks had to be cancelled when the Military Staff thought their plan had been compromised by prisoners or ralliers.

Quick Advance: The attack force left their camps at dusk and marched to the assembly point while sappers started cutting a way through the target's perimeter defenses.

Quick Attack: The attack would begin in the early hours, leaving time for the attack force to escape before dawn. Attacks were carried out according to the 'Three Strongs' principle:

Strong Fight: To achieve and then exploit surprise

Strong Assault: The assault troops would overrun a weak point in the defenses

Strong Pursuit: Reserves would exploit the breach and create havoc inside the base

Quick Clearance: The attack usually only lasted a few minutes and the men withdrew before the Americans deployed their firepower.

Quick Withdrawal: The men regrouped at a rendezvous point before splitting into small groups and dispersing.

NVA SAPPERS

To begin with, the People's Liberation Armed Force trained sappers to support attacks by the regular infantry, but early failures due to inadequate planning and inexperience left them with a poor reputation. At first there was a sapper battalion in most of the NVA military regions and companies or platoons were attached to regular units when required. Numbers grew steadily and the creation of a dedicated headquarters and staff in the spring of 1967 ensured that sappers soon became the elite troops of the NVA. Sappers received up to three months extra training, either at a base near Son Tay or with units in the south, in the following areas:

Reconnaissance and scouting of military installations
Camouflage and silent movement
Crossing surfaces unseen, including mud, water, ditches, leaves, sand and grass
Explosives and how to destroy perimeter defenses and installations
Disarming traps, mines and flares and how to silently enter a base

Sapper cells were used to target military bases, government buildings, ships and bridges, often leading attacks by regular units, and they relied on secrecy and stealth to break through the installation perimeter. Sappers carried out many of the suicidal high-profile attacks on American installations during the Tet Offensive in February 1968 and the battle with sappers in the United States' Embassy compound in Saigon grabbed the American public's attention.

After the Tet attacks, sapper platoons were combined into companies and battalions. A sapper battalion had four or five companies, each with three platoons of up to twenty men. Platoons were split into two squads which were in turn divided into three-man cells.

By the summer of 1969 there were twenty-seven battalions and thirty-nine companies of sappers and they were attacking fire bases, major installations and government buildings every week. Attacks on American targets would eventually cause an average of over $1 million damage per raid.

THE SAPPER ATTACK

The target was observed and intelligence was gathered while the sapper commander developed his plan and his men trained for the attack. Success depended on stealth, surprise and coordination. A security cell stood guard as the troops assembled and weapons teams moved into position.

The sapper raiding party was divided into two or more assault teams, called arrows, each with four- or five-man cells. The three-man penetration cell, wearing only shorts and smeared with mud for camouflage, approached the target at dusk, and began the slow crawl through the barbed wire, mines and trip wires, marking the route with cloth strips. While cutters could snip wire, the sappers preferred to use poles to lift concertina wire or mats to lay over sections. Mortars fired random shots and the explosions covered up noisy activities. If the penetration cell was spotted it would either try and blast its way through the wire with explosives or withdraw rapidly.

Assault cells used Bangalore torpedoes or plastic explosive charges to blast a way through the final barrier, and the explosion signaled the start of the attack. Time was of the essence and the sappers moved fast, firing their weapons to drive the defenders into their bunkers. Explosives were thrown inside to cause maximum casualties while demolition charges were placed on predetermined targets. meanwhile the support cells engaged targets in the open, drawing the defenders' attention from the assault cells.

The sappers withdrew as soon as their main targets had been destroyed. Support cells gave covering fire as they fell back through the perimeter and headed to their assembly point.

STAND-OFF ATTACKS

As the perimeter defenses at American bases improved, the VC and NVA increasingly relied on using mortars, rockets and recoilless rifles to inflict damage on the crowded targets. Military staff could plan an attack at their leisure, moving their weapons into position on the night of the attack and then removing them as soon as it was over.

Reconnaissance teams observed the base layout for lucrative targets while civilians working inside the base were questioned; feint attacks assessed the perimeter defenses and base response times. Security was paramount and the weapons teams were only told their target a few hours before the attack.

There would be no time to fire registration rounds at the target so survey teams plotted the launch area and the target, calculating the direction and elevation the weapons would fire at. They placed aiming stakes at each location (bamboo or branches stuck in or laid on the ground) and decided if ramps, pits or tripods would be used to support the rocket tube.

Local labor had established a supply cache in advance close to the chosen site leaving the crews to carry their weapons to the launch site on wooden

Artillery fire was often used to draw attention away from a sapper attack; this shell has set off a huge explosion in the fuel depot at Dong Ha base. (Marine A191778)

cradles; the cradles were then converted into tripods and lashed together with vines. The crews arrived after dark and while some teams prepared the launch site, others cut a trail to the ammunition dump. Mortars were usually grouped in a semicircle, with each weapon in a camouflaged foxhole while recoilless rifles were often hidden on high ground overlooking the target. Weapons were usually wired together in batteries with regular spacings in case of an accidental explosion. Whatever the weapon, the crews were usually ready to fire in less than an hour.

Rockets and mortars were usually fired at area targets, including ammunition and fuel dumps, aircraft parking areas and buildings, while recoilless rifles, RPGs and machine guns were aimed at bunkers and command centers. 57mm and 75mm recoilless rifles took time to assemble and dismantle and they had to be set up with a direct line of fire to the target, leaving them vulnerable to return fire. Pack howitzers were powerful but cumbersome and they needed animals to carry them to the firing area. Mortars were popular, but the 60mm versions only had a short range and their projectiles were easily to spot, making them an easy target. Crews often hid in bunkers or tunnels, sometimes under hamlets where they were safe from return fire. Larger 81mm and 82mm mortars had to be protected by emplacements but as US anti-mortar tactics improved, many were moved across the border with Cambodia or Laos. By 1966 rockets were the weapon of choice. They were lightweight, easy to set up and able to deliver a rapid high-impact attack from longer ranges. The 122mm rocket could fire up to 11,000m, nearly twice the range of the 120mm mortar.

The flashes from the weapons were easy to spot and the attack had to be completed before the base helicopters and artillery could respond, and they generally lasted anything from 2 to 20 minutes. The crews had no time to congratulate themselves as once they had fired their weapons, it was a race against time to escape before the American helicopters and artillery returned fire.

A rocket attack on Can Tho Air Base has destroyed a CH-47 Chinook helicopter. (111-CC-53439)

NORTH VIETNAMESE AIR DEFENSES

Pilots flying over North Vietnam had to contend with a coordinated anti-aircraft system ranging from machine guns to sophisticated surface-to-air missiles. A network of early-warning and fire-control radars were linked by comprehensive communications capable of giving ample warning of an air raid. Surface-to-air missiles began to appear at the start of 1965 and there were over 300 three years later which accounted for many of the planes shot down (over 400 by 1968).

The North Vietnamese Air Force was armed with over 100 jet fighters based at ten airfields across the country. However, the mixture of MiG-15, MiG-17, MiG-19 and MiG-21s rarely engaged the US Air Force and US Navy planes in air-to-air combat.

CHAPTER 19

THE AFTERMATH

THE WITHDRAWAL OF COMBAT TROOPS

In January 1969, Richard Nixon was inaugurated as the President of the United States and his administration immediately began planning how to withdraw ground troops from what was becoming an increasingly unpopular war. Plans to hand over greater responsibility to South Vietnam's Armed Forces, a range of programs known as Vietnamization, were announced in March. The plan's implementation on 8 June coincided with Nixon's public declaration that the first withdrawal of 25,000 troops from Vietnam would begin the following month, the start of a three-year long process. They left in the following order:

1969
July / August	1st and 2d Brigades, 9th Infantry Division
November	3d Marine Division

1970
April	3d Brigade, 4th Infantry Division
October	3d Brigade, 9th Infantry Division and 199th Infantry Brigade
December	1st and 2d Brigades, 4th Infantry Division
December	1st and 3d Brigades, 25th Infantry Division

1971
March	11th Armored Cavalry Regiment and 5th Special Forces Group
April	1st Marine Division and 2d Brigade, 25th Infantry Division
May	1st and 2d Brigades, 1st Cavalry Division
August	1st Brigade, 5th Infantry Division (Mechanized) and 173d Airborne Brigade
November	11th and 198th Brigades, 23d Infantry Division
December	3d Brigade, 101st Airborne Division

1972
January	1st Brigade, 101st Airborne Division
February	2d Brigade, 101st Airborne Division
June	3d Brigade, 1st Cavalry Division and 196th Infantry Brigade

COMING HOME

The final years in South Vietnam caused a host of problems as troops became frustrated while they waited for their tour to end. The cessation of offensive activity increased the men's boredom, and resentment grew as the units were withdrawn, leaving the rest behind to continue what was considered by

Cheers resound around the cabin as this planeload of released prisoners takes off from Gia Lam Air Base near Hanoi. (111-CC-1155658)

the majority to be a lost cause. By 1971 morale started to disintegrate and the number of cases of crime, racially motivated incidents, drug abuse and disobedience rose; fraggings, shootings and accidents also increased.

Many veterans had no interest in serving out the rest of their time once they had returned from Vietnam, and their discontentment spread to new recruits as they waited to be discharged.

News reports during these troubled times helped to create a feeling of mistrust, one which was felt between the Vietnam veterans and those of the Second World War and Korea for many years. Few Vietnam veterans became involved in Veteran organizations or the American Legion and those who joined were rarely accepted in the years following the conflict. Only in recent years has it been acceptable to say that they were proud of their service in Vietnam.

OPERATION HOMECOMING

Between 12 February and 29 March 1973, 591 US prisoners were released in four stages timed to coincide with the final withdrawal of US troops from South Vietnam. Men captured by the Viet Cong were taken to Saigon, those held in North Vietnam were taken to Hanoi, and a few imprisoned in China were taken to Hong Kong. All three parties were then flown to Clark Air Force Base in the Philippines where they were the focus for a wave of admiration across America as they stepped off planes and met their waiting families. Their welcome was a complete contrast to the reception many other veterans received when they returned home.

Some of the men had survived years of mental and physical torture while they were held in inhumane prisons such as the infamous 'Hanoi Hilton'. Many had been forced to make humiliating statements denouncing their 'war crimes' while others had been paraded and filmed for propaganda purposes by their North Vietnamese captors. Following extensive debriefings and medical examinations they were taken to a hospital to begin their long road to recovery.

An ARVN tank stands guard during the 1972 NVA offensive; three years later chaos overtook the South Vietnamese Armed Forces. (111-CC-81756)

THE FINAL OFFENSIVE

By the spring of 1975, the NVA was ready to enter South Vietnam in force once again and on 10 March the first attacks fell on Ban Me Thuot and Pleiku airfield. Ban Me Thuot fell after only four days of fierce fighting and, with only one of

the main roads through the Central Highlands open, President Thieu ordered his forces to withdraw from the mountains around Kontum and Pleiku. Rather than regrouping and counterattacking, confusion reigned as the ARVN fell back in disorder and panicking air crews concentrated on evacuating their families and friends to airfields across the south rather than engaging targets. When the NVA attack resumed on the 16th, the ARVN fell back quickly towards Qui Nhon, abandoning over sixty aircraft and large quantities of fuel and ammunition.

As the NVA attacked Phu Cat Air Base, the situation in I Corps to the north rapidly deteriorated. With the road to Qui Nhon threatened and Da Nang air base under attack, thousands (including many soldiers) headed to the port where American ships waited offshore. Chaos reigned in the city as armed deserters fought their way through the crowds to try and escape, leaving only a few to defend the air base; it soon fell leaving over 180 planes and huge supply dumps in the NVA's hands.

With I and II Corps taken, the Vietnamese Air Force abandoned Nha Trang and Cam Ranh Bay air bases as thousands of soldiers and civilians fled ahead of the advancing NVA, hoping to be evacuated by sea or air. Thousands withdrawn from Da Nang had to re-embark on waiting ships so they could be taken to the Gulf of Siam. By the beginning of April thirteen NVA divisions had cut all the roads leading to Saigon and on 9 April Xuan Loc, only 40 miles from the capital, was under attack. There was heavy fighting at the town but it finally fell on 23 April; both Bien Hoa and Tan Son Nhut nearby were abandoned a few days later, ending the aerial evacuation of South Vietnam.

On 29 April President Ford ordered Operation Frequent Wind, the helicopter evacuation of Saigon, but as US Navy helicopters worked around the clock to evacuate American personnel and Vietnamese officials, Vietnamese pilots flew their families to Thailand or one of the US carrier ships off the coast; many had to be pushed overboard while other crews crashed into the sea in desperation. The following day Saigon fell as North Vietnamese troops moved into the capital the and remaining elements of the South Vietnamese forces were ordered to surrender. The struggle for South Vietnam was over, almost ten years to the day after American ground troops had landed near Da Nang.

EVACUATION OF THE US EMBASSIES

In both Cambodia and South Vietnam, the final places to be evacuated were the US Embassies. Plans to evacuate the Cambodian Embassy had been prepared in August 1973 when Khmer Rouge units advanced towards Phnom Penh. A few Americans and their support staff were evacuated from outlying towns but by 15 August the Cambodian Army had stopped the attack. In April 1975 the Khmer Rouge once more advanced on the capital and Operation Eagle Pull began on the morning of the 12th. Marines were flown in and established a perimeter around Landing Zone Hotel before escorting the Embassy staff to waiting helicopters. In just over an hour 276 people, including eighty-two Americans, had been airlifted to safety on US Navy carriers in the Gulf of Thailand. Cambodia fell five days later.

The final evacuation of Saigon was far from well planned. Operation Frequent Wind was initiated on 29 April when over 850 Marines landed and held a defensive perimeter while nearly 400 US citizens and 4,500 Vietnamese, many of them government officials and their families, were evacuated. As the last Marines prepared to withdraw, their commander learnt that several hundred Americans

Helicopters deliver American staff to the aircraft carrier USS Midway during Operation Frequent Wind. (Navy-1165122)

and thousands more Vietnamese had gathered at the US Embassy in the city; he was left with no other option than a large-scale airlift from the small compound.

As crowds surged forward around the Embassy, one helicopter at a time landed in the compound while others used the tiny helipad on the roof of the building. Operations continued throughout the night but the number of people waiting continued to grow. During the early hours of 30 April Washington gave the order to concentrate on evacuating Americans, forcing many to leave their Vietnamese assistants behind, and at 0500 hours Ambassador Martin boarded a helicopter, one of the last of over 2,000 evacuated. Three hours later the last of the Marines had been withdrawn. Several hundred Vietnamese had to be left behind in the compound while thousands of others were stranded across the city as the North Vietnamese troops closed in.

THE HUMAN COST

The number of men and women who served in South Vietnam was around 2,600,000, nearly 10 per cent of America's young men and women. They were divided between the services as follows:

Army	1,736,000	Air Force	293,000
Marine Corps	391,000	Navy	174,000

Around 50 per cent, or 1.3 million, either saw combat or provided close support. The following tables chart the human cost of the conflict:

HOSTILE DEATHS	US ARMY	US NAVY	US AIR FORCE	US MARINE CORPS	US COAST GUARD	TOTAL
Killed in Action	25,358	1,115	537	11,491	4	38,505
Died of Wounds	3,566	150	49	1,476	1	5,242
Died while Missing	1,960	325	1,130	108	0	3,523
Died in Captivity	45	36	25	10	0	116

NON-HOSTILE DEATHS	US ARMY	US NAVY	US AIR FORCE	US MARINE CORPS	US COAST GUARD	TOTAL
Accidental Death	4,907	579	531	1,436	2	7,455
Illness or Injuries	1,437	69	170	314	0	1,990
Died while Missing	928	281	141	3	0	1,353

TOTALS	US ARMY	US NAVY	US AIR FORCE	US MARINE CORPS	US COAST GUARD	TOTAL
Totals	38,196	2,555	2,583	14,837	7	58,178

The first US casualty occurred in 1957 and the deaths were still being confirmed in recent years. However, 97 per cent of the men lost their lives between 1965 and 1973.

One sobering fact is that approximately 11,500 of the men who died were 20 years old or younger. Over 303,000 men were wounded; 75,000 of them were severely disabled.

REMEMBERING

REMEMBERING THE DEAD

The Vietnam Veterans Memorial Fund was set up by a group of veterans in April 1979 as a non-profit charitable organization to raise funds for a memorial to remember the 2.7 million men and women who had served in Vietnam, particularly those who died there.

One member of the group, Jan Scruggs, lobbied Congress for a plot of land and in July 1980 President Jimmy Carter signed the legislation for a memorial site in Constitution Gardens close to the Lincoln Memorial.

The design of Maya Ying Lin, an undergraduate at Yale University, was chosen in May 1981 by a panel of judges following a national competition and work started the following March. The memorial comprises two partially sunken walls laid out in a large V-shape. Each wall is 250ft long and they start at ground level while a path leads the visitor down to the apex as they increase in height. Lists of names fill the walls and the polished black granite reflects the visitors' profiles and their surroundings. The memorial was dedicated on 13 November 1982, after a week of commemorations for Vietnam veterans. The whole project had been paid for by individual and corporate donations.

The Stars and Stripes always flies on a nearby flagpole and on memorial days it is joined by the black and white POW/MIA flag. A traditional bronze sculpture of three Servicemen staring towards the wall was added in 1984 and a memorial remembering the 7,500 women who served in Southeast Asia

Thousands of names fill the polished black granite walls of the Vietnam Memorial Wall. (Author's collection)

Veterans, the bereaved and tourists mingle as they file silently past the Vietnam Memorial Wall. (Author's collection)

Above left: *The POW-MIA flag: 'You are not forgotten.'* (Author's collection)
Above right: *The statues of three comrades in arms face towards the Memorial Wall.* (Author's collection)

Remembering the 7,500 women who served in Vietnam. (Author's collection)

completed the area. The memorials and the surrounding park were handed over to the National Park Service and the area was accepted by the President of the United States on 10 November 1984.

In 2006 there were 58,253 names on what is known by many as 'The Wall'; around 1,200 are still missing. Names of men who died of wounds received in Vietnam have started to be added in recent years, but the fight goes on to include those who contracted terminal illnesses from the controversial defoliant, Agent Orange.

REMEMBERING THE MISSING

At the end of the Vietnam conflict there were 2,583 unaccounted-for servicemen and their families have fought a never-ending search for their loved ones. With the help of search teams and information given by the local population, many unmarked graves were located and the remains identified so they could be returned to the United States. Nearly 2,000 possible sightings have been reported over the past forty years but many have turned out to be false sightings or missionaries working in isolated areas. In January 2007 forty-seven sightings were still on file as unresolved while 1,788 Americans are still listed as Missing in Action.

Newton Heisley had designed a flag for the National League of Families of American Prisoners and Missing in Southeast Asia as early as 1971 so they could fly it in memory of their loved ones. The stark black background has a white, silhouetted head bowed below a guard tower in the center and the words 'You are not forgotten' at the bottom.

The fight to remember the missing was initially the concern of their families and loved ones, but by the mid-1980s the message had spread across the nation and the third Friday of September was declared National POW/MIA Day.

The POW/MIA flag was flown over the White House for the first time in 1988 and it was put on display in the Capitol Rotunda the following year as a permanent reminder of the plight of the missing. On six days of the year, Veterans Day, National POW/MIA Day, Independence Day, Armed Forces Day, Memorial Day and Flag Day, the flag is flown over the White House, the Capitol, national cemeteries and war memorials, military bases and post offices.

FURTHER READING

Numerous books and articles have been written about the Vietnam conflict, covering all aspects from a variety of angles. Many contemporary documents are available online, either to view or download. Professor Edwin E. Moise, of Clemson University, SC, and Professor Richard Jensen, of the University of Illinois, have compiled extensive online bibliographies covering books, articles and online resources for the Vietnam War. Their home pages are:

Professor Edwin E. Moise:
http://www.clemson.edu/caah/history/FacultyPages/EdMoise/bibliography.html

Professor Richard Jensen:
http://tigger.uic.edu/~rjensen/vietnam.html

INDEX